TIPPER
G.A.A. B

A Millennium Production

Collected & Compiled
by

Seamus J. King, Liam Ó Donnchú, Jimmy Smyth

IRELAND

First published in 2000
by
County Tipperary Board G.A.A.
Lár na Páirce,
Slievenamon Road,
Thurles,
Co. Tipperary.

Tipperary's G.A.A. Ballads

A Millennium Production

Collected and compiled by
Seamus J. King, Liam Ó Donnchú, Jimmy Smyth

ISBN   0-9538423-0-4

Printed by:
Kilkenny People Printing Ltd,
Purcellsinch, Carlow Road, Kilkenny, Republic of Ireland.

No man will love his land and race
Who has no pride in his native place,
Nor will traditions linger long
Where local poets make no song

CRIOSTÓIR O'FLYNN, *Centenary*

Parochial map of County Tipperary

Contents

Part One
Games and Activity prior to
The Twentieth Century

1

Part Two
County Achievements

3

Part Three
Club Victories and Rivalries

Part Four
Hurling

Part Five
Laments and Tributes

9

Part Six
Miscellaneous Items

11

Preface

The Tipperary ballads, poems and recitations have an instinctive sense of what is apt. Many of them are simple, uncomplicated and powerful. They give emphasis to the games as a special ingredient in the make up of Ireland; a capacity to give the nation an individuality and a self-consciousness and they point to a specific entity different to other nations. They reveal the contentment, independence, satisfaction, special value and identity that Gaelic games bring into the lives of Tipperary people, young and old, at home and abroad. They ring out a special sophistication of their own.

The texts have something to say about life, that awakens a reader's recognition. They communicate their insights into people and the world. The authors have different backgrounds and some would be influenced by the pattern of language of a local area that has survived from earlier times. This can be attractive and noble. It can be enriching and refreshing. It can be original and eloquent.

We may not be able to apply literary exactitudes or expect the approval of literary critics to all these compositions but in many we find a taste for heightened language and a sweet mixture of haziness and magic. All the texts are spontaneous and straightforward and in each item we always find lines that are both imaginative and vigorous. They tell us who we are, where we come from, and where we stand.

The ballad gives emotional insight to the vital role played by Gaelic games in Irish society. The balladmaker is the mouthpiece of the grassroot Gael, who passionately breathes and lives our games. He has his finger on the local pulse; he recognises the social significance of local events, which he faithfully records with an extra flair borne of an intimate local insight.

The texts portray the feelings and thoughts of people with whom we can imaginatively identify ourselves. They give an insight into their character, their problems and their world. They have something to say about life and they present features of the real world, which heighten and enhance experience in some way; qualities of human life, joy, and sadness, serenity and tension, humour and tragedy. They give a deeper understanding of the nature of Irish society and its national personality. The authors are content in the knowledge that they have great games, great heroes, great people and great places.

This collection came from an initiative of Tipperary G.A.A. Millennium Committee. The items were collected from club publications, G.A.A. yearbooks, newspapers, personal collections and submissions from clubs and individuals. The collection is divided into six sections: (1) ballads, poems and recitations relating to games and activity prior to the start of the twentieth century; (2) items in which county achievements are remembered; (3) ballads and recitations highlighting club victories and rivalries; (4) items which deal exclusively with the game of hurling; (5) a section, which pays tribute to individuals and/or laments their passing; (6) other miscellaneous items of a general nature.

The book has been compiled and collected by Seamus J. King, Liam Ó Donnchú and Jimmy Smyth.

Seamus J. King, native of Lorrha in the North of the county has been residing in Cashel, where he is a teacher since 1965. He has been interested in historical and G.A.A. affairs for a long time and has written exclusively in both areas. His publications include club histories, county histories and the well-received, *A History of Hurling*, which was published by Gill and Macmillan in 1996. He has also served at the administrative level, having been chairman of the Cashel King Cormacs and of the West Division of Tipperary G.A.A. He is currently chairman of the Yearbook Committee. He is presently completing the history of the North Division of Tipperary G.A.A., which will appear next March in conjunction with the Board's centenary.

Liam Ó Donnchú, Hollyford, has resided at Thurles and Moycarkey for many years. He is very much associated with communication in the G.A.A. through his involvement with match programme production at Semple Stadium and his role as secretary of Tipperary G.A.A. Yearbook since 1982. On the G.A.A.'s administrative side, Liam has been chairman of Thurles Sarsfield's G.A.A. Club (1989-1999) and is treasurer of Lár na Páirce – the Gaelic Games interpretative centre in Thurles. He is currently researching the history of Thurles Sarsfields. He holds an M.A. from the

History Department of U.C.C. and is Principal Teacher at Moycarkey N.S., Pouldine, Thurles.

Jimmy Smyth, Clontarf, Dublin (formerly Ruan, Co. Clare) was an outstanding Clare hurler from the fifties. He was selected on Munster's best hurling team in 2000. As well as being a fine ballad singer, Jimmy has also written numerous ones, including a number, which appear in this collection. Also, he is an authority on the tradition of the G.A.A. ballads, having presented his thesis on the subject for his Master's Degree at University of Limerick some years ago. Two years ago he published *Ballads of the Banner* on the G.A.A. ballads and poems of County Clare, which was received with popular acclaim.

Also, worthy of our thanks is the Millennium Committee of North Tipperary County Council, whose generous grant alleviated some of the financial worries involved with the publication. We are also very grateful to South Tipperary County Council who through the Arts Act, assisted us financially.

We hope that this book will bring pleasure and satisfaction to its readers. It recognises the widespread practice of capturing in verse the highlights of county, club and individual Gaelic sporting achievements. The book if of historical interest, including as it does items from the distant past as well as those of quite recent events. It contains a rich heritage which has been collected in book form for the first time and which will give it a deserved permanence.

Is le mórtas cine a chuirimid an cnuasach seo ós comhair an phobail mar chuid de cheiliúradh na Mílaoise. Tá sé lán go béal le seoda luachmhara a dheimhníonn stádas ár gcluichí agus meoin traidisiúnta Gaelach atá fós go láidir, forleathan i saol ár muintire i gContae Thiobraid Árann. Is gné fíor thábhachtach dár n-oidhreacht bailéid, filíocht agus amhráin na ndaoine.

Gurbh fada buan iad.

Tipperary G.A.A. Millennium Committee

Meán Fómhair 2000

~ PART ONE ~

Games and Activity prior to The Twentieth Century

[Established over a Century.]

THE COMMERCIAL AND FAMILY HOTEL,

AND POSTING ESTABLISHMENT,

THURLES.

LIZZIE J. HAYES, Proprietress.

Birthplace of the G.A.A. – November 1st, 1884

Corcaigh v Tiobraid Árann 1741

(Níor chuibhdhe dhon ghasraidh)

Le Seán na Ráithíneach
Foinse: Seán na Ráithíneach
Torna do chuir in eagar
Oifig an tSoláthair, Baile Átha Cliath
Preas Dún Dealgan 1954

Níor chuibhdhe (1) dhon ghasraidh, (2) tharraing ón áird adtuaidh, (3)
maoidheamh a ngaisce, mar cantar le dámh go buan;
's cér chruinn bhur scaitheamh (3a) ag freagairt do láthair sluaigh,
do scríobh na Barraigh an barra 's an báire uaibh.

Uaibh do sciobadh, le cumus gan chlaon (4) ar bith,
Buadh gach cluiche (5) d'ár imir (6) ár laochradh libh;
's cé buaireadh sibhse fá thuitim an scéil mar sin,
san uachtar tuigidh gur mhionaca i n-éachtaibh sinn.

Sinne nár coigil gach cothrom do leigean timcheall (6a)
Sinne do bhrostuigh (7) go foirtil I bhfeicsin daoine;
Sinne do chothuigh gan osna go deireadh an coimheascar;
is sinne go follus tug solus bhur gcreidimh dhíbhse.

Díbh (8) ní mheasaim gur masla ná náire fós,
I dtír ná i dtalamh, go ndeachaidh an áit seo (9) romhaibh,
i gcroidhe 's i gceannas, i n-acmhaing, (10) i gcáil 's I gcló;
's dá bhrígh sin feasta ná tagaidh chun láithrigh (11) leó.

Leó ba mheallta an mheabhair, don fhuirinn táinigh,
Fógairt geall go leabhair i n-imirt báire,
I gcomhgar Ghleann na nGall, 'na gcrithid námhaid,
's a ngeóbhadh (12) 'na dteannta ann badh linne an láitheach.

Do láthair Mhic Ádaim, ceann uirid (13) na gcríoch,
's gach árdfhlaith do ráinig (14) i n-ionad an ghnímh (15)

d'fáiscamair báire go cliste chun (16) cinn,
is d'fág sin bhur ndánta, 'na mustar gan bhrígh.

Brígh an chúrsa má's fonn libh a thagairt go cóir:
do bhí an súgradh go clúmhail, is fanadh go fóill;
an rí (17) Fionn is a chongnamh (18) dhá dtagadh 'na (19) gcomhar
ba thrí thúisce (20) bheadh túirseach 'ná Barraigh na slógh.(21)

Slóighte sonaidhe (22) molfaidhear (23) choidhche ag dáimh,
le códacht, chloistí, (24) chosnáid (25) tír gan táir;
leóghain gan lochtaí , (26) is sochroidhe (27) chím ar fagháil;
lucht fórsa I gcogaidhibh (28) ghoirtigheas naímhid (29) go tláth.

Tláth níorbh iongnadh (30) an fhuireann do reidheag 'na gceann,
I ndeáidh gach cruinnighthe rineadh I bhfeidhil teacht ann;
's nár fágadh oiread an duine bhí i scidhil (31) go seang
gan cárnadh chugainn, 's sinne tug faghairt don dream (32)

Dream cheannais gan locht nách loiceadh d'aon sa tír;
Dream dhearbha I dtroid ná coirfeadh (33) céadtha dhíbh;
Dream fearamhail foirtil d'oscail réidh an tsnaidhm;
Dream Bhaile na gCloc, cur ortha, féach, níor chuibhdhe. (34)

1.chaoi; 2. –sradh; 3. attuaig; 3a. sgathamh; 4.claon; 5. cluithe; 6. imthir; 6a.
tímpchioll; 7.-tuig; 8. dhíbh; 9. áitso reomh-;10. anacfuinn; 11.-rig; 12. sa ang- 13.
urruid; 14.-nidh; 15. An ionnad an ghníomh; 16.chum; 17. rígh; 18. chúghnamh;
19.ina; 20.thúsga; 21. slóg; 22. sonaoi; 23. –fuigher; 24.chloistíghe; 25. chosnaoid;
26.-taoi; 27.-chraoi; 28. accogaoibh; 29.naoid; 30. –gna; 31.aseidhl; 32.'dram' tríd
síos; 33. -theadh; 34.chaoi; agus 'ut supra' scríobhtha fé, ag ceangal an chonchlainn.

'Ar bháire mhór Ghleann na nGall .i. iomáin chomórtais do tugadh san bhliadhain
1741, idir Chonntae Chorcaighe agus Chonntae Thiobrad Árann. Donnchadh Mac
Craith (o Choill Beithine) agus Mac Ádaim.i. Colonel Barry, Ghleann na gCárr, ba
chinn ar an mbáire sin. Do bhíodar filidhe Thiobrad Árann dá mhaoidheamh gur aca
féin do bhí an lá, is ag déanamh rabhchán air sin. Do bhí Seán na Ráithíneach, an uair
sin, 'na chomhnuidhe i gCarraig na bhFear, I Mhúscraighe, agus I mbéal an doruis,
dar leat, ag Barraigh Mhóra Bhaile na gCloc óna bhfuighead comaoine móra go
minic'.

It is not fitting for the group that came from the north
to boast about their exploits, as is sung by poets everlastingly;
And although your effort in responding to the opposition was accurate,
the Barrys snatched the victory and the game from you.
From you was snatched by faultless ability
the victory in every game that our heroes played against you;
And although you were distraught at that outcome,
Understand that we are most often victorious in exploits.

We, who did not deny justice to anybody;
We, who hastened energetically in the view of the people;
We, who without sigh endured the combat until the end;
It is we who vanquished you decisively (*lit*. it is we clearly, who gave the light of your
faith to you)

I do not think that it is any insult or shame for you
whatsoever that you were defeated,
In heart and in authority, in ability, in fame and in appearance;
And therefore henceforth do not go into combat against them.

They were mistaken, those who came
in proclaiming copiously wagers in hurling
at Gleann na nGall, where enemies quiver,
And no matter who might accompany them there,
we would be the victors.

In the presence of McAdam, chief of the territories
And every prince, who came to the site of the deed,
we skilfully advanced the game
and that left your exploits (or ballads) worthless.

If you wish to have an accurate account of the day's events:
The contest was notable, and (? that is not all):
If king Fionn and his helpers were to come to their assistance,
They would thrice more quickly be exhausted than Barrys of the hosts.

Prosperous hosts they will forever be praised by poets;
Bravely, it was heard, they defend (their) land without reproach;
Faultless heroes, the best I see;
Fighters in wars, who vanquish (their) enemies

It is no wonder that those who were against them were weakened
After every encounter that occurred there;
And that not even a single person was left (? standing)

Who was not laid low by us,
And it is we who tempered the host.

A band of leaders without fault, who would not yield to anyone in the land;
A firm band in battle, whom hundreds would not weary;
A manly strong band who easily opened up the knot;
The band from Balinaglough, to challenge them,
See, it was not fitting.

Corcaigh v Tiobraid Árann 1741(A Translation)

By Seán Ó Murchú na Ráithineach-one of the Gaelic poets of Carrignavar and translated by Tom Barry, Garrynacoole.
Source: Bride Rovers Abú-The story of Gaelic Games in Rathcormac Parish by John Arnold, Garryantaggart, Bartlemy.

'Twas improper of the Northern party
To boast its feats in lasting poetry
Whatever result they bandied about,
The Barrys won without a doubt.

Mistaken was the team that came
Loudly boasting of its hurling fame
In the fearsome gap of Glenagoul
To find that we instead prevail.

Before McAdam leader of the district
And every noble at the conflict
With skill we wrung the match ahead
To leave your verses larne and dead.

The winning band not easily swept away
This fighting band untiring in the fray
This able band to open any lock
Be aware these men from Ballinaglough.

This is a part translation of the Corcaigh v Tiobraid Árann item on page 7.

In 1741, a game involving teams from Cork and Tipperary met in what is widely regarded as the first ever Cork v Tipperary Inter County game. The game took place at Glenagoul near Rathcormac. It was in essence a challenge between a side drawn from Tipperary organised by Donnacha McGrath of Kilbehenny and a Cork side organised by Colonel McAdam Barry of Lisnagar in Rathcormac. On the Cork side for this match were several Barry brothers from Ballinaglough in Carrignavar. Tradition relates that there were seven or eight sons of William Fitzredmond Barry on this team. They were cousins of Colonel McAdam Barry of Rathcormac. There would have been no knowledge of this game were it not for the fact that the result was disputed. A bard from Tipperary who had accompanied his team to Glenagoul (Glenagowl) put it about and boasted that the Tipperary team had won. This was denied by the Cork side and

Seán Ó Murchú na Raithineach-one of the Gaelic poets of Carrignavar put down in verse a rebuke to the Tipperary poem and in fact claimed that the Cork team won.

There were actually ten verses to the poem and the foremost significant verses were translated by Tom Barry and given above.

The tradition that the match was played in the locality has survived down through generations in Rathcormac and also in the Carrignavar district. In his book 'The Banks of the Bride' the late Patsy Barry, the local historian remembered that it was a much talked of event in the locality in years gone by and the actual field of play which is on the roadside in Glenagoul is still pointed out. Tom Barry of Garrynocole in Rathcormac who had done considerable research on this particular game points out that the year 1741 was a particularly disastrous year for Ireland. There was a great frost the previous year in 1740 which almost totally destroyed the potato crop and led to a scarcity of food. Whole villages were reported as being wiped out. The crisis finally came to an end about August or maybe earlier in 1741 when an exceptionally good harvest was recorded. It is possible that the Glenagoul hurling match marked the ending of the local crisis or famine and if not organised for a wager it could have been organised to restore spirits and morale generally Whatever the reason the fact remains that the earliest known Cork v Tipperary hurling match was played in the parish of Rathcormac. (Bride Rovers Abú The story of Gaelic Games in Rathcormac Parish by John Arnold, Garryantaggart, Bartlemy.)

21

Na Sláintí

*Foinse: Londubh an Chairn le Maighréad Ní Annagáin
agus Séamus de Chlanndiolúin*

Ó Slán chum na cnuic is chum árd ghleanna'n tsuilt,
Agus slán leatsa Thiobruid Árann.
Chum Sheaghain ghil Uí Chuirc agus Séamus gan choir,
Le saor chead óm thoil céad slán chughaibh.
Gach lá bíodh againn cead *vault* agus con,
Báire as ruith t'éis snáimh seal ó,
Ar mhóintibh mhín bhog, ag cur seóladh faoi phuic,
Sin slán lem ghoin go dtí an ráig sin.

Slán chum na habhann, mo ghrádh Lios na nGall
Is gach pháirc dheas dá ngabhmaois tríthe.
Slán chum an dream, as chum árd ghuth na ngleann,
Do fhágamar in am aoibhinn.
Tá mo shláintese go fann ó ráinig mé anonn,
Is ná thráchtaid ar am na baoise,
Mbíodh báire is greann le fághail ann go Samhain,
Agus slán le nár liúnta Bridhde.

Slán chum na Mumhan, is chum Sheaghain ghil de Búrc,
Agus slán chughaibh go dluth le chéile,
Slán chum na Cúlach, mar a mbíodh an greann,
Agus scáirdeach de'n bhrannda daor leis.
Tá mo shláintese go fann ó ráinig mé ann,
Is ná tráchtfadh siad liom ar Maothaill ó.
Do chaill mé mo shiubhal, mo *vault* is mo luth,
Ó d'fág mé an tSiúir 'san Raechoill.

Cá bhfáfainn tú a Philib, mo shlán chughat do chuirim,
Is shlán chum tuille ded' chomharsain
Shlán chum mo chumainn tá i gCnoc na gCuradh,
Is slán agus fiche dom' stórach.
Go dtráighfidh an tuile tá 'dir mé's tusa,

Ó grádh bhéidh agam I gcomhad duit ó.
Mo láimh ar an ngloine, slán chughat do chuirim,
Do shláinte tar muir 'nois ólaim.

Na Sláintí (The Farewells)

Mairéad Ní Annagáin writes: 'The place-names mentioned in the Gaelic version were in the border-territory of the Déisi and south Tipperary. The song was composed by an ecclesiastical student in Rome. The words are interesting as showing the hold athletics, jumping, running, swimming, hurling, etc., had on the people then as now. The writer's great regret is that deprived of the freedom of the green fields he has lost his fine physical training. His companions in the hurling and hunting field are mentioned with affection. This song was sung in my memory by the older generation, people who, if alive now, would be bordering on the century. I got the words from Patrick Power of Stradbally, Co. Waterford, as I had forgotten most of them, having been so long away from the Déisi.'

Londubh an Chairn was published in 1925 and if the song was only sung by people born in 1825 it could relate to any period in the 19c if not to the previous century.

23

Na Sláintí (A Translation)

Foinse: Londubh an Chairn le Maighréad Ní Annagáin
agus Séamus de Chlanndiolúin

Farewell to the hills, the glens and the rills
An farewell to my old Tipp'rary,
From the friends of my youth, in sorrow and ruth,
I'm parting, in truth, heart-weary.
Where we leaped and we ran, where we hunted and swam,
Where we fished in the Suir's bright waters,
To the bog and the mere, where we hunted the deer,
To Clonmel's gallant sons and fair daughters.

Farewell to the streams I see in my dreams,
The fields where I used to ramble.
Farewell to my friends, from the hills and the glens,
Farewell to the brake and the bramble.
I've bartered my health in seeking for wealth
And I'm grieving in stealth to leave ye,
The hurling and fair, the comradeship rare,
And the good friends that ne'er would deceive ye.

Old Munster! Goodbye! For thee till I die,
With tears in my eyes I'll be grieving;
Thy laughter and fun, thy stormclouds and sun,
Till my brief days are done, I'm leaving.
Till dry is the sea that parts me from thee
My heart's love Machree! —unending,
With glass in my hand, to Munster's bright strand
From far foreign land I'll be sending.

The Hurling 1798

By Edward Mandeville
Source: National Library and
Séamus Ó Riain, Moneygall

Of all the sports that please the rural throng,
The goal first claims the effort of my song;
Where mimic war its evolutions shows,
To sly, to harass, to pursue and close.
By games like these the Rome began,
Where beardless childhood play'd the warlike man.

Some hoary sage, rever'd by all the train,
Who long had been the champion of the plain,
With placid smile, not with tyrannic sway,
Waves back the crowds, the willing crowds obey.
With knowing ken he marks the level ground,
And plants the *willow* at the well-known bound.   *1
Reflection fans the half-extinguished flame,
With fond remembrance of his former fame;
Where oft he Nisus-like skimmed o'er the plain
Or stood the butt of ev'ry tilting swain
When shouting maids extoll'd him with their cries,
The rolling orb dim fading in the skies;
Whilst won'dring they the cloud-veiled ball pursue,
And whisp'ring ask the place to which it flew:
Fain wou'd he join the youthful band once more,
His heart yet willing—but his strength is o'er.
Affection kindles in each swelling breast,
And all his fame unenvy'd is confessed.
When thus the sage, of former prowess proud,
Becks the attention of the prattling crowd.
'Such were my pow'rs when once I here have stood,
When strongly flow'd the current of my blood;
Ere envious age an hoary winter spread
O'er the thin'd honors of my silver head'

The lusty lads advance in equal rows;
Each parent's breast with blushing transport glows;
Silk kerchieves bind their close compacted hairs;
Each strong-nerv'd hand a polish'd hurly bears;
Contrasted wreaths their hardy breasts display,
To mark each partner thro' the mazy play.
With ribbon gay which her fair head array'd,
Or homely garter that herself had made,
Which from her leg with native blush she stole,
Of her chaste love the great, tho' humble dole,
Each buxom lass her fav'rite lad intwines,
Each sturdy band in rustic splendor shines.

The signal made aloft is flung the ball,
All anxious watch impatient for its fall:
The steady *back* their bossy weapons rear,   *2
And twirl them nimbly in th'intrenchant air;
Men above men in quick succession bound,
Hips jostle hips, the clashing hurlies sound;
'Till one, essays, versed in the wiles of play,
And nimbly sends th'elastic ball away.
The cause remov'd here ends the contest too,
The active whips with hasty steps pursue;
Scud o'er the plain swift as the fleeting wind,
Or tilting leave the prostrate foe behind,
(Foe of the hour, hence harmony and peace,
And friendship clasps them in its close embrace.)
Back to the green the pliant orb they roll,
Each party pointing to the adverse goal;
Now high it flies, then skims the turf below,
As chance, or skill, directs the sounding blow;
'Till stop'd its course the flying *wings* essay,   *2
Or sturdy force, or quick finesse of play.

Close as the phalanx fam'd in ancient song,
They crowding press the rolling ball along;
Now those succeed, now these reluctant yield,

26

As crested legions on the embattl'd field.
O'er some fall'n hero wage the stubborn fray,
To bear triumphantly the spoils away.

True to his charge the goal-man calm surveys
The various efforts, and the winding maze.
Hopes, doubts and fears, alternatively arise,
As friends or foes possess the bounding prize.
To lend his aid, tho' eagerly inclin'd,
Still duty binds him to the post assign'd.

Enough, the prowess of each swain display'd,
He, bids them cease, who first the bands array'd.

*1   willow—The goal is usually made of arched willow twigs.
*2   The different divisions into which hurlers are formed.

Edward Mandeville, the author was one of the land-owning gentry of Ballydine .

A number of factors determined the distribution of the southern game. 'The most
important was the patronage of the local gentry families particularly those most
closely embedded in the life of the local people. They picked the teams, arranged the
hurling greens and supervised the matches, which were frequently organised as
gambling events…Landlord patronage was essential to the well-being of the southern
game; once it was removed, the structures it supported crumbled and the game
collapsed into shapeless anarchy…. the gentry's disengagement from immersion in
the shared intimacies of daily life can be seen not just in hurling, but in other areas of
language, music, sport and behaviour, as the gradual reception of metropolitan ideas
eroded the other loyalties'. (Kevin Whelan, Bicentennial Research Fellow at the Royal
Irish Academy, History Ireland)

Príosún Chluain Meala

Foinse: Londubh an Chairn 1925, le Maighréad Ní Annagáin agus Séamus de Chlanndiolúin

Ar maidin lae 'lé Pádraig
'S mé ag fágáilt an bhaile
'S mé ag dul go hÁrd Pádraig
'Cur lásaí lem' hata.
Bhí Bríainín is Máirín
Dá shíorrádh liomsa casadh,
Agus mé go socair sást'
I bhfochair Sergeant ag ól leanna

Éir' id' shuidhe a bhuachaill
Agus glúais ar do ghearrán
Go ragham 'triall ar an stúairín
Tá thuas ar an gcnocán.
Mar bhí sí dá luadh liom
Ó bhí sí 'na leanbh bán,
Agus is binne liom naoi n-uair' í
Ná'n chuaichín ar an ngéagán.

Tá mo shíain is mo dhiallaid
Ar iasacht as baile
Is mo chapall ag fiadhach aige
Buaichaillí an airm
Tá mo chamán ag fiaradh
Is ag líathadh fa mo leabaidh,
Agus mé go dúbhach díachrach
I bpríosún Chluain Meala.

Ó do bhí mé im'buachaill
Ba stuamdha bhí 'sa mbaile,
Dhéanfainn súgradh nó gáire
Nó pléirách ar faithche.
Do bhuailfinn poc báire

28

Chomh hárd leis na fearaibh,
Is a dhaoine na n-árann,
Nach cás libh mo dhalladh.

The air was also sung to Edward Walsh's song with English words, 'Máighréad Ní Cheallaigh.' First published in 'An Lonndubh' 1904

The Jail of Clonmel

By. J.J. Callanan
Source: Londubh an Chairn 1925, le Maighréad Ní Annagáin agus Séamus de Chlanndiolúin

How hard is my fortune
And vain my repining;
The strong rope of fate
For this young neck is twining.
My strength is departed,
My cheeks sunk and sallow,
While I languish in chains
In the jail of Cluain-Meala.

No boy in the village
Was ever yet milder,
I'd play with a child
And my sport would be no wilder.
I'd dance without tiring
From morning till even,
And the goal-ball I'd strike
To the lightning of heaven.

At my bed foot decaying
My hurl bat is lying,
Through the boys of the village
My goal-ball is flying;
My horse 'mong the neighbours
Neglected may fallow,
While I pine in my chains
In the Jail of Cluain-meala.

Next Sunday the 'Pattern'
At home they'll be keeping,
And the young active hurlers
The field will be sweeping;

With the dance of fair maidens
The evening they'll hallow,
While this heart, once so gay,
Shall be cold in Cluain-Meala.

Written about 1850 and has appeared in many publications under the name of The
Convict of Clonmel., or the Gaol of Cluian Meala.

J.J. Callanan was a poet, born in Cork in 1795. He studied for the priesthood for a
period. Entered Trinity to prepare for the Bar but did not continue. Returned to Cork
in 1823 to act as a tutor in a local classical school. Accepted tutorship in Lisbon and
died there in 1829." It is Callinan's great distinction that he was the first of the Anglo
Irish poets to give adequate versions in English of old Gaelic poems". (The Minstrel
of Éirinn by Terence O'Hanlon 1930)

Little is known of the youth, whose name was O'Donnell, Iveragh, Kerry, but relates
to a happening about the middle of the 18c. The Whiteboys (Buachaillí Dána) were his
companions. He was to be hanged in Clonmel jail on the following Friday—
apparently with two fellow victims. Their heads would be severed from their bodies
and exhibited on spikes at the gate of the prison, as a warning to others.

The Whiteboys were a movement of country (agrarian) protest. The were so called
because of the white shirts worn over everyday clothing—partly for disguise and
partly for shared identification at night. Protest began in County Tipperary in 1761.
The evils of lanlordism—absentee lanlordism — were at their height. Tithes on corn,
rents and evictions were the main grievances. The people had no redress as they were
denied parliamentary privilege and debarred from election to any public body. The
Whiteboys were guilty of many excesses. They burned homesteads, hocked cattle and
sometimes 'carded' their victims, i.e scraped the naked back with a steel wool card.
But the people, in general, supported the Whiteboys as they considered such excesses
a measure of their grievances.

'Success to the Whiteboys; we've a few of them here
We'll toast their good health in both whiskey and beer;
And long may they reign over country and town,
For they are the boys that keep land-jobbers down.'

The Whiteboy Acts, 1766, 1776, 1787, created numerous capital offences connected
with protest.

31

The Men of Tipperary

By Thomas Davis

Let Britain boast her British hosts
About them all right little care we,
Not British seas nor British coasts
Can match the men of Tipperary.

Tall is his form; his heart is warm,
His spirit light as any fairy,
His wrath is fearful as the storm
That sweeps the hills of Tipperary.

Learn him to fight for native land
His is no courage cold and wary,
The troops live not on earth would stand,
The headlong charge of Tipperary.

You meet him in his cabin rude
Or dancing with his dark-haired Mary,
You'd swear they knew no other mood,
But mirth and love in Tipperary.

You're free to share his scanty meal,
His plighted word he'll never vary,
In vain they tried with gold and steel,
To shake the faith of Tipperary.

Soft is his cailín's sunny eye,
Her mien is mild; her step is airy,
Her heart is fond; her soul is high,
Oh! she's the Pride of Tipperary.

Let Britain too, her banner brag,
We'll lift the green more proud and airy,
Be mine the lot to bear that flag,

And lead the men of Tipperary.
Though Britain boasts her British hosts
About them all right little care we,
Give us, to guard our native coasts,
The matchless men of Tipperary.

The author, Thomas Osborne Davis was born on the 24th October 1813 and died on the 9th September 1845. With Gavin Duffy and John Blake Dillon he founded the Nation in 1842. Love of Ireland and pride and glory in its past were the ruling passions of his life. As a leader of the Young Ireland movement he was greatly esteemed. His charisma and powerful writings made him undisputed leader of the Young Ireland group, and he sought to bring their sense of nationality to the public through his popular ballads.

J. D. Mehigan writing under the pen name of Carberry writes, 'the fact that in three years 1842, 1843 and 1844, the prodigious pen of Davis in the Nation newspaper, both in prose and verse, thrilled the Irish people as they were never thrilled before and awoke a slumbering spirit of nationhood, fed the smouldering fires of tradition and forgotten history, fanning them into an eternal flame of Island love'

Davis loved Tipperary. He spent long holidays in Tipperary (Monaquill, Templederry) in his youth. Many of the Tipperary hurling songs of the 1930's for instance, seem to be influenced by the verses in the above poem. Jim Hurley, Secretary U.C.C. who fought in a famous IRA column, and won four hurling All-Irelands with Cork and who wrote under the pen name S.O.M writes, ' Yes! To have the manhood of your district described as matchless by 'The Kingliest King that Ireland ever saw' might even excuse the almost insufferable pride noticeable at times in my friends Breen and Leahy'.

'Home Longings, ' or 'Slievenamon'

By Charles J. Kickham
Source: The Valley Near Slievenamon-a Kickham anthology compiled and edited by
James Maher. 1941

Alone, all alone, by the wave- washed strand,
All alone in the crowded hall;
The hall it is gay, and the waves are grand,
But my heart is not here at all.
It flies far away, by night and by day,
To the time and the joys that are gone—
Ah! I never can forget, the maiden I met,
In the valley near Slieve-na-mon.

It was not the grace of her queenly air,
Nor her cheek of the rose's glow;
Nor her soft black eyes, nor her flowing hair,
Nor was it her lily-white brow:
'Twas the soul of truth, and of melting ruth,
And the smile like a summer dawn,
That stole my heart away one mild May day,
In the valley near Slieve-na-mon.

In the festive hall-by the star watched shore—
My restless spirit cries—
'My love—Oh, my love—shall I never see you more?
And, my Land—will you ever uprise?'
By night and by day, I ever, ever pray—
While lonely my life flows on—
To see our flag unrolled, and my true love to unfold
In the valley near Slieve-na-mon.

'Home Longings' or **'Slievenamon'** as it is popularly known, was first published in
Dr. Cane's Kilkenny magazine, the 'Celt', where it was introduced as a vocal item in a
tale by Charles J. Kickham, entitled 'Never Give Up'—from the motto which
sustained James Maher, the central figure of the story, who had been unjustly evicted
from his holding. This story was afterwards contributed to the magazine 'Young

Ireland,' in November 1875, under the title of 'The Home of Slievenamon: in A Story of Irish Country Life,' by Charles J. Kickham. Our version of the song is taken from the 'Celt,' which presumably printed it from the original manuscript of its composer, who was, of course, Charles Kickham himself.

The setting of the song, is revealed thus: —Edward O'Neill a former law student, who was forced to return home to take charge of his deceased father's affairs, had incurred the enmity of his landlord because of his part in the Insurrection of 1848. More recently Edward had provided his enemy with a fresh grievance by voting as conscience directed, but contrary to 'orders'. The landlord, accordingly, has resolved to ruin him, and the young man comes to inform his sweet heart that the only course left open to him is to leave Ireland.

….Edward O'Neill paused at the door of the back drawing room, to collect himself for what he knew would be a painful interview. The happy hours he had spent in the society of Susan Maher; the radiant smile, the glad light in the soft dark eyes, and the warm trusting clasp of the little white hand, that always greeted him; pleasant summer rambles, with her arms linked in his; winter nights made brighter than summer, by the sunshine of her smiles and the music of her voice; tender, lingering, oft repeated 'good-byes'; all, crowded upon his heart.

'O, slavery, through how many channels can your embittered waters be poured into the heart!'

He recognised in the air, which Susan at that moment commenced to play, an old Irish melody, which he knew she had adapted to a little ballad which he himself had written while a law student in Dublin. This effusion of 'wild youth passed,' sung in a clear sweet voice, created such a tumult of contending feelings in his breast, that he could not help smiling at what he considered his own weakness—(The Valley Near Slievenamon-a Kickham anthology compiled and edited by James Maher. 1941, p 61.)

In the 'Tales of Tipperary' Kickham writes: Old Slieve-na-mon! —did we ever indulge in daydream of which you were not part and parcel? Its sweetest draught was to contemplate the happy homes round thy base, freed forever from the despoiler! Was the dream of love? It was to thy azure outline the beloved one turned her eyes to hide the blush and tear called up by the impassioned avowel. And when the trembling hand was at length yielded, and the pure heart wooed and won—you, Old Mountain! peeped in, through woodbines and sweetbrier, upon a home scene, the like of which— alas! —is but too seldom to be found save in the visions of the dreamer. And when the time for such visions was gone by, and despair crept in where hope had been—when the cup of sorrow was drained to the very dregs—was it not to thee we fled—like a child to its mother's lap—and thou hast heard the groan which torture and the rack would fail to wring in the hearing of human ear!
And when earthly hope had withered, save one—what was it? —to sleep the last long, peaceful sleep beneath thy shadow. And saddest thought of all, is this too, but a dream, destined never to be fulfilled? We do not wonder at the reply of the United Irishman, when asked, after a life long exile, why he returned to a land where there

was not a single friend or acquaintance left to bid him welcome—'I came back,' said the exile, 'to see the mountains!'

And Brian O'Higgins in his poem I Love You, Tipperary writes,

'I love you Tipperary dear, for sake of him who told
The tale of homely 'Knocknagow' —its hearts as true as gold—
For sake of 'Matt the Thresher's' strength, and Nora Lahy's grace,
I love you Tipperary, tho' I never saw your face.

I love you Tipperary, for sake of one dear friend,
Within whose eyes your smiles and tears forever meet and blend,
Whose trust and friendship freely given, no change could e'er efface,
O! I love you Tipperary, tho' I never saw your face.

I love you Tipperary dear, for sake of each and all;
By night and day on you, a stór, may kindly blessings fall;
May sorrow pass you lightly o'er, and never leave a trace;
God bless you Tipperary, tho' I ne'er may see your face.

Inscription over Kickham's Grave

C.J.Kickham
Born 9th May 1828,
Died 22nd August, 1882.
Journalist, Novelist, and Poet,
But Before All Patriot.
Traitor to Crime, Vice and Fraud,
But True to Ireland and to God.

R.I.P.

The Farmer's Song

By Charles J. Kickham
Source:The Valley Near Slievenamon—A Kickham Anthology compiled and edited by
James Maher

I've a pound for to lend, and a pound for to spend—
And *céad míle fáilte* my word for a friend;
No mortal I envy, no master I own—
Nor lord in his castle, nor king on his throne.
Come; fill up your glasses, the first cup we'll drain
To the comrades we lost on the red battle plain!
Oh, we'll cherish their fame, boys, who died long ago—
And what's that to any man whether or no?

The spinning wheels stop, and my girls grow pale,
While their mother is telling some sorrowful tale,
Of old cabins levelled, and coffinless graves,
And ships swallowed up in the salt ocean waves.
But, girls, that's over—for each of you now
I'll have twenty five pounds and a —three year old cow;
And we'll have *lán na mhála* at your weddings I throw—
And what's that to any man whether or no?

Come here, *bhean na tighe*, sit beside me a while,
And the pride of your heart let me read in your smile.
Would you give your old home for the lordliest hall?
Ha! —You glance at my rifle that hangs on the wall.
And your two gallant boys on parade-day are seen
In the ranks of the brave 'neath the banner of green;
Oh! I've taught them to guard it 'gainst traitor and foe—
And what's that to any man whether or no?

But the youngest of all is the 'white-headed boy'—
The pulse of your heart, and our pride and our joy:
From the dance and the **hurling** he'll steal off to pray,
And will wander alone by the river all day.

He's as good as the priest at his Latin I hear,
And to college please god, we'll send him next year.

Oh, he'll offer the Mass for our souls when we go—
And what's that to any man whether or no?
Your hands, then, old neighbours! one more glass we'll drain
And *céad míle fáilte* again and again!
May discord and treason keep far from our shore,
And freedom and peace light our homes evermore.
He's the king of good fellows, the poor, honest man;
So we'll live and be merry as long as we can,
And we'll cling to old Ireland through weal and through woe—
And what's that to any man whether or no?

Editor's Note—'The Farmer's Song' was sung by Matt the Thresher in 'Knocknagow' where it appears under the title of 'The Peasant Farmer's Song—for the time to come.'

Gurtdrum Big Field

*By Shelley of Cutteen, Solohead, circa 1860. Received by Seamus J. King,
Boherclough, Cashel from Micheál Ó Riain, Ballydota, Monard*

Dear Thomas, sit by me a stór
And tell some tales of home,
That will take my wandering spirits back
O'er the ocean's leaping foam.
Back to the old land I love so well
Where my young footsteps strayed—
Where the honey bee and butterfly
I chased from shale to shade.

And farther from the old land I roam
The more it appears to be,
And the merry days I spent at home
In the joys of infancy.
With good neighbours all around
And comrades one and all,
Assembled in Gurtdrum big field
For to kick the round foot-ball.

No more dear Thomas we will roam
When Solohead mass is o'er,
To share our joys with the Gurtdrum boys
Whom I will see no more.
Through the Tileyard Grove no more will we roam
Or nest beneath its shade
Or wander through Gurtdrum big fields
Where to the dances we strayed.

I love the path we trod to school
With comrades by my side.
Day after day they fled away
Across the ocean wide.
Now some of them in their father's graves

Beneath their native clay
I met some here that gave me cheer
Out in America.

And now before I'll end my song
Indeed I'm well inclined
To bid farewell to all my friends
In Ireland far behind.
No matter, should I travel earth
Around from pole to pole
I love the spot that gave me birth
Within my Irish soul.

Micheál Ó Riain received this song from Mrs Helen Hayes (nee Perry) formerly of
Ballyryan, Solohead, who died in New York in her 100th year in 1986. Old GAA men
locally say that this is the first reference, that they are aware of, relating to GAA
matters in Solohead—the song is deemed to date from circa 1860.

Tipperary v Clare 1844

Anon
Source: The Clash of the Ash in Foreign Fields by Seamus J. King.

And first in the field were the gallant old Tipps,
With strength in their arms and smiles on their lips;
Like the fast heaving surge of their own royal stream,
The sons of the Shannon in ecstasy came;
While famed Garryowen poured its tribute along,
And Clare's sturdy peasants were thick in the throng.

'There were occasional references to hurling in Australian newspapers even before the founding of the GAA. One such is from the Brisbane Courier of March 24, 1874 in a report of St.Patrick's Day celebrations at Gatton 'Amongst other things the playing of a hurling match was introduced, for the first time, we believe, in Queensland. The game is thoroughly Irish, and bears about the same relation to the national sports of the Emerald Isle that cricket does to those of England. Usually the picked athletes of one parish are matched against those of some neighbouring district and, as the number of men playing is frequently very large, and thousands of persons throng to the scene of contest and take almost as active an interest in the proceedings as the players themselves, an Irish hurling match is about as lively an affair as anyone would wish to see.'

There's an earlier reference in 1844. It announced a hurling match to take place at Batman's Hill, in the neighbourhood of Melbourne, on July 12 between the men of Clare and Tipperary for a bet of fifty pounds. The match was arranged as a counterblast to an Orange procession to the same place to which all-good men who hated 'Pope and Popery, brass money and wooden shoes' were expected to give their assistance. The hurling match attracted five hundred stalwart Irishmen armed with hurleys, staves and shillelaghs and they had a great day's fun while the Orange procession shivered out of existence.

The Golden Fontenoy's Hurling Team 1870

By J. Dalton, Glendale, N.Y. U.S.A., July 20th 1969
Source: Golden-Kilfeacle: The Parish and its People by Senator Willie Ryan.
Received from Seamus J. King, Boherclough, Cashel.

These verses about a hurling team, composed of men and boys,
Whose deeds upon the Gaelic fields are known as no surprise.
They have vanquished all who came their way without making any
noise
They're the pride of all Tipperary, the Golden Fontenoy's.

Their captain is a valiant youth, a hero true and brave—
His gallant sires came here of late across the exiled wave,
To plant the tree of liberty in the land he idolised;
'Long may he live, his aid to give to the Golden Fontenoy's'.

Young Burke come first upon the list, no doubt our number one—
An athlete great his limbs complete, he's healthy, stout and strong.
Each day with heartful pleasure, he cheerfully supplies
Poteen pure mixed with the Suir for the Golden Fontenoy's.

There are others too I'd wish to name, and indeed I love them well,
When on the field, their camáns wield, and few can them excel.
There's young Hourigan, brave Thady Ryan and Pat Lynch devoid
of noise,
Carmody and Mickey Blake, for the Golden Fontenoy's.

Here comes three men from Cloughaleigh in jerseys neatly dressed,
With Fontenoy, in letters bright conspicuous on their breasts.
They are powerful on the field and when their spirits rise,
They'll surely win through thick and thin for the Golden Fontenoy's.

In Golden Michael Kennedy first saw the light of day.
He is now the champion's athlete by Hudson's stormy bay.
May happiness attend him, under occidental skies
And may he soon return home to the Golden Fontenoy's.

Success attend this gallant band in life as they pass on.
Halcyon days may they enjoy, elation grow among.
May angels guide and guard them, until the day they die,
And here I'll end what I have penned, long live the Fontenoy's.

Olympic Games in Roscrea

By The Rhymer from Roscrea
Source: The Nenagh Guardian, July 26, 1873. Received by Liam Ó Donnchú from
local historian Joseph Tobin, Thurles.

Descend O Muse! Perch on my pen: inspire me what to say;
I'm going to sing a song again, a song about Roscrea.
A dear, familiar, ancient place, is this old town Roscrea,
'Twas there we had a sporting race and jumping th' other day.

As in the Guardian I've not read one word about the sport;
It shan't be by the neighbours said; you had not some report.
Happ'ning in Corville's green retreats (Good Count O'Byrne's
place),
Some sketch of these athletic feats, in rhyme I'll try to trace.

The Roscrea band, all dressed so grand, was there to make us glad
And played until the crowd were set all musically mad.
Oh, how we pranced and how we danced, while on us glanced the
eyes,
With looks half-bold and half askance, of maidens that we prize.

Oh, 'twas a glorious day indeed; the sun with splendour shone
And paused to see the man, whose speed, the Silver Lover won.
The first prize was a £5 watch, the second, shillings ten;
Six fine athletes formed the match, all young and stalwart men.

Brave Daniel Reardon's foremost man, the watch his power rewards,
For of Patt Murphy, in the van, he held the ground six yards.
And ratt'ling in Patt Murphy's wake, Dan Stapleton appeared;
For the third best, there being no stake, Dan's thunderously cheered.

The other men who tried their luck were Tierney, Cantwell, Dwyer,
Three boys of stamina and pluck and all that you'd desire.
Next year, if they but practice well, the chances are they'll win;
For 'tis by practice most excel, so let them soon begin.

44

The next race is fully fifty yards short of the previous run,
And poor indeed, was their reward, who first and second won.
For these three hundred yards the first, ten shillings got for meed,
While but one half that paltry sum fell to the next in speed.

No matter, sure 'tis all for fun: we all for pleasure came;
What signifies who's lost or won; th' amusement is the same.
Seven started, each one strove to win; Jem Dwyer kept clear ahead;
Ned Maher, he came second in, P. Rice the others led.

Now comes the Boy Race, 'tis sooth, a truly pleasant sight,
To see the sinless brow of youth, thus mantling with delight.
Each eager to outstrip the rest; each restless at delay;
They're off—a score, perhaps, three score; how close they run,
Hurra!

The race is yards, twice seventy-five, just fit for tender years;
Good gracious! How that youngster strives in front of his compeers.
Young Menton leads, Brave boy! What ho! E.Quinlan has him
passed,
At what a rapid pace they go: see Sharp there hurrying fast—

Closer and closer, see, he nears E.Quinlan in the run;
Between them small the space appears—Hurrah! the race is won!
E. Quinlan wins by 'bout a yard; D.Sharp is second scored,
Young Menton pressed the victors hard; he counts a close up third.

The rest now come careering in, jostling and making fun;
May it be theirs in Life to win, when the world's race they run.
May long in memory be enshrined the day's enjoyment and
Hereafter oft recalled to mind, when in some foreign land.

Next comes the running jump, a feat, which, for success requires
Agility with strength should meet in one whom praise inspires.
Dan Stapleton, just half an inch, beat Murphy P., whose best
Was four-eleven—close was the pinch—but these beat all the rest.

T. Treacy, Tooher, Harrold, Maher, and Cantwell, also, tried:
Their jumping powers, but all declare it was in vain they vied.
Other amusements followed fast, till Sol far in the West,
His farewell rays on Corville cast, telling 'twas time to rest.

Had I poetic Pindar's power or my lyre like his was strung,
What sunshine o'er these sports I'd shower, sublimely they'd be sung!.
Accept the will, then, for the deed, nor spurn my humble lay;
Insert, that those who've run may read The Rhymer from Roscrea.

This poem predates the foundation of the GAA. Athletics were more popular in the early days of the GAA than hurling or football. Athletic meetings were drawing bigger crowds. The new association, at the beginning, concentrated largely on athletic meetings and hurling and/or football games were played as curtain raisers.

It wasn't until 1886 that hurling , football and handball were given equal prominence to athletics. In time, the GAA ceased to control athletics and concentrated mainly on hurling, Gaelic football and handball.

The Hurlers of Glenn-acos- lán

By J.J. Finnan (Myles)
Source: The Patriotic Songs and Poems 1865-1912
Received from Séamus Ó Riain, Moneygall.
Also: Our Games Annual 1958

'Tis well I remember the good olden time,
When I was a fine strapping boy in my prime;
When young men had spirit and plenty of brawn,
Who belted the leather at Glennacoslán.

Of that famous spot I would have you take note,
It might be the scene of the 'Peeler and Goat'
For it lies close to Bansha and Lowe's of Kilshan,
That 'field of the hurlers' famed Glennacoslán.

I know the place well; I was there in my day,
With camán well polished, prepared for the fray.
For with 'parish bullies' I then took my stand,
Although you could blow me today from your hand.

Not mine to disparage, not mine to run down,
Our hurlers today of the country or town;
Nor say that the best is the merest *spriosán*
Compared to the hurlers of Glennacoslán.

We sported no tights that pure modesty hurts,
Bu wore our knee- breeches and bandlecloth shirts,
With handkerchiefs over our *nappers* well drawn,
To show our true colours at Glennacoslán

Our rules were so simple that all understood,
Except some pure drone or a 'stick-in-the-mud';
'Twas shoulder to shoulder, 'twas brawn against brawn,
The sight was entrancing at Glennacoslán

47

There was Delany, the best known of all,
Whose duty was always to strike up the ball;
Whose cabin stood near on the slope of Kilshane
He was the old stand-by at Glennacoslán

And there from Kilfeakle came Paddy Guilfoyle
Who long felt to tyrants as sore as a boil;
With Kellys and Hogans, from Kyle to Grenane,
And tested their mettle at Glennacoslán.

And from ancient Emly came Jacky McGrath,
And many bold boys who despised Saxon law;
The Finnans, of Latteen; Matt Ryan of Kilross–
All stripped for the fray when the ball got the toss.

There were Ryans from Shronell, and Ryans from elsewhere,
And Caseys and Condons from Mitchelstown square;
While 'Boland the fiddler', who hailed from Brockbawn,
Astonished the natives at Glennacoslán

From nigh Ballyneety came Kennedy Mór
As strong as Cú Chulainn that hero of yore;
With doughty Tom Bradshaw, from Cullen's green bawn,
To loosen their muscles at Glennacoslán

Brave Bansha, Kilmoyler and Aherlow Glen,
Prepared for those meetings, the pick of their men:
Old Tubberadora sent Billy Marnane,
As dauntless as any at Glennacoslán.

To name all my heroes would make a big book,
Who went with their parties to goal or to puck;
Their deeds should be blazoned as bright as the dawn,
They honoured old Ireland at Glennacoslán.

But Alas! For our land, in those strenuous hours,
We then could if only aware of our powers,

Have chased the vile Saxon and all his vile spawn,
Like chasing the leather at Glennacoslán.

So now to conclude and to finish my rhyme,
The 'boys' were superb in your grandfather's time;
Then heed well the tales the old 'Seanachie' tells,
And treasure them all, while the heart proudly swells.

The author, J.J. Finnan ('Myles'), 1865-1912, was born in the Glen of Aherlow; emigrated to U.S.A.; wrote many poems and in his own words—'though I lay no claims whatever to a place among the bards of my country. I claim to be what is perhaps better—an Irish patriot. The lessons of true nationality that I learned at my father's knee more than sixty years ago I have never forgotten and never will.'

Gleanncoslan is situated in the townland of Kilshane, half way between Tipperary town and Bansha. The field on which they played is known as Deerpark. There is no local lore regarding the exploits of the hurlers and there is nothing known about them apart from the poem. Folklore has it that every Sunday, hurlers congregated at Deerpark, played matches between themsleves, commencing early morning and finishing at dusk. Seeing that the author J.J. Finan was born in 1865 and passed away in 1912, and he seemingly was writing about his own father's time when he himself was a fine strapping boy in his prime, it is likely that the hurling he remembers was being played between 1880 and 1887.

In Thurles Town

By Criostoir O'Flynn
Source:Centenary F.N.T. 1985, Atha Cliath 1

In Thurles town on All Saint's Day
A hireling in Dublin Castle's pay
Spied on the valiant men who came
To Hayes's Hotel, noting each name;
He little knew that each would be
Remembered long after he
And Empire's lords had passed away
Like morning dew on summer's day
When Freedom's sun rose to renew
The glory our Celtic race once knew
And rank old Erin in rebirth
With all free nations of the earth.
Proudly today we remember all
Those patriots who rallied to the call
When Cusack threw his challenge bold
At snobs, shoneens and all who sold
Their nation's heritage on the field
Of manly sport. Seven men sealed
Their names as spokesmen for their race,
Rainbow of hope on the tearstained face
Of Roisín Dubh, as seven men more
Would sign at Easter's rising hour.

The Founders and Patrons

By Criostoir O'Flynn
Source: Centenary, F.N.T.1985

53   Brave Cusack first, the Man from Clare,
        Reared on the Burren, bleak and bare
        But rich in monumental stone,
        In Language and ancestral lore.
        Born into hunger, Cusack saw
        How British rule and British law   '
        Sent famine scything through a land
60   Of emerald green that God's own hand
        Made fertile as Eden. Trained to teach
        In so-called National Schools that preached
        English culture and English ways
        In England's tongue, he knew the days
        Of Ireland's language and traditions
        Were numbered. Improving his position
        To Catholic colleges, where gombeen men
        Paid fees to have their children learn
        To parrot Anglo-Irish Protestants
70   Still echoing English antecedents,
        He suffered, till it made him sick,
        The cream of the country, rich and thick,
        Unwilling cog as he had been
        In the imperialistic Murder Machine
        He ventured then to earn his bread
        Independently in the "empty trade"
        The poet Donncha Rua tried.
        At Gardiner Place by Liffeyside
        Cusack's Academy soon had grown
80   Famous as Plato's Athenian grove.
        Like Plato too he knew that man
        Needs more than bread, no spirit can
        Survive, no nation will endure
        That loses self respect; the cure

For Ireland's slouching servile soul
Would start with making bodies whole
In games that were our nation's own

88   Games that would link each Irish town
With Tara and the plains of Eamhain.

90   Next Maurice Davin, athlete supreme,
Clear-souled and true as Carrick's stream,
He learned to row on pleasant Suir,
Became a champion of the oar,
Built his own boats with skill and pride
And won as if he owned the tide.
In boxing too he was renowned
Never by any champion downed,
At hammer and shot he oft out-threw
The best that English brawn could do.
100   But more than all pastimes Davin loved
The games of Erin and often proved
An athlete of as great renown
As Matt the Thresher in 'Knocknagow'.
And yet his mighty hands could hold
The fiddle and the fighting bow
As gentle as a fairy wand
Playing the airs of his native land.
And everywhere on fields of sport
By every class and creed and sort
110   The name of Maurice Davin stood
As high as any hero could
For honour, fair play and manhood.

From Dublin came John Wyse-Power,
Fenian and Editor, this quiet hour
More revolutionary than armed victory
Would earn for him a place in history.

A sound Belfastman, John McKay,
On the *Cork Examiner* earned his pay,
So, no man there knew more about
120 The differences between North and South,
Or how language, games, class and creed
Can be used maliciously to breed
Dissension for political ends
And make us only count as friends

Those who believe and speak and play like us.
Wolfe Tone dreamed of a day
When labels of class and creed would be
Anacronisms, and the world would see
An Ireland reborn in unity.
130 Today, McKay and Tone would pity
New birthpangs of Ulster cursed by spells
Concocted in bigotry's darkest hells.

And what did the snooping Castle spy
Think when he saw the tall D.I,
Thomas Mc Carthy join those men
In that billard room turned seditious den?
An inside man, no doubt, he'd say,
Not knowing that the man from Dingle Bay
Had crammed to join the R.I.C.
140 At Cusack's Dublin Academy.
Like the poet Eoghan Rua in Rodney's fleet
Under his English belt there beat
A heart as true as to his native land
As any in Fionn mac Cumhaill's command.

From Templemore another came,
J.K. Bracken the builder: the name
Of patriots he preserved forever
In marble monuments, but never
Could his own patriot soul perceive
150 The cards in Fate's capricious sleeve:

A Fenian father in that company
Whose second son would one day be
Sitting on London's Cabinet board
And end his days a British lord.

The youngest name of all we praise,
P.J.O'Ryan, evokes no blaze
In glory's deeds, but let him stand
For those who at that meeting sat
And served unnamed, and for all those
160   Unnamed whose glory is the cause
They love and serve from year to year,
To God's own heart such names are dear.
So round a billiard table green
They met, nor could they have foreseen
How that symbolic cloth would spread
Like Brigid's cloak in years ahead
To make the myriad ordered lawns
Where men and youths would wield camáns
And chase the ball in sporting life
170   As part of an Irish way of life
Not chauvinistic, nor xenophobic,
But national, recalling our heroic
Past, legends of Setanta brave,
Of Táin Bó Cuailnge and Queen Maev,
Of Diarmuid Ó Duibhne on Tara's plain
Whose hurling valour won the game
And won him Gráinne's fatal love.
Heroes and saints in heaven above
Saw God's own blessing on our nation
180   On that All Saint's Day at the creation
Of the Gaelic Athletic Association.

Like Patrick's three-leafed shamrock bright
Three patrons spread the movement's light
By radiance reflected from their fame:
Davitt, Parnell, and Croke, each name

A beacon on Freedom's long dark road.
Croke's patriot pen from Cashel flowed
In Pauline epistle urging his flock
To revive the traditions of their stock,
190   By awakening pride in parish and town
He roused a people long trodden down
In servile apathy.
             Davitt had seen
His family evicted in Mayo, had been
A child worker in a Lancashire mill
Where he lost an arm. In Dartmoor cell
Or breaking stones in the convict yard
He meditated long and hard
On Ireland's miseries, shaping the plan
That would restore the ravaged land
To its own people.

200   Parnell of Avondale
Might well have been content to avail
Of privilege of class and creed
Like others of his landlord breed
And squander in London luxury
Rents racked from his tenant's misery.
His American mother had taught him well
To know the sound of the Liberty Bell,
That all are born to be free
That God gives life and liberty
210   To every human soul and race
And no man, no power can halt the pace
Of a nation's march to its rightful place.

Notes by the Author:

75   P.H. Pearse described the educational system as a "Murder Machine". His
essay makes sad reading seventy years later--nothing has changed except
that there is a vast increase in the numbers being processed through the
cramming factories.

55

77   In his comic poem Eachtra Ghiolla an Amarráin (The Adventure of the
      Luckless Fellow), the Clare born poet Donncha Rua Mac Conmara (1715-
      1810), about whom Francis Mc Manus wrote a trilogy of novels says:
          Ag múineadh scoile dob obair dom laethibh,
          'S a rún don phobal gur folamh an cheird sin!
      (Teaching school was the work of my days, and everyone knows that's an
      empty trade)
80   Plato's Athenian grove: the garden near Athens where Plato taught was
      called the Academy.
89   Tara. the palace of the High King of Ireland was situated at Tara in County
      Meath. In Irish it is often called Teamhair na Rithe. (Tara of the Kings)
      Eamhain. The ancient capital of Ulster, seat of the king and of his warriors,
      An Craobh Rua (The Red Branch), of whom the Irish Superman, Cú
      Chulainn, is the most famous in legend.
103   Knocknagow. The novel, sub-titled the Homes of Tipperary, by Charles J.
      Kickham, published in 1873.
126   Wolfe Tone. Theobald Wolfe Tone, Dublin Protestant barrister, the leading
      idealist in the United Irishmen and 1798 revolutionary movement . His
      grave at Bodenstown is the Mecca for annual pilgrimages by republicans,
      true and false, and inspired the fine ballad, the final verse of which goes
      thus:

127   In Bodenstown churchyard there is a green grave
                      And freely around it let winter winds rave—
                      Far better they suit him, the ruin and gloom,
                      Till Ireland a nation can build him a tomb.

141   The Kerry poet Eoghan Rua Ó Súilleabháin (1748-1784) renowned for his
      mellifluous aislingí (political poems in which the poet encounters Ireland
      in the form of a beautiful ethereal woman) was press-ganged into the
      British Navy and served under Admiral Rodney at a naval battle against
      the French in the West Indies on April 12ᵗ, 1782. Eoghan composed a
      laudatory poem, Rodney's glory, to commemorate Rodney's victory and in
      the hope (vain as it proved) that the grateful Admiral might let him go
      home to Kerry.
152   Brendan Bracken,, second son of Joseph Kevin Bracken, was born in
      Templemore in 1901. He was destined to become Minister of Information
      in Churchill's wartime cabinet. In 1952 he was elevated to the peerage as
      Vicount Bracken of Christchurch. He died in 1958. See the comprehensive
      biography by Charles Edward Lysaght, Brendan Bracken (Allen Lane,
      London, 1979)
166   The legend of St. Brigid's cloak was know to every child in Ireland in my
      school-days, when school reading-books were, in the best sense of the
      phrase, 'racy of the soil' written by Irish writers and published by wholly
      Irish publishing companies. A rich man to whom Brigid appealed for a bit
      of land to found a convent mockingly told her that he would give her as
      much as her cloak would cover (the sneering agnostic is not a new

phenomenon, in Ireland or in humanity). Brigid having prayed to God, took off her cloak and spread it on the ground; the sneer was wiped off the agnostic's face as he saw the cloak stretch until it had covered just about the amount Brigid herself had in mind.

174 Táin Bó Cuailnge .The most famous story in the Irish saga, telling of the war between Queen Maev of Connacht and King Conchúr (Conor) of Ulster. Cú Chulainn being the principal character in what is really a sequence of tales.

175 Diarmuid Ó Duibhne. One of the heroes of Fianna Éireann . He was a glamour boy, irresistible to women because of a magic 'love spot'. The High King's daughter Gráinne, betrothed to the widower Fionn (Diarmuid's boss), fell for Diarmuid when she saw him winning a hurling match single-handed on the plain at Tara and forced him into eloping with her. The tale of Fionn's vengeful pursuit is one of the great stories of the Fenian cycle.

Extract from The GAA—A History by Marcus de Búrca, 1980 -page.24

'At 3o'clock on Saturday afternoon November 1, 1884 Cusack opened the meeting in the hotel billiard room Probably not more than 13 people, and possibly only eight were present. The accepted number of founder members is seven: they do not include F.R. Moloney of Nenagh, who undoubtedly attended. Soon afterwards Cusack put the number at a dozen; twice later in uncontradicted statements made publicly when all concerned were still alive, he changed to nine. In addition to the seven accepted founders—Cusack, Davin, John Wyse Power, John McKay, J. K. Bracken, Joseph O'Ryan and Thomas St. Mc Carthy—the following were reported in reliable papers as having attended: William Foley of Carrick-on –Suir and Dwyer Culhane, William Delahunty, John Butler and M Cantwell, all of Thurles itself. The absence of anybody from Galway is surprising: but illness prevented John Sweeny of Loughrea from travelling.

The proceedings were brief, Cusack alone being long-winded. Davin took the chair and Cusack read the convening letter. Davin in a short statement pointed out the incongruity of Irishmen permitting Englishmen to organise Irish sport, emphasised that his had led to the decline of native pastimes and called for a body to draft rules to aid in their revival and to open athletics to the poor. Cusack followed with a longer speech, censuring the press for not reporting Irish sport and reading 60 messages of support; McKay also spoke. On the proposal of Cusack with Wyse Power seconding, Davin was then elected president of what was initially called the Gaelic Athleltic Association for the Preservation and Cultivation of National Pastimes; Cusack, Wyse Power and McKay were elected secretaries. After agreeing to ask Archbishop Croke, Charles Stewart Parnell and Michael Davitt (the founder of the Land League) to become patrons, the meeting adjourned'.

The author Criostoir O'Flynn was born in Limerick City and now lives in County Dublin, He is one of Ireland's best-known and prolific bilingual writers, having written over fifty books and plays in English and Irish. He uses the Irish form of his surname, Ó Floinn, when writing in Irish. He worked in teaching, broadcasting, journalism and public relations, but has been a full time writer since being elected to AOSDÁNA, the state sponsored body of writers, artists and composers who are considered to have made a significant contribution to the arts in Ireland .

Seven Men of Thurles

By Gerard Ryan, Inch, Bouladuff, Thurles
Source: Liam Ó Donnchú, Ballymoreen, Littleton

Seven men of Thurles
Gathered from afar
To rejuvenate the people
To believe in what they are.

A historic meeting
Surely did take place
To give the people back their games
And take pride in their race.

Seven men of Thurles
Their contribution it was great
The changed the pattern of men's lives
In the twentieth Century state

Old Kilcash Football Team

By Ned Kelly
Source:Cill Sioláin-100 Years and More of Gaelic Games in the Parish of Kilsheelan
and Kilcash 1884-1988. Received from Seamus J. King, Boherclough, Cashel.

Warm and bland like the fair vale around them
Were the boys of Kilcash we once knew
Their rivals they say that they often found them
An invincible team to subdue.
In the football arena they shone oftentimes,
As they lined up for victory's dash,
Like heroes in battle they broke through the lines
For the name and the fame of Kilcash.

Their spirits were high as the mountain behind them
As friends they were loyal and true
Brave and undaunted their country did find them
When called on to dare and to do,
Gladly the maidens bedecked them with florals
When visiting teams they outclassed.
Oh, 'tis often they brought home the laurels
In the glorious days of the past.

While manhood and manhood they strongly possessed
Every one was a typical Gael:
Oh, Erin, with sons such as these you are blest
When the enemy comes to assail
Then here's to the boys of Kilcash in my day
May these lines find them happy as then
Tho' no more the game of football they'll play
'Tis a pleasure to know they were men.

'Tis many a day since they answered the whistle,
Yet back thro' the ages will memory flash:
Let who will toast the shamrock, the rose and the thistle,
Here's a health to the men of Kilcash.

Gone are the comrades who marched by our side
And the girls we loved long ago
And the kind hearths that sheltered and fed us
In our fight 'gainst the blackhearted foe.
Gone are the days when we shouldered our guns
Gone in the mists away;
Gone are the leaders and gone are the men
And gone is the old I.R.A.

This is a tribute to the famous Kilcash Redoubtables, a noted football side in the Kilsheelan- Kilcash parish from 1884 to the end of the 19th century.

The parish of Kilsheelan and Kilcash were well to the fore in the early days, having a team in 1884 and two clubs being formed in the parish in 1885, Kilcash and Gambonsfield.

The first team in the parish was the Kilcash-Redoubtables (1884-1923). They were the most dreaded team in the county at the time. They were a team of giants of powerful physique and they used all their attributes to the best advantage particularly when taking part in wrestling which was a feature of the games at the time. The members of the first team were Tommy Kelly, Ned Kelly, Pat Ryan, Jim and John Kehoe, Tom and James Butler, William and James O'Shea, Mick and Peter Tobin, Tom and Pat Lawless, Pat and John Stokes, Mickey Dee, Jim Slattery, Tom Carey, Jack Cummins, Tom Prendergast, Mike Fleming, Willie Gibbs, Dick Crotty, Phil Callinan, Mick Lyons, Jim Hennessy, John Harvey , Patsy O'Neill and Patsy Foran. The team recorded a win over a Waterford selection played in Hurley's field in Glen Kilsheelan. Football was the dominant game in the parish before the turn of the century but it has reliably been established that a hurling team from Kilsheelan played Boherlahan towards the end of the century and was beaten by 47 points. There are few references to hurling after this until it was revived around 1928.
The last line of verse two also comes in another version: 'To place o'er the brow of Kilcash'
The author Edward Kelly was a famous son of Kilcash. He was born near the village in 1860. He was educated in De La Salle College in Waterford and in Belvedere College, Dublin. He came to Carrick-on –Suir in 1888 and taught in the Workhouse there for twelve years. While in Carrick he played football with Kickham's. He had previously played for the Kilcash Redoubtables. In 1900 the Workhouse was demolished and Edward Kelly emigrated to America. He settled in Chicago where he secured a position in the City Hall as a Civil Service employee and worked there for twenty-three years. His first poem Ormonde Lodge was published in the Irish Times around the end of the century. In Chicago he had a book of poems mainly about the Valley of Slievenamon and his native Kilcash published by J. Ringley Corp. in 1930.

The Kellys were noted athletes and footballers. A field across from their residence in Kilcash was known as the Sportsfield and major athletic events took place there around the turn of the century with athletes like the Davins from Deerpark and the champion Kiely from Ballyneale taking part. Thomas Kelly, nephew of Edward Kelly was a renowned athlete.

Moycarkey and Moondharrig

By Father. J. B. Dollard
Source: History of the GAA 1910-1930 by Phil O'Neill

When from her sleep of ages renowned Tipperary woke—
Her sister fair Kilkenny, right courteously she spoke.
'The Gaelic sun has risen, your champions call in line,
For Erin's olden glory, to clash camáns with thine.

Chorus:

Moondharrig, Moondharrig, ye leaped into the fray
Moondharrig, Moondharrig, how gloriously that day.
Moycarkey and Moondharrig, a stubborn fight ye fought;
Mondharrig, Moondharrig, what wonder works ye wrought.

God prosper old Moondharrig and keep her sons secure,
Within the sun-kissed valleys where rolls the stately Suir.
And when the wars red beacon o'er Erin's mountains glows
You'll find them in the vanguard that sweeps upon her foes.

Chorus:

Moycarkey and Two-Mile Borris.

By Monsg. J. B. Dollard.
Source: Moycarkey-Borris GAA Story 1984)

From her sleep of ages
Renowned Moycarkey woke
Her sister Two-Mile Borris
Right courteously she spoke—
That the Gaelic sun had risen,
 Her champions call in line,
For Erin's olden glory
To clash camáns with thine.

Moycarkey won the 1899 All-Ireland Hurling Final v Wexford (Blackwater) at
Jones's Road, on March 24, 1901 by 3-12 to 1-4. The game was unfinished. Tipperary
was awarded the title.

Tipperary (Two-Mile-Borris)) won the 1900 All-Ireland Hurling Final v London
(Desmonds) at Jones's Road, October 26, 1902. Tipperary 2-5, London 0-6).

For notes on Fr. Dollard (later Monsg.) see notes on All Ireland Hurling Final 1913,
in Part 11 and The Hurler in Part 1V. +

The Tubberadora Team

Tom Leahy, President of Club
Source: The Tubberadora-Boherlahan Hurling Story By Philip F. Ryan.
Air: God Save Ireland.
Chorus after each verse.

Now I'll sing in praise of home no matter where I roam
And the many games and pleasures of the years.
And to see the Gaels all round upon the hurling ground,
There is none to beat the Tubberadora team.

Chorus:

Then cheer boys cheer for these young heroes,
With victory smiling on their way.
And the ladies to compare with their voices rent the air,
When they meet to greet the Tubberadora team.

In the ball-alley you'll see, those boys crowned with victory—
The hurling is their joy and heart's delight.
And like brothers one and all they are ready for the call
With the beams of victory shining on their way.

It was in the month of May when first they went to play,
Against the 'Holy Terrors', they being champions of the day.
They were champions of renown and they hailed from Thurles town,
But the boys from them their laurels stole away.

They played in Dublin town, that great city of renown,
Where the Galway men cried out 'side your own'   **
But our boys being left and right made a dash with all their might,
And the leather they drove whistling though the poles.

In Golden as we know, to their colours they were true,
'Gainst Racecourse men they made a heavy score.
But in justice I must say, they showed our boys some gallant play,

65

But like others they were forced to fall away.
Drombane in ninety-four made Tipperary's taverns roar,
And the championship secured most manfully.
But our boys as you know well, did those champions overthrow,
Amidst ringing cheers of victory on the field.

Now Bawnmore being last to try for Tipperary's final tie,
And old Erin gazed on them most anxiously.
But 'twas then our boys did show where the medals were to go,
And the championship secured most manfully.

Now we will toast those fearless boys, who bring joy beneath the skies,
To the weary and the crazy and the old.
And their 'colleens' I am sure their poor aching hearts will cure,
And will cheer them on the victory once more.

**Side your own—An Br. Liam P. Ó'Caithnia explains 'Side your own' in his book Scéal na hIomána, Ch.8. 'Side your Own' meant that each player had to be to his right, that is, with his right hand towards the goal he was defending and his left hand towards the other goal. The other team would be directly opposite in the same way. Each hurler would have to stay on his own side and could not encroach on the other side without being on his right. This seemed to eliminate left-handed play. There is more evidence of this in East Cork where old people were heard to say that odd word 'deisigh' (right) in a way that would suggest that the ball was to be hit with the right side only. When the rules of the Association, which were drawn up by Maurice Davin were considered and committed to print in The United Ireland, 7 Feb. 1885 a short note as follows was put at the end of the hurling rules—N.B. 'Hitting both right and left is allowable.' Michael Cusack was of the opinion that the ball could be struck from whatever position it was in and this reduced the inclination to deal with the ball except with the hurley. In 1883 he wrote in the Shamrock, 'While the game was decaying in the hands of the youth of wise parents because the eldest of them were gathered together in exile, robust people whose courage, speed and endurance gave them a capacity for the game when played for the first time—the weakling of misery called 'side your own' was introduced and the game was shorn of its pride.'

The Tubberadora Hurling Story describes Tubberadora as 'just a townland a mile *from* Boherlahan village. A straggle of houses, a close knit farming community was the basis of the club, which was the making of Tipperary hurling tradition, and the achievement of singular distinction for the place itself. Twenty eight All-Ireland medals were brought home to five houses within a half a mile from one another from 1895 to 1898.. Raymond Smith, Decades of Glory 1966, p.40 writes, 'they would have won many more than three, with which they retired undefeated, sated with triumph, but like Alexander of old they had no more worlds to conquer.' Smith relates the story of Mickey Maher, the fair-haired giant from Nodstown, who captained Tubberadora, getting his forwards to prepare for the All-Ireland final of 1898 by shooting at the

band of a wheel in Walsh's kiln field in Tubberadora. —and their willingness also to make sacrifices in an era when cars were not yet known. Ned Maher and Ned Brennan

would walk six Irish miles into Thurles to Mass in the Cathedral with their hurleys, boots and togs slung over their shoulders, then take a slow train to Dublin and on their return to Thurles, after winning an All-Ireland title, walk home again to Tubberadora'.

In the History of Hurling published in 1946, Carbery writes that 'Thurles, Clonoulty, Moycarkey, Toomevara and Drombane—all had slashing sides before Tubberadora's star arose in 1895. Led by the fair-haired Mikie Maher, this powerful team crashed their way through all opposition, taking three All-Ireland titles between 1895 and 1898. Many grand Tipp. teams we have seen, but nothing quite like Tubberadora. '

Very Rev. Philip Canon Fogarty, P.P. V.F. pays the following tribute to the Tubberadora team in Tipperary's G.A.A. Story (p84)
'They were a master combination of hurlers; a team without parallel in Gaelic history. Three national titles and no defeat in any championship contest are standing memorials to their worth. To date, they had played fourteen championship matches, and their total score was 71 goals, 108 points to 17 goals and 46 points for their opponents. Though now saying 'goodbye' to the Association, the champions could have still held on without in any way endangering their imperishable name. But finding their neighbours from the Jockey and Borris ready and willing to take the flag from their hands, they resigned it without misgiving, knowing that it was in safe keeping.

Officials of the team: Thomas Leahy, President, Michael Conlon, Secretary, Paddy Costelloe, Treasurer, Mike Leahy, Denis Walsh, John Doyle, Jim Shanahan, John Maher, William O'Brien and Tom Fitzgerald.'

The all-Ireland final results were as follows:

1895 Played Mar 15, 1896. Tipperary (Tubberadora) 6-8, Kilkenny (Tullaroan) 1-0.
1896 Played Mar. 27, 1898. Tipperary(Tubberadora) 8-14, Dublin (Commercials) 0-4
1898 Played Mar.25, 1900. Tipperary,(Tubberadora) 7-13, Kilkenny (Threecastles) 3-10

1895 Team: M. Maher (capt), E. Maher, Phil Byrne, W. Kerwick, John Maher, D. Walsh. John Walsh, Peter Maher, T. Flanagan, Jas. Flanagan, P. Riordan, Jas. Gleeson, Fergus Moriarty, John Connolly, J. Maher, E. Brennan, W. Devane.

1896 Team: M. Maher (capt), J. Maher (F), Phil Byrne, W. Devane, M. Wall, E. Maher, E. Brennan,J. Walsh, T. Condon, J. Connolly, J. Flanagan, T. Ryan, P. Scanlon, T. Flanagan, E. Ryan, P. Doherty, D. Walsh.

67

1898 Team: M. Maher (capt), E. Maher, E. Brennan, J. Walsh, J. Connolly, T. Ryan, W. Devane, E. Ryan, P. Byrne, W. Dunne, T. Condon, J. O'Keeffe, J. Maher (M), D. Walsh, J. Maher (F), Dick O'Keeffe

Tubberadora

(Where the beautiful springs do flow)

By T. Leahy, Club President.
Source: the Tubberadora-Boherlahan
Hurling Story

When I lived in sweet Tipperary, my heart was light and free
Among my dear old neighbours, I always longed to be.
'Twas with the Gaels I always rambled and with them I'd like to go,
But I'll ne'er forget the brave young lads where the beautiful springs
do flow.

Well do I remember when first they went to play,
Against the 'Holy Terrors' in the merry month of May
When the ball was put in motion, their camáns they let go,
First victory crowned these brave young lads where the beautiful
springs do flow.

The teams from dear old Ireland they conquered o'er and o'er
On Limerick, Clare and Tullaroan they made a heavy score.
The Corkmen too, they did subdue, three times they were laid low,
By these young matchless heroes where the beautiful springs do
flow.

Despite all strife and jealousy, those heroes had to stand
Invincible, unscathed, unconquered through the land.
And for three years in succession they let the world know
They were All Ireland champions where the beautiful springs do
flow.

Farewell my loyal comrades, farewell my native shore,
'Tis with you I spent happy days and hope the same once more.
All my friends residing here desire to let you know
They send best wishes to the boys where the beautiful springs do
flow.

The Hurlers of Tubberadora

Anon
Received from Liam Ó Donnchú, Ballymoreen, Littleton.

The county has men from the mountain and glen,
Strong active, gay, manly and burly.
Expert at ball, in practises all,
With hand or the foot or the hurley,
That mother and sire and relation admire,
And maidens as pretty as Flora,
Especial a team with their medals in gleam,
From famous old Tubberadora.

With action and art and intelligent, smart,
To battle on centre and border.
With magical force in a mighty resource,
In line, regulation and order.
With national scarf, like the men of Clontarf,
Led on by the chief of Kincora,
And splendour sublime in athletical prime
Of the hurlers of Tubberadora.

With cheers high and long from the gazers in throng,
A wonder and ecstasy wrapt in;
At martial display, in hilarity gay,
Of referee, hurlers and captain.
With pleasure and smile on the maidens of style
The Molly and Nelly and Nora,
In glances and looks at the wonderful pucks
Of the heroes from Tubberadora.

Success to the team by its fame and esteem,
On hill and on plain and on hollow.
For favourite sport for the cottage and court,
With merits and honour to follow.

With praises profound from admirers around
And lovers, the Maggie and Flora,
The printers and bards showing love and regards
For hurlers of Tubberadora.

The Suir View Men

By Thade Connell, Kilbreedy-the song was collected by Queenie Taylor (Nee Ryan) from her father Phil.. S ource: Suir View Rangers 1895-1898-A History. Received from Seamus J. King, Boherclough, Cashel. Chorus after each verse.

When first they went for championship it was 'gainst Killenaule
To the Racecourse of Cashel, they went both one and all.
Their opponents didn't turn up, they were nowhere to be seen
So they hurled the ball right through the goal and shouted for victory.

Chorus:

Hurrah for the Suir View men, they are the lads of mirth,
They belong to Boherlahan; it's the land that gave them birth.
No wonder they are victorious, it's plain to be seen,
When they have the boys from Bawnmore, Longfield and Clareen.

To Golden town they next did go with heart and right good will,
To face Knockgraffon bullies on the plains of Mantlehill.
They thought that by their bull-work that they would surely win
But they hurled the ball right through the goal and shouted for the Suir View men.

To the Deerpark they next did go where they had a sporting day,
To face the Ballytarsna boys, their value to display.
They were in great rotation, we heard they oiled their joints
But the Rangers oiled them o'er again with four goals and three points.

We have a noble captain; Jack Fogarty is his name
He belongs to Boherlahan; he is a man of greatest fame.
Two men from Clonoulty along with them did join
And another man from Clonmore, you all know him Tom Ryan.

Suir View as a hurling club no longer exists. The area for which the catchall name
Suir View was decided upon could best be described as that represented by the old

civil parish or Ardmayle, or the present western portion of the modern parish of Boherlahan-Dualla. Included in this area are the townlands of Ardmayle Ardmayle West, Ballyroe, Bawnmore, Clonmore, Clune, Clareen, Ballydine, Longfield, Kilbreedy, Gortnaglough, Camus and Slatefield. The club existed for four years, 1895, 1896, 1897 and 1898. In this four years, they had played in three consecutive county finals and won one (1897) and had met and overcome most of the leading sides in Tipperary and adjoining counties. There is a doubt as to whether they ever got the medals for the county final win. The most thorough and diligent searches have failed to locate even one at this stage. They were beaten on three occasions only-twice by Tubberadora, one of which was drawn and lost only in extra time, and once by Cork.

The above song , The Suir View Men was composed by Thade Connell whose family lived at the Camus end of Kilbreedy in a house later known as 'Croke's old house' during the period of the Suir View club's existence. Thade was born in 1879 and attended school at Ardmayle N.S. where he was a contemporary of some of the younger team members. He and his brother Ned were well known musicians, as also were some of Thade's sons. He was father of the O'Connells of Gaile and uncle of the O'Connells of Ardmayle East . The song was written before the 1895 county final. It ends rather abruptly leading to the belief that a number of verses are missing.

Team (1887): Jack Fogarty (capt), Patsy Morrissey, Danny Morrissey, Con Maher, Peter Maher, Paddy Maher, Simon Moloney, Tim Heney, Jim Heney, Ned Pennefather, Will Dwyer, Tommy Dwyer, Con Dwyer, Pat Dwyer, Tom Ryan, Pat Ryan, Phil Fogarty.

Bohercrowe Ballad 1889

Source:The Arravale Rovers Story
By Tom O'Donoghue.

Bohercrowe is the darling
Bohercrowe is not dead yet,
Rosanna may be snarling
But they need not fret.
For when they can beat Fethard
The medals they'll get–
Good luck to gallant Bohercrowe
They are the champions yet.

For when the match was called for
The referee lined up the teams.
The Bohercrowe boys bashed away
And shattered Fethard's dreams.
The Fethard boys got savage then
And made an aweful rush,
When Brian O'Brien caught the ball
And kicked it into touch.

But when full-time was called upon
The crowd they did rush in,
Shaking hands with Bohercrowe
Saying they were great men.
They looked at one another
And held up their fists saying,
We have the county championship
Going home to night to Tipp.

When coming to Kilfeacle
It was a glorious sight,
To see the furry hills of Crogue
Ablaze with fire that night.
And coming up the Spittle

With neither dread nor fear,
There were better men in Bohercrowe
Than Gubbins, Quane or Peare.

In 1889, thirteen teams entered for the football championship—Rosanna, Bohercrowe, Cahir, Poulmucka, Solohead, Tipperary Commercials, Bansha, Boherlahan, Cullen, Knockavilla, Carrick, Grangemockler, and Ballycullen. Bohercrowe defeated Knockavilla at Kilfeacle and then travelled to Clonmel to face Grangemockler. . According to Very Rev. Canon Fogarty in *Tipperary's GAA Story:*

The final was in Thurles, between the winners and Carrick who were unprepared, because of Land War activity. Mr Davin's team had to leave the laurels to Cavanagh and his brilliant group of footballers by the decisive score of 2-7 to nil. As champions of Tipperary, Bohercrowe Independents got a walkover from the Clare champions and faced Midleton in the Munster final at Mallow. The Tipperary men won by 1-2 to 0-3. The All-Ireland final was played at Inchicore, on October 20, 1889. Final Score, Tipperary (Bohercrowe) 3-6. Laois (Maryboro') 0-0.

Team: Gil Kavanagh (capt), Jack Cranley (vice capt) Joe Ryan, Willie. Ryan, Ned Ryan, Billy Ryan, Joe Ronan, Paddy Buckley, Willie Shea, John Daly, Paddy Hall, James Keating, Mick Wade, Bryan O'Brien, Patrick Ryan, Laurence Fox, John Ryan, Paddy Finn, Tom Dwyer, Dick Whelan, Paddy Glasheen.

Substitutes and earlier member of the team were Mick Ryan, Pat McCarthy, Pat Hogan, Willie Sheehan, Jack Pickham, Jim Murphy, John Griffin, John J. Hayes Ned Ryan, Jack Power.

The deeds of the Bohercrowe champions are recalled in the locality around Tipperary in the Bohercrowe Ballad. This remembers not just the great victory over Fethard in the county championship, but also, the intense local rivalry with Rosanna. The lines that speaks about 'coming up the Spittal with neither dread nor fear' is a direct challenge to Rosanna; their main power base was in the Spittal area. 'There are better men in Bohercrowe than Gubbins, Quane or Peare,' refers directly to three of Rosanna's famed players.
In his *History of Gaelic Football*, p.25, Carbery says that the final was played in very bad weather. There were many pools of water on the ground. Disputes were many, and spectators were as often in the grounds as outside. It was a rough disorderly game, and Mr. T. O'Driscoll, referee had a busy time. Portlaoighise played a strong vigorous game, but they were no match in skill and resource for the fast and brilliant Tipperary team. Five Ryans played for Tipperary and five Cushions for Laoighis.

Honeymounts v Ballingarry/Shinrone 1889

Source: Received from Liam Ó Donnchú,
Ballymoreen, Littleton.

In the summertime of eighty- nine
All in that pleasant year,
When Ballingarry and Shinrone
Came to hurl the mountaineers;
From Honeymount the word went round
As to what would be their doom
They would win the day
Or men they would slay
Before they would go home.

The Honeymounts had a reputation as 'holy terrors' on the field. In 1889 a strong challenge was issued to them by a combined team from Ballingarry and Shinrone. The venue was 'The Big Park' in Cooraclevin. Honeymount won by one point. One of this team, James Nolan, Summerhill was selected on the hurling team that went to America in 1888, a tour that was known as The American Invasion. The ball which he took with him on that historic tour is still a treasured heirloom.

The names of the men who played with the Honeymounts have an honoured place in the records of the club.
Thomas Corcoran, Honeymount (Captain and Manager), James Nolan Summerhill, Michael Tierney, Castleroan, John Hogan, Castleroan, John Keane, Castleroan, Michael Maher, Rathnavogue, Daniel Brereton, Rathnavogue, Philip Maher, Clashegad, Pat Byrnes, Loughawn, John Maher, Loughawn, Martin Maher, Loughawn, Patrick Ahearne, Ballintemple, Edward Ahearne, Ballintemple, Timothy Gleeson, Springmount,, Richard Stapleton, Emill, James Guilfoyle, Rath, Pat Guilfoyle, Rath, Patrick Maloney, Moneygall, Denis Maloney, Moneygall, Con Dwan, Derrycallaghan, Martin Dwan, Derrycallaghan, Patrick Maher, Castleroan, Malachi Maher, Castleroan, Michael Maher, Castleroan, Tim Morkan, Summerhill, Jack Morkan, Summerhill, Mick Morkan, Summerhill, Mick Treacy, Moneygall, Mick Dunne, Foxborrow, Jack Dwan, Foxborrow, Paddy Bowen, Longfordwood, Denis Reid, D.Madden.

The Ballyhane Boys

Courtesy of Sean O'Neill, Clonganhue.

Source: The Cappawhite GAA Story,1886-1989. Received from
Seamus J. King, Boherclough, Cashel.

On the sixth day of January the year of ninety-nine
The morning it was misty, the evening cleared up fine.
The Ballyhane boys started though light was their escort
To meet the Templederry boys, the champions of the North.

When they landed in Currenny the people all did say.
'Ballyhane boys you'll be beaten, Templederry'll gain the day'.
'O Yes', said Fr. Donoghue, 'and that without delay,
For I have picked the best of men from Nenagh unto Rea'.

They had the pick of Keeper, likewise sweet Magherclay
All around the Silvermines and down along to Rea.
They had the pick of Keeper, likewise sweet Garavane
They brought the pick to play and kick the boys from Ballyhane.

When the game got underway, such a sight was never seen
Eireann's pride like Sarsfield's Boys, they wore their jackets green
They ran the ball up through them all, to the forwards it did stroll
Young Duggan he got under it and quickly scored a goal.

Fr. Donoghue rushed in to see what it was all about
He rushed into the goalman and thought to put him out.
Now tell the truth, you can't deny, you know more about a sleán
Than to stand a goal—defend against the boys of Ballyhane.

This tournament took place on January 6th 1899, at Ballycarron, Curreeney. Ballyhane
(Erin's Pride) played Templederry and according to Ballyhane had to wait one and a
half hours for the arrival of Templederry. Ballyhane also claimed that they scored one
goal and one point which the referee did not give them. Templederry in reply claimed
that they got no official notice of the match from Ballyhane. Templederry won by 1-3
to 0-3.

Cappawhite/Ballyhane Team selection for 1899 was Paddy, Matt and Jim Duggan, Slattery, Casey, Bill Schofield, Pat Hammersley, Bill Sadlier, Tom Kearns, Jim Dwyer(Mason) and Dick Ryan, Jack Quinlan, Jim Davern, Dan Flynn, Jack Whelan, 'Scientific Johnny',Donoghue, Jim Buckley, Paddy, Bill and Mick Ryan (Coopers), Dan Quirke, Jim Fitzgerald, Joe Bradshaw, Pat Kennedy and Mick O'Brien.

The Irish Foot-Ball Game 1896

Words and Music by Safford Watters.
Source: Harding Sheet Music Collection Vol.7 at the
Irish Traditional Music Archive, 63, Merrior Square, Dublin 2.
Chorus after each verse.

Thanksgiving Day was over and the boys upon the height,
Had watched old Yale and Harvard in their yearly football fight,
When Casey says to Dolan, 'let's get up a team,' says he,
'And challenge all the sheenies that live on the bowery'.
And so it was decided and the day at last was set;
The place was Murphy's vacant lot; the ground was soft and wet.
The story of the massacre is what I'm going to tell,
And if you'd been within a mile, y'd have heard Pat Casey yell:

'Line up, stand up, don't yez hear me call?
The audience is waitin' and we cannot find the ball.
Murphy, Dolan, can't yez quit yer scraps?
And when the game is over, yez can kill them sheeny chaps.

If you'd 'a' seen the uniforms the boys had on that day,
Their rubber boots and rubber snoots would take your breath away;
With liver pads and bandages they swaddled ev'ry limb, —
Pat Casey's dad stuffs furniture, so he upholstered him.
And Casey had the dandy scheme to win that football game,
'Twas tough upon the other team, but got there all the same.
Says he, 'each one pick out yer man and do him up', says he,
'And then we'll simply rush the ball to glorious victory'.

We followed out his orders and in just ten minutes more,
We'd made a hundred touch down and we'd kicked goals by the
score;
We sailed into the other team and wiped the earth with them;
We grabbed them by their top-knots and we yanked 'em limb from
limb.

We danced on them, we sat on them, we stamped them in the ground;
The fragments of that other team were strewn for blocks around.
And Casey says, 'at three gold balls' them fellows may have luck,
But when it comes to one pig-skin, it takes old Irish pluck'.

The Athletes of Erin

By T.D. Sullivan: Source: Cashel Sentinel, 11th July 1896,
Received from Seamus J. King, Boherclough, Cashel.
Air: O'Donnell Abu

Here's to the health of the athletes of Erin
The sons of Cú Chulainn and great Fionn Mac Cumhaill
Fame they bring home from each field they appear in
From Thurles to Texas, from Cork to Cabool.
Theirs are the wind and limb, to jump, run or ride and swim
To press for the goal or to strike up the ball.
Stout hearts and able hands, may be in many lands
But Ireland's brave boys take the shine from them all.

Think of great Davin, the pride of his nation
The Creans and the Bulgers, the Lees and Du Cros;
Think of young Conneff, who makes a sensation
Midst racers and pacers wherever he goes.
Think of the Tug of War—the sight was worth living for—
Pulled by our Polis against the Scot's Greys.
After a strain or two, off went the boys in blue,
Haulin' the sojers all over the place.

Mullen and Meredith, Carrol and Carey
Horgan and Morgan are known and renowned.
Ryan, whose jump is so lofty and airy,
You'd think 'twas a bird springing from the ground!
Who'd set a man agin, Reynolds and Flanagan?
A hammer of Cyclops to fling o'er the field.
Long may their strength remain, muscle and nerve and brain
Erin is proud of their names on her shield.

'Tis true that our youth can't be always victorious
Reverses they sometimes but seldom will meet.
But aye may their conduct be noble and glorious
In sunlight of triumph or shade of defeat.

81

Holding that any day, 'fair play is bonnie play'
Cheerful and kindly what're may befall—
So shall we ever hear, shouted from far and near
Ireland's brave boys take the shine from them all.

'For the first few years of its life the GAA was much more concerned with athletics than with games. To Cusack the need for nationalists to control Irish athletics and the desire to open athletics to every social class were at this stage more important than the revival of hurling and Irish football. Until 1887 or so hurling and football games were usually subsidiary events at athletic meetings: Often they did not figure on the Programme at all. ' *(The GAA—A History by Marcus de Búrca, p23)*

Verse 2   **Maurice Davin** was born on June 29th, 1842, the eldest of a family of four boys and a girl born to John and Bridget Davin in Deerpark near Carrick-On –Suir. The family lived by farming and a thriving business transporting goods in barges on the river Suir from Carrick to Clonmel.

In his youth he gave promise of being a powerful athlete and concentrated his active participation on rowing, scoring many successes at regattas in Waterford, Clonmel and Carrick. He built his own boat the Cruiscín, which is preserved in a barn in Deerpark.
In his late twenties he turned his attention to athletics; he studied the rules and techniques of the events he chose, worked out training schedules, studied diet and general rules of health for the serious athlete. From 1875 to 1879 he won numerous Irish championships in the weight throwing events.

In 1881 he and his brother Pat challenged the English champions at the Championships in Birmingham and swept all before them in the weights and jumps.

He was deeply concerned that athletic sports in Ireland were carried out in accordance with English laws and that the majority of Irish people were excluded. In 1877 he stated, 'We are very much in the want of some governing body for the managing of athletes in this country'. And he promised his support for such a body.

Michael Cusack was well aware of Davin's popularity and the high respect he had earned so he turned to him to discuss plans for a new association.
He was the unanimous choice to lead the Gaelic Athletic Association. He was well equipped for the task, to draft new rules and a constitution was adopted at the second Annual Convention in 1886.

He resigned when a new executive adopted rules contrary to the constitution, but he returned to reconstruct the association in 1888; finding his position untenable he resigned a second time but he retained his interest in the welfare of the association up to his death in January 1927 in his eighty-fifth year. His coffin was borne from the church of St. Nicholas by prominent officials of Tipperary County Board, Johnny Leahy, Wedger Meagher and Joe Maloughney, two of his famous students T F and

Larry Kiely, and his life-long friend Dan Fraher of Dungarvan. His last journey was across the Suir to the family burial place in Churchtown.

Verse 2 **Tommy Conneff** was a native of Clane, Co. Kildare. A champion world-class runner from half mile to four miles. He won many Irish championships at those distances from 1886 to 1888, the year he emigrated to the U.S.A. There he competed for many years. His world record of 4 min 15 3/5 secs for the mile remained unbeaten for sixteen years.

Verse 3 **Jim M. Ryan**, Tipperary town won international fame as a high jumper. He cleared 6ft. 3½ inches at Nenagh Sports and 6ft 4½inches at Tipperary Sports in 1890, setting up a new world record..

John Flanagan from Kilmallock in Limerick was a champion at the long jump and throwing the hammer. He emigrated to America in 1896 and subsequently won three Olympic gold medals: Paris 1900; St. Louis 1904: London 1908, an extraordinary achievement.

Denis Carey, Kilfinnan, Co. Limerick: Won championships at throwing the hammer and hurdle racing. He was active in top-class competition for over thirty years.

Denis Horgan, Banteer, Co. Cork: Was Ireland's most renowned athlete at putting the shot. From 1893 to 1912 he won forty-two national titles in Ireland, England and in the United States. In 1904 he set an Irish record in the shot at 48ft. 10ins. which remained unbeaten for half a century.

(The notes on Davin, Conneff, Ryan, Flanagan, Carey and Horgan were compiled by Séamus Ó Riain, Moneygall. Séamus served the GAA in an administrative capacity at club, county, provincial and national level. He was President of the Association from 1967 to 1970. A noted hurler and footballer with his club, Moneygall and county, Tipperary, he was also a champion athlete. He is a retired national teacher, and has written two books including **Maurice Davin (1842-1927)**, **Geography Publications 1994**, *and numerous articles on local history and the GAA.*

The Pattern of Emly

By Edmund C.Murphy, 2011 First Street, N.W.,Washington D.C. Dedicated by the author to his sister, Mrs James O Neill, Moanmore, Emly. Received from Micheál Ó Freaghaile,Imleach, Tiobraid Árann and from Seamus J. King, Boherlough, Cashel..

At Emly's pattern you might see old maids their long beads telling
And young ones moved with piety, flock from their humble dwelling;
Where some were there the truth to tell, who did not know their prayers so well,
But merely out for pleasure; who sauntered through the streets all day
Past tents where pipers used to play, where crowds were feeling very gay and drinking at their leisure.

Until, well strung, they view the games, encouraging and hearty.
Where strong men bare their sinewy frames, 'mid plaudits of their party.
For when their heads were growing dizzy, 'twas then their sticks were getting busy,
But athletes sway the crowd: Jumps they'll contest both broad and high,
The hurdle race they'll run close by but first the heavy weights they'll try, for here are champions proud.

Both Ryan and Bradshaw, gossips claim were looking very sullen,
The one from Cloghaready came; the other came from Cullen.
Then Jack McGrath, a stalwart lad, said, I am on my native sod
And I will yield to no man'. Jack Dingley, too, well known to fame.
All Ireland honours he could claim. Such legs, such arms, such neck, such frame, ne'er graced a Greek or Roman.

The workmen called the judge aside, and said, 'we're through with preparin'
This place, come let them now decide the championship of Erin!'

But on the crowd that stood around fell silence deep, prolonged,
profound,
Showing interest ran high; though one small diocese might them
claim
All Ireland could not bound their fame: Well might Clanwilliam's
sons exclaim, 'They did the world defy'

Then Jack McGrath first toed the cut; the weight heaved yards
eleven.
But William Ryan beat that a root, he stood just six feet seven.
Then Dingley, massive, tall and grand, the stone threw with his good
right hand,
And shot it through the gate; Tom Bradshaw grasped it in his hands,
His muscles firm as iron bands, away past Dingley's mark it lands,
The cheering now was great.

Though Jack McGrath tries all his might, 'twas plain his star was
setting.
But Jack Dingley was 'out of sight', on him the crowd was betting.
Though why should I attempt to tell, how far they threw, who threw
so well,
Who filled the crowd with wonder; Save that Will Ryan so tall and
straight,
The capstone raised, nine hundred weight, while Bradshaw jumped a
six-foot gate, 'mid cheering loud as thunder.

But on the road returning home, just at the Hill of Cullen;
Some spectre, whether ghost or gnome, in accents gruff and sullen,
Said, 'why do you with evil fate, pursue this haunted road so late,
When mortals should be sleeping; Though you might throw a
hundredweight
And fling it through an iron gate; if you're caught here again so late,
Good cause you'll have for weeping.

Let fools in Emly's ancient town of patterns cease their jesting.
The men who brought it wide renown, are in their graveyards resting.
No more their prowess will they show, not more the heavyweights they'll throw,
Now humble are the great. But while their memory will live,
This tribute to them I will give, that our descendants may yet strive,
Their deeds to emulate.

Charles J. Kickham

By Edmund Murphy, Washington D.C.
Received from Liam Ó Donnchú, Ballymoreen, Littleton.

Along the winding Anner banks no walks he'll longer take,
Nor on the slopes of Slievenamon, the echoes lightly wake,
Nor tell us of some brawny man how far he threw the stone
That saved that day the honour of his own Mullinahone.
While to deter our restless youth from fighting England's foe—
He struck off 'Patrick Sheehan from the Glen of Aherlow.'

Had he but lived until this day, we'd have in epic bold
The triumphs of Tom Kiely, in the new world and the old,
The greatest athlete of our time, Tipperary's famous son,
Who twice the world's championship, decisively had won,
A niche in Erin's Hall of Fame, he surely yet will fill,
Nor cherished less is he who left us 'Rory of the Hill.'

Some few have won immortal fame upon the battlefield,
Whose matchless skill and valiant deeds, compelled their foes to
yield,
And some possessing wondrous strength, their country's pride
uphold,
Till glory wreathes her hallowed name, like Greece in days of old
But dearer still the fearless man, with kindly heart I vow,
Slieveardagh's son! The author of pathetic 'Knocknagow'.

John Devoy regarded by Padraig Pearse as the greatest of the Fenians wrote:
'Kickham was born in Mullinahone, on the 9th May 1828. His mother's maiden name
was O'Mahony and she was a cousin of John O'Mahony, the founder of the Fenian
movement. He came of a very well-to-do family and received the training of an Irish
boy of his class up to fourteen years of age, when the accident happened which
changed the whole course of his life. He was holding a flask of powder near a fire to
dry and it ands it exploded with the result that he was rendered nearly blind and
almost completely deaf. Kickham had great literary ability and a wide knowledge of
modern litreature. His principal stories are 'Knocknagow', 'Sally Kavanagh' or the
Untenanted Graves, For the Old land and Tales ofTipperary. Kickham was one of the
four most prominent men in the old movement, and as chairman of the supreme

council for several years before he died was the unchallenged leader of the reorganised I.R.B. Kickham's ability is not to be measured by his writings although they give him a place. He displayed knowledge of men that was remarkable on account of the paucity of his information about them and his inability to see and hear them but his estimates of their character and ability were all correct. It was the same with public events and foreign affairs. He was the master of Irish politics. His reading had to be done with his spectacles lifted up on his forehead, his hand shading his eyes and the book, paper or letter held within a couple of inches from them. Conversation with him for many years had to be carried on by the aid of an ear trumpet and for a long time before he died by means of the deaf and dumb alphabet. When Kickham died in 1882 there was a great funeral procession in Dublin, which the Freeman said exceeded in numbers that which followed the remains of John O'Mahony, the American Fenian leader, to Glasnevin in 1877. The IRB was then 35,000 strong and the members came from all over Ireland and from England and Scotland to pay their respects to the chairman of the supreme council.

William O'Brien in an editorial in the United Ireland 1882 wrote: Charles Kickham possessed the soul of a hero, free as virgin gold from fear or stain. A dreamer by the Anner, a child with merry children in the cabin of Phil Lahy, his darkened sight could flash with pride in the dock, and his soldier heart grow none the fainter for being buried in an English felon-tomb. A nation that can produce such sons and return their love with passionate increase cannot fail in the destiny whose vision illumined Charles Kickham's years of penal suffering and brightened his dying eyes. His works and his example will be a precious legacy long after Death in his chilly chamber has left nothing of the mortal part of the poet, novelist, and patriot, except the 'bare ruin'd choir where late a sweet bird sang'.

And John O'Leary wrote:'but there was another kind of knowledge, beside that of books, possessed by Kickham, and in this I have never met with anyone who excelled him. He knew the Irish people thoroughly, but especially the middle and so-called lower classes, and from thoroughness of knowledge came thoroughness of sympathy. It was not that he at all ignored the faults or shortcomings of the people, but he was convinced that these were far more than counterbalanced by their virtues, and anyway, whatever merits or demerits they might have, they were *his* people, to whom he was bound to cling, through life unto death, and this he did with a strength and force excelled by no man of his generation, if equalled by any.'

(The above information was extracted from '*The Valley near Slievenamon*, a Kickham Anthology, edited by James Maher, 1941.)

Thomas F.Kiely-The Champion 1869-1951

By Rody Kirwan, Waterford
Received from Liam Ó Donnchú, Littleton.

In a sylvan setting by the River Suir in the far-famed Golden Vale,
Near the Southern slopes of Slievenamon lies the village of
Ballyneale.
Famous in local history for its strapping men and tall,
With Thomas Francis Kiely, the finest of them all.

The atmosphere was athletic that he lived in as a boy,
'Till he became a champion under Davin's watchful eye.
At the championships in Dublin, he decided to have a go,
And when the programme ended, he'd won seven in a–row.

Conscious of his prowess, now great confidence he gained.
And ambitious for higher honours, methodically he trained.
In ninety-seven and for some years, to England he made trips,
And beat the world's best to win five hammer championships.

At St. Louis Exposition, the all-round championship he won.
Defeating amongst others the Yankee champion —Adam Gunn.
At Boston, two years later—he won for the second time
At an age when athletes normally are years beyond their prime.

He was a star attraction for some twenty years or more.
The prizes won in all those years numbered quite a hundred score.
Including seventy championships at home and overseas,
For which there were gold medals and he won with perfect ease.

He's a credit to his county, to his country, to his name,
For through these years of active sport, he always played the game.
He set a fine example to our up-and-coming youth,
To follow in his footsteps the ways of manliness and truth.

A man of courage and of iron, a man with nerves of steel,
Who far surpassed his fellow man and made admirers feel

That Kiely's name and Kiely's fame should live forever on,
Lies now in a deep and peaceful sleep, 'neath the slopes of
Slievenamon

Thomas Francis (Tom) Kiely was an all round athlete. Born 25th Aug. 1869 at
Ballyneale, Carrick –On-Suir. He died in Dublin in 1951. He was a neighbour of the
Davin brothers, who coached him. He won a total of fifty-three athletic titles, 18 in the
hammer, and on one day, 10th Sept. 1892, he won seven GAA titles. He also won 16
British Crown gold medals, including 7 in succession, 1890, 1891, 1892, 1893, 1894,
1895 and 1896. He won the British A.A.A. hammer titles 5 times, in 1897, 1898,
1899, 1901, and 1902. He set a world record in the hammer of 162 ft. He was told he
would get a free trip to the 1904 Olympic Games at St. Louis, if he represented Great
Britain but he declared for Ireland and thus had to pay his own way to America. He
won the gold medal, at the age of 35, in the all-round championship, (now Decathlon)
the only time this event was competed for. Competing in 10 events all in one day, he
won 4 events and triumphed by a margin of 119pts, with a total of 6036 points. In
1906 he won the all-round championship trophy of America at the age of 37. As a
younger man he played in the first ever hurling inter-provincial for Munster against
Leinster in 1896.

PART TWO

County
Achievements

ALL-IRELAND MEDAL
1930

All Ireland Hurling Final 1906

By Edmund Murphy, Washington D.C.
Source:Moycarkey-Borris GAA Story and New York's Irish World. Also received
from Liam Ó Donnchú. There are slight differences between both versions.

You who delight in feats of strength and skill,
And ever aid such contests as is meet;
Let echoes of the game bide with you still,
That on Kilkenny's field did lately thrill
The anxious crowds, who, spellbound waited till
In thunder tones the victors proud they greet.

From out the nation's capital there came,
A wonderful outpouring of her sons,
Inspired by Faugh a Ballagh's sudden fame
The worthy wearers of the ancient name.
Besides, their deeds of valour she could claim.
And now she sends them forth 'mid orisons.

At every station through Kildare crowds greet
The train that scarce can haul its living freight.
All anxious on the hurling field to meet.
The contestants for to observe and greet
And carefully to note each brilliant feat
That helps All-Ireland prize to captivate.

And now contingents from the South draw near,
From Shannon's spreading flood to Slievenamon.
And many a shout and many a rousing cheer
Greet Thurles team wherever they appear.
Lives there a Tipp! Who feels the slightest fear
But that his side will come out champion?

They now line up all ready for the fray.
And men of finer mould on field ne'er stood.
If Dublin looked assured, right well they may,

All Ireland's team they beat without delay.
Besides 'The Shields' they won the other day.
Come, Faughs, assert your sway; Come Tipps, make good!
The ball's thrown in and bounding o'er a knoll—
Before they scarcely knew it was in play.
Will Leonard registered a pretty goal,
And still another point, Faughs promptly stole.
Nor did Semple's splendid stroke the ball control
For Harty made a point without delay.

The game's still young and anxious crowds review
Each play that helps to favour either side.
The Faughs by Harty led again, renew
The contest, 'till another goal's put through.
Then loud applause, Will Leonard greeted you;
Of Dublin—you're undoubtedly the pride.

The ball's sent down and Shelly striking low,
Helped by Gleeson, through the crowd it sizzling rips
With such force, past their goalposts it would go—
But 'Keeffe at once corrected with a blow—
And quickly the white flag a point did show
For the slashing, headlong, dashing, peerless Tips.

The cheers and plaudits loud of the crowd
Intensifying the struggle in the field.
The camáns poised, their purpose had avowed—
Such combat ne'er was seen they all allowed.
Each one so determined and so proud
He'd die e'er to opponent he would yield.

Ten minutes more will see the contest end
And still more resolute the struggle grows.
The camáns,men and ball,more freely blend.
This,through their posts Patrick Riordan tries to send.
Semple and Gleeson to their aid,did lend
And Dublin seems to waver 'fore their blows.

Tipperary's forwards now press hard their goals;
Faughs, hope you still, the cherished prize to grasp?
Then back the tide of victory, you must roll,
The Tipps are simply now beyond control.
Kenna scores a point and Riordan shoots a goal;
The prize is surely 'scaping Dublin's grasp.

'Tis now five minutes to the final bell.
Gauge well the ball—you're making history.
The Tipps now rush; can Faughs their charge repel?
Strike! Strike! With all your might, now blows will tell—
But hark! That swelling roar! That deafening yell!
Hurrah! Tipperary's wins the victory.

Final Score: - Tipperary (Thurles) 3-16, Dublin (Faughs) 3-8. The game was played at Kilkenny on October 27, 1907.

Tipperary: Tom Semple (capt), J. Hayes, J. O'Brien, P. Burke, M. O'Brien, T. Kerwick, P. Brolan, H. Shelley, J. Mockler, T. Kenna, P. Riordan, T. Allen, P. Maher, J.Burke, J. Gleeson, J. O'Keeffe, T. Gleeson.

Dublin :D.McCormack (capt), A.C. Harty, P.Hogan, J.Cleary, J. O'Riordan, M.Murphy, J.Quinlan, J.O'Dwyer, P.Kennedy, W.Leonard, W.Murphy, T.Warner, B.O'Brien, M.O'Callaghan, J.Grace, M.Quinn, W.O'Callaghan

Magnificent Tipperary 1906

By Risteard M. O'Hanrahan on October 30th, 1907.
Received from Liam Ó Donnchú, Ballymoreen, Littleton
Air: O Donnell Abu

Cheer after cheer broke forth from the thousands strong
Greeting our hurlers in 'Ye Fair Citie'.
Loudly in praise rose the voice of the great throng,
Crying 'Magnificent Tipperary'
On then brave Knocknagow; show them your prowess now,
Let not your spirit or courage vary.
Thurles and Borris men; fleet Tubberadora men,
Work for Magnificent Tipperary.

Swift as the wild deer that roams the great mountains
Keen as the eagle guarding his eyrie.
Strong as the force of the wild rushing fountains
Such are the men of bold Tipperary.
Oh, then brave Knocknagow; win back your laurels now,
Be not in strength or skill ever chary.
Toil now with all your might; strive in the noble fight,
Work for Magnificent Tipperary.

The battle's half over, the Capital's leading
But 'Kickham's' men are not cold and weary.
They will triumph yet—danger unheeding—
And win the day for old Tipperary.
Play up brave Knocknagow, show your opponents how
To play a game cool, deft and airy.
Prove now that you are men, ready to win again,
All-Ireland honours for Tipperary.

Then onward they rushed with a wild , fierce hurrah
Yet quite graceful and light as the fairy.
And loud cheers rent the air as out from the fray came
The victorious men of Tipperary.

Hurrah! Brave Knocknagow; you've kept the Thresher's vow,
And crowned yourself by a grand victory.
Ireland is proud of you, grand sons of Róisín Dubh,
And of Magnificent Tipperary.

Tipperary Boys Again

By Dan English, Rossmore-Also credited as author is
F.A. Gleeson, Templemore.Source: Gaelic Echo, Sat. July 11, 1942
Air: A Nation Once Again '

.

When Semple to Kilkenny came
In the year nineteen-o-seven
Of gallant Tipp to uphold the fame
With five men and eleven.
'McCormack brave' says giant Tom
'You'll need those mighty men
To battle with the swift and strong
Tipperary Boys Again.'

You'll need those mighty men
You'll need those mighty men,
To battle with the swift and strong
Tipperary Boys Again

The Thurles boys marched out quite calm
With the lads from Borris 'knacky',
And two stout veterans from Drombane
Backed up by brave old ' Jockey'.
Tipperary ne'er before had known
Such stalwart hurling men
Go forth at dawn— with sweet camán,
Tipperary Boys Again.

Such stalwart hurling men
Such stalwart hurling men
Go forth at dawn —with sweet camán
Tipperary Boys Again.

The coin is spun, camáns are crossed,
Hurrah! The Tipps are slashing—
The bounding leather as 'tis tossed
By Barna's fierce ash crashing;

The play was right magnificent—
Tho' poured the drenching rain;
Still on they went, with one intent —
Tipperary Boys Again.

Tho' poured the drenching rain;
Tho' poured the drenching rain;
Still on they went, with one intent —
Tipperary Boys Again.

The whistle shrill rings out 'full-time'
Tipperary is victorious;
'O'Riordan, Gleeson, 'Hawkeyed' Brien
Bear on the flag before us'.
The honours of All –Ireland
We have not sought in vain,
Oh splendid team, sweet seventeen,
Tipperary Boys Again.

We have not sought in vain,
We have not sought in vain,
Oh splendid team, sweet seventeen,
Tipperary Boys Again.

Munster Hurling Final 1906

By E.Murphy, Washington D.C.
Source: Boston Pilot.
Received from Liam Ó Donnchú, Ballymoreen, Littleton.

Hurrah! For the gallant Thurles team
That Munster failed to beat:
There lurks in their frank and fearless mien
And in their dark eyes fiery gleam
A pride that scorns defeat.

When Holycross for honours tried
A stalwart aggregation
Their hopes were quickly dashed aside
Though Horse and Jockey with you tied—
You beat them in rotation.

In each encounter since you've shown
You're masters of the field.
First Limerick's defeat was known—
Then Clare's picked team was overthrown
And Cork was forced to yield.

Excitement ne'er was more intense
Since Cork had picked its best.
Besides the gathering was immense,
For a championship was in suspense,
With giants to contest.

Tipperary! Scarce the shout arose
Before you smashed the ball
And dealt it out such telling blows
That though you met with stubborn foes
Proud Cork was doomed to fall.

Borris great triumphs gained in vain,
Discretion's what they lacked;
Or else upon Kilmallock's plain
To clinch their victory they'd remain
Nor leave themselves side-tracked.

Such follies Thurles will avoid,
No chances they'll let slip:
Semple with wisdom will them guide,
The Gleesons and Mahers at his side
Will win the championship.

Tipperary , Cork and Clare had easy victories over Limerick, Waterford and Kerry
respectively. Tipperary qualified for a final clash with Cork. The game was played on
the 19th August 1907 at Tipperary. Tipperary 3-4, Cork 0-9. The last two verses
probably refer to the semi-final between Cork and Tipperary at Kilmallock on the 28th
Oct. 1905. With twenty minutes remaining and Tipperary leading 2-4 to 2-3, a dispute
arose over the non awarding of a seventy yards free to Tipperary and they left the
field. The game was refixed but did not take place and Cork won their fifth successive
Munster title with a victory over Limerick.

Team: 1906 Munster Final: T.Semple (capt), J.O'Brien (goal), J.Hayes, T.Allen,
T.Kerwick, T.Condon, P.Bourke, T.Gleeson, J.O'Keeffe, P.Maher, J.Burke,
J.Mooney, J.Mockler, H.Shelly, T.Gleeson, M.Gleeson, P.J.Riordan.

The Borris Boys

Source: Moycarkey—Borris
GAA Story

I'll sing in praise of the Borris boys
No matter where I roam.
They brought fame to Two-Mile- Borris
And to friends across the foam.
When first they went to Carrick
To give a grand display,
And the Leinster men were certain
That they would win the day.

To play for forty minutes more,
They asked the Leinster team,
But the team refused and left the field,
No longer would they play
For well they knew the Borris boys
Would win the Shield that day.

So the second time they journeyed on
To the same old hurling field,
Prepared to suffer, bleed or die
Or win those Railway Shields.
Fifteen in green played their sixteen,
Right manfully and well
They were overthrown, the Leinster men,
When dark night on them fell.

The ball was put in motion
And it filled our hearts with joy,
More especially when first blood was drawn
By a Two -Mile Borris boy.
The ball was then struck out again
To the centre of the field
It was plainly seen that the boys in green
Would make Kilkenny yield.

100

Fox Maher was shaping with the ball
When Hayes both cute and keen,
He made the umpire toe the line
And wave the flag of green.
A glorious tussle then ensued
And man and ball did roll
Such great applause and ringing cheers
When Borris scored a goal.

It was after fast and brilliant play
They let Kilkenny know
That into Two- Mile Borris
The Railway Shields would go.
So give three ringing cheers again
For heroes great and grand
Who shone so bright and glorious
The emblem of our land

And may their young successors
On every Gaelic field
Bring honour, fame like Borris gained
With Championship and Shield.

In 1906, Tipperary represented by Two-Mile-Borris defeated Kilkenny in the replay of the final of the Railway Shield.
The Railway Shield competition was an inter-provincial championship inaugurated in 1905.
Odds were in favour of Munster for the replay. Leinster's team consisted of thirteen from Kilkenny, two from Wexford, one from Dublin and Bob O'Keeffe from Laois— later President of the Central Council, and a native of Mooncoin

Very Rev. Canon Fogarty, in his book Tipperary's *G.A.A. Story* gives the history of the Railway Shields: In hurling and football, interprovincial competitions for the trophies mentioned were inaugurated by the Central council in 1905. The Shields— worth £50—were presented by the Railway Company, and were to become the property of the teams winning them, twice in succession, or three times in all. The selection was given to the winners, or runners up in each province, and the proceeds, after paying expenses, went to players injured in the All Ireland Championships'.

Canon Fogarty also relates in his book (p 131) that a day or so before his death on November 29th 1906, Michael Cusack (Founder) was told that the Munster v Leinster Shield's game, would be postponed if he died. 'No' said he, 'let the game go on', and then.....'I will be there'. He was buried the day of the match, and a striking spectacle in his funeral procession from the Pro-Cathedral to Glasnevin, was the Tipperary and Leinster hurlers with draped camáns and mourning rosettes forming a bodyguard.

Selection— Ned Hayes (capt), Tom Allen, Paddy Hayes, Jimmy Burke, Mick Purcell, Billy Maher (Borris), Jim, Joe and Dick O'Keeffe, Jack, Bill and Billy Gleeson, Tim Condon (Moycarkey), Watty Dunne, Jack Doherty (Ballytarsna), Tom Semple (Thurles) Con Brewer (Ballymackey), Hawk O'Brien (Thurles), Tommy Riordan (Drombane), Tim Gleeson (Drombane) Paddy Maher, Mike Wall.
The Tipperary team was as in Deerpark, (first game) except that it included Tim Gleeson, Mike Wall and Paddy'Best' Maher, replacing three who were off through injuries. Munster won by 4-10 to 4-4.

Tipperary's Railway Shield 1906

By J.J. Downey: Templetuohy.Source: Gaelic Sportsman, Sept 1, 1951
Chorus after each verse.

You sons of sweet Tipperary, no matter where you roam,
Your hearts I know will throb with joy when you hear of the news
from home.
How our dashing Borris hurling team so bravely took the field,
And defeated brave Kilkenny for the much prized Railway Shield.

Chorus:
So, hurrah three times hurrah! For our dashing Borris Gaels,
Whose victory shall now resound thro' Erin's verdant dales;
For the honours they've achieved on many a Gaelic field,
And their victory o'er Kilkenny for the much prized Railway Shield.

That gallant band of heroes, they bravely withstood
The onslaught of four counties, which sent forth, their bravest blood,
To do battle for their province, but soon were forced to yield,
And surrender to our Borris Gaels the much-prized Railway Shield.

It was the third occasion, on which those heroes met,
But our boys went forth to battle with features grim and set;
Determined to gain victory, they never meant to yield
Or relinquish to Kilkenny the much-prized Railway Shield.

The Premier County well boast such dashing men as these,
They're a credit to Tipperary and their exiles o'er the seas;
And when next they go hurling may they well the camáns wield,
And gain another victory, like that of the Railway Shield.

Tipperary and Two-Mile-Borris

Anon:
Source: Johnny Ryan, Littlelton

She walked fast with the captain
And they both sat down to rest
And the next to pass
Was the famous Paddy Best   *1
She kissed his wounded eyebrow
And held his brawny hand:
'You're a credit to your county
And dear old Ireland.'

Big Bill whose manly form   *2
Was blushing scarlet red
Before the queenly lady stood   *3
And she to him kindly said,
Your heart it is so warm,
And your arms are too strong,
For any Leinster champions
That lives to Nora Long.   *4

Mick Wall, whose graceful bearing,   *5
With his handsome Celtic face,
Well known at crossroad dancing,
Was the noblest of his race.
Tim Condon's manly form,   *6
She looked with mother's joy,
 He was standing like a heckler
Outside the walls of Troy.

My sons she cried in ecstasy
As three more passed along,
Drombane, the Horse and Jockey   *7
Tell the Gleesons of their song,
Of battles waged and victories won

And mighty deeds galore,
The names of Tim and Billy
And Jack so grand to score.

And Tubberadora's champion,   *8
You're struggling hard once more
For the honour of your county
As you did in days before.
And yonder from the fertile fields
Near Cashel's honour pile,
I see a son to Cormac
He is the noblest of the royal.

And sure it is Jack Doherty;   *9
'Come here a mhic mo chroí
And bring Watty Dunne along with you
Until you both I see.
Ah Billy, you're broken-hearted,
They did not let you play
For the honour of your county,
In this great Olympic fray.

Then passed her by the youngest,
The bravest of the brave;
Jimmy Bourke, who said they'd conquer,   *10
Or die their names to save.
Tom Allen the grandest hurler,   *11
Of all the Gaels among;
'How is your wounded ankle'
From out her heart was wrung.

So softly sadly sighing,
As a tear stood in her eye,
To each and every hurler,
She bade a fond goodbye.
I am going to my mountain home
Near Galtees purple tide,

To give a place to Fionn Mac Cumhaill
On Slievenamon tonight.

So as she parted, blessed them
And bade them not to fear
They rose like a matador
Of a wild Tipp'rary cheer
That echoes in the shield
And rebaying as it fell,
Into the heart of Leinster,
And every mossy dale.

This was a Two-Mile Borris /Tipperary selection in 1906—Railway Shield.

*1	Paddy 'Best'Maher
*2	Big Dill Gleeson, Horse and Jockey
*3	Johnny Ryan claimed that the Queenly lady was a Queen of Leinster.
*4	A line that doesn't make much sense—Nora Long?- Johnny Ryan thought that Nora Long was the Queen of Leinster.?
*5	Mick Wall from Horse and Jockey.
*6	Tim Condon (Ballinure)—Captain, Horse and Jockey.
*7	There were three Gleesons from Drombane—Billy Gleeson, Little Billy Gleeson and Timmy Gleeson. Jack Gleeson was from the Horse and Jockey.
*8	Tubberadora's champion was Mickey Maher
*9	Jack Doherty,Watty Dunne and Billy Gleeson. Billy Gleeson, Drumbo, Horse and Jockey, won two All-Ireland medals.(1899 with Horse and Jockey and 1900 with Two-Mile-Borris) Watty Dunne also won two All-Ireland medals (1898 with Tubberadora and 1899 with Horse and Jockey)
*10	Jimmy Bourke from Coolcroo,, Two-Mile-Borris.
*11	Tom Allen fromTwo-Mile-Borris.

See notes attached to *The Borris Boys*

Sunday's Shield Match 1906

By P.D. Keevan, Dundrum (late Fethard)
Received from Liam Ó Donnchú, Ballymoreen, Littleton.

It was at Jones's road, to be right in my code,
The second cold day of December,
Moondarrig and Tipp to hurl did strip—
A game I will always remember.
The Tipps for to lick, Moondarrig did pick
Three counties and Ye Citie Fairie,
But all was no go; the boys let them know
That they'd bring home the Shield to Tipperary.

The first time they played, the Tipps so well stayed
That the score of Moondarrig diminished.
The referee's call declared 'eighteen all'
So the match was a draw and unfinished.
But, true to their core, Tipp would play half-an-hour more,
But Moondarrig so cute and so hairy,
Declined for to play, for they knew on that day
That the Shield would be won by Tipperary.

Moondarrig worked hard, defeat to retard,
But the Tipps did grand shooting and striking.
'Fox' Maher roared out with a terrible shout,
'The game is not played to my liking
But never give in, the match we must win,
Though the Tipps are all getting contrary'—
For they ordered 'The Fox' to unlock his box
And hand out the Shield to Tipperary.

The game from the start was furious and smart,
And Moondarrig are sterling, good players;
Although not from scratch, they had more than a match
In the Tipps , who are terrible stayers.
For according to play, on that wintry day,

The famous De Wet or Delarey,
Couldn't check the onslaught of the men who have fought
For the honour of gallant Tipperary.

The game is all o'er, the referee's score
Declare Knocknagow to be winners;
It was a great feat, for the men they have beat,
Moondarrig are no new beginners.
So let all hands be right, let no man have spite,
Think of Stephens, 'CJ.' and O'Leary;
Let no tyrant see but we all can agree—
Kilkenny! Shake hands with Tipperary!

See notes attached to *The Borris Boys*

Tipperary v Kerry 1906

By James Quinn (formerly from Ballypatrick, Kilsheelan/Kilcash.
Source: Cill Sioláin-100 Years and More of Gaelic Games in the Parish of Kilsheelan
and Kilcash 1884-1988.Received from Seamus J. King, Boherclough, Cashel.

Ours is a team of gallant men
When playing you'd like to see them.
None can withstand that noble band
That loves the call of freedom.

The name you bet—victorious yet
For with stalking determination
And with courage bold they mean to hold
The county's reputation.

Unequalled yet is our brave Barrett
O may you never vary,
That magic name that has gained such fame
For gallant Tipperary.

Just see them when they played their men
With tactics like Napoleon,
And famous Kelly whose kick is sure
To send a point or goal in.

From far and near you'll ever hear
Them sing with heartfelt praises
Of young Rockett who will yet go down
In all of history's pages.

The Kerrymen came and tried to gain
That trophy prize so glorious
But Tipperary fought with might and main
And made sure of being victorious.

To see that day brave Butler's play
It filled the crowd with rapture.
I hope they have the medals rare
Of Irish manufacture.

O may that team forever feel
The strength to kick the leather
And may they stand with hand in hand
United all together.

May their every game be crowned with fame
And may they never vary
And still maintain the honoured name
Of good old Tipperary.

This team defeated Kerry in the American football championship. Jack Rockett, born
approx. 1882 from Kilsheelan/Ballypatrick was probably captain of this team. Ned
Kelly Kilcash was also on the team.

The All-Ireland Championship 1908

By Edmund Murphy:
Source:The Voice of the People (Songs and History of Ireland)
Song 18: McCall Collection, NLI, Dublin.
Received also from Liam Ó Donnchú, Ballymoreen, Littleton.

Two stauncher teams never did camáns wield
Than in Athy for highest honours met:
Dublin's athletes marched proudly on the field.
Tipp's matchless sons composed the other set.
What Gaels their deeds of valour can forget?
Or ever saw them on the battleground,
Against the greatest odds to fume or fret,
Although by difficulties oft beset,
But press the foe to meet the ball's dull bound,
Nor yield one inch before they heard the whistle sound.

From far and near the anxious Gaels had come,
To see those teams already known to fame,
Nor lacked their martial sounds of fife and drum,
Although such things might then appear quite tame,
Compared with the excitement of a game,
Which brought into the field eight thousand souls,
To see the capital make good its claim.
While still the human tide through benches rolls,
The ball's thrown in and rushed down to the Dublin's goals.

But Grace was there and promptly sent it back,
To Kelleher whose blow had changed its course,
And won first blood, and staved off the attack.
So the metrops are yelling themselves hoarse,
While Leonard from the side a goal did force,
And with unerring aim he shot it through,
But to long pucks the Tipps had now recourse,
Then back to Leinster's posts the leather flew,
And twice the flag went up for Semple's aim was true.

Tipperary's puck-out now was closely watched;
Fast work was done and Dublin's uprights raided,
Burke, Shelly, Kenna, Fitz, some plot have hatched,
And in full force the east preserves invaded
And points banged in while Leinster's smile had faded.
Quinn's blow caused now a lull in the assault—
A splendid stroke and few that could have made it,
Which ended in a point through no one's fault,
The pace had grown so hot both sides were glad to halt.

The second half has opened like the past—
Strong hopes of victory each side has swayed.
They've struck a gait, which surely cannot last,
So fast and furious the game they played.
So grand is the impression they have made
That the vast crowd looks on with bated breath
While Grace against the South directs a raid,
And Dublin's fans shout, 'victory or death'
While Tipps with grim resolve strike for their native heath.

Forth comes Will Leonard cheered by Dublin's hosts,
Imparting to the Faughs both hope and pride,
As dashing with their swift and powerful stride,
They shot the ball down through the other side.
Intense and more intense excitement grows
As on the ball they land with all their power,
For this great contest now drawn to a close.
Should Leinster prove the master of the hour?
Else Tipp. holds still of Ireland's youth, the flower.
Stiff pucks both Fitz and Shelly quickly land,
And Dublin's backs before their goalposts cower.
For Semple now was using head and hand,
And Carew's fresh attack was deemed superbly grand.

The nervous tension still was at its height,
Though the Metros. could scarcely hope to win,

Yet shouts arose of 'Dublin to the fight',
As Tipps the onslaught led through thick and thin.
Till Carew's smashing drive a goal shot in.
Then Leinster's chance seemed hopelessly to slip,
While Semple flagged amid the deafening din,
Then swelled the roar, 'Hurrah for gallant Tipp',
The Premier county's sons have won the championship'

All_Ireland Hurling Final played at Jones' Road 25 April 1909: Tipperary (Thurles) 2-5, Dublin (Kickhams) 1-8. Replay at Athy on June 27, 1909. Tipperary 3-15, Dublin 1-5.

Tipperary Team:Tom Semple (capt), T. Kerwick, J. Mockler, J. O'Brien, H. Shelley, A. Carew, J. Mooney, T. Kenna, P. Burke, P. Brolan, J. Moloughney, J. Burke, T. Gleeson, M. O'Dwyer, J. Fitzgerald, P. Fitzgerald, Martin O'Brien.

Note: Jack Gleeson, Joe O'Keeffe, Bob Mockler and William Herns played in the drawn game for Tipperary. Michael O'Dwyer, John Fitzgerald, Pa. Fitzgerald and Jimmy Burke came on for replay.

Champions-The Thurles Team

By Edmund Murphy, Washington D.C.
Received from Liam ó Donnchú, Littleton, Thurles.

A sláinte to fair Thurles Town
May no dark clouds above it frown
To mar its proud display;
But there let sunshine long endure
In fertile fields, along the Suir,
Rich smiling harvests to secure
Those who hold hurling sway.

In nineteen-seven we went to meet
The team that Connaught then did greet,
As champions of the West.
We met by Shannon's waters blue
And won by thirty five to two,
But like game men they fought it through
Resolved on doing their best.

'Twas thus last year our team did fare—
We walloped Kerry, shattered Clare
Beat Limerick out of fun,
And in Fermoy the Corkies met;
What Gael that meeting can forget
'Twas uphill work 'gainst Cork, but yet
The victory we won.

What team has beaten Munster so,
And left them all with tales of woe,
While Tipps look on and cheer?
That Waterford beat in a thrice,
And 'cleaned up' Limerick so nice
And vanquished gallant Cork twice
Within the present year.

To Dublin, too our mettle showed
When we met them at Jones's road
And later at Athy.
Though Dublin sought that second meet,
We trailed their colours in defeat,
And Scotland beat a quick retreat
For their old home in Skye.

Hurrah! Hurrah! For the Thurles team,
The grandest that was ever seen
Throughout the GAA.
Who proudly battled, nobly fought,
Though not supported, as they ought;
Men who indulged no selfish thought,
But worked and won the day.

Thurles Aboo!

*By Templemorensis, Sept. 1909. Received from Liam Ó Donnchú,
Ballymoreen, Littleton. Chorus after each verse.*

Nearer the 'final' is coming, beware boys!
The great day's at hand when you'll take to the field.
And battle once more for the laurels of fame, boys
Determined that never shall the gallant Tipps yield.

Chorus:

Forward to victory, then, on for the Leinster men,
Let Erin see what 'the blue' boys can do;
Practise at dawn and noon, train hard and train soon,
On! On! The battle cry is Thurles Aboo.

What is your fear boys while Semple is with you,
That gallant old captain who leads in the fray?
Why should you doubt when you think of the past boys?
That one word 'Dungourney' ought all trouble allay.

Send in your best boys, your fleetest, your bravest,
The fight will be fierce, you must use your best shot.
Pick out the keen-eyed, the sure stroke, the swift man,
Another 'All Ireland' then you'll notch to those got.

This was written after Tipperary had beaten Cork in the Munster final on the 29th
August 1909. Tipperary 2-10, Cork 2-6. In the All- Ireland Final, Tipperary (Thurles)
were beaten by Kilkenny (Mooncoin) by 4-6 to 0-12 on the 12th Dec. 1909 at Cork.
On June 27th, 1909 Tipperary had defeated Dublin in the All-Ireland hurling final
replay at Athy for the 1908 title.

Team: Tom Semple (capt), J.O.Brien, T.Kerwick, P.Burke, J.Fitzgerald, J.Mockler,
J.Moloughney, A.Carew, M.O'Brien, P. Fitzgerald, J.Mooney, R.Mockler, H.Shelly,
T.Gleeson, J.Burke, P.Brolan, J.Hackett. Sub: E. Hayes.

Munster Hurling Final 1909

By Edmund Murphy, Washington D.C. Sept 14, 1909.
Source: Tipperary Star 1909 received from Liam Ó Donnchú, Ballymoreen, Littleton.

Of contests Tipp was oft the scene where Arra flows the hills
between,
But never had Tipperary seen excitement run so high:
As when the Corkmen took their stand against the champions of
Ireland,
The Munster Championship to land, conclusions for to try.

Then high enthusiasm ran; each hurler swung his gay camán–
There was not on the field a man stood listless at the call.
So prompt were they to take their place— to watch the ball each
other face
For they were leaders in the race, now one of them must fall.

Then for the sphere the rebels go, but Gleeson checked them down
below,
And Shelley hit a frightful blow for one who looked so mild.
Then Kelleher for Cork did score and he and Ronayne scored once
more
While Fleming made the green flag soar and Cork roared themselves
wild.

Not yet Cork's winning gait grows slack, 'tis Walsh now leads the
attack,
But gallant Thurles beat them back; the play was very hot.
The Tipps were not to be denied, in every blow was local pride,
Cork's forwards Semple threw aside, while Mockler made the shot.

A point and goal at once they score, Tipp's sympathisers cheer and
roar,
Throughout the half, which now is o'er, they played against the
wind.

But favoured with the wind and weather; although opposed not
caring whether,
Unsparingly they welt the leather and Cork's uprights they find.

Then furious shots Tipp's forwards gave and many a goal did Fitzy
save,
For never yet worked backs so brave as he and 'Hawk' O'Brien.
Though Cork had victory almost earned; a bitter lesson yet they
learned,
Tipp's speed and strength the tables turned, they win for the third
time.

Tipp's gallant captain worked things through, James Burke was there
and Brolan too,
And to crush Cork—in rushed Carew and piled up score on score.
And keener now excitement grew, to end it all the whistle blew
'Mid shout s of Tipps! Long life to you! —You're champions o'er
and o'er.

Played at Tipperary Town on the 29th August 1909. Tipperary 2-10, Cork 2-6.

Tipperary (Thurles)— T. Semple (capt), T. Kerwick, M. O'Brien, J. Mockler, P.
Brolan, H. Shelley, A. Carew, J. Mooney, J. 'Hawk' O'Brien, P. Burke, J.
McLoughney, M. O'Dwyer, J. Burke, J. Fitzgerald, T. Gleeson, R. Mockler, P.
Fitzgerald..

118

The Munster Final 1913

By Sliabh Ruadh (Phil O'Neill)
Source: History of the GAA 1910-30 by Phil O'Neill.

'Twas an autumn day and the sun shone down
With a cheerful ray o'er the seaside town,
And dense the crowds that thronged then there
And joyous the crowds that rent the air:
For there were gathered our country's pride
From Lee, Suir, Nore and Shannon's side:
And came they too from Sarsfield's town
And forth from the shadow of Knockmealdown:
E'en from the west were gathered there
Young men comely and maidens fair:
And with anxious step and eager pace,
Hurried they on to the trysting place,
For here today in contest fleet,
Tipperary's best and Cork will meet—
Here beneath the Comeragh's frown
They'll cross camáns for the Munster crown.

Now, the hour's at hand and the crowds throng round,
Soon the hurlers invade the ground:
Deafening the cheers that greet these braves,
Each one the call of battle craves.
Tipperary decked in gold and blue,
Cork in jerseys of crimson hue;
Sturdy, lithe -limbed, well-set men,
Stout of arm and stern of ken.
Scions true of our ancient race,
Sternly they marshal face to face,
And soon the trumpet of battle speaks
And then in a flash the phalanx breaks!

Onward they press with might and main!
Onward, backward and on again!

Here they rush; there they meet,
Centremen, backmen, forwards fleet.
Then list to the click and creak and crash
As hero meets hero, ash to ash;
Now a bang, now a bound,
As the horseskin flitters across the ground:
Another moment it soars on high
Like a hunted bird through the autumn sky:
Now like hare by greyhounds chased,
That nimble ball is pressed and paced,
Whilst thousands watch with hearts a-beat,
The fortunes of that contest fleet—
From some a shout, from some a moan,
As the leather enters the danger zone.
Then see that surging, swaying pack,
As they parry and poise and hurl and hack;
Multi-colours blend together
Clashing ash and flying leather
Mind and muscle, might and brawn,
Behind each stroke of the stout camán.
'Go on Rockies' 'Go on Tipp!'
Such the cry from every lip;
Then suddenly a thunderclap stirs your soul,
And thousands clamour 'A goal, a goal'
The green flag waves in a moment more
And proclaims to all 'tis indeed a score.

Thus for an hour the battle raged,
Hotter and fiercer they each engaged:
Those stalwarts bold, unknowing fear,
Their county's honour alone held dear;
Seeking no gain or paltry pelf,
Reckless of limb and life itself:
Each heart true and stout and brave,
No spirit there of serf or slave!
So never let old Ireland fear
That none are left her cause to steer;

For should proud freedom call again,
For gleaming lines of fighting men,
The first to lead the noble work—
The men of Tipp. and Rebel Cork!

This Munster Hurling Final was played at Dungarvan on September 21, 1913. Tipperary 8-2, Cork 4-3. The author notes (p 361) that the last lines have proved prophetic, for the boys of Tipp. and Cork led the van during the Black and Tan regime'.

This was the first time that distinctive county colours were worn. Tipperary wore bright crimson and gold jerseys and on the breast the crossed keys of the Kings of Cashel. Cork had saffron jerseys with blue collars and cuffs and a large C on the breast. Both counties were to change later to the colours they wear today.

1913 Team Selection—P. Wedger Meagher (capt); W. Kelly, J.Harty, E. Cawley, S, Hackett, F. Mc Grath, M. Ryan, J. Kennedy, E. Gilmartin, J.'Skinny' O'Meara, J. Raleigh, J. Murphy, H. Shelly, P. Brolan, E. O'Keeffe, Paddy Kennedy, Bud Keeffe, Stephen Hackett, Jim O'Meara.

Toomevara Abú

By Michael Bourke, Newport
Source: Newport in Song and Poetry
Published by Michael Bourke Festival Committee.
Air: O'Donnell Abu

By the banks of the Suir whose waters run so calm and pure,
There is terrible commotion in alley, street and lane.
For the bold Tipps are advancing on Waterford City,
To bring back fresh victories to Tipperary again.

Chorus:

'Up Toomevara' then, the cream of Ireland's hurling men,
I wish to God Ned Carson could get one good look at you.
He'd stow away his foreign guns, run home and stick to eating buns,
If he heard Tipp'rary's war cry, 'Toomevara Abú'.

Limerick, Cork and Galway fell, the Kilkenny boys they played right
well—
Poor Sim Walton boasted loudly that it's easy to beat you.
And when you met the 'College boys' the devil's lads for fun and
noise,
You wrote for them a headline that their masters never knew.

Chorus:

We had followers from each town and glen, village boys and
mountain men,
A braver band ne'er mustered since the days of Brian Boru.
Then up with your battle cry, give a cheer to rend the sky,
Hurrah for Knocknagow and 'Tommevara Abú.

Chorus:

122

Tipperary always led the van; they beat the tyrants to a man
And now upon the Gaelic field, they've proved their mettle too
You come from noble stock and place, a mighty, fighting hurling race
You're a credit to Tipperary and 'Toomevara Abú.

Chorus:

Now brave boys pull together, keep banging at the leather,
Let no disturber come between you, stick together loyal and true.
For you are a gallant little band, there's not your match in Paddy's land,
Led on by Wedger Meagher and bould Fr. Donoghue.

Chorus:

Tipperary's road to the Munster final in 1913:

15 June at Waterford: Tipperary, 6-0, Waterford 2-2 Referee M. Mehigan, Cork.
17 August at Market's field, Limerick. Tipperary 3-2, Clare 2-0 Referee A Quillinan, Limerick.
21 Sept at Dungarvan, Tipperary 8-2, Cork 4-3. Referee J McDonnell, Kerry.

Tipperary (Toomevara) 1913 Team Selection—P. Wedger Meagher (capt), W. Kelly,
J.Harty, E. Cawley, S. Hackett, F. Mc Grath, M. Ryan, J. Kennedy, E. Gilmartin,
J.'Skinny' O'Meara, J. Raleigh, J. Murphy, H. Shelly, P. Brolan, E. O'Keeffe, Paddy
Kennedy, Bud Keeffe, Stephen Hackett, Jim O'Meara.

Clare v Tipperary 1913

By Michael Bourke, Newport
Source: Newport in Song and Poetry by Michael Bourke Festival Committee

'Twas the seventeenth of August, I remember well that day,
When Tipp and Clare selections for the championship did play.
The boys from Clare are manly Gaels, great dash and skill have
shown,
But they had to bow to Wedger's men in far-famed Garryowen.

Then success to bold Tipperary, your past records are not few,
There's not a team in Erin's Isle can play the game like you.
We'll sing their praise o'er hill and dale, let no bluffers run them
down,
They vanquished Clare's bold dashing Gaels that day in Limerick
town.

Our hurlers came from Emly and Templetuohy's plain—
Horse and Jockey and famed Thurles, where they hate a coward's
name;
And the Toomevara champions, men our country ne'er did shame—
All came together manfully to uphold the hurling fame.

More power to Clare's great stalwart braves, dash and skill forced
you to yield,
But we won't forget your daring deeds on Bodyke's bloody field.
You fought for home and country, met the redcoats face to face,
But in Limerick town your boys went down—they could not stand
the pace.

Tipperary's scrolls of hurlers bold are packed with deeds of fame,
Tubberadora and Moycarkey, may the heavens bless your name.
I think with pride on the Borris boys who in front are always seen,
We have men as brave to day Thank God, the boys in gold and
green.

God bless you Wedger Meagher, may your courage never fail,
In many a hard fought contest, you were never found to quail.
When I think on Semple's daring deeds, my heart o'erflows with joy,
We have a hero still to take his place, in the Toomevara boy.

Then assemble all Tipperary Gaels in every glen and town,
And swell up the testimonial to those heroes of renown.
'May God guard our camán wielders' be the prayer on every lip
By the storied walls of Garryowen, they won the championship.

Tipperary's road to the Munster final 1n 1913: See notes attached to the previous item
Toomevara Abú.

Verse 4   *Bodyke's bloody field*—Bodyke lies about three miles west of Scariff and
sixteen miles east of Ennis. This comment refers to the evictions at Bodyke, in 1887.
Bodyke up to the 1880's had not made any remarkable contribution to Irish history
and to people living outside County Clare was totally unknown. But the year 1887
was to see a change. Bodyke was destined to be on the lips of men and women
throughout the length and breadth of Ireland wherever people gathered to discuss the
land question and the evils of landlordism.

Michael Davitt founded the Land league at Irishtown in Co. Mayo in 1879. Its radical
nature was to be seen in its constitution: The land of Ireland belongs to the people of
Ireland to be held and cultivated for the sustenance of those whom God decreed to be
inhabitants thereof. Land being created to supply mankind with the necessaries of
existence, those who cultivate it to that end have a higher claim to its absolute
possession than those who make it an article of barter to be used or disposed of for
purposes of profit or pleasure. The end for which the land of a country is created
requires and equitable distribution of the same among the people who are to live upon
the fruits of their labour in its cultivation!'

The Bodyke landlord called on the law to support him in the exercise of his property
rights against an obdurate tenantry who resisted his rack rent claims. The tenants of
Bodyke had combined very effectively with the support of the Land League. Bodyke
played a most significant part in the land revolution of the late 19c. The eviction of
twenty eight families began on Thursday, June 2 and lasted until Wed. June 25. 1887.
Bodyke was to be used as a battleground between landlords and tenants. What the
tenants sought was revolutionary. Bodyke played a most significant part in the land
revolution of the late nineteenth century. Its contribution to the total overthrow of the
prevailing land holding system was immense. It was not just a local reaction to a local
experience but was a most important battleground which tested the fundamental issue
of the day—rights— the landlords versus those of the tenants. The law was on the side
of the landlord and the law must be upheld and seen to be so. What Bodyke sought
was revolutionary and if they succeeded then a major revolution was at hand.

Certain patterns emerged during the course of the evictions. Church bells greeted the arrival of the evicting party each morning. Attempts were made by the evicting party to outwit the crowds and tenants attempted to lure the sheriff into evicting the wrong person. The normal defence procedure was simple. Doors were usually removed and blocked up with some suitable material. The windows were barricaded and large bushes were placed at vantage points around the house. Inside the house the tenants waited armed with buckets of hot porridge, boiling meal and boiling water. The task of forcing and entry was left to the emergency men who were hired to do this work. These were not from the locality and were 'imported' specially for the occasion. Since the battering ram had not yet come into general use, this group operated long iron crowbars to attack the walls of the house while the occupiers continued to drench the crowbar brigade with the stuff which they had stored inside. Much of the defence in Bodyke was in the hands of the womenfolk.

One tenant made the following preparations before an eviction. *A dozen large tubs and pans of water stood about; a heap of peat, six feet square, blocked up the corner where it was believed the crowbar men would attack; half a dozen pitch forks were disposed ready to hand; long poles were prepared to push off the scaling ladders which the stormers might employ; a great thornbush was cut to block the door between the two parts of the house in case one of them should be carried by assault; and in the odd corners left by these elaborate preparations the beds of the family were stowed away, and screened off by temporary partitions, and the best of the furniture had to be removed to under a hedge in the next field.*

At the conclusion of the evictions of the first day Michael Davitt addressed the people as follows:

'When I listened to a man today inside one of the cabins regret that he had not a rifle in hand by which he could have defended the home his father built, I echoed the wish in my own heart, and wished the the people here had equal weapons and we would have taught these exterminators a lesson which they could never forget, and would have given an example which crushed humanity in other parts of the world would have profited by, but I feel my words here today are merely an expression of vain regret......'

But the Bodyke tenants were the victors in the long haul. Four years prior to this hurling game between Clare and Tipperary in 1913, the Land Commission in 1909 acquired the property compulsorily. The Bodyke section of the estate was acquired in one lot. And undertakings to purchase from this body were quickly entered into by the tenants. Tenant ownership had become a reality. Without the sacrifice of the Bodyke tenants that solution would have been delayed. Twentieth century Irish society has been tardy in recognising and acknowledging the tremendous debt, which is owed to the 'Bodykes' of the later nineteenth century.

(Information extracted from *The Bodyke Evictions* by John S, Kelly, published by Fossabeg Press, Scariff, 1987)

United We Stand

By Patrick Connor, Prospect Park, Kilkenny
Source: The Gaelic Echo, St. Patrick's Day Number 1942,
The Kilkenny Moderator, Nov 15, 1913 and Famous Tullaroan (Ó Dúill)

'Twas in November, we all assembled, to see the final at Jones' Rd.
Where the grand old champions as game as bantams, in many a
battle the line have toed.
Half past two was the hour appointed, the ground was wet and the
going dead,
When Ireland's champions in black and amber, line out with
Munster in gold and red.

Drug, Sim and Rochford are first to enter, three old veterans we love
so well,
And the piper's band before them marching—the sight should ever
in memory dwell.
Ah, here comes Munster in gold and scarlet, the finest hurlers we'll
meet again,
And only once have they been defeated—their deeds are told by
many a pen.

The coin is tossed and Kilkenny win; 'Drug' Walsh the captain calls
out the roll:
The backs are marching to take their places and Power is gone to the
Clonliffe goal.
Woeful Gargan is first to trespass and then commences a fierce
attack,
By Doctor Grace and J.J. Brennan, for speed and courage they do not
lack.

But Walton waltzes through his opponents and the white flag rises
for our first score
And the green flag soon in the breeze is waving, by good old Gargan
beside the Nore.

Dick Grace and 'Drug' beat all before them and up dashed Kennedy
the mighty giant,
His fine long pucks relieving greatly and from a 'seventy' he scores
a point.

With Tipp bombarding and Power still guarding, the leather
travelling at lightning speed,
Our heroes dashing and hurleys clashing, they're still maintaining
their two points lead:
Their combination is a revelation, in every station our boys excel,
As camán wielders and splendid fielders, the Munster champions
alone can tell.

Tipp's great forwards again are pressing but Keoghan and Rochford
are quite at home,
From the Boyne to Shannon, who'd conquer Lennon, that fine
performer from Erin's Own.
Ah, what could equal the Doyles and Doherty and Jim Kelly,
Moondarrig's Gael?
Their splendid passing, the Tipps outclassing, there's none could
beat them in Inisfail.

Oh look at Walton, their posts assaulting, at last he raises the final
score,
Our shouts are heard on the hills of Clara, when he beat O'Meara,
the 'barn door'
Our colours shining more bright than ever and more determined our
champions play,
To win the battle, once more they rattle, the hounds are failing, they
cannot stay.

The clouds are lowering, the light is fading, the hounds are sinking
behind the hares,
Kilkenny's pussies are fast escaping—they'll never catch them into
nets or snares.
Another rally from Toomevara saw Power defending his net once
more,

128

The glorious victory is at our mercy—God bless our hurlers beside
the Nore.

Oh, thanks to heavens, there goes the whistle; Tooomevara's
Greyhounds' long course is o'er,
And when in slips they can call to memory, the loose limbed hares
by the river Nore.
Oh, sweet Kilkenny, your victories many, have styled you
champions from both far and near:
Hang up your camáns and wear your laurels, you won with honour
from year to year.

You beat the best they could send from Munster, the pride of
Leinster before you fell,
The Glasgow exiles you too defeated and the Liverpool Irish you
beat as well.
One word in favour of Toomevara, the greatest sportsmen we've
ever met,
We'll grasp their hands as worthy foemen and hope to see them
victorious yet.

On Jones' road when the match was over, we chaired the champions
into their room,
The Tipp contingent went home downhearted, they ne'er expected
the fall of Toom.
But where's the team in Irish Ireland or in any country beneath the
sun,
Could stand an hour before the champions at Jones' road where
they've always won.

Oh, where is Limerick, those splendid hurlers, that play on paper and
not on grass,
Will they deny that you're Ireland champions but talk feels always as
smooth as glass.

Oh, gallant veterans, don't leave your places, though years be stealing on you, don't fret.
For fit and well by God's own graces, you're worth a dozen All-Irelands yet.

All honour to you, Dan O'Connell, also Jim Nowlan, true Gaels you are,
Likewise John Lalor and Johnnie Kealy and our guard of honour is brave Tom Maher.
But Peter Dunne the champion's mascot is always with them through storm and hail,
On Sunday last when the match was over, with fair excitement he jumped the rail.

Farewell old champions, I'll close my verses, in hopes to meet you again next year,
May you win the cup you hold at present, that you can do it I have no fear.
So keep united and stand like brothers, there's more All-Irelands for you in store,
I love to hear the ash a'clashing along the banks of the lovely Nore.

All-Ireland Hurling Final at Jones' Road, November 2, 1913. Kilkenny (Mooncoin) 2-4, Tipperary (Toomevara) 1-2.

In this year teams were reduced from 17 aside to 15 aside. Limerick hurlers defeated Kilkenny in a classic at Jones' road on July 28th 1913 in the Fr. Matthew Hall Tournament. The reference to Limerick's hurlers in the third last verse is probably an unhappy memory relating to this defeat. Limerick were led by Tyler Mackey. O'Meara (Barn door reputation in verse 7) was Jack (Skinny) O'Meara)

The victory over Tipperary in the 1913 All-Ireland Final was particularly sweet to Kilkenny as Tipperary (Toomevara) had defeated Kilkenny (Moondarrig) the previous June in Dan Fraher's field, Dungarvan. It was also very sweet because this was Kilkenny's third All-Ireland win in a row.

'The Greyhounds created an image in the public mind as distinctive as that created earlier by Tubberadora, Dungourney and Thurles Blues. Paddy Leahy described them as 'the hard-luck team of hurling history', for the other teams mentioned all inscribed their names in the All-Ireland roll of honour, the 'Greyhounds' failed to win the one game that mattered most of all. The Toomevara 'Greyhounds' got their name, from their fleetness of foot.

Kilkenny—R. 'Drug' Walsh (capt), J. Power, J. Keoghan, J. Rochford, J. Lennon, D. Kennedy, R. Grace, M. Dargan, J.J. Brennan, P. Grace, R.Doherty, R. Doyle, S. Walton, M. Doyle, J. Kelly.

Tipperary—P. 'Wedger' Meagher (capt), J. O'Meara, F. McGrath, S. Hackett, B. Mockler, J. Raleigh, T. Gleeson, J. Harty, E. Gilmartin, E. Cawley, P. Brolan, H. Shelley, J. Murphy, W. Kelly, E. O'Keeffe.

Kilkenny Still

By Pat Long, Tullogher
Source: Gaelic Echo, St. Patrick's Day Number 1942.
Also Kilkenny Journal, Nov. 29, 1913.

Dear Sir, you may remember, I wrote to you last December
About Kilkenny's famous hurling men.
I said, I'd cross the ocean but I took another notion,
And here I'm writing poetry once again.

It's again the same old story; they've again won fame and glory,
In the last All-Ireland final lately played.
With confidence so airy, they outpointed Tipperary,
And put the pride of Munster in the shade.

Oh, magnificent Tipperary, how you struggled, never weary,
'Tho' Kilkenny's ceaseless rushes drove you back.
How you came anew again and your gallant hurling men
Returned ever fiercer to attack.

Only those who saw can tell, how Tipperary fought right well,
Though beaten and defeated in the fray:
How stubborn their defence mid excitement wild and tense,
As they strove to keep Kilkenny still at bay.

Oh, it was a gallant sight, when Kilkenny in their might,
Rolled back Tipperary's desperate forward play:
An our county's needs must honour those who won such glory for
her,
'Tis for what I write this simple little lay.

We do not want to crow o'er Tipperary's overthrow,
Or boast of what Kilkenny's players have done:
For Kilkennys and Tipperarys have been friendly since the fairies
Taught them hurling in the ages dim and gone.

All Ireland Hurling Final 1913

By Rev. James B. Dollard,Mooncoin.
Source: Received from Liam Ó Donnchú, Ballymoreen, Littleton.

Sounding their corded harps, the bards of old
Sang of Cuchulainn's prowess when he struck
With swift camán the whirling ball in air
And met it ere it fell, whipping it back
To meet it as before. And too! They tell
Of the great Fenians meeting on the plain
In mimic warfare when the hurleys clashed
And Dhiarmuid O'Doon showed wondrous skill
With ringing blows forcing the stubborn goal
While thousands cheered him on—so may I sing,
To a theme worthy of my lyre.
I sing the great All-Ireland championship
Lately in Dublin fought, when from the South
Came up Kilkenny's champions, fitly trained
And captained by 'Drug' Walsh, a manful Gael,
Modest, yet brave, with him Moondharrig's best:
Kelly, the Doyles, Dick Doherty and Power
The goalman came and Tullaroan sent there
Jim Walton, Keoghan, Kennedy and Grace.
And yet another champion famed, whose name
Was like the last—Kilkenny sent Brennan and Drennan,
Drawn from Erin's Own and the strong hero Gargan—
Last I name though far from least, Rochford,
Threecastles pride, eager, indomitable!. Against these
Tipperary's choice were fitted—men whose deeds
Through Munster wide were famed a gallant band
From Toomevara and from Thurles drawn
From Horse and Jockey and the fertile vales
Of Templetuohy—Meagher captained them
Young and impetuous, eager like his team
To sweep aside opponents and possess
The ribands blue of Erin's championship!

Vast were the throngs that crowded Jones' Road
To see the combat. As the teams lined up
A silence fell—as before the rush
A whirl and roar that marks the hurricane
An awful hush pervades the waiting world.
And nature bates her breath—so quiet fell
Upon the mighty multitudes. At once the
Dreaded suspense was broken, as the ball
Was cast to ground and the swift players rushed
Hither and thither, driving towards the goal.
Ash tested ash and the far-echoing sound
Like the repeated din at Clontarf
Was heard, and from the sideline rose a roar
Like the hoarse surf upon a stormy coast.
'On, On, Moondharrig ' 'Tipperary On'
Then it was that the Tipps like lions roused
Leaped at their foes remembering great deeds
Done by their forebears when old 'Knocknagow'
Led all the world. And Matt the Thrasher's strength
Matched Golls and Ossians! Then Moondharrig's choice–
Dodged not the issue but against them bore,
And all their craft and conscience called to mind
To stem that fierce attack—so the swift battle raged
And quick as thought the ball shot here and there,
Now menacing the Tipperary goal.
Which from the strong Kilkenny citadel
With matchless mettle forced. There rose a shout
That echoed to the Galtees, when at length
Tipperary bulged the net, and fates looked black
For brave Moondharrig, but with courage grim
They marked up point for point until ahead.
Then Gargan shot a goal, and wild unrolled
The deep-toned Leinster cheer as when the sea
Fretted by eastern gales strikes Wicklow's coast
In volleying thunder! As when summer fields
Are thick with flowers— all around the hive
The bees are humming, rushing towards the comb.

So 'gainst the Munster fortress dashed and drove
Kelly and Walton, Doherty and Doyle
The posts bombarding! And again the ball
Travelled Kilkennywards till Walsh held up
The Leinster net like a wall of brass;
With Rochford, Threecastles prodigy,
Broke the fierce charge, till half-time whistle blew!
The second half began with lightning speed
And Tipperary anxious to retrieve their
Threatened fortunes, broke into the fray
With desperate will. Their captain urged them hard
Leading them on, but the strong defence
Of Lennon, Keoghan, Rochford and John Power
Held out intact—at last the leather shot
Down the left wing from Doherty to Doyle
From Doyle to Kelly—Kelly struggled strong
With a tall adversary, then freed the ball
And shot to Walton with unerring aim
Who doubling, found the net. Then sudden rang
Tumultuous cheers from all the Leinster host
Shaking the skies—as when a western gale
Piling the seas on Staffa's stormy coast
Fills Fingal's caves with clangor and resounds
With din reverberant to the clamouring north.
But yet brave Tipperary had not shot
Their latest bolts. With frenzy of despair
They hurled their strength upon the Leinster goal
Seeking a score—but Rochford nullified
Their frantic efforts and then the ball rolled wide.
Then it was that the captain Richard Walsh
Shook Rochford's hand and spoke him words of praise
More pleasing to the hurler than the shrieks
Of frenzied thousands. Then again the ball
Zig-zags the field, in scientific play.
From Keoghan's stroke to Lennon swift it flies,
Lennon to Gargan sends the leather on
Gargan to Michael Doyle—to Kelly he

135

Flashes the sphere and Kelly shoots on goal!
A wondrous play that sure deserved a score.
But Tipperary's backs were sound and true
Fighting a glorious battle though losing game
Till the 'long whistle' blew—Moondharrig then
All-Ireland champions were declared.

Fr. Dollard, (later Monsg.) the author, born 30th August 1872 was a Kilkennyman from Ballytarsney, Mooncoin. He wrote numerous poems and articles about hurling. In Carberry's Annual 1946/47 Carberry writes, 'Dear kindly Mooncoin man who loved the hurling and the hurlers with an abiding love...Fr. Dollard's book of sacred poems, written in exile has won him a high place in church literature. His droll tales of Myles na gCamán, his ballad of The Little Villages; his beautiful translation of Donnaca Rhua's Bán-Chnuic-Éireann-Ó; his beautiful poems perfectly balanced and brimful of Celtic imagery, on the fairies, sports, romances of his homeland; his descriptive verses of Suirside and Clontarf, all endeared him to our hearts'. He died in Toronto in 1946. (*History of the GAA*, 1910-1930, Phil O'Neill, (Sliabh Ruadh).

Edward O'Keeffe, Mooncoin writes, 'Very early in life Fr Dollard became a student of the mystery and folklore of Ireland. With his great talents and gifts of expression he developed a love for poetry, drama and short stories. His many literary works in later life reflected that love. Having completed his classical studies in Ireland he left for Canada in 1890 going to New Brunswick... He immediately began his studies in the Grand Seminary in Montreal...Fr Dollard was ordained to the priesthood in 1896; he served successively as curate at St. Mary's and St. Luke's churches in Toronto. For nine years he served as P.P. at Uppergrove where he erected a new church. He later served at St. Monica's and Our Lady of Lourdes parishes.

While devoting his life to the spiritual well being of his parishioners, Fr. Dollard found time to carry on his writings. At least four volumes of his poems were published in Canada. His books *Irish Ballads and Lyrics*, *Irish Mist and Sunshine* were some of his most popular and best known works. In *The Gaels of Moondarrig*, a volume of short stories chiefly describing Mooncoin hurlers, it also depicts a way of rural life over a hundred years ago. As well as following the fortunes of the Mooncoin and Kilkenny teams, several of his poems of that period (1904-13 were written in praise of the hurlers of Cork, Kilkenny and Tipperary, and his writings under the pen name 'Slievenamon' were widely read.

Fr. Dollard's vital position in the maintenance of the Irish refusal to submerge the national dignity has seldom received the acknowledgement it so richly deserved, but it is there in his writings and in his life for all to see.... as well as being a great lover of his country, he particularly liked his old home at Ballytarsney. In one of his best known poems the Bridge of Ballytarsney the nostalgia for home may be easily noticed.'

Hurrah for Toomevara

By Michael Bourke
Source: Newport in Song and Poetry
Published by the Michael Bourke Festival Committee.
The Gaelic Echo, Dec. 12, 1941
Air: The Wearing of the Green.

On June the first nineteen-thirteen, to Dungarvan town so fair,
Our bold Tipperary hurlers went with hearts as light as air;
To meet Moondarrig's champions, it's the first time they did meet,
But bold Wedger Meagher's 'Greyhounds' soon ran them off their feet.

Chorus:

Then hurrah for Toomevara, may your banner never fall,
You beat Galway and Queen's county and you levelled Cork's stone wall:
But I never will forget the day Kilkenny's pride went down
Before the skill of Wedger's men in sweet Dungarvan town.

For some time past your fame went down thro' causes I won't name,
But the Toomevara 'Greyhounds' have brought Tipp in front again
You're a credit to your county, better men were never seen,
Under bold Tipperary's banner in your colours gold and green.

Chorus:

God bless you Meara and Mc Grath, Raleigh and Hackett too,
Likewise brave Bobby Mockler, you were always loyal and true.
There's Kelly and Gilmartin; they never miss a ball
And Thurles boy Hugh Shelley, he could hole a four foot wall.

Chorus:

Now Thurles, Toom, and Jockey boys take one advice from me,
If you mean to keep on winning, united you must be.

137

If you win the Munster final, I'll fling up my old caubeen
And give a cheer for Toomevara and the boys in gold and green.

Chorus:

Give one cheer for Timmy Gleeson, the hero tried and true—
There's Harty, Ryan and Cawley; they all know what to do.
And our hero Wedger Meagher, he is the lad can fly—
No forgetting Murphy and O'Keeffe, the Templetuohy boy.

Chorus

Now to conclude and finish, I must bid you all adieu—
You showed Kilkenny's stalwarts what Tipperary men can do.
You knocked out all-Ireland champions; poor Sim Walton's heart is broke
So now we'll build a monument to our glorious Dr. Croke.

In 1896 the Croke Cup inter-county competitions were instituted to mark the Silver Jubilee of Archbishop Croke's episcopal appointment.
This was the Croke Cup Memorial tournament final played at Dan Fraher's field, Dungarvan in 1913. Later on in the year (Nov) Kilkenny reversed the result in the All-Ireland final. See *Kilkenny Still* and *United We Stand*.

Final Score: Tipperary 5-4, Kilkenny 1-1.

Team—P.'Wedger' Meagher, F. McGrath, J.Harty, E.Cawley, M.Ryan, W.Kelly, S.Hackett, J.O'Meara, E.Gilmartin, (Toomevara) H.Shelly, T.Gleeson, (Thurles) R.Mockler, J.Murphy, (Horse-Jockey) J.Raleigh, (Emly) E.O'Keeffe Templetuohy).
Subs: J.Leahy, T.Mockler, J.Fitzpatrick, P.Fitzgerald, M.McKenna, J.Kennedy.

The Thomond Feis Shield 1915

By Michael Bourke, Newport
Source: Liam Ó Donnchú, Ballymoreen, Littleton.

Tipperary men stand up and wherever you be
At home in the green isle or far o'er the sea.
Give three mighty cheers for those men of renown
Who brought home the Shield and who now wear the crown.
This team of young heroes and on this we agree,
They conquered them all from the Foyle to the Lee.
No doubt the bold Claremen a grand team did field
But dash, science and pluck made those brave heroes yield.

'Twas a soul stirring sight when the train it slowed down,
To see our boys marching through old Limerick Town.
Led on by bold Wedger, who was ne'er known to yield—
In a short time we've taken the old Market's Field.
At three-o-clock sharp, the match did begin.
The teams toed the line and the ball was thrown in.
Clare warriors were nimble, lithe, active and fit,
But the boys of Tipperary were all steel and grit.

Then Shanahan gave a huge drive to the ball.
It was met by Bob Mockler before it did fall—
A beautiful shot sent it flying to the stand,
From the hop, Hughie Shelly a nice goal did land.
Then score after score through the posts Tipp did drive,
They swarmed round the Clare backs like bees round a hive.
The ashen sticks crashed and the ball soared on high—
'Tis netted once more by the bold Thurles boy.

Then fill up your glasses and give them a toast.
Tipperary of those gallant heroes may boast.
Here's luck to Jack Kennedy, Dwan and Raleigh,
O'Meara, Bill Kelly, O'Keeffe, and Cawley.
There's Hackett, Mick Hammonds and Shanahan too,

Paddy Brolan and Murphy, all good men and true.
Jack Harty and Mick Ryan are crowned with renown
But there's no match for Shelly from famed Thurles Town.

I must now conclude for my feelings are high.
May the Gaels in Tipperary and Clare never die.
I sounded their praises as well as I could,
Through village and valley, o'er hill and wild wood.
If mistakes I have made, you'll forgive me I'm sure,
For I'm not in the same class as Davis and Moore.
The Hip, Hip, Hurrah for Tipp's heroes so rare,
And a cheer for the boys from the bare hills of Clare.

They may boast of their hurlers in Galway and Clare,
Roscommon, Queen's County, Wexford, elsewhere.
Cork and Kilkenny can hurl the ball,
But the boys from Tipp'rary can leather them all

'The Thomond Shield, a magnificient trophy value £50, was presented by the Gaelic
league in Limerick in the year 1913 for competition amongst the county hurling
selections of Limerick (Castleconnell), Tipperary (Toomevara), Clare (O'Callaghan's
Mills) and Cork (Redmonds), with the condition it became the property of any county
winning it twice in succession or three times in all. Toom selected for Tipperary and
though they went out of the running to Lmerick in 1913 and to Cork in 1914 they felt
that they could yet win the cherished prize. Returning to their old status in 1915, the
'Greyhounds' dashed through Limerick, 4-1 to 0-1 and through Clare 4-5 to 1-0. A
feature of the games, played of course in Limerick, was the presence of armed
Irishmen where they were not seen since Sarsfield. In 1916, the trumpets rang triumph
for the 'Greyhounds' and the Shield was brought home by a second successive
victory—first over Clare by 4-5 to 1-0, and then over Limerick by 5-0 to 2-2. For the
Cork match in 1916, the Tipps entered the arena wearing mourning armlets in memory
of the dead of Easter Week, and in doing so, acted contrary to British military orders.
Their action—loudly applauded—was a fine lead to Gaeldom just when everything
seemed lost in the rebellion save the honour of the men who took part in it. No trains
were allowed for the final with Limerick, but the gathering was large and pipe bands
added variety to the proceedings.' *(Tipperary's GAA Story, by Very Rev. Philip Canon
Fogarty, P.P., V.F. Templemore, p204)* Because of the War of Independence the
competition lapsed from 1917 to 1919. It resumed in 1920 and it was not until 1925
that a new trophy was presented- a replica of the Ardagh Chalice, which Tipperary
also made their own, winning it both three times in all and twice in succession in
1931. The last final was played at Páirc na nGael, Limerick on 2nd May 1957. (For a
full account of the Thomond Feis, see *One Hundred years of Glory*, A History of

Limerick GAA, by Séamus Ó Ceallaigh and Sean Murphy published by Limerick GAA Publications, 1987, p147)

The above game was played on May 16, at the Market's Field, Limerick 1915. Clare (O'Callaghan's Mills) were the reigning All-Ireland champions and fielded ten of the championship team. The following is the successful victory team of 1916:

'Wedger' Meagher, J.O'Meara, S. Hackett, J. Kennedy, M.Ryan, J. Harty, W.Kelly, R.Minogue, J.Collison, J. Ryan—Lanigan, T.Ryan—Lanigan, M.Hammonds, H.Shelly, J.Murphy, J.Raleigh. Subs: F.McGrath, E.Cawley, E.O'Keeffe.

Boherlahan 1916

By George Denney, Ballypatrick, Clonmel.
Received from Liam Ó Donnchú, Ballymoreen, Littleton.

Of years 'tis full a score
Since thy trusty heroes bore
Tipperary's name before!
Boherlahan.

Now by Dungarvan's strand,
From all corners of the land,
Many thousands take their stand,
Boherlahan.

From Desmond's vales so fair,
From the wind-swept hills of Clare,
All Munster greets ye there
Boherlahan

And from each fairy haunted glen,
Round Moondarrig's storied plain
Come the pride of Leinster's men,
Boherlahan.

From old Galtee's towering crest,
To Slievenamon's dark rugged breast,
Tipp's hopes upon thee rest,
Boherlahan.

Well, that trust has been repaid—
Well the might of Cork ye've stayed;
Grand the game of Fionn, ye've played,
Boherlahan.

Wearers of an honoured name,
Bearers of Tipperary's fame,
Victors of a grand fought game,
Boherlahan.

Munster Hurling Final played at Dungarvan on the 1st October 1916.

Tipperary (Boherlahan), 5-0, Cork 1-2.

Tipperary Team: J.Leahy (capt), J.Doherty, A.O'Donnell, J.Power, R.Walsh, D.Walsh, P.Leahy, W.O'Dwyer, N.O'Dwyer, J.Murphy, J.Fitzpatrick, H.Shelly, T.Devane, J.Collison, T.Shanahan.

The Hurling Final 1916

By D.B.English, Rossmore
Source: Received from Liam Ó Donnchú, Ballymoreen, Littleton.

Did you hear the news today? says the Shan Van Vocht.
Boherlahan's cleared the way, says the Shan Van Vocht.
They put Kilkenny on the run, for they whacked them every one,
Till the All-Ireland they had won, says the Shan Van Vocht.

'Twas January twenty-first, says the Shan Van Vocht.
Sure our throats we nearly burst, says the Shan Van Vocht.
When the lads in jerseys blue; Tubberadora wore them too,
Thro' the goalposts sure they flew, says the Shan Van Vocht.

I'll sing to every name, says the Shan Van Vocht,
That brought our county all this fame, says the Shan Van Vocht.
This parish sure before, brought All-Irelands to our door,
For three and one makes four, says the Shan Van Vocht.

What about the team? says the Shan Van Vocht.
Must I name the full fifteen? says the Shan Van Vocht.
So here goes to every man; find a fault sure if you can,
When every name you scan, says the Shan Van Vocht.

The Leahys—brothers two—says the Shan Van Vocht.
If they only knew, says the Shan Van Vocht.
Their fame's on every lip, when Kilkenny's wings to clip,
They played for gallant Tipp, says the Shan Van Vocht.

In Walshes, we had Dick, says the Shan Van Vocht.
And Denis, oh! So quick! says the Shan Van Vocht.
We could bet our very lives, that he never made such 'drives'
Since the days of ninety-five, says the Shan Van Vocht.

Doherty and O'Donnell, says the Shan Van Vocht.
They're sons of old Tyrconnell, says the Shan Van Vocht.

They were lined across the back, the forwards for to crack,
But they seldom crossed their track, says the Shan Van Vocht.

There's a brace of the Dwyers, says the Shan Van Vocht.
Kilkenny say they're fliers, says the Shan Van Vocht.
Oh! Sure every ball they got, they stuck it to the spot—
They surprised a bloomin' lot, says the Shan Van Vocht.

There is gentle Hughie Shelley, says the Shan Van Vocht.
Of his deeds, sure, I could tell ye, says the Shan Van Vocht.
He's little but he's wise; he's a terror for his size
And he doesn't advertise, says the Shan Van Vocht.

Murphy, Power and Fitz, says the Shan Van Vocht.
They made some 'terrible hits', says the Shan Van Vocht.
If you were to see them stride as they raced along the side,
Whilst Tipperary cheered with pride, says the Shan Van Vocht.

I'd say my memory's gone, says the Shan Van Vocht.
Not to mention Tom Dwan, says the Shan Van Vocht.
He was placed between the 'sticks', where he played some of his
tricks,
And put Kilkenny in a fix, says the Shan Van Vocht.

The North Tipperary boy says the Shan Van Vocht.
He filled our hearts with joy, says the Sean Van Vocht.
When e'er he got the ball, every Tipp. I heard them call,
'Go on rale Moneygall', says the Shan Van Vocht.

Shanahan made the pace, says the Shan Van Vocht.
As he bottled up 'Dick Grace' says the Shan Van Vocht.
No brag or boast I'm sure; he's the pride of Ballinure,
No hurler could be truer, says the Shan Van Vocht.

Then a cheer from all the Gaels, says the Shan Van Vocht,
Within Tipperary's vales, says the Shan Van Vocht.
Thro'Boherlahan and Moneygall, from Rossmore to Killenaule,
Here's a hearty wish to all, says the Shan Van Vocht.

The 1916 All-Ireland Final played at Croke Park on January, 21, 1917. Tipperary
(Boherlahan) 5-4; Kilkenny (Tullaroan) 3-2.
'Fitz' of verse 10—Joe Fitzpatrick, Twomileborris.
'The North Tipperary Boy' of verse 12 — Jer Collison, Moneygall, uncle of Séamus
Ó Riain, ex-President of the GAA. See Tipperary Abú 1916 for team.

Tipperary Abú 1916

By James J.Healy
Received from Liam Ó Donnchú, Ballymoreen, Littleton.

Shrilly the referee's whistle is sounding—
Shouts of 'Up Tipp' resound through the field.
The boys to their favourite places are bounding
To play the All Ireland to win the old shield.
    Go on the blue and gold
    Strike as ye struck of old,
Show them all what you so well can do.
    Muscle and sinew tight,
    Strike out with all your might,
Rush to your slogan—'Tipperary Abú.

Wildly around them Kilkenny men are racing—
Fearless as lions the Tipps hover near.
The captain—the right sort—the ball now is chasing,
Like a dart he goes through them a-tossing the sphere.
    Deftly he lifts the ball.
    Drives it clear over all,
Right through the goalposts it finds its true way.
    Camáns are whirled high
    Caps are flung to the sky.
'A goal for Tipperary— 'Tipperary Abú'.

What cheers rent the air when the battle is finished,
And Tipp and Kilkenny grasped hand in hand.
Their loyal friendship not one whit diminished,
For they fought for the love of the dear old land.
    Up! Every Munster man!
    No matter of what clan.
Cheer the 'All Irelands' —hurru boys, hurru.
    Connaught and Leinster men
    Don't ye feel proud of them?
Up the 'All Irelands'—Tipperary Abú.

Team—J. Leahy (capt), T. Dwan, J. Doherty, W. Dwyer, T. Shanahan, J. Power, J. Fitzpatrick, J. Collison, P. Leahy, H. Shelly, J. Murphy, R. Walsh, D. Walsh, W. Dwyer, A. O'Donnell.
Se notes attached to The Hurling Final 1916

Up Tipp 1916

By T.J.Keating Brookhill, Fethard. 1916
Received from Liam Ó Donnchú, Ballymoreen, Littleton.

From the Suir to Shannon's shore,
From Slievenamon to Galteemore,
Ev'ry true heart proud
Of Tipperary's fame,
Is now full of hope again,
That her gallant hurling men
Will uphold the stainless honour
Of her name.

Think of exiles o'er the foam,
Whose fond hearts are e'er at home.
Now they're waiting, longing,
Wishing day and night,
For the news upon the tide,
That shall make them glow with pride—
'Up men! And for their sakes
Put fervour in the fight.

Fight for Boherlahan's name,
Think of Tubberadora's fame,
Of Moycarkey, Two-Mile-Borris
And Thurles too.
Strike for Horse-and-Jockey bold,
For kingly Cashel famed of old,
And for gallant Toomevara,
Good and true.

Hear the cry on ev'ry lip—
'Forward, forward, gallant Tipp!'
Let the silken flag of vict'ry
Flutter now.

Put your best into the fray
Bring the laurels of the day
Back to anxious hearts at home
In Knocknagow.

God Bless You Boherlahan

By D. B. English, Rossmore- Source: Tubberadora—Boherlahan Hurling Story
By Philip F. Ryan Also credited to T.J.Keating by Nationalist Jan. 27th 1917

O God bless you Boherlahan!
From our hearts we wish you now,
You've hoisted victory banners o'er
The cots of Knocknagow.
There's joy in every hamlet,
In valley, hill and glen
You're the pride of Tipperary,
Gallant Boherlahan men.

Ever worthy Boherlahan
Of the hurling men of old:
You have steered to gallant victory,
Tubberadora's blue and gold.
Laurels after twenty summers,
You have won for them again—
You're the pride of Tipperary,
Gallant Boherlahan men.

Linked in honour, Boherlahan
May your name forever be,
With Moycarkey, Two Mile Borris
And old Thurles fair and free.
With renowned old Tubberadora,
Writ with honours golden pen,
You're the pride of Tipperary,
Gallant Boherlahan men.

Oft at evening in Boherlahan,
Round the cheery kitchen fire,
Will be told the deeds of Leahys   *1
Of the Walshs and Dwyers,   *2
Of Fitzpatrick, Murphy, Shanahan,   *3

Shelly, Dwan, ODonnell, Power, *4
Of Doherty and Collison, *5
Heroes of a thrilling hour.

God be with you, Boherlahan!
Cries an exile far from home,
As the joyful news is wafted
O'er the creamy, crested foam.
Their hearts with joy are swelling
And the silent tear drops flow,
As they picture pleasant hours
In Tipperary long ago.

O God spare you Boherlahan,
Long may men like you remain,
To uphold Tipperary's honour,
Free from blemish and from stain.
Give one ringing cheer of victory,
On the mountain, in the glen—
You're the pride of Tipperary,
Gallant Boherlahan men.

*1   Leahys—Johnnie, Paddy, Mickie and Tommy
*2   Walshs—Johnny, Denis, Dick.
      Dwyers—Willie, Paddy, Nodstown.
*3   J. Fitzpatrick, J. Murphy, Coffey, Horse and Jockey,
*4   A.O'Donnell, J. Power. T. Dwan, Holycross. H. Shelly Thurles.
*5   Jack Doherty, J. Collison.

The Boys of Boherlahan

By Phil O'Neill (Sliabh Ruadh)
Source: History of the GAA 1910-30
Air: The Risin' of the Moon

In Ireland's hurling history
Tipperary holds first place,
For many a glorious victory
Has been won by Kickham's race.
And whilst we give due credit
To each team and to each man,
We now must sing the praises
Of the boys from Boherlahan.

Chorus:

Up the boys from Boherlahan,
Gallant hurlers every man,
Ireland's choice and Ireland's champions
Are the boys from Boherlahan!

Then here's to Tippperary,
To her hurlers bold and brave,
To her homesteads bright and cheery,
Where they never reared a slave.
And now a toast I give you,
And let each one fill a can,
'Here's many more All-Irelands
To the boys of Boherlahan'

After Tipperary (Boherlahan) beat Kilkenny (Tullaroan) in the 1916 All-Ireland
Hurling final played at Croke Park, on January 21, 1917, the author composed this
song and sent it to the captain Johnny Leahy. The above were the first and last verses.
Final score, Tipperary, 5-4, Kilkenny 3-2.

All-Ireland Champions 1916

By Jim Croke, Grallagh, Horse and Jockey.
Source: Moycarkey Borris GAA Story

Lead on my bold Tipperary,
May your courage never weary,
And I sing of Boherlahan's fame galore.
Yes, Boherlahan's famed fifteen
The bravest ever seen
And to morrow will be champions for once more.

Chorus:

Cheer boys, cheer, for those young heroes,
Victories smile on every side,
There has never been a foe
These brave men couldn't overthrow,
So now they are Tipperary's pride and joy.

And Toomevara of great fame,
Yes, they bore a glorious name,
For they never met their match upon the field.
But in Thurles famed old town
With its field of famed renown,
It was there you forced these gallant men to yield.

Chorus:

Before you Limerick's fame went down
In Dungarvan of renown,
And their heroes you left feeling very sore.
And on the same old field,
County Cork's team had to yield,
To the champion team of Munster for once more.

Chorus:

In Athlone by Shannon's side,
You have beaten Galway's pride,
A team ye thought of might and strength and power.
But you played so fast and quick
That the pace they could not stick,
And all had left the field in half an hour.

Chorus:

Then the Leinster champions came,
To uphold their glorious name,
'Twas the boys of famed Kilkenny took your hand.
But the power with which you play,
Brought you victory on that day,
And now you are the champions of the land.

Chorus:

And to help you with the game
Up from Moneygall they came,
With Borris and Moycarkey ever true.
And from Thurles famed old town,
With its Gaels of great renown,
Came the men who wore the famous colours blue

Chorus:

And those colours famed of old,
 Tubberdora's blue and gold,
Are the jerseys that are proudly worn by you,
And those colours day by day
Come victorious through the fray,
With your lovely little caps of violet blue.

Chorus:

155

Tipperary Over All 1917

By William F. Quillinan, Bonerea,Cappawhite.
Received from Liam Ó Donnchú, Ballymoreen, Littleton.

Once more the battle's fought and won—once more Tipperary's men
Have vanquished all opponents and are victors once again.
Come every Gael from hill and dale and hearken to my call,
And let ten thousand voices shout,'Tipp'rary Over All'.

Oh! Boherlahan, you're the pride and joy of ev'ry Gael.
Your fame today has gone beyond the shores of Innisfail.
And far across the ocean's deep, Tipp'rary's sons will call
For lusty cheers for you, who've placed 'Tipp'rary Over All'.

On January the twenty-first, the famous match was played.
The wished for day had come at last, although 'twas long delayed.
Kilkenny's men lined out to win and thought not of downfall
Till Boherlahan proved they meant, 'Tipp'rary Over All'.

Oh! When that thrilling game began, excitement did run high.
And thousands watched the leather as it soared into the sky.
And when o'er Kilkenny's crossbar, brave Leahy drove the ball,
Three thousand lusty voices cheered, 'Tipp'rary Over All'.

Sure eight long years have passed since last our county was supreme,
But, thanks to Boherlahan now, we've got the champion team.
With a pick from Thurles, Borris, Jockey and Moneygall,
Kilkenny's flag was lowered and 'Tipp'rary Over All'.

Then here's to Boherlahan and long may they reign supreme.
Both Limerick and Cork went down before that brave fifteen.
May fortune and success be theirs—ill luck them ne'er befall,
But long their slogan cry be, 'Tipp'rary Over All'.

All-Ireland 1916 senior hurling final at Croke Park.

All Ireland Football Final 1918

By T.J.Keating, Ballinasloe, Co. Galway.
Received from Liam Ó Donnchú, Ballymoreen, Littleton.

Brother Gaels of Tipperary hear the call to battle sound,
Tro' the valleys, o'er the mountains, filling all the land around;
Gallant Gaels from Suir to Shannon , hands and hearts must now unite—
Forward, forward Tipperary! Gird your armour for the fight.

You have conquered Cork and Kerry, Waterford and proud Mayo,
Now the sons of famous Wexford you are out to overthrow;
'Tis a task for men of daring—they are doughty foes to face—
But you're sons of Tipperary—of a daring dashing race.

Ah! 'Tis long ago Tipperary—nearly twenty summers now,
Since the gallant Clonmel Shamrocks won renown for Knocknagow.
Oh, God bless them! —aye, God rest some too—for sake of them will you
Dash onward, Tipperary, and prove yourselves as true?

Arravale and Bohercrowe have writ in lustrous lines of gold   **
The name of Tipperary in the Gaelic days of old.
Now your native county calls for true men once again,
Oh, does she call in vain to you, brave, brave Tipp'rary men.

Cast aside all jealousies; fling feuds and favour to the wind:
Choose fifteen, the bravest men, Tipp'rary now can find;
Hearts that beat for motherland, oh, come they far and near,
Muster gallant hearts like these, Tipperary need not fear.

Hear you not the exiles' voices calling far across the foam?
Hark: that thund'rous appeal to you from anxious hearts at home!
Can you now resist their pleading? Is your fiery spirit dead?
Is magnificent Tipp'rary's grand old bygone fled?

On to battle Tipperary! flashing, crashing, dashing on,
Sweeping like the swollen torrents down the slopes of Slievenamon.
On for honour, on for glory, on for home and kith and kin,
On for gallant Tipperary—and God strengthen you to win!

Played at Croke Park on February 16th 1919. Wexford (Blues and Whites) 0-5,
Tipperary (Fethard) 0-4) This was Wexford's fourth title in a row.

Tipperary—Arthur Carroll, Jim McNamara, Ned O. Shea, (capt) Jerry Shelley, Willie
Ryan, Ned Egan, Tommy Powell, Tom Quinlan, Jim Ryan, Tommy Ryan, Bill Grant,
Jack Skinner, Dick Heffernan, Gus McCarthy, John O'Shea. Subs. Ned Duhy,
Mick.Hogan, Pat Butler, Martin Shanahan, Gus Dwyer and Bob Redmond.

**Bohercrowe, Arravale Rovers and Clonmel Shamrocks had represented Tipperary
and had won three All Ireland Football championships in 1889, 1895 and 1900.

Clare v Tipperary

Anon

To Garryowen of Treaty Stone one day in hot July,
Came Clare and Tipperary teams, their hurling skills to try
Now Amby Power leads on his men, 'mid crowds of lookers on,
To meet those daring Galtee boys, as strong as Slievenamon

The ball's thrown in, Power and his men; their hurley sticks now swing.
Those heroes mean to fight this day and trophies homeward bring.
The battle rages fast and fierce, they fly like birds on wing,
I'd rather captain either team, than reign as England's king.

Tipperary boys by Meagher led like a tempest onward tear:
'Keep on the ball, drive men and all out through the goal of Clare'
But Power replies, fire in his eyes, 'dash on my men dash on'
The anxious eyes of Munster men are gazing proudly on.

Tull Considine, long life be thine, I never doubted you:
Ev'n though your stick is broke in bits, the ball is flying through.
Now 'neath the Tipp crossbar 'tis shot, wild cheers, Hurrah, Hurroo
Only one minute now remains Tipp you must die or do.

Then Pat O'Brien strikes out the ball, 'tis caught at centre-field
ByTommy Ryan from Silvermines, a boy that ash can wield.
Up to the gap of Clare it flies, 'Quick, Quick;' too late Mc Caw—'
The ball flies in a goal for Tipp, the match ends in a draw.

Tipperary v Limerick 1922

By Tim Crowe, Dundrum-An Irish champion athlete
Air: Kelly the boy from Killane
Chorus after each verse

On the first of July nineteen twenty-three
In the sportsfield of famed Thurles town
Thousands did throng to witness a game
Twixt those two teams of hurling renown.

Chorus:
Then hurrah for the boys in the blue and the gold
Give a cheer from your hearts for such men
And a cheer for the side from the famed Shannon side
Whom, we thought the championship would win.

'Twas a grand sight to see those two teams take the field
As thousands did cheer from all o'er.
As the men they lined up, they looked in the pink
And a smile for each other they bore.

Now each man takes his place and the ball is thrown in
And a great dash for honours is made.
The great Limerick boys rushed all over the place
But Tipperary were not to be dismayed.

From goal post to goal post the ball travelled fast
While Limerick they dashed through in style.
Tipperary defended and challenged like men
But Garryowen sure were there all the while.

At half-time Limerick were four points ahead
And victory was shining in its face.
While thousands around gently breathed a prayer
That Tipperary would still hold its place.

When play was resumed the Tipps set to work
And quickly they netted the ball.
Limerick attacked but all was in vain
For Tipperary was like a stone wall.

The game being fast, excitement ran high
And Tipperary like reindeers they flew.
While the crash of the ash and the swift hurlers dash
Brought many a wild 'hurroo'.

A seventy was taken by young Donnelly
He sent the ball soaring o'er the bar.
The white flag went up amidst thunderous cheers
For the scoring was standing now at par.

Now for the honours was everyman's cry,
And the play was ten minutes to go;
The Limerick boys got playing in splendid style
But Tipperary never yielded to the foe.

The boys from the city were again pressing hard
And like lightning they rushed with the ball.
The gay Tipps were never ever seen to flinch
But defended like heroes one and all.

Now all of you who saw and who witnessed this game
Will praise every man on each team
Tipperary and Limerick remember the name
And long life to the true-hearted Gael.

The 1922 Munster Final was played at Thurles on the 1st July 1923.

'The Munster final between Tipperary and Limerick at Thurles was a game of thrills.
The hurling was exceptionally good. An unusually fast pace was set from the throw-in
and ruled right to the end. In the end a draw was a fair result, each team scoring
2-2. The replay was at Limerick and carried with it a set of medals presented by the
Directors of the Irish Independent but it failed to provide the feast of hurling
anticipated. Tipperary won by 4-2 to 1-4.

Tipperary went on to defeat Galway by 3-2 to 1-3 in the All Ireland semi-final at Ballybrit racecourse and after looking clear winners in the decider against Kilkenny they were stunned by a late rally which produced two goals in as many minutes. Final score: Kilkenny 4-2, Tipperary 2-6. *(Munster G.A.A. Story)* Tipperary's centre-field, John Cleary, was so disappointed that he dumped his hurley and boots into the Liffey as he walked to the train at Heuston Station.

Tipperary—John Leahy (capt), J. O Meara, A.O'Donnell, J.Power, P.Power, P.Browne, J.Cleary, M.Kennedy, S.Hackett, J.Darcy, T.Dwane, W.Dwane, J.J.Hayes, J.Fitzpatrick, P.Spillane.

All Ireland Final 1925

By Francis Phillips, Cashel
Received from Liam Ó Donnchú, Ballymoreen, Littleton.

The Gaels in fiercest clash they met
Last Sunday in September,
Croke Park the spot 'tis you may bet,
And others will remember.
'All Ireland cry' it filled the air
The final stroke and smasher,
Tipperary men were everywhere,
 Likewise the Galway Rasher.

Now twenty thousand throttles roared
And hands and hats were 'waven'
As still from Jones' Road they poured
Like ships into a haven.
They surged and crushed to see the sight
'Tis Gaeldom gives the greeting,
'All-Ireland Final' is the fight,
See Tipps and Galway meeting.

O thunderlike the roar I hear
The ash is sourly clinching.
'Up Tipp!' they yell in Galway's ear
But Galway she's not flinching.
'The West's Awake' pulse through their blood
Like fire runs through a prairie
The Connaught boys they bravely stood
To conquer bold Tipperary.

Up, Up, nigh in the clouds and down
The ball is sent like lightning,
Camáns they shine like heather brown
Around the goal are tightening.
One desperate rush for Galway's win

Faint echo in Dunleary,
While victory shrieks 'mid battle's din,
Magnificent Tipperary.

And far and near the news will go
How Galway took her beating.
For Tubberadora blood you know
Those Claddagh boys were meeting.
But Gaels are Gaels where're they meet
Our hearts are light and airy,
'All-Ireland Final' at our feet
And the victory's for Tipperary.

Played at Croke Park on the 6th Sept 1925. Tipperary 5-6, Galway, 1-5.

Tipperary—Johnny Leahy (capt), A.O'Donnell (goal), M. Mockler, M.D'Arcy, J.J.Hayes, M.Kennedy, S. Hackett, J.Power, P.Leahy, P.Cahill, T.Duffy, J.D'Arcy, W.Ryan, P.Power, P.O'Dwyer. Subs: W.Quinn, S.Kenny, J. and P. Kennedy.

All-Ireland Final 1925

By T.J.Keating, Brookhill, Fethard.
Received from Liam Ó Donnchú, Littleton.
Air: Clare's Dragoons
Chorus after each verse.

Oh listen to that deaf'ning cheer
That fills the air afar and near,
'Tis vict'ry's slogan ringing clear
For grand Tipperary's hurling men.
O'er Ireland's best they hold the sway,
For Connacht's beaten in the fray
No hosts on earth could safely stay
Tipp'rary's fearless hurling men.

Chorus:

Give three loud cheers my countrymen,
For gallant Tipperary now,
Whose sons have honoured once again
The name and fame of Knocknagow.

On famed Croke Park's historic field
Where stalwarts struggled, fought and reeled,
The Galway hosts were forced to yield
Before Tipp'rary's hurling men.
What power could say the onward dash
Of men who swept like lightning flash
Like torrent down a mountain crash?
Tipp'rary's gallant hurling men.

From silv'ry Suir to Shannon's shore,
From Slievenamon to Galteemore,
The praise is chanted o'er and o'er
Of Tipperary's hurling men.
The news is swept across the sea

To fill the exile's heart with glee
And make him long again to be
With Tipperary's hurling men.

Around the fireside's cheery blaze,
When work is o'er you'll hear them praise
The Darcys, Leahys, Powers and Hayes—
Tipperary's matchless hurling men.
O'Donnell, Duffy, Cahill, Ryan,
Are names Tipp'rary's hearts enshrine,
For fearlessly they toed the line
With Tipperary's hurling men.

Of Kennedy's deeds you'll hear them tell,
Before whom many a fortress fell,
Of Hackett too, who fought full well
With Tipperary's hurling men.
They'll sing of Dwyer's and Kenny's fame
And talk with pride of Mockler's name
The heroes of a thrilling game
With Tipperary's hurling men.

God bless these men of fighting mould,
Who donned the famous blue and gold,
And fought like heroes did of old—
Tipp'rary's champion hurling men.
And Ireland's cause is ever sure
When she has some as brave and pure
As these from Shannon's shore to Suir,
Tipp'rary's fearless hurling men.

Played at Croke Park on the 6th Sept 1925. Tipperary 5-6, Galway, 1-5.

166

Welcome to Tipperary Hurlers 1926

By Francis Phillips, Cashel
Received from Liam Ó Donnchú, Ballymoreen, Littleton.

Hurrah! They're landed back again
The pride and pick of hurling men
A shout we hear now up the glen
Like thunder far 'tis rolling,
Or Yankee cheers that Sunday when
In Polo Park—the goaling.

We missed you since the month of May,
Yet watched your courses as day by day
New victories won, you cleared the way
From Cork to Colorado.
Some said, 'twas Kelly, Burke and Shea,
Who wrecked the Procadaro.

Our kith and kin from shore to shore
Showered honours never known before;
They felt like 'Paddies' ever more
As sung in song and story.
With banners gay from roof to floor,
Tri-colour and 'old glory'.

And sure Columba's noble hand
Held out her feeling, friendly hand
To Erin's Gaelic hurling band
She knows their brawn and muscle,
That gripped her starry banner grand
In days of blood and tussle.

And noticed they among the crowd
Some veteran hearts who cheered them loud
And felt that Ireland could be proud
Of men so light and airy.

'Tis Knocknagow they all avowed
They're sons of Tipperary.

Hurrah! My bold unconquered men
No praise too great with voice or pen
You vanquished all and will again
Be victors in the battle;
And laurels now will crown you then,
While ashen sticks they'll rattle.

'Whereas hurling was only one of the many sports to feature in the Tailteann games it was to hold centre stage in the 1926 visit by Tipperary to the U.S...A party of twenty players and three officials made the trip. Also included was the trainer Tim Crowe, a legendary figure from Dundrum, Co. Tipperary...The first match was before thirty thousand spectators at the Polo Grounds. The next stop was San Francisco. The tour was a splendid success. All seven games had been won. The crowds were large and enthusiastic and the total number that witnessed the games was about one hundred thousand.' *(The Clash of the Ash in Foreign Fields* by Seamus J. King) See also *God Speed You O'er The Ocean.*

Welcome to Tipperary

By T.D. Shanahan, Limerick and U.S.A.
Source: Gaelic Days (Illustrated Handbook) published by Gaelic Athletic
Publications, San Mairéad, Ballinacurra, Limerick.

You're welcome Tipperary,
To California's shore!
We hail you and acclaim you,
And welcome you once more.
For you the drums are beating,
Your Celtic hearts are true
To dauntless Kickham's teachings,
And Erin's pastimes, too.

You're welcome sweet Tipperary,
Thou peerless paragon!
You hurlers from Moycarkey,
And hearts from Slievenamon.
True sons of Toomevara,
Aye, victors in the fray,
And matchless Boherlahan,
You're welcome here today.

I greet you famed Tipperary,
Long may your records grow!
Grangemockler, Youghalarra
And gallant Bohercrowe.
Blest Croke—your spirit's with us,
My heart with rapture rings,
Recalling Erin's glories
And Cashel of the kings.

Success to you—Tipperary,
The glory of our land.
We hail you as the champions
Of camán -wielders grand.

The game that kings and chieftains
Of Erin used to play,
Then here's to you, Tipperary,
You're welcome here today.

God speed you o'er the ocean

By Egan Clancy
Source: The Tubberadora—Boherlahan Hurling Story
By Philip F. Ryan.

God speed you o'er the ocean, to that old home once again,
To Munster hills, its rippling rills, fair land of golden grain.
Where a fáilte breá awaits ye, and blessings too galore,
While bonfires bright will light on Slievenamon and Galteemore.

At the Boherlahan cross- roads, where the hurlers congregate,
When the practise match is over, to discuss the news of late.
They hear of the victories, of their sturdy brother Gaels
And they plan a big reception; your homecoming now entails.

The merits of O'Donnell, the Leahy brothers, Hayes—
Are compared with star opponents, of the games of other days.
Well may they say for cunning play, unerring aim and dash,
An equal for young Kennedy, never swung the crooked ash.

The science of Phil Cahill, the speed of Paddy Dwyer,
The great defence of Hackett, Duffy's tactics sure inspire.
The Powers, Martin Mockler, Steve Kenny, Willie Ryan,
Can tackle, pass and double, that's where those gossoons shine.

There's joy in Toomevara; Frank McGrath just paid a call,
To the home of Wedger Meagher, once the greatest of them all.
For the honour of the village, they have parted well, I vow
Like the days of Matt the Thresher, in the grand old Knocknagow.

Take this message to the homeland of your exile brothers here:
You thrilled us with your glorious play, fond memories to hold dear.
Yours the fame to play the game, like real men staunch and true,
God speed you o'er the ocean, Tipperary Gaels adieu.

171

Tiobrad Árann Abú

By Tom Keating, Fethard
The Treble Crown printed by The Tipperary Star,Thurles.
Air: Kelly of Kilann or Billy Byrne of Ballymanus.
Chorus after each verse.

Tiobrad Árann Abú! Tiobrad Árann Abú!
That's our watchword and war cry foraye;
For Tipp'rary's brave men from the hill and the glen
Are the champions of Ireland today.
Fling the new on the breeze; let it ring o'er the seas,
On the moorland and wild mountain blue.
How the boys on the field forced all rivals to yield
With the cry Tiobrad Árann Abú!

Chorus:

Then hurrah boys hurrah, 'tis our glory today,
How the seniors and brave minors too,
Showed the juniors the way to win fame in the fray,
With the cry, Tiobrad Árann Abú!

In the land of our birth—purest gem of the earth—
Writ in bright flashing gold of the dawn
Is Tipp'rary's fair name and her far flowing fame
In the swing of the Irish camán.
Let the bright blue and gold of our banner unfold
And we'll swear to be loyal and true
To the men of renown who won victory's crown,
With the cry Tiobrad Árann Abú!

'Tiobrad Árann Abú!' Let it ring loud and true
'Till it shakes heather crown'd Sliabh na mBan;
For no power could e'er smash Tipperary's swift dash
With the clash of the ash sweeping on.
While of vict'ry we boast, let each now drink a toast
To the brave men, the tried and the true.

172

Who so oft in the past nailed our flag to the mast
With the cry, Tiobrad Árann Abú!

In the games of the Gael, may our men never fail
To be loyal to Éire's fair name;
May they ever march on like the men who are gone,
True to gallant Tipp'rary's great fame.
Yes, with Ireland's camán and the speed of the fawn,
And the blood of the Gael thro' and thro'
Feeling proud of the past they will fight to the last,
With the cry, Tiobrad Árann Abú!.

In 1930. Tipperary achieved the rare feat of annexing All-Ireland hurling titles in senior, junior and minor grades. To commemorate this event, Very Rev. John Meagher, P.P., chairman of the Tipperary County Board offered a prize of £5 for the best poem to mark the achievement. This was the winning effort. The adjudicators were Very Rev. W. Fitzgerald, Adm. Thurles: Rev. J. M. Hayes C.C. Castleiney and Rev. N. Kevin MA St. Patrick's College, Thurles.

Senior Team—J.J. Callanan (Capt), J. O'Loughlin, J. Maher, M. Ryan, J. Harney, J. Lanigan, T. O'Meara (goal), M. Kennedy, P. Mc Kenna, P. Purcell, P. Cahill, M. F. Cronin, T. Butler, T. Leahy, T. Treacy. Sub. J. Heeney.
Played at Croke Park on Sept. 7, 1930 . Final Score: Tipperary, 2-7, Dublin 1-3

Minor Team—M. Maher, J. Russell, M. Coffey, W. O'Neill, L. Burke, G. Heavey,, J. Lanigan, T. Coffey, J. Dunne, J. Semple, E. Wade, P. Ryan, J. Close, T. Harney, J. Quinlan. (Tipperary 4-1, Kilkenny 2-1)

Junior Team: Pat Harty (capt), Tom Harty, Willie Ryan, Tim Connolly, Mick Mc Gann, Martin Browne, Ned Wade, Tom Rainey, Jack Dwyer, Mick Ryan, Dan Looby, Pat Furlong, Wm.Gorman, Joe Fletcher, Sean Harrington. Subs: Joe Maher, Tom Hayes, Tom Power, John Connolly, Mick Kennedy, Mick Ryan. (Tipperary, 6-8, Kilkenny 3-2)

173

Tipperary 1930

By Miss Brigid Hayes, Camas Park, Cashel
Source: The Treble Crown:
Printed by The Tipperary Star, Thurles.

It's not a crown of diamonds
Nor yet a crown of gold,
But a Treble Crown of laurels
That speaks of fame untold.

The Triple Crown

By Jack Hughes, Reiska
Source: Received from Liam Ó Donnchú, Ballymorreen, Littleton, Thurles
Air:The Bold Manchester Three

Have you seen Tipperary's champions, hurling Clare in Cork's own town,
When they won the Munster final, the first step to the Triple Crown.
I have seen some Munster finals but none with can compare
As that match in Cork's Athletic Grounds, between the champions, Tipp and Clare.
At half time we were leading with just one point to spare
With the wind and sun against us, sure it looked a win for Clare.
But our own experienced trainer, Tom Semple is his name,
He gave our boys a lecture as to how they'd play the game.

The match again re-started and we could plainly see
That Tipp would be the champions that day beside the Lee.
They drove men and ball before them with their old Tipperary dash—
Tommy Daly in the goalposts, sure he saw their coming rush.
He set himself to save his net, but it was all in vain:
They made railroads through the backlines, the green flag went up again.

Chorus

Here's a health to our great champions and to brave Tom Semple too,
Who trained them to perfection, in their colours gold and blue.
With Father Maher in the lead, our flag we have unfurled,
The Triple Crown of high renown will broadcast o'er the world.
And Tipperary sons so far away in many a foreign shore,
Will hear with joy and shout a Hip, Tipperary ever more.

Our next encounter was at Birr for the semi-final test,
Where we beat the pick of Galway, they're the champions of the
West.
They're a sturdy combination, each man being tried and true
But they failed to hold our champions in their colours gold and blue.
They set a pace to hurling, I'll ne'er forget once more,
And they won the semi-final with an overwhelming score.

The great all-Ireland final, it was a gruelling hour,
'Twas broadcast on the wireless, O'Loughlin holds up Power.
He's that great all Ireland forward, but he had to stand at bay,
While Loughlin cleared to Cahill, who sent it down the way,
Unto the centre forward, who let with it on the ground,
'Twas pounced on by Murt Kennedy and soon the net was found.
When Treacy, he got wounded, our spirits, they were low
But when he did resume again, he set our hearts aglow.
He sent the leather soaring and as it did come down,
'Twas banged between the goalposts for to win the Triple Crown.

Our minors and our juniors, Kilkenny's pride brought down,
When they won their two All Irelands and their title to the crown.
In Croke Park, our minors battled, 'twas on football final day,
Against Kilkenny's trained fifteen, who thought they'd take the
sway.
But when the match was over and the final whistle blew,
Our minors were the champions, they'd won All-Ireland number
two.

Our juniors, they were confident, their county's honour to uphold,
When they lined out in Waterford, in their colours blue and gold.
Kilkenny, they were hopeful, they'd take victory to the Nore,
But soon their hopes were shattered, by Tipperary's awful score.
We rallied round them cheering, their flag for to unfold
And through Waterford's proud thoroughfare, we paraded up and
down
We had won the three All Irelands and that glorious Triple Crown.

Father Dollards tribute: 'Surely the homes of Tipperary will be happy this Christmas, having the hay saved, Cork and Clare 'bet', Galway and Dublin in the shade, and dear old Slievenamon proudly gazing on prostrate Kilkenny. I always thought that the old mountain rejoices when Tipperary hurlers are triumphant and weeps when they are defeated—and why shouldn't it? Hurling and Slievenamon are the two most ancient survivals in Tipperary; they have been friends for thousands of years'. (*Tipperary's G.A.A. Story, p295*)

Tipperary's Road to the Triple Crown 1930

Senior

13 July	Dungarvan	Tipperary 2-5, Waterford, 0-1
27 July	Cork A.G.	Tipperary 6-4, Clare 2-8
17 August	Birr	Tipperary 6-8, Galway 2-4
7 Sept.	Croke Park	Tipperary 2-7, Dublin 1-3

Junior

27 April	Tralee	Tipperary 5-5, Kerry 0-5
14 Sept.	Clonmel	Tipperary 4-7, Limerick 4-7
24 August	Limerick	Tipperary 5-4, Limerick 2-5
1 June	Thurles	Tipperary 7-4, Clare 1-2
	Dublin	Tipperary 11-5, London 1-0
	Waterford	Tipperary 6-8, Kilkenny 3-2

Minor

3 August	Mallow	Tipperary 7-1, Kerry 4-2,
14 Sept.	Thurles	Tipperary 4-0, Waterford 2-1
24 Sept.	Mardyke, Cork	Tipperary 4-3, Cork 3-0
28 Sept.	Croke Park	Tipperary 4-1, Kilkenny 2-1

The Triple Crown

By P. Bowe, Longfordpass
Printed by the Tipperary Star.
Air: The Risin'of the Moon.: Chorus after each verse.

In Ireland's hurling history
Tipperary holds first place,
For many a glorious victory,
Has been won by Kickham's race.
And whilst we give due credit
To the man of old renown
We'll sing you of the boys today,
Who won the Triple Crown

Chorus:

Yes, we've won the Triple Crown
When they thought Tipperary down,
We've speed and dash; we've got the ash
To win the Triple Crown.

We're proud of Kickham's county,
Her hurlers brave of yore,
Who brought her fame and honoured name
From Suir to Shannon shore.
We think of all who held the ash
When tyrants tried to drown,
The noble pride of those who tried
To win the Triple Crown.

We'll mention Tubberadora
With the heroes of the past:
Moycarkey's name, Boherlahan's fame
With Ireland's game will last.
We pride in Two-Mile Borris
And the Blues of Thurles town

Who fed with fire our heart's desire
To win the Triple Crown.

Then here's to Tipperary
To her hurlers bold and brave,
To her homesteads bright and cheery
Where they never reared a slave.
And though Ireland seemed against us
When we held the ashen brown
They're glad to say 'Tipperary's Way'
Has won the Triple Crown.

Another entry to commemorate the feat of annexing All-Ireland hurling titles in
senior, junior and minor grades.

Tipperary wears the Treble Crown

By Frank McGrath, Nenagh
Source: The Treble Crown
Printed by the Tipperary Star
Air: Clare's Dragoons

From Slievenamon to Shannon's wave
Tipp'rary's athletes swift and brave,
In far off days her flag upheld
No tyrant's threat e'er made them yield.
Adown the years that spirit went
That titled her mag-ni-fi-cent.
Today as then that headlong dash
Still sweeps the field where hurleys clash.

Chorus:

Tipp'rary's year! Clear comes that call,
On, on, her stalwarts sweep the ball,
Through serried ranks they smash their way
Brave Kickham's spirit's here today.
The nation's game, her honour, pride,
Tipp'rary clasps them to her side
With Ireland's greatest teams gone down
Tipp'rary wears the Triple Crown.

Dungarvan's hosting saw the day
Her seniors onward fight their way
To Cork where Clare's proud spirit dies
Tipp'rary takes old Munster's prize.
Then steadily as Cashel's Rock
At Birr they stand the West'rn shock
And scoring true they qualify
'Gainst Leinster's best, their chance to try.

At Croke Park where Mick Hogan bled
And joined the roll of martyred dead,
Like greyhounds speeding from the leash
Through Dublin lines the Tipp. men crash.
Tipp'rary's flag is hoisted high
That cheer goes echoing to the sky
And distant exiles weep for joy
Tipp'rary's spirit ne'er shall die.

The minors harking to the call
Like Fionn and Oisín drive the ball,
Her juniors bending to the work
Unconquered too they make their mark.
In future years at each fireside,
Tipp'rary's deeds are told with pride,
Her children list with hearts aflame
All burning to uphold the name.

Frank McGrath , (1885-1965) the author, was a Youghalarra, Toomevara and
Tipperary senior hurler. He was Tipperary's representative on the Central Council for
eight years up to 1928 and manager of the Tipperary team that toured the States in
1926. He was also responsible for the admission of Britain as the fifth Province in
1928. The McGrath Cup, North Tipperary's senior hurling trophy is named in his
honour. He was chairman of the Munster council in 1937. (See p.439 *Munster GAA
Story*). This was another entry for the competition in 1930. The adjudicators were

Very Rev. W. Fitzgerald, Adm. Thurles: Rev. J. M. Hayes C.C. Castleiney and Rev.
N. Kevin MA St. Patrick's College, Thurles.

Triumphant Tipperary

By Tom Keating, Fethard
Source: The Treble Crown
Printed by the Tipperary Star
Air: Eoghain Chóir—the Men of the West.

Here's a song of triumphant Tipp'rary—
Oh, sing it in village and town,
On the moorland, the hill, and the prairie,
For it tells of great deeds of renown.
'Tis a tale that will yet live in story,
Of might, and of muscle, and brawn;
How her hurlers won honour and glory,
In wielding the Irish camán.

Chorus:

Chorus: Then here's to immortal Tipp'rary,
And her hurlers as fleet as the fawn,
Who are famed for their dash and their daring
In wielding the Irish camán.

Nineteen hundred and thirty's the year boys—
'Tis a tale fit to tell o'er and o'er—
When Tipp'rary accomplished a feat boys,
That ne'er was recorded before;
For her minors, her juniors, her seniors,
Are champions as fleet as the fawn—
In the harvest of hurling the gleaners,
In wielding the Irish camán.

As the torrent that sweeps down the valley,
Tipp'rary rushed onward until
Rousing cheers of sweet victory's rally
Re-echoed o'er hamlet and hill.
Oh, no power could withstand such a test boys—
The finest e'er seen on a bán—

182

And they crown'ed old Tipp'rary the best boys,
For wielding the Irish camán.

And while grand old Tipperary rejoices,
From Shannon to sweet Sliabh na mBan,
Let us raise up our hearts and our voices,
To honour the men who are gone:
For undaunted they played Eire's game, boys,
With a dash like the flash of the dawn,
And made famous Tipp'rary's fair name, boys,
For wielding the Irish camán.

Let our banner float high o'er the mireland,
O'er valley, and village, and town,
And we'll vow to be true to old Ireland,
And Tipp's gallant Gaels of renown.
Yes, the men of the past will inspire us
To hope for to-morrow's bright dawn,
And their hist'ry with courage will fire us,
In wielding the Irish camán

This was a second effort by Tom Keating to commemorate the three hurling All-Ireland wins in 1930.

Tipperary's Triple Crown Win 1930

By Michael Bourke, Main St. Newport.
Source: The Treble Crown(An entry in the competition to comemorate the event)
Printed by Tipperary Star, Thurles.
Air: The Wearin' of the Green.Chorus after each verse.

O, Paddy dear and did you hear them speak of gallant Tipp?
They say they're now the holders of the world championship.
They conquered all from Derry's wall right down to Wexford town
And now they are the winners of the famous Triple Crown.

Chorus:

Then hurrah for bold Tipperary you're the boys know what to do:
There's not a team in this wide world can play the game like you.
You beat them all both great and small from Cork to Donegal,
Then God bless you bold Tipperary, senior, junior, minors , all.

Moycarkey, Thurles, Boherlahan, Templemore and Moneygall,
Lorrha, Toom and Holycross; you're the boys can play the ball.
God bless those dashing hurlers be the prayer on every lip,
Now where's the team that can compare with the peerless Gaels of
Tipp.

Success to those brave heroes, may their courage never fail
In many hard-fought contest they were never found to quail.
I'll sing their praise in stirring lays till the great God on me calls,
Then a cheer for bold Tipperary, Tipperary over all.

I must now conclude this little verse—my feelings, they are high.
May the dashing peerless hurlers of Tipperary never die.
They have conquered Ireland's bravest, best, which crowned them
with renown,
Then God bless the boys of gallant Tipp, that won the Triple Crown.

The Treble Crown 1930

Anon:
Received from Liam Ó Donnchú, Ballymoreen, Littleton.
Chorus after each verse.

Ye Gaels, Ye Tippmen far and near,
In one loud chorus, one loud cheer,
Proclaim the glory of the year
And gallant Tipp's renown.
Our seniors bravely led the van.
Our juniors fought as Tippmen can,
Each minor proved himself a man,
In bringing home the crown.

Chorus:

We hail the men whose grit and dash
And skill to wield the seasoned ash.
Made Tipp. this year of fair renown,
Proud holders of the Treble Crown.

In famed Croke Park was seen the clash
When thirty stalwarts crossed the ash—
'Twas there they proved again their dash
The men in blue and gold.
In Waterford was also seen
Another competent fifteen,
Whose hurling was as swift and keen
As ne'er was seen of old.

With men like these in Innisfail,
The grand tradition of the Gael,
Will stand in spite of wind and hail—
Its splendour will not vary.
Our nation's spirit will not die,
But foreign influence defy.
Then here's once more our slogan cry,
'Tis gallant Tipperary.

All-Ireland Victory 1930

By Francis Phillips, Cashel: Source: The Treble Crown
Printed by the *Tipperary Star.*
Also Cashel and Rosgreen GAA History 1985
(Séamus J. King)

In hurling days round Tara's Hall
'Twas Brian Boru first struck the ball
And sent it whirling 'mongst them all,
'Till stopped by wan O'Cleary,
A Prince who came to win or fall,
And take it to Tipperary.

He said that Meath, tho' Royal your name
To Premiership you have no claim,
Let Ireland, too, dispute the same,
And then we're not contrarie,
For Championship in hurling game,
Belongs to Tipperary.

And strange as centuries rolled away,
In truth his words are proved today,
From Tubberadora to Lough Neagh,
Our victories never vary,
But brighter shines when all decay,
The fame of Tipperary.

On well-fought fields we showed our might
A million hearts cheered with delight,
While eager eyes peered through the flight,
Aye! Watch the ball so airy,
And thunder cheers in fury's fight,
'Magnificent Tipperary'.

Undaunted yet by boast or power,
All Ireland men stand to this hour
Upon the spot where first they flower,

186

Foretold by Prince O'Cleary,
The home where Gaelic praises shower
And bloom in Tipperary.

'Tis known beyond the ocean's roar
The shock that shook Dungarvan's shore,
When Cork went down as ne'er before
To rise if only dare he.
Our Boys have yet the same in store—
Who'll match against Tipperary?

Come nerve we now—our venom pour
Brave hearts beat fast while thousands roar
The 'Munster Brogue' is here galore
There's Ned and Mick and Mary.
The victory's ours—All-Ireland o'er,
'Tis heard in Tipperary.

Who thought that Knocknagow was gone,
And ashen sticks both stout and strong,
And brain and bone lived but in song
Like tales of ghost and fairy.
'Me sowl' we're there like Slieve-Na-Mon
Magnificent Tipperary.

The following extra verse is to be found in the *Cashel and Rosgreen GAA History*
1985 (Séamus J. King)

But fame well won is never vain,
We're hearts and hands in Ireland's game,
And brain and bone to smash the chain
That binds us yet in slav'ry.
Could right but rule, where might doth reign
Then freedom in Tipperary.

Another entry to commemorate the 1930 achievement.

Hurling Triple Crown 1930

By Dan English, Rossmore
The Treble Crown printed by The Tipperary Star, Thurles.
Air: Glory, Glory, to Old Ireland. Chorus after each verse.

There's a spot that's dear to mem'ry—it is linked with hurling fame,
Where Gaelic sons foregather—Tipperary is its name;
Within its storied history, fill'd with valour and renown,
We'll inscribe those names with honour that have won the Triple
Crown.

Chorus:

So we'll sing their name and their fame boys
And cherish all those that are gone.
Join hands together for old Ireland
As we go marching along.

My boyhood's early fancies form an album of the past—
And memories proud and golden cling together to the last.
Of immortal Tubberadora where the Suir flows gently down—
Gave the sons of hurling champions to win the Triple Crown.

Moycarkey filled with honour boys, the year of ninety-nine,
The Blues and Two-Mile- Borris next stepp'd into line
Toomevara and Boherlahan kept our flag from going down
And sent Kennedy, Wade and Butler to snatch the Triple Crown.

To win the Triple honours came heroes once again,
From Lorrha on the Shannon and Solohead as well,
From Cappawhite and Golden with their patterned hurleys brown,
Killenaule and Newport to win the Triple Crown.

You can grasp the hand of hurlers in the homes of Borrisoleigh,
The game has found its stalwarts in that little town Roscrea.
Clonoulty's fame we'll mingle that day 'gainst Cork's own town
When they broke the ranks of Gower Street, long before the Triple
Crown.

Holycross of ancient story with its abbeyed ruins of fame,
Can blend its olden glory with Cahill's hurling name.
With O'Meara and the Leahys and the men of Thurles town,
That marked the road to victory that won the Triple Crown.

Oh should the lure of Erin call her wandering children home,
Whom centuries of sorrow have forced across the foam.
Then with the Powers and Mahers we'd have neither sigh nor frown:
We'd entwine the harp and shamrock round another Triple Crown.

This was an entry for the 1930 competition.

189

All-Ireland Final 1930

Anon:
Source:Séamus Mac Mathúna, An Clár, Neil Fogarty, Templemore, John Murray,
Templederry, Patrick Hackett, Two-Mile Borris, Mickie Hayes, Two-Mile Borris, and
Christy Fogarty, Thurles. Air: Master McGrath.

The seventh of September was the date of the year
When Tipp'rary and Dublin once more did appear,
In the All-Ireland final at old Dublin town,
When the laurels of Dublin old Tipp. did pull down.

Just about three o'clock at the venue we found
Thirty thousand spectators had all gathered round,
When Dublin marched out for to die or to do
And the colours they wore were their famous light blue.

Next came Tipp'rary those boys of great fame,
Through the States and old Ireland they've earned their name,
Led on by their captain so fearless and bold
And arrayed in their jerseys the blue and the gold.

That day in Croke Park was a sight, it was grand,
When the two teams lined up just in rear of the band.
To march to the line like their fathers of old,
We felt proud of our county, the blue and the gold.

The teams they lined up and the backs were sent out—
The bookies were hoarse as for bets they did shout.
'Even money Tipp'rary' we soon heard them say,
The champions of Munster will carry the day.

The ball was thrown in and then started the fray
For the hurling *blue riband* in battle array.
And the old Dublin mountains re-echoed each clash
Every whizz of the ball, every whish of the ash.

A foul on the right brought Tipp'rary a free,
That ball was soon placed by the good referee.

Phil Cahill he struck it, Lord how it did soar
Sailing over the bar for Tipp'rary's first score.

Now the hurling was keen and the tackling was fast,
We had thrills there in plenty right up to the last.
One mad dash by Dublin, our backs failed to save,
'Till the gallant O'Meara made a wonderful save.

Now Dublin they pressed Tipp'rary all round
'Till a stubborn resistance they very soon found.
From McKenna and Purcell, those stars of the pack
Of Tipp'rary's fleet greyhounds, who soon drove them back.

The work done at mid-field by Treacy was grand
And the cheers for that hero that came from the stand,
Will live in our memory until we are dead
And the crimson-stained bandage he wore round his head.

Here's a health to you Kennedy, long may you reign—
You're the pride of all Ireland, the star of the game
And you Tommy Leahy, we'll never forget
When you passed bang by Campion right into the net.

Two goals, seven points and the long whistle blew
To the spot where our flag was unfurled we flew.
We surged round our heroes and bid them good cheer
To be All-Ireland champions for many a year.

Hats off to those heroes, this dashing fine pack,
Coached by Leahy and Semple, who stood at their back.
To those two past masters all honours are due,
For the victory they gained when the long whistle blew.

My tale is unfurled, the end it is near—
There is one thing for certain; there's no cause to fear,
That the hearts in our bosoms will ever grow cold
Whilst those stalwarts of ours wear the blue and the gold.

Hurrah for Gallant Tipp 1930

By Seán Ó Carra
Source: Gaelic Sportsman, Jan. 6, 1951

We hail their very name,
The fifteen whose splendid game
Has loaded Tipp. with fame
For aye

With good Tipperary ash,
And old traditional dash
Like coursers from the leash
 They bound

They played a stalwart game,
They upheld the county's name,
Broadcasting more its fame
Far and wide

My heart with joy doth bound
As I hear the cheers resound
From the blazing hills around
Galteemore.

Come boys; give one more cheer,
Which all Tippmen far and near
With voices loud and clear
Will prolong.

Without mistake or slip
It will pass from lip to lip
The 'Hurrah for gallant Tipp'
Every time'

Ham Sunday

By Robbie O'Connell
Source:Close to the Bone, LP-Side B

'Twas back in the year of nineteen-thirty-two
That the great event happened in Carrick-on-Suir
A big match was planned for the new Davin Park
And Kerry and Tipp were the teams to take part.
The news of this match it was carried all round
'Twas thought droves of people would flock to the town
And word it came down from a GAA club
There'd be thousands of people all looking for grub.

And everyone thought here's a chance to get rich
We could make a small fortune on an ould ham sandwich.
We could charge what we want and it wouldn't be hard
There'd be so many here they're all bound to be starved.
So the butchers and bakers got busy straight off
To make sure everyone would have more than enough
And the valley was full not of reels or of jigs
But the smell of fresh bread and the squealin' of pigs.

And when the great day it at last came around
And an air of excitement pervaded the town.
A brass band was out and they marched through the park
Just waitin' for someone the signal the start.
There were lookouts and runners and great agitation
To warn when the first train pulled into the station
There were signs up all over proclaimin' quite clear
'The best ham sandwiches are on sale here'

Oh the streets were all full as the tension it rose
And the men were all out in their best Sunday clothes
With the children all waitin' this great sight to see
While the women stayed home boilin' kettles for tea.
There was one poor man full of such anticipation

When he heard what he thought were the sounds of invasion
That he stumbled and fell down the stairs in a fright
But 'twas only some farmer in parkin' his bike.

Oh, 'they're comin. they're comin.' some one cried 'they're here'
And the people got ready to raise a loud cheer
But no one understood and no one could explain
When only two people stepped off the train.
So they waited around 'till the next train came in
And they couldn't believe it was empty again
Then the most of them left and went off to a pub
To decide about what they would do with the grub.

Well they argued all day 'till the match it was over
About what they ought to do with the left-overs
And they all were agreed 'twas a wicked disgrace
Every dog in the town had a smile on his face.
There were hams in the pantries and hams on the shelves
'Twas said that some people made pigs of themselves
There were still loads of hams when a week had gone by
But not even a dog could look one in the eye.

And now to conclude and to finish this song
For I'm sure I've already been singin' too long
Every song has a moral of that I've no doubt
This one's no exception as I'm sure you'll find out.
So remember 'Ham Sunday' it could be your salvation
Make sure you're not caught in the same situation
For it's all very well being prepared that I'll own
But you're better off cuttin' it close to the bone.

Munster senior football final played at Carrick-On-Suir on the 7 Aug. 1932. Kerry 4-
5, Tipperary 1-4.
Michael Coady, Carrick–on-Suir, gives an account of the event in 'the Nationalist' ,
Clonmel, Feb. 11, 2000.
'Robbie O'Connell, the author, is the son of the late Seán and Cáit (neé Clancy)
O'Connell. He lives in the U.S.A. and has a high profile in Irish folk song circles. His
witty ballad is on the Green Linnet Label, the 1982 album SIF 1038 entitled *Close to
the Bone*. This was Robbie O'Connell's first recording, with sidemen Tommy Keane

and Tom Phillips. The sleeve illustration by Carla Frey shows a streetscape of Carrick's West Gate and Town Clock, with, in the foreground, a pack of assorted dogs and hounds, some devouring hams and loaves, others so stuffed with food that they're helplessly belly up on the Main Street.

On the face of it that Sunday was a very big event. The new Davin Park was being officially opened, and named, of course after Maurice Davin, the renowned athlete of Deerpark and co-founder and first president of the GAA. Maurice had died in 1927. The Treacy Park housing estate, now bordering Davin Park, had not yet been built. In its place stood the ruins of Carrick Workhouse. Some of the stone from the latter was used as trunking under the terraces of the new sports ground.

For hard information I looked up my copy of Canon Fogarty's Tipperary's GAA Story.Davin Park was officially opened by W.P.Clifford, a former president of the association. Amongst the dignitaries present were the great veteran athletes Pat Davin and T.F. ('Champion') Kiely. The latter also a director, along with Jerry Shelly, Tipperary footballer and survivor of the infamous 'Bloody Sunday' game of 1921. Carrick Brass Band was there, under the direction of my grandfather, Michael Coady, who died a few months later.

Canon Fogarty's comment on the game was: 'In the final the Kerrymen let the Tipps expend themselves before the decisive offensive which was somewhat akin to a tornado, and left no shadow of doubt as to their superiority'

Fogarty's line out of the Tipp team on the day, with club affiliations was as follows: - Mick Healy, Chris Murray, Tom Cormack, Pat Arrigan (Grangemockler): Dick Power, John O'Leary, Mick Lonergan, Jack Weston (Clonmel Shamrocks): John Cummins, Martin Lonergan (Kilsheelan): Jim Noonan (Cloneen): Dick Allen (Fethard): Jack Scott (Mullinahone): Con Keane (Thurles): Mick Barry (Bansha):

There is no doubt about the fact that the massive crowds expected to swamp the town did not materialise on the day. When people travelled to matches in 1932 they did so on foot, by bicycle, or by train. Special excursion trains pulled into Carrick station on Ham Sunday. They say that the Brass Band was standing by to welcome the first train. Two people got off. Others dispute that and claim that four people arrived.

Times were very hard in the early nineteen thirties but scores of households and shops in Carrick had gone into debt and danger to buy foodstuffs and set themselves up as caterers for the day; hoping to capitalise on the famished hordes that were expected. Others set up their yards and gardens as parking places for bicycles....It looks like very few Kerrymen made the long journey or, if they did, they may have carried their own rations along with them from the Kingdom.

Anyway, we can imagine the recriminations on that Sunday night in Carrick. The whole town stuffed with unsold ham and cold meats, much of it still to be paid for. No doubt people found someone to blame; they always do in such circumstances. And no doubt the Carrick dogs did well in the succeeding week until as Robbie O'Connell's song says, they just could not take any more'.

195

Tipperary v Kilkenny 1937

By Michael Bourke, Newport.
Source: By the Mulcaire Banks—
By Michael Collins and Denis Floyd.

Tipperary men stand up again wherever you be
At home in old Ireland or over the sea.
Give three ringing cheers for those men of renown
Who conquered Kilkenny in Killarney's fair town.

What a wonderful sight when the train did slow down
To see the bold Tipps march through Killarney's fair town.
Led on by Lanigan who was never known to yield
In a short time we'd taken this grand hurling field.

At three o'clock sharp the match did begin
The teams toed the line and the ball was thrown in.
The boys from Kilkenny were active and fit
But the men from Tipperary were all steel and grit.

When Butler gave a huge drive to the ball
'Twas met by Tommy Treacy before it did fall
And the beautiful shot sent it flying towards the stand
From the hop Jimmy Coffey a nice point did land.

Then ball after ball through the posts Tipp did drive
They swarmed round Kilkenny's backs like bees round a hive.
The ashen sticks clashed and the ball soared on high
And 'twas netted once more by our own Newport boy.

The Ryans of Moycarkey were brave men and true
Cornally and Maher to mention but few.
Wall and O'Donnell have won great renown
And there was no match for Cooney from famed Carrick town.

They mustered from Nenagh, Newport and Shallee,
Roscrea, Templederry, Toome and Borrisoleigh,
In thousands they came there from Thurles and Cahir
County Roscommon, Wexford and elsewhere.

From down below Carrick, from above Templemore
From New Inn and Cashel, Clonoulty, Rossmore:
Horse and Jockey, Kilcommon and Rearcross too,
Not forgetting Birdhill, Ballina and Portroe.

And now to conclude while my feelings are high
May the Gaels of Kilkenny and Tipp. never die
I've sounded your praises as well as I could
O'er mountain and valley, through glen and wildwood.

If mistakes I have made, you'll forgive me I'm sure
For I'm not in the same class as Davis and Moore.
And the bold Tipps they gave Kilkenny the slip
And brought back the cup to the green hills of Tipp.

All Ireland Hurling Final 1937 at Killarney on 5 Sept 1937: Tipperary, 3-11, Kilkenny, 0-3. The GAA in 1937 was in the process of building the Cusack Stand but had expected to be able to stage the 1937 All Ireland Final in Croke Park. By the late summer of 1937 the greater part of the stand apart from the roof and the seating had been built. However, a strike in the building industry held up work for the best months of that year. It was found necessary to find an alternative venue. The council decided to play the match in the new Fitzgerald Stadium in Killarney.

Tipperary— T. Butler (goal), D. O'Gorman, G. Cornally, J. Lanigan (capt), J. Ryan, J. Maher,, W. Wall, J. Cooney, J. Gleeson, Jim Coffey, T. Treacy, T. Doyle, W. O'Donnell, D. Murphy, P. 'Sweeper' Ryan. Subs: D. Mackey, T. Kennedy.

Tipperary v Cork 1941

By Michael Bourke, Newport
Source: Newport in Song and Poetry
Published by the Michael Bourke Festival Committee

Tipperary men will you stand up, wherever you may be
At home in old Ireland or far o'er the sea.
Give three mighty cheers for these men of renown,
That conquered the Cork men in famed Limerick town.
Good luck to those brave boys so airy and free,
That conquered them all from the Foyle to the Lee,
No doubt the bold Cork men a great team did field,
But science, dash and pluck made those brave heroes yield.

Chorus:

They can boast of great hurlers in Galway and Clare,
Queen's County, Roscommon, Wexford and elsewhere—
Cork and Kilkenny can hurl the ball,
But the boys from Tipperary have beaten them all.

'Twas a soul stirring sight when the train did slow down,
To see our boys marching through old Limerick town—
Led on by bold Maher, who was ne'er known to yield
In a short time we have taken the grand hurling field.
At three o'clock sharp, the match did begin—
The teams toed the line and the ball was thrown in.
The Cork men were nimble, light, active and fit,
But the boys of Tipperary were all steel and grit.

Maher, then, gave a huge drive to the ball,
'Twas met by Cornally before it did fall.
A beautiful shot sent it flying towards the stand,
From the hop, Tommy Doyle a nice goal did land.
Then score after score through the posts they did drive,

They swarmed round the Cork backs like bees round a hive.
The ashen sticks cracked and the ball soared on high,
'Twas netted once by the bold Thurles boy.

All the Gaels of bold Tipp. were in Limerick that day,
Right active in seeing Tipp's selection so gay.
They mustered from Nenagh, Newport and Shalee
Roscrea, Templemore, Toom and Borrisoleigh.
In thousands they came there from Thurles and Cahir,
Horse and Jockey, Kilcommon and Clonmel known as rare.
Cashel, Tipperary, and from around Rearcross too,
Not forgetting Birdhill, Ballina and Portroe.

Then fill up your glasses and give them a toast,
Tipperary of those dashing hurlers can boast.
Here's luck to O'Gorman, Tom Hayes and Bill Smee,
Cornally, Ryan's three, Mahers two, Tom Doyle and Heaney.
There's Condon, Tom Treacy, and Flanagan too,
Young Semple and Murphy, all good men and true.
Peter Ryan and Pat Leamy are crowned with renown,
They're no match for O'Donnell from fair Golden town.

I must now conclude for my feelings are high,
May the Gaels of Tipperary and Cork never die.
I sounded their praises as well as I could,
Through village and valley, o'er hill and wildwood.
If mistakes I have made, you'll forgive me I'm sure,
For I'm not in the same class as Davis and Moore.
Then Hip, Hip Hurrah for Tipp's heroes so rare,
And a cheer for the boys from Cork county so fair.

Played at Limerick on the 26 Oct, 1941: Final Score—Tipperary 5-4, Cork 2-5.

Team: James Maher (goal), Denis Gorman, Ger Cornally, Tom Hayes, John Ryan
(capt), John Maher, Tommy Doyle, Wm. O'Donnell, N. Condon, M. Ryan, James
Heaney, P. Flanagan, J. Ryan, T. Treacy, J.Looby.

The 1941 championship was disrupted by an outbreak of foot and mouth disease,
which lasted from February to October. In an attempt to minimise the spread of the

disease, the Department of Agriculture restricted travel in the affected area which were mainly Munster and south Leinster. The main casualties as far as the GAA was concerned were the provincial championships of Munster and Leinster.

'Tipperary defeated Waterford by 4-7 to 3-4 to qualify for a semi-final meeting with Cork. All-Ireland champions Limerick had an easy victory over Clare by 8-3 to 1-5 in another first round game. Cork and Tipperary were scheduled to play in Cork on August 17, but the Premier County was not permitted to travel. The Leinster Council had a similar problem when Kilkenny were not allowed to play the Leinster final…the Central Council requested both Munster and Leinster councils to nominate teams to take part in the All-Ireland series. Leinster nominated Dublin. In Munster it was decided that Limerick and Cork would meet for the right to represent the province in the All-Ireland final. The winners would meet Tipperary for the Munster championship when travel restrictions were lifted. Cork who had been without an All-Ireland title since 1931 had an easy victory over a Limerick side minus the Mackey brothers and Paddy Scanlan (goalie) on September 14—Cork 8-10, Limerick 3-2. Two weeks late Cork regained the McCarthy Cup with a 5-11 to 0-6 victory over Dublin. By the middle of October travel restrictions were lifted and so Cork and Tipperary were able to play the Munster final in Limerick. Dublin spared the Leinster Council any embarrassment when they had a goal to spare in the delayed Leinster final.' '
(Extract from the Munster G.A.A. Story pp 184/185)

Tipperary wins Today

Anon
Source: Gaelic Echo, Sept, 22, 1945 Also John Joe Roberts, formerly of Portroe,
Seafield, Kilmacthomas, Co. Waterford.

Sliabh na mBan looked up to Galtee on a clear September morn,
When the Golden Vale was gleaming with its fields of new-cut
corn—
And the Shannon River shouted to the Suir across the way,
There's a hurling match in Dublin, Tipperary wins today.

Flashed the message over Munster from Dungarvan to Tralee,
From the falls of Castleconnell down to Bandon by the sea.
And the hills of Cork made answer up to Galtees wild hurrah—
We have cause to know their mettle—Tipperary wins today.

Thundered up the train to Dublin by Kilkenny's marble town—
Thundered over by the Tholsel, you may tear those streamers
down—
'Tis Mooncoin and Boherlahan once more into the fray—
By the kings of conquering Cashel, Tipperary wins today.

Now ye blades of bold Kilkenny on this field of verdant green
Shall be played the game to grace one flag with victories thirteen;
If this added glory shines along the black-and-amber way,
We will proudly hail you victors—Tipperary wins today.

Wildly cheers the gathered thousands as the teams are coming thro'
In Kilkenny's black-and –amber, in Tipperary's gold and blue.
And the cheers are hushed to silence as they hear the anthem play,
Then they cry above the tumult, Tipperary wins today.

Now there's Maher in the goalmouth and there's Maher leads the backs,
And there's Coffey in defence and there's another leads attacks.
There's Ryan left-full-forward and another o'er the way,
And their hearts beat out the message, Tipperary wins today.

Mark them down for history's record—Devitt, Murphy, Purcell, Wall—
Goldsboro, Cornally, Gleeson, Brennan, first of all—
Tommy Doyle is just behind them and they keep that ball in play,
And it sings between the uprights, Tipperary wins today.

Kilkenny nobly rallied, point for point and goal for goal,
Swiftly passed those crowded minutes as young Blanchfield took his toll.
But a hero countered briskly in that dazzling grim affray,
Maher stopped them in the goalmouth, and Tipperary wins today.

Oh, 'twas glorious there to see them, foremost of the hurling Gael,
Were you listening Sliabh na mBan to hear the breezes from the Pale?
Shout it up to grand old Galtee, up Thurles and Roscrea,
O'er the plains of Cluain na Meala—Tipperary wins today.

Hands across to Castlecomer, send a greeting to Mooncoin,
Tullaroan deserves a tribute from Moycarkey, Shevry, Moyne;
For the boys of grand Kilkenny, hear John Maher nobly say,
'We were mighty proud to meet you though Tipperary wins today.

Final score—Tipperary, 5-6, Kilkenny, 3-6. Played at Croke Park on Sept 2, 1945.
Team—Jim Maher, J. Devitt, G. Cornally, F. Coffey, M. Murphy, John Maher (capt),
T. Purcell, H. Goldsboro, T. Wall, 'Mutt' Ryan, T. Doyle, E. Gleeson, John Coffey,
A. Brennan, P. 'Sweeper' Ryan.
John Joe Roberts says that Shevry pronounced Shev-roy is near Upperchurch towards
Borrisoleigh, and that there's an ould saying in Tipp. 'Beyant Shevry there's no
religion and beyant Upperchurch, there's no God'
The Tholsel is a market place in the centre of Kilkenny City.
Writing about this game in the *History of Hurling*, p.89, (1946), Carbery says,'
Kilkenny forwards were good: it was Tipperary's high grade backs, cool and resolute
and strong, confident, accurate, ambidextrous hurlers, that made those stocky

Noreside speed merchants look moderate betimes. Not all the time of course; for we saw the most brilliant diagonal pattern-weaving of the hour when Kilkenny staged the rousing rally in the second half...Then the fur flew, splintering ash crashed round the Tipperary goalie, Jimmy Maher, who had radar eyes on his wee hurley: 'five feet eagle-eyed, between hurling posts. Jer Cornally crowded round; Devitt, Flor Coffey, and Captain Maher swarmed in to help. Full-blooded pulling of ash fair and free. Fit bodies crashed together with resounding thud; Kilkenny black and amber boys like wasps at a hive; heads went in where hurls should be. And what Thomas Davis called 'The matchless men of Tipperary'' weathered the autumn storm that battered down but did not destroy, their plenteous harvest, won with so much pains and care in Munster and Leinster fields last spring and summer'

The Blue and Gold 1945

Anon
Air: the Men of the West

The rocky old road seemed much longer
With transport so scarce and unsure
Yet on bike and on dray, each wended his way
With the joy of an exile's return.
'Twas a scene that an artist might envy
The gathering of clans to the fold;
Black and amber were flashed in the sunshine
With lacings of blue and of gold.

Loud cheers rent the air with sweet music
From hearts full of zeal and of grádh
Whilst our isle has such Gaels and such Gaedhilge
There's no fear for Érin go Breágh.
Croke Park was full to o'erflowing
The clash of camáns was in swing
'The laurels we'll take, said the Nore boys,
But the lads from the Suir said, 'we'll win'.

In the air the leather went flying
Kilkenny played manly and bold
But the ball, you may bet, soon lodged in the net
By the heroes in blue and in gold.
The Nore boys attacked fast and fiery
The cup seemed at times in the van;
In defence for the gallant old county
Tipperary was there to a man.

We're proud of you Gaels of Tipp'rary
We cherish our gallant fifteen
Who have fleetness and strength to attack and defend
With marking decisive and keen.
You thought of 'The Homes of Tipp'rary'

Your aim was so fearless and true
And your lustre I'll pen when you step out again
In the loop of the gold and the blue.

I never did doubt you Tipp'rary
Reliable e'er in the fray;
You've brought home another all-Ireland
God bless and God keep you I pray.

Final score—Tipperary, 5-6, Kilkenny, 3-6. Played at Croke Park on Sept 2, 1945.

Team—Jim Maher, J. Devitt, G. Cornally, F. Coffey, M. Murphy, John Maher (capt), T. Purcell, H. Goldsboro, T. Wall, 'Mutt' Ryan, T. Doyle, E. Gleeson, John Coffey, A. Brennan, P. 'Sweeper' Ryan.

Come On, Tipp'rary 1945

By Ceitinn

O God bless you Boherlahan!
From Slievenamon to Shannon shore
Round stately Cashel of the kings
From Aherlow to Templemore.
'Come on, Tipp'rary' Never yet
You shirked a challenge on the field
Of fame or hurling when you met
With foemen worthy of your shield.

Yours is the land by Kickhan sung,
By Cormac's gesture sanctified,
Where valiant Geoffrey's fiery tongue
Rebuke the spoiler in his pride.
A land by nature doubly dowered
With purple hills and dreaming vales,
Whose sons to tyrants never cowered,
The cradle of resurgent Gaels.

Though Tubberadora's day be gone
And dim the memory of its sires,
Their sons have seen another dawn
Another Maher the beacon fires;
Telling to all who see it blaze
O'er rock and river, hill and plain,
As in the old heroic days,
'The kings of hurling reign again'

Gallant Tipperary 1945

By Rev. John J. Lambe P.P. Gurtnahoe-Glengoole
Source: The History of Gortnahoe-Glengoole GAA. Received from Seamus J. King,
Boherclough, Cashel.
Air: Gallant Tipperary Boys. Chorus after each verse.

At Fermoy town we won renown
Hurrah! for gallant Tipperary, boys.
Jim Ware and Waterford went down
Hurrah! For gallant Tipperary, boys.
Our backs stood fast, our forwards goaled,
The old Tipp dash its story told
And victory came to the blue and gold
Hurrah! For gallant Tipperary, boys.

Chorus:

Then hurrah! hurrah! hurrah! again,
For bold John Maher and his merry men
Hurrah!hurrah! hurrah! again
For the old Tipp dash is here again.

At Thurles town we Cork did meet
Hurrah! For gallant Tipperary, boys.
Jack Lynch, Jim Young and Kelly fleet,
Hurrah! For gallant Tipperary, boys.
They hurled with skill and they hurled with heat
But they could not cope with the flying feet
And the lightning strokes of our hurlers neat
Hurrah! For gallant Tipperary, boys.

Mick Mackey's men to Thurles came
Hurrah! For gallant Tipperary, boys.
The Munster crown to win and claim
Hurrah! For gallant Tipperary, boys.
Right fiercely went the crack of ash

And man for man gave clash for clash
And Tipp all Limerick attacks did smash
Hurrah! For gallant Tipperary, boys.

With Antrim 'bet' then came the test
Hurrah! For gallant Tipperary, boys.
To see who were our country's best
Hurrah! For gallant Tipperary, boys.
Kilkenny's pride before us stood
The were keen and quick, they were more than good,
And the question was; Win? Who should?
Hurrah! For gallant Tipperary, boys.

Kilkenny's forwards drew first blood
Hurrah! For gallant Tipperary, boys.
Tipp never flinched but staunchly stood
Hurrah! For gallant Tipperary, boys.
Then the old Tipp dash came to the fore
The goals flashed in, one, two, three, four
And the whole field shook to a mighty roar:
Hurrah! For gallant Tipperary, boys.

Kilkenny battled bravely on
Hurrah! For gallant Tipperary, boys.
But they could not beat Tipp. and captain John
Hurrah! For gallant Tipperary, boys.
As he came to the stand to receive the prize
Sure pride shone out in Tipperary eyes,
And with him we say Tipp will continue to rise
Hurrah! For gallant Tipperary, boys.

Onward Tipperary 1945

Sean O'Carra, Thurles
Received from Liam Ó Donnchú, Balymoreen, Littleton.

Now men of Tipp. you're on your mettle surely,
With rivals who are worthy of esteem.
Be nothing daunted by their blazoned glory—
Remember you're Tipperary's chosen team.

Yes, pride of Tipp, it's yours to do it honour.
Conquer again with Tipp's traditional dash,
With first-time striking, pull and never dally.
The black and amber hopes you're bound to smash.

To write your names on Tipp's long roll of honour,
Among the stalwart's names in memory's keep.
Crash through Kilkenny's back lines like a whirlwind,
With clashing ash and headlong clashing sweep.

We'll light you home with bonfires blazing gladly,
Your victory we'll extol with voice and pen.
Your fame we'll blazon bright that all may read it
Among the names of Tipp's great hurling men.

This is reputed to be a poem of encouragement to the Tipperary team, urging them to repeat their 1937 win. If this is so, then it refers to the Tipperary v Kilkenny All-Ireland final to be played at Croke Park on September 2nd 1945.

Champions of '49

By 'Top Hat'
Received from Liam Ó Donnchú, Ballymoreen, Littleton.

On the fourth day of September in the year of forty-nine
When Laoghis and Tipperary in sporting fray did join.
In Croke Park's famed arena where thousands came to cheer,
Those sturdy camán wielders who for honours did appear.

When Cashel's beloved Archbishop set the teams to play
The Tipperary forwards began their great display.
Tho' each stout Laois defender was working like a giant,
The flying Pat Stakelum sent over Tipp's first point.

Then sharp shooting Jimmy Kennedy was taking steady aim,
'Twas then the Laoghis supporters were fearing for the game,
As Shanahan and Kenny kept the forwards on their toes,
'Twas pass the ball to Kennedy and between the posts it goes.

The man from Toomevara then added to the score—
Then Paddy Kenny's goal and points increased the margin more.
Helped on by Sonny Maher of Boherlahan fame,
From then on it was easy guess, the outcome of the game.

Here's health to Tony Reddin, may he guard the posts for long,
To Brennan of Clonoulty, a full back brave and strong.
And Bannon, pride of Nenagh, who gave a great display
And the brothers Ryan of hurling fame who came from old Roscrea.

And Tommy Ryan of Thurles would be a much-felt loss
With the Stakelums, Doyles and Gorman from far famed Holycross
And Sean and Paddy Kenny from dear old Borrisoleigh
Their play was well worth going a long way 'for to see'.

Sonny Maher and Flor Coffey recall Boherlahan fame
And Toomevara's Shanahan brought memories back again.

There was Sarsfield's Mickey Byrne as nimble as could be
And our star man Jimmy Kennedy as yet with U.C.D.

Well done we say good neighbours in the county of O'Moore
The craft of Tipperary your boys could not endure.
May we always have such sportsmen who we know in praise will join
For Ireland's hurling champions in nineteen forty-nine.

All-Ireland Hurling Final at Croke Park on September 4th, 1949, Tipperary 3-11, Laois 0-3.

Team: A. Reddan, M. Byrne, A. Brennan, J. Doyle, P. Stakelum (capt), F. Coffey, T. Doyle, S. Kenny, P. Shanahan, Tommy Ryan, Mick Ryan, J. Kennedy, J. Ryan, 'Sonny' Maher, S. Bannon. Sub. —P. Kenny (for F. Coffey)

* Verse 6— Dinny Gorman, native of Holycross. Dinny played in the 1937 All-Ireland winning side.

Tiobrad Árann Abú 1950

By P.B.Ryan, New Line Dundrum
Source: Received from Liam Ó Donnchú, Ballymorreen, Littleton
Chorus after each verse.

Tiobrad Árann Abú !Tiobrad Árann Abú!
Let it ring ever proudly and high.
Let it ring o'er the vale, o'er the hill and the dale,
'Til in music it swells to the sky.
Let it travel with pride, o'er the deep ocean wide,
O'er the plain and the wild moorland too,
How the men of renown won the All-Ireland crown
With the cry Tiobrad Árann Abú!

Chorus:

Then hurrah, shout hurrah; proud are we boys today,
For our brave hurlers, dashing and true.
Through the field sweeping down, won the all-Ireland crown
With the cry, Tiobrad Árann Abú!

Peerless and bold, with the grand style of old
And nimble and swift as the fawn,
Are those all-conquering men from the plain and the glen,
In the swing of the pliant camán.
Let it bravely be told how the grand blue and gold
Was carried triumphant and true.
By that gallant fifteen, dashing hurlers and clean,
With the cry, Tiobrad Árann Abú!

Bonfires blaze bright as the morning's sunlight
On the mountains and high hilltops green,
For the men, who with pride, every effort defied
Of Kilkenny's brave stalwart fifteen.
And again as of yore, our brave men to the fore,
Will hasten with courage anew,

And add further fame to Tipperary's fair name
With the cry, Tiobrad Árann Abú!

All-Ireland Hurling Final at Croke Park on September 3rd 1950. Tipperary 1-9, Kilkenny 1-8.

Team: A. Reddan, M.Byrne, A. Brennan, J.Doyle, J.Finn, P. Stakelum, T.Doyle, S.Bannon, P.Shanahan, E.Ryan, Mick Ryan, S.Kenny (capt), P. Kenny 'Sonny'Maher, J. Kennedy. Sub: Tommy Ryan for 'Sonny' Maher.

Tipperary's Hurling Men 1950

By R.Frewen
Source: Received from Liam Ó Donnchú, Ballymorreen, Littleton

They're talking of our hurling men from Cork to Donegal—
They're telling of their battles grim by the crags of wild Imaal.
The wild Atlantic waves have heard the echo of their fame—
Oh! Could we write in letters bright, their story and their name.

God bless you Jimmy Kennedy, you're loved round Slievenamon.
You thrilled our hearts—you broke the hearts of foes and followers on.
You're backed by men we're proud to own, but they would each recall,
'In truth we never won a match, 'twas Jimmy won them all'

A blessing on you Reddin Dubh, when we were most in doubt,
The balls like hail were whistling round, with grit you kept them out.
Before you on the ramparts stands Brennan cool and still,
Oh! Anthony, You're grand, you're brave —in peril we trust your skill.

Do you hear the foe a'roaring wild where our lines in danger stand?
But hold! Those wings that seem to shake, by Byrne and Doyle are manned.
And Tommy Doyle—Ah, Tommy Doyle, bounds in to save the day,
And Thurles and all Ireland are shouting 'Doyle Hurrah!'

Another whom Tipperary boasts, the pride of every Gael,
Is Bannon—brawn and sinew, defender non-pareil.
With him in line is Stakelum strong, determined, firm and stout.
No words could write of Stakelum's might—no one did e'er him doubt.

And you remember 'ninety-eight' and Kelly of Killane,
Who died for lonely Ireland's cause, where smiling Slaney ran.

But born again and in our ranks, is Kelly, kingly tall;
Phil Shanahan, a chieftain, in battle, lord of all.

Sean Kenny, captain, leads his men, with dash and do or die,
And Borris gives a Kenny too, to raise the green flag high.
The Ryans we cheer, Mick, Jack and Ned, grand hurlers one and all,
And Tommy Ryan, a stylist and Maher a stone wall.

Look down, oh Emerald Galtees high! Look down, oh Keeper Hill!
Behold with pride those men who guide and gap of danger fill.
Sure well we know the valour of our sturdy rivals bold,
But our heart's blood throbs for Kickham and our flag of blue and
gold.

Tipperary Fifty-One

By Jack Ryan, Beechwood Drive,
Greystones, Limerick. (formerly Newport)

The flags are proudly waving and Croke Park is gold and blue,
And the haunting strains of Slievenamon would thrill you through
and through.
We have won three titles in a row, forty- nine to fifty-one—
Let victory's cry be held on high and joy to everyone.

With Pat Stakelum as our captain, we beat Laois in forty-nine—
In fifty, 'twas Sean Kenny's men, who kept the 'Cats' in line.
In fifty-one, Jim Finn's brave lads retained the championship
And brought sweet victory home once more to the gallant hills of
Tipp.

Here's to Tony Reddan then who manned the Bearna Baoil
Against the finest forwards from Wexford, Cork, and Clare.
A cheer for Tony Brennan our peerless sound full-back
Who kept the forwards all subdued and stemmed each fierce attack.

With the 'Rattler' Byrne on the right, faith there was no way
through—
The cry was, 'whip it on the sod' like every Thurles Blue.
While on the left we had a man to stop the lads from Ross
Son of the soil, his name John Doyle, from historic Holycross.

At right –halfback was Jimmy Finn, a hurler fine to see,
He played it tight with left and right, true son of Borrisoleigh
At centre-back was Stakelum, all honour to you Pat,
You let the sliotar do the work and sailed it o'er the lath.

And by your side was Tommy Doyle who has five All-Irelands now—
May he wear his honours many years in his own sweet Knocknagow.
Two greyhounds from gallant Toom, oh we had a centre-field,
John Hough and Philly Shanahan were never known to yield.

The half-forward line we filled with Ryans, from Borris and Roscrea,
With Ned and Tim out on each wing and Mick to take the sway.
In front were Sonny Maher and Seamus Bannon from the Ragg
And Paddy Kenny, tried and true, to raise the famed green flag.

Here's a toast to you Phil Purcell and Paddy Leahy too—
Who trained our gallant hurling lads who wore the gold and blue.
'Tis proud you feel this blessed year—another championship,
We'll keep your memories evergreen in the vales and glens of Tipp.

Then raise your glasses here to night for the men from Slaney side,
Their day will come, I have no doubt, to honour Wexford's pride.
With men like Flood, the Rackards, Wheeler and Kehoe,
There's not their likes on Gaelic fields wherever you may go.

Where're the clash of ash is heard and hurlers take the field,
No other game is quite the same and to it all must yield.
So raise a cheer for all to hear for hurlers one and all,
Who graced our fields and raised our hearts with stout camán and ball.

All-Ireland Hurling final at Corke Park, September 2, 1951. Tipperary, 7-7, Wexford 3-9.
Team: A. Reddan, M. Byrne, A. Brennan, J. Doyle, J. Finn (capt), P. Stakelum, T. Doyle, P. Shanahan, J. Hough, E. Ryan, Mick Ryan, Tim Ryan, P. Kenny, 'Sonny' Maher, S. Bannon. Sub: S. Kenny for P. Kenny.

Tipperary v Kilkenny 1958

By Bill O'Keeffe
Source: Cill Sioláin-100 Years and More of Gaelic Games in the Parish of Kilsheelan
and Kilcash 1884-1988. Received from Seamus J. King, Boherclough, Cashel.

The whistle blew, the game was on, now came our greatest test,
Before us on Croke Park's green sod we faced Kilkenny's best.
Our hearts were bold, our courage strong, we feared not any man,
The clashes were so thrilling as to please the greatest fan.
O'Grady kept a right goal and safe was Michael Maher,
Young Carey held his man subdued, Mick Byrne was a star.
When hurleys clashed and battles raged, John Doyle charged with
the ball,
Or Jimmy Finn lashed sharp and quick or maybe Tony Wall.

Chorus:

Up from the country came Tipperary's hurling men
A dashing, daring bunch of lads those fifteen stalwart men.
They knew no fear; they held their ground and pulled hard on the
ball
Our gallant Tipperary team with captain Tony Wall.

John Hough and Theo English were always to the fore,
And Jimmy Doyle—a treat to watch—piled up a winning score.
Lar. Keane and Donie Nealon were ever in the fray,
Devaney and Tommy Larkin all helped to win the day.
Mc Grath and Liam Connolly both stood the trying test,
This gallant Tipperary team will rank among the best.
A toast to our great hurling men on this wet August day,
And credit to Moondarrig's men for a thrilling hour's display.

Chorus:

All Ireland Hurling Semi-Final at Croke Park on August 10. Tipperary, 1-13,
Kilkenny, 1-8.

218

Tipperary v Galway 1958

By Paddy Noonan, Killenaule
Source: Received from Liam Ó Donnchú, Ballymoreen, Littleton.
Air: the Men of the West.

Tipperary have done it again,
So raise up your voices and sing
We've beaten the cream of the country
Including the great Christy Ring.
We've beaten the men from the Shannon,
The Lee and the Suir and the Nore
We've beaten the best of the men of the west
As we did many times before.

We first met the boys from the Shannon
And gave Mackey's boys quite a shock
Our troubles were many; we hadn't Devaney
And had to line out without Hough.
But we discovered young Nealon
And Carey the man from Roscrea,
Men from Fethard, Clonmel and Kilsheelan;
All helped Tipp to carry the day.

Then came the men from the Lee-side,
We beat them with little to spare,
And those who like me, could not go to see,
Sat and listened to Micheál Ó hEithir.
The game to be sure was a thriller,
It had Munster's traditional sting,
Like the cheer that arose, as the crowd on their toes,
Watched the duels between Byrne and Ring.

Next came the champions of Munster,
The men from the banks of the Suir
And though they were fast, their pace did not last
And Tipp had the medals secure.

Our centre-field pair, Hough and English,
Every Waterford plan they did foil,
While their forward's attacks, seldom passed our half-backs
Jimmy Finn, Tony Wall and John Doyle.
Then on the tenth day of August,
Croke Park was both slippy and wet,
And Kilkenny then knew that their chances were few
When young Doyle sent the ball to the net.
And as the half-time whistle sounded
Each Kilkenny face wore a grim smile
They had no chance at all against Tony Wall,
Carey, Finn, Byrne, Maher and Doyle.

Then we had a date in September
To keep with the men of the West,
And Tipp's hurling team, every member,
Proved that he was one of the best.
So again we're champions of Ireland,
Seventeen senior titles we hold,
We can wear our best smiles while we've men like the Doyles,
To carry the blue and the gold.

All-Ireland Hurling Final played at Croke Park on Sept. 8th 1958.

Final Score: Tipperary, 4-9, Galway, 2-5.

Team: J. O'Grady, M. Byrne, M. Maher, K. Carey, J. Finn, A. Wall (capt), John +
Doyle, J. Hough, T. English,, D. Nealon, T. Larkin, Jimmy Doyle, L. Keane, L.
Devaney, L. Connolly.

Munster Final 1961

By James Armshaw
Source: Received from Liam Ó Donnchú, Ballymoreen, Littleton, Thurles.
Air: God Save Ireland-Chorus after each verse.

Come raise your glass on high,
Let your cheers reach to the sky
For those brave and gallant hurlers of renown.
Who that day in sixty-one,
Mid the thunder of the throng
From Limerick brought the Munster crown.

Chorus:

Rise up men of Tipperary
Rise up and fling your hats on high.
We have a worthy team
In this wonderful fifteen
Those splendid boys
They are our pride and joy.

The Shannon flowed along
And it seemed to sing a song
Of deeds of fame that happened long ago.
But another day of fame,
Is now coupled to its name
And bonfires blaze where Suir waters flow.

O'Brien, he stood the
And in that mighty crush
No Corkman ever scored a single goal.
And our sons will yet relate
How he sealed the rebels fate
And how he played with all his heart and soul.

The Moloughneys and O'Riain,
The finest ever seen
The Cork backs could not stop those forwards bold.

221

And McKenna left no doubt,
When Moloughney got knocked out
That we still have men to wear the blue and gold.

Sean McLoughlin stood the pace
And with that easy grace
Of a hurler who has hit the highest mark.
He gave a grand display
In that fast and furious fray
And we hope to see him often in Croke Park.

Donie Nealon led the van,
He's a hurler and a man
His splendid shots went blazing to the net.
And our hero Jimmy Doyle
With daring skill and style
Through the Cork defence went flying like a jet.

In mid-field we had two men,
Their praises we will sing
For they blasted everything that came their way.
It was sheer delight to see,
The ball go high and free
From English and Devaney on that day.

Now all that I could say
Would not our debt repay
To that brave and gallant man from Holycross.
Resurged by three or four
And sometimes even more
With those rebel boys John Doyle played pitch and toss.

Mick Maher true to form,
Never wavered in any storm
And Carey too he had his man at bay.
O'Gara and Mick Burns,

With their magic twists and turns
With Matt Hassett, finished Cork that glorious day.

From Keeper to Clonmel,
The story we will tell,
For many a year of this great victory.
Here's to the blue and gold—
'Up Tipperary's hurlers bold
May their names live long in history'

Munster Hurling Final at Gaelic Grounds, Limerick, 30, July 1961. Tipperary 3-6, Cork 0-7. Referee: Mick Hayes, Clare.

Tipperary Team: D.O'Brien (goal), M.Hassett, M.Maher, K.Carey, M.O'Gara, John Doyle, M.Burns, T. English, L.Devaney, Jimmy Doyle, D.Nealon, T.Ryan, T.Moloughney, W.Moloughney, S. McLoughlin. Sub: J.McKenna.

'The official attendance was returned at 61,175, the biggest crowd ever to witness an Irish sporting event outside Croke Park. It was a never to be forgotten day and the recorded crowd by no means represents the real attendance. The gates to the popular enclosure were thrown open midway through the minor game to avoid panic as the huge crowd swayed dangerously. Some thousands then gained free admission whilst many more turned back on the Ennis Road when they heard of the situation at the Grounds. Some estimates put the crowd at Limerick on that day at well over 70,000. The Cork team, which togged out in its usual hotel in the city had to leave their cars halfway up the Ennis Road and force their way through the throng of spectators to get to the Grounds.

Although he continued to wear the county jersey for another two years, this was to prove Christy Ring's seventeenth and last appearance in a Munster final. Coincidentally, it was also his seventeenth championship game against Tipperary.'
(Munster GAA Story p.244)

223

Matt Hassett's Hurling Men

Anon
Source:Toomevara G.A.A.1885-1985
Received from Seamus J. King, Boherclough, Cashel

To Garryowen of Treaty Stone one day in hot July,
Whose deeds on Ireland's playing fields are the toast of hill and glen.
From Ollatrim south by Keeper's Height to distant Sliabh na mBan,
You've upheld our county's honour and your eighteenth All-Ireland
win.

On the verdant green of Limerick's field you humbled rebel Cork.
And as Munster's leading champions met Dublin at Croke Park.
With these gallant boys you fought it out and matched them score for
score
As the far off sun kissed Galtees they heard the victory roar.

O'Brien of Knockavilla who manned the barn door
Was fronted by those heroes, Carey, Hassett and Maher Mór.
Mick Burns and Wall from Sarsfields, John Doyle from Holycross
Repelled those Dublin forwards and resolved they'd never pass.

Theo English, Matt O'Gara from historic Toome nearby
Supplied the balls for Nealon and the wonder Thurles boy.
We toast you Liam Devaney from the spot called Borrisoleigh
By your courage and your daring, you've made hurling history.
The Mc Loughneys and Mc Kenna, they fought for every ball
And that vital one point victory came at Fitzgerald's final call.

So from Kickham's Premier County, from every hill and glen,
They toast you Matt Hassett and your gallant hurling men.
That recall those days of 'Wedger' bold and Johnny Leahy too—
Here's many more All Irelands is our fervent wish for you.

Commemorates Tipperary's 1961 All Ireland hurling win v Dublin on September 3.
Tipperary, 0-16, Dublin 1-12.

Team—D. O Brien, M. Hassett, (capt), M. Maher, K. Carey, M. Burns, T. Wall, John Doyle, M. O'Gara, T. English, Jimmy Doyle, L. Devaney, D. Nealon, John 'Mackey' McKenna, W. Moloughney, T. Moloughney. Subs—T.Ryan (Killenaule) for Mc Kenna, J. Hough (for O'Gara), S.McLoughlin (for Wall)

Tipperary Champions 1962

By Bill O'Keeffe
Received from Liam Ó Donnchú, Ballymoreen, Littleton.

Well done Tipperary's hurling men, you filled our hearts with pride
Hats off to Wexford's stalwart sons, stout men from Slaney side.
Your speed and skill brought many a thrill as the battle raged full
blast,
But our boys in blue in sixty-two showed courage to the last.

We cheered O'Brien's daring saves and Maher's pull and dash:
Kieran Carey and the fearless Doyle broke through in many a clash.
A hero tall stood Tony Wall with O'Gara by his side,
And Mick Burns's long and raking pucks rolled back the Wexford
tide.

Theo English and Devaney played their best when things were worst:
McKenna of the flying feet made many a daring thrust.
Tom Ryan's goal was brilliant and McLoughlin tough and quick,
While Nealon chased the rolling ball and glued it to his stick.

The captain Jimmy Doyle took scores with grace and skill and ease
And Tom Moloughney roamed about for any chance to seize.
The subs Tom Ryan and Connolly did well for their short while,
And showed that they are moulded in the real Tipperary style.

Now down the years we'd had fine teams who brought us great
renown,
The Greyhounds, Blues and Boherlahan, De Wets from Nenagh
town.
Moycarkey , Jockey, Holycross, won many a gallant test,
But our men in blue in sixty-two now rank among the best.

All-Ireland Hurling Final, Sept 2 at Croke Park. Tipperary 3-10, Wexford 2-11. This
was two-in a row for Tipperary.

Team—D. O'Brien, John Doyle, Mick Maher, Kieran Carey, Matt O'Gara, Tony Wall, Mick Burns, Theo. English, Liam Devaney, Jimmy Doyle (capt) J. 'Mackey ' McKenna', T. Ryan, (Killenaule), D. Nealon, T. McLoughney, S. McLoughlin. Subs: Liam Connolly for (Matt O'Gara), T. Ryan, Toomevara (for Jimmy Doyle.)

'The author Bill O'Keeffe was born in Kilsheelan in the early years of the century and was educated at Kilsheelan N.S, St. Mary's C.B.S. and St. Patrick's Training College, Dublin. He was first secretary of the Kilsheelan club, which was formed in 1924. He taught for a while in St. Mary's C.B.S. He later became principal of Loughbrickland National School, County Down and assisted the local Glenn GAA club for many years. He wrote poems on many subjects including ones on his native Kilsheelan and the valley of Slievenamon. He died in 1984 and is buried in Newry, Co. Down'. (*Slievenamon in Song and Story* edited by Sean Nugent 1996)

The Hurlers of '62

By Rev. Bro. Joseph Perkins, C.B.S. Thurles.

We've often heard our fathers tell in the far off days of old
Of great deeds done, of men who shone for the famous blue and
gold.
But we today have seen men play as fearless, staunch and true,
Who did uphold the blue and gold, the men of sixty-two.

Before the Saxon's cruel yoke, Tipperary would not bow.
We read with pride by our own fireside, great Kickham's
Knocknagow.
We've got them still with that dash and skill,' Matt the Threshers'
brave and true
Who play the game, win honour and fame, like the men of sixty-two.

In goal O'Brien does always shine, John Doyle still shows us how.
Six times he's won the major crown, this star of Knocknagow.
And by his side Holycross's pride, Mick Maher keeps all at bay,
And on the wing—men fear the swing of Carey from Roscrea.

When danger shows its angry head, when the tide of battle turns,
'Tis then we see the gallantry of O'Gara, Wall and Burns.
Ne'er known to yield at centre-field, English comes sweeping
through
And Devaney's name is honoured with fame with the men of sixty-
two.

Like Mick Mackey of yore, McKenna tore, then parted with the ball.
We'll ne'er forget how he shook the net, the man from Killenaule.
From play or frees, 'gainst sun or breeze, like a typical Thurles blue,
With speed and style—great Jimmy Doyle, was skipper of sixty-two.

And down the wing did Nealon spring and sent it o'er the bar.
Around the square on ground or air, McLoughney was the star.

228

McLoughlin's stick was sure and quick, Connolly came racing through,
And Toom's Tom Ryan did also shine in nineteen –sixty- two.

Then here's to all that gallant band, who beat the Wexford boys,
Ye did uphold the blue and gold, Tipperary's flag still flies.
Subs Mounsey, Slevin, Murphy and ex-captain Hassett too,
Who won renown and the nineteenth crown in nineteen sixty-two.

Then, three cheers for Tipperary, come raise your glasses up!
May our gallant men bring home again, the Liam McCarthy cup.
To those who won, we say 'well done' to our sporting losers too,
Hip-hip, hurrah, let us sing today for the hurlers of sixty-two.

All-Ireland Hurling Final, Sept 2 at Croke Park. Tipperary 3-10, Wexford 2-11. This
was two-in a row for Tipperary.

Team—D. O'Brien, John Doyle, Mick Maher, Kieran Carey, Matt O'Gara, Tony
Wall, Mick Burns, Theo. English, Liam Devanney, Jimmy Doyle (capt) J. 'Mackey
McKenna', T. Ryan, (Killenaule), D. Nealon, T. McLoughney, S. McLoughlin. Subs:
Liam Connolly (for Matt O'Gara), T. Ryan, Toomevara (for Jimmy Doyle.)

All Ireland Champions 1962

By Matt Kirwan
Source: Received from Liam Ó Donnchú, Ballymoreen, Littleton.

'Twas in September, I well remember,
To see our hurlers at Jones' road,
When Doyle led out the Munster champions,
Facing Wexford's heroes led by Rackard bold.
The anthem over, the backs in places,
And Tipp defending the Clonliffe goal.
John Dowling's whistle had barely sounded,
When Mc Loughney snatched a major score.

Another followed and our hearts beat faster,
But Wexford stormed us in days of yore.
And points from Lynch, Tim Flood and Kehoe,
They narrowed the margin of a victory score.
Those Wexford lads, they fought courageous—
Their hurling valour we'll oft recall,
And names like Rackard and Nick O'Donnell,
Will long illumine Mount Leinster's call.

We hail our champions from sweet Tipp'rary—
O'Brien, who guarded the barn door,
John Doyle, Mick Maher and Kieran Carey,
We'll sing their praises for evermore.
Mick Burns of Nenagh, with Matt O'Gara,
In the centre covered by Tony Wall.
Those brave midfielders, Devaney and English,
They met the challenge of every ball.

There's Jimmy Doyle from Thurles Sarsfields,
Whose deeds of glory we oft recall,
At Dúrlas Éile, or Limerick City,
Or against the famous Cork stonewall.
The fair-haired Nealon from Youghalarra

And that grand young hurler from Killenaule.
Tom Ryan's goal brought shouts exultant
To distant firesides at Mullinahone.

There's Sean McLoughlin and 'Mackey'McKenna,
With Tom McLoughney from Kilruane.
Those are the heroes we'll toast together,
Like the champions brave of sixty-one.
Let's sing the praise of brave Tipp'rary,
Likewise those heroes from stout Killane,
Who played the game like worthy sportsmen
And upheld the honour of all Irishmen.

All-Ireland Hurling Final, Sept 2, at Croke Park. Tipperary 3-10, Wexford 2-11. This
was two-in a row for Tipperary.

Team—D. O'Brien, John Doyle, Mick Maher, Kieran Carey, Matt O'Gara, Tony
Wall, Mick Burns, Theo. English, Liam Devaney, Jimmy Doyle (capt) J. 'Mackey
McKenna', T. Ryan, (Killenaule), D. Nealon, T. McLoughney, S. McLoughlin. Subs:
Liam Connolly for (Matt O'Gara), T. Ryan, Toomevara (for Jimmy Doyle.)

Tipperary's Twentieth Crown

By Rev. Bro Joseph Perkins, C.B.S. Thurles.

Ho! See the great Tipperary host march forth with faces wan
From the lovely homes of Knocknagow, 'neath the shades of
Slievenamon.
They come with courage in their hearts, from county and from town
To beat the black and amber boys and win the twentieth crown.

They had won the National Hurling League, at home and in New
York
And had whipped the bonny Banner boys and lashed the boys from
Cork.
The Premier county forges on, who'd dare to keep them down?
They were steeled to go and meet the foe and win the twentieth
crown.

John Doyle again did take the field, six notches on his gun
Nor did he leave Croke Park's fair sward, 'till the seventh's proudly
won.
When John stood there around the square, we never had cause to
frown,
For solid as a rock he withstood each shock and won the twentieth
crown.

John O'Donoghue was sound and true, that former Harty star.
In the Bearna Baoil never known to fail was the sturdy Michael
Maher.
In the thick of the fray was the man from Roscrea, with Mick Burns
from Nenagh town.
Tony Wall strong and tall lashed on every ball that gave us the
twentieth crown.

Michael Murphy skippered this famous team, right well he did the
same
And many's the year by Marlfield side, they have heard of Theo's
name.

Like a great Carrick swan going swiftly on, when the Suir moves gently down
Great Michael Roche flew and full well he too helped us win the twentieth crown.

Jimmy Doyle with style no man can foil, so graceful and so cool,
And galloping through like a bolt from the blue was Larry Kiely from Glengoole.
Up goes the hand, Mick Keating's in command; the ball comes quickly down,
The Ballybacon star sends it over the bar when we won the twentieth crown.

Now see the fleet-footed Nealon race, the ball glued to his stick.
And Mackey McKenna dashes in, so strong, so sure and quick.
The sliotar 's in McLoughlin's hand, and now he's bearing down
Upon the goal and palms it in to make sure of the twentieth crown.

How straight does Liam Devaney's shot go sailing towards the net—
Mick Lonergan did nobly play, ne'er once had we to fret.
Our sub goalman was Peter Sullivan, Pat Ryan of Moycarkey renown,
And Len Gaynor too was willing to do, when we won the twentieth crown.

Let us raise our glass to this mighty team from Ballybacon to Roscrea.
Burgess, Cashel, Holycross, Moycarkey, Borrisokane.
Marlfield, Thurles, Borris(oleigh) Glengoole, Kilruane, Tipp and Nenagh town,
Sixteen parishes helped us to win the Premier's twentieth crown.

Here's to Paddy Leahy and his band, who picked the very best.
Ossie who saw that all were well and fit to stand the test.
Trained to the last, trained to the last, they had trod the upward way,
And Tipp now leads with twenty crowns gained on all-Ireland day.

All-Ireland Hurling Final played at Croke Park on Sept. 6 1964. Tipperary, 5-13, Kilkenny 2-8.

Tipperary— John O'Donoghue, John Doyle, Mick Maher, Kieran Carey, Mick Burns, Tony Wall, Michael Murphy (capt), Theo English, Mick Roche, Jimmy Doyle, Larry Kiely, Michael Keating, Donie Nealon, J. 'Mackey' McKenna, Sean McLoughlin. Subs—M.Lonergan (for Maher), L. Devaney (for Kiely)

The Champions 1964

By Michael Hayes, Ballingarry
Source: Phil Cashin, Brittas, Kilnamanagh, Co. Kilkenny.

Tipperary are the champions of nineteen sixty-four.
They beat the black and amber, Kilkenny from the Nore.
Our team was underrated as the game we did approach
By our GAA sports writers, Mick Dunne and Andy Croke

Here's to John O'Donoghue, he played a brilliant game—
He was fronted by a back line, who are worthy of their name.
Lonergan, Maher, Carey and dauntless John Doyle,
Who won his seventh medal and his first in forty-nine.

The three Tom's from Kilkenny were outhurled and outran,
By the full-backs, who had stamina and the speed of Royal Tan
Murphy, Wall and Burns, their men they did subdue,
And McLoughlin's handball efforts put Ollie in a stew.

Gallant Theo English and Roche from Carrick town
Produced a brand of hurling that helped to win the crown.
Kiely, Doyle and Keating, the backs they did outwit,
And paved the way for Nealon to shake Kilkenny's net.

The hero Liam Devaney, when called he did his bit—
He centred in a beauty that was finished to the net.
McKenna and McLoughlin, two forwards of great fame,
Their bustling style of hurling put Ollie off his game.

The forwards were goal hungry, they chalked up five-thirteen
To take the twentieth title, one more than Cork's nineteen.
The trainers and selectors, the champions you let go
On the soil where Michael Hogan gave his life so long ago.

Tipperary are the champions of nineteen sixty four,
They beat the black and amber, Kilkenny by the Nore.
Great sportsmen from Kilkenny, you have kept the game alive,
With the help of God we'll meet again, in nineteen sixty-five.

Notes: See Tipperary's Twentieth Crown

The Men of Sixty-Four

By Patrick Power, Drangan
Received from Liam Ó Donnchú, Ballymoreen, Littleton
Air: Roddy McCorley

We often heard our fathers tell how in the days of old
Of fearless men from hill and glen who wore the blue and gold.
But there that day, we saw men play as ne'er were seen before
They did uphold the blue and gold those men of sixty-four.

O'Donoghue, both staunch and true, John Doyle still shows them how–
Seven times the premier award he's won, that star of Knocknagow.
And by his side Holycross's pride, Mick Maher bars the way,
While on the wing, men fear the swing of Carey from Roscrea.

Our great half-line did always shine, three cheers for Tony Wall–
Mick Murphy too, our captain true, who always played the ball.
And on the wing, the praise we'll sing of Mick Burns, who played so
well
And when danger came, we heard the name, Theo English from
Clonmel.

When the game is won and the day is done, we'll recall the Carrick
giant–
We'll ne'er forget and speak of yet how you scored that lovely point.
You tore up field and would not yield, like the Walls in days of yore,
And Babs from Grange, sure he found the range with the men of
sixty-four.

From the other side, we'll recall with pride the deeds of Jimmy
Doyle–
When taking frees, he's at his ease, he gave us cause to smile.
The Thurles star taps them o'er the bar, with that swing so neat and
cool
Helped on his way by the fiery play of young Kiely from Glengoole.

McLoughlin too, the brave and true, the net sure he did find—
When he jumped in the air, just outside the square and then left Ollie
blind.
Then Mackey bold like the star of old, through Kilkenny's backs he
tore—
Donie Nealon's three will make history for the men of sixty-four.

Then Devaney came to add his name to that band so loyal and true—
Though he failed to score, he did far more, and his presence they
well knew.
When like a flash, he made a dash and placed Nealon for that score,
Mickie Lonergan too, we'll remember you with the men of sixty-
four.

O'Sullivan, the brave Pat Ryan, and the lad from Kilruane—
Len Gaynor is that hero's name who starred with the twenty-one.
They took their seat, prepared to meet, the challenge from the Nore,
Now their names are well in history's page with the men of sixty-
four.

Now the year is gone and the title won and we can proudly say,
That you played the ball both one and all and carried off the day.
Now play the game, keep up your name and please God if we're
alive,
We will see you in that twenty first, in the coming sixty-five.

Notes: See Tipperary's Twentieth Crown.

Heroes of Tipperary 1965

By Gerard Ryan, Inch, Bouladuff, Thurles.
Source: Received from Liam Ó Donnchú, Ballymorreen, Littleton.

Once more the cup is back at home in storied Thurles Town.
The vanquished have retreated, the victors won renown.
But all combined in sportsmanship, a heritage to uphold—
A Gaelic pastime to renew, its pleasures to unfold.

The crowds at Croke Park looked aghast; what grandeur filled their sight?
As before them on the emerald sward the champions showed their might.
The guiles of age, the speed of youth, a unit to the core,
Brought exultations from the stands as each score followed score.

In homesteads around Munster, stories will be told
Of illustrious teams and famous figures, who donned the blue and gold.
But the men who won the twenty-first will hold a special place
In the hearts of the premier county folk, exemplars of our race.

John Doyle's name forever linked with number twenty one—
From monastic Holycross he comes—their honour-laden son.
Synonymous of the Thresher in Kickham's Knocknagow,
A legend with a hurley, a Hercules with the plough.

The hurlers of Tipperary, kingpins of the code—
Gaeldom's standard-bearers with a permanent abode.
Befitting Davin's county, where many years ago
A small fire was started, that seems to grow and grow.

All Ireland Hurling Final at Croke Park, September 5th 1965. Tipperary, 2-16, Wexford 0-10.

Team: J.O'Donoghue, John Doyle, M.Maher, K.Carey, M.Burns, A.Wall, L.Gaynor, T.English, M.Roche, Jimmy Doyle (capt), L.Kiely, L.Devaney, D.Nealon, J. McKenna, S.McLoughlin.

All-Ireland Hurling Champions 1965

By Matt Kirwan
Source: Received from Liam Ó Donnchú, Ballymoreen, Littleton

'Twas in September, 'I well remember,
To see the final of sixty-five,
When Tipperary champions met the men of Wexford,
For All-Ireland honours they both did strive.
In days to come around our firesides,
We'll tell our sons and oft recall,
Those deeds victorious and hurling glorious,
Of Tipp'rary's twenty- first All-Ireland call.

The anthem over, the backs in places
And Tipp. defending the Railway goal,
Mick Hayes's whistle had barely sounded
When Wexford sought an early score.
Tipp'rary's forwards were soon in action
And McLoughlin crashed home a vital goal,
McKenna's points brought shouts exultant
From Hill' 16 to Mullinahone.

The men of Wexford, they fought courageous,
'Gainst Tipp'rary backs so sorely tried.
John Doyle, Mick Maher and Kieran Carey,
They met the challenge from every side.
In front Mick Burns with Len Gaynor
And Tony Wall to guard the line,
Where the eagle eye of John O'Donoghue
Was there to save the net each time.

We'll toast Mick Roche and Theo English
And our stalwart captain, Jimmy Doyle,
With Larry Kiely, Liam Devaney
And Donie Nealon to complete the line.
They'll talk today of Cork's own maestro,

The peerless forward Christy Ring
Of Martin Kennedy, of Limerick's Mackey
And of Nick Rackard in praise they'll sing.

But at Dúrlas Éile by Shannon's waters
Or where Cork City meets the Lee,
Let's toast John Doyle, the Holycross defender,
Who for Tipp'rary's honour made history.
So let's toast the champions from sweet Tipp'rary,
Likewise the losers from Killanne,
Whose deeds of valour and of hurling glory,
Is the pride today of Irishmen.

Let the bonfires glow on the heights o'er Keeper
To the far off Galtees above the Suir
And Tipp'rarys honour, like the faith of Kickham,
Live on in her homes and forever endure.

All Ireland Hurling Final at Croke Park, September 5th 1965. Tipperary, 2-16,
Wexford 0-10.

Team: J. O'Donoghue, John Doyle, M.Maher, K.Carey, M.Burns, A.Wall, L.Gaynor,
T.English, M.Roche, Jimmy Doyle (capt), L.Kiely, L.Devaney, D.Nealon, J.
McKenna, S.McLoughlin.

Kilkenny by the Nore 1967

Anon
Source: *Famous Tullaroan, (O Duill)*

'Twas the third day of September and all-Ireland day as well,
With hurling fans from everywhere, the crowd began to swell.
At three-fifteen, Croke Park was packed like sardines in a tin
And then the six mark question was, 'which team was going to win?

The Munster champions, gallant Tipp, were confident no doubt
And the ninth All-Ireland medal for John Doyle was sticking out.*1
But the Leinster champions said No! No! —He will not get one
more,
We will win today and bring it to Kilkenny by the Nore.

Well you all know what happened—who won and all the rest—
The Kilkenny hurlers proved to all that they were Ireland's best.
And in spite of all the obstacles that Tipp. put in the way,
They crowned themselves with glory on this all-Ireland day.

Now I needn't tell you how they hurled—all that came on the air
From our darling commentator, renowned Micheál Ó hEithir.
Then you read it in the papers so I cannot add much more
To the praise already given to Kilkenny by the Nore.

To the black and amber champions, much more than praise is due,
But I have no more to offer them, so then what can I do.
Only sit here in the armchair with paper and with pen,
And write once more what I said before about our hurling men.

So, good luck to you Kilkenny and may you enjoy the trip,
When you win the world cup against New York, instead of gallant
Tipp.
And remember when you do return, we will welcome you once
more,
Our grand All-Ireland champions, Kilkenny by the Nore.

All -Ireland hurling Final played at Croke Park on Sept. 3, 1967. Kilkenny 3-8, Tipperary, 2-7.

*In this match John Doyle, Holycross, probably the most versatile Tipperary backsman of all times was attempting to win his ninth all-Ireland senior hurling medal. John had already won eight all-Irelands, played in all six back positions, won eleven National League medals, represented Tipperary for nineteen consecutive years, and was never substituted during this period.

Na Ceithre Cúinní

Le Liam Prút
Leabhar: An Giotar Meisce
Foilsitheoir: Coiscéim 1988, lch 14,

Breathnaigh go maith ort féin I gceithre cúinní an scátháin:
Is le dua a fhéachfaidh tú gan náire is fonn reatha ort ó d'áit sa slua
ar Shráid Uí Chonaill
Dhá oiche roimh an gcluiche mór idir Gaillimh is Tiobraid Árann.

B'in tusa ar chlé ag éisteacht le radió comharsan I mbliain a 49;
Tusa agus siceolaíocht gliondair úd uisce athnuaite Thiobraid Árann
(agus Corcaigh scólta!)
B'in tusa.

Annsin tú imeacht idir na camáin bíodh le cúthaile nó le fonn
scórála:
Tusa é sin go neoid tá ag tabhairt na gcor ón slua
sa chúinne ar dheis?
Breathnaigh go maith ort féin do leathmhaoile ródháiríre,
Do dhithneas mallsiúil is do chamán alabaird
Sa triú cúinne.

'S nuair a bhéarfaidh ar do chúinne deiridh
an é cluiche an amadáin clóis agat é
na ceithre cúinní líonta
'S tú fós ar bóiléagar?

Look well at yourself in the four corners of the mirror:
With difficulty will you look without shame and desire to run away
from your place in the crowd.
On O'Connell Street
Two nights before the big match between Galway and Tipperary.

That's you on the left listening to a neighbour's radio in 49;
You and the psychological delight of that renovating Tipperary
water. (and Corcaigh scalded!)
That's you?
Then you escaping between the hurleys either through shyness
or on a scoring spree:
Is it you timidly twisting and turning from the crowd
in the right hand corner?
Look hard at yourself and your overserious half-baldness
Your slow-going urgency and disproportionate hurley
In the third corner.

And when you reach your final corner
Is it still the schoolyard fool's game with you?
The four corners filled
And you still off your guard?

Níochlas Inglis agus laochra eile '87 a spreag an dán seo. Tagraíonn téama an teidil do
chluiche a d'imrímís i seantán clóis na scoile, cúigear ag imirt. Bhíod an cúigiú duine
ag faire ar a dheis mar a tharlaíonn sna cathaoireacha ceoil.

Nicholas English and the other '87 heroes were the inspiration for this poem. The title
theme refers to a game with five participants we use to play in the schoolyard shed in
Cill Bhairrfhinn (Kilbarron). The fifth pupil had to be smart to find a vacancy when
one or other pair or both pairs swopped places.

Champions of '71

By Matt Kirwan
Source: Received from Liam Ó Donnchú, Ballymoreen, Littleton.

'Twas in September, I well remember,
To see the final on Croke Park soil,
When the Munster champions led by Tadhg O'Connor,
Faced the Noreside challenge in epic style.
The anthem over, the backs in places
And Tipp. defending the Clonliffe goal,
Frank Murphy's whistle had barely sounded
When Francis Loughnane snatched a minor score.

Those points he scored with regal splendour
And soon Tipp. pierced the 'barn door'.
Noel O'Dwyer's great goal brought shouts exultant
From lordly Keeper to Galtymore.
Kilkenny's forwards, they fought tenacious,
And Keher found the net once more.
But Tipp'rary's backs and the peerless O'Sullivan,
Reminded us of the days of yore.

The mighty Keating of Ballybacon
And dauntless Ryan from historic Toom,
Oh, how he plied that perfect pass
That gave Moycarkey's Flanagan a major score.
The men of Carrick, they hurled with grandeur,
Mick Roche was there at a vital call
And P.J.Ryan sent our hearts a soaring
As he lofted over a mighty ball.

Kilkenny fought back with goals by Keher,
And one from Purcell that rocked the goal.
But Tipp. came back with fire and fury
As Dinny Ryan flashed home that winning score.
Let's toast Kilruane's Gaynor, Kildangan's Hogan,

And stalwart Gleeson from Moneygall,
Cappawhite's John Kelly, Liam King of Lorrha,
And O'Sullivan, who held many a torrid ball.

Let's toast the champions from sweet Tipp'rary,
Likewise those hurlers from the Nore,
Whose deeds of valour and hurling glories,
Wrote a special page in our Gaelic lore.
Let's toast the men that Davis spoke of,
And for whom Sean Treacy fought and died.
May the Gaelic spirit live on to inspire them,
Those matchless champions from Anner's side.

All-Ireland Hurling Final played at Croke Park, on Sept.5th, 1971. Tipperary, 5-17, Kilkenny, 5-14.

Team: P.O'Sullivan, L.King, J.Kelly, J.Gleeson, T.O'Connor (capt), M.Roche, L.Gaynor, P.J.Ryan, S.Hogan, F.Loughnane, N.O'Dwyer, D.Ryan, J.Flanagan, R.Ryan, M.Keating. Subs: Jimmy Doyle for S. Hogan, P.Byrne for J.Flanagan.

248

Munster Final 1987

By Frank Shanahan
Celtic Park, Dublin

Here's to the heroes who won us acclaim
On the fields of Killarney, oh! 'What a great game'
They beat the proud Corkmen like Tipp'rary of old
A marvellous day, we were in from the cold.

The match it began at half-three on the dong
At a quarter to six Tipp. were still hurling strong.
And the Cork boys who strove to lead for so long,
Were bewitched and bewildered, 'Oh boy! 'What's gone wrong'

Let's start with the goalie, who made 'what a save'
In the Stadium in Thurles, all the fans they did rave.
The Cork forward Kingston, he surely let fly,
But the valiant Ken Hogan pulled it down from the sky.

In the square Con O'Donovan proudly did stand,
So safe and so sure with his hurley in hand.
And Heffernan and Gibson were like a stone wall
When the going was tough, they came out with the ball.

At centre-half-back sure it wasn't a wonder
The Corkmen stood back as John Kennedy did thunder,
With ball on his stick as he cleared it upfield—
The man from Clonoulty was ne'er known to yield.

Our captain tall Stakelum from Borrisoleigh—
He makes us feel proud and fills us with glee
As he sends the ball goalwards, 'Get ready, Get set',
We're in for a score as Cork backs are upset.

There's Paul Delaney from the town of Roscrea,
So dashing and daring, he keeps all at bay.

In charge of the centre Fitzelle and Bonnar
Were holding full sway with style and with honour.

At centre-half forward some heads often roll
As Donie O'Connell takes off for the goal.
While out on the wings with a skill and flair
The style of Jerry Williams and Aidan so fair.

In front of the goal there is no denyin'
The power and the drive of our own Bobby Ryan.
From play and from frees whether near or afar
Pat Fox sends the sliotar right over the bar.

There's English from Cullen so agile and quick,
With one minute to go with the ball on his stick—
As he headed for goal, we all let a roar
For we knew that our 'All Star' was certain to score.

So three cheers for the team, who so hurled with style,
Not forgetting Ger Stapleton, McGrath and Mick Doyle.
Our trainers so brilliant, three heroes of old,
Who knew what is best for the blue and the gold.

This was a very important game for Tipperary because they hadn't won a Munster
Final since 1971. The Tipperary captain, Richard Stakelum, began his victory address
after the game with the memorable words; 'The famine is over'

Team: Ken Hogan, John Heffernan, Conor O'Donovan, Seamus Gibson, Richard
Stakelum (capt), John Kennedy, Paul Delaney, Colm Bonnar, Pat Fitzelle, Gerry
Williams, Donie O'Connell, Aidan Ryan, Pat Fox, Nicky English, Bobby Ryan. Subs:
M.McGrath, M.Doyle, G.Stapleton.

Up the Blue and Gold 1987

By Paddy Power
Source: Liam Ó Donnchú, Ballymoreen, Littleton.
Air: Where the Mulcaire river flows

I'm forced to take my pen again, these few notes to write down
About a group of hurling men, who have brought us great renown.
They brought honour to Tipperary like the teams in days of old—
So now, once more, as oft before, it's three cheers for the blue and
gold.

Huby Hogan's son, to you 'well done, you're a goalie tried and true'
O'Donovan, both brave and strong, his presence they well knew.
While on the wing they fear the swing, of the lad from Kilruane
And on the right, with all his might is the brave John Heffernan.

Our great half line did always shine, John Kennedy was great.
Sure high and low he let them go and Cork soon knew their fate.
From the other side we'll recall with pride, Delaney's great display
And in years to come, they'll be saying 'well done' to the stalwart
from Roscrea.

The Stakelum name is engraved in fame, since the year of forty-nine,
When a man called Pat, then wore the hat, when all the stars used
shine.
Our centre-field, they did not yield, with Bonnar playing so well
And by his side was Cashel's pride, the dauntless Pat Fitzelle.

Our forwards all, both big and small, they did not let us down.
With the Killenaule man for to lead the van, from that place of high
renown.
McGrath and English, the Ryans and Fox, they gave us cause to
smile—
Gerry Williams, Gerry Stapleton and our hero, Michael Doyle.

If I had space, I'd spare no praise of that sturdy boy Joe Hayes.
'Twas in the draw, that his skills we saw as he set the scene ablaze.
To all the subs, I'll say 'well done' and we'll give a loud hurrah
And we'll not forget the part you played, Liam Stokes and John McGrath.

Now your hour has come and the crown is won and we can proudly say
That you played the ball both one and all and carried off the day.
Now raise your glasses up on high and we'll give another cheer.
And we hope to see the McCarthy Cup in the Premier next year.

Celebrating Tipperary's win in the Munster Championship Final 1987.

Team: Ken Hogan, John Heffernan, Conor O'Donovan, Seamus Gibson, Richard Stakelum (capt), John Kennedy, Paul Delaney, Colm Bonnar, Pat Fitzelle, Gerry Williams, Donie O'Connell, Aidan Ryan, Pat Fox, Nicky English, Bobby Ryan. Subs: M.McGrath, M.Doyle, G.Stapleton.

Cluiche Ceannais na Mumhan 1988

Le Liam Prút
Leabhar: Loch Deirg-Dheirc
Foilsitheoir: Coiscéim, lch. 10,11, 1994
Fonn: 'Fuaireasa cuireadh chun dul ag an bposadh!

D'iarrasa ticéad chun dul ag an gcluiche
Fox-tí Nicky-tí Bobby- tí Pa
Is olc a chuaigh an ticéadsan domhsa
Fox-tí Nicky-tí Bobby-tí Pa
Cuiread sa phost é agus d'fág sé an tAonach
Fox-tí Nicky-tí Bobby-tí Pa
Ach chugamsa níor tháinig go raibh sé ródhéanach
Fox-tí Nicky-tí Bobby-tí Pa

Chuas ar an gcluiche 's b'álainn an scór é
Fox-tí Nicky-tí Bobby- tí Pa
Ach níorbh fhada a mhair sin gur ligeadh an tóin as
Fox-tí Nicky-tí Bobby- tí Pa
Tháinig Mac Cnáimhsí agus sheachain mé taom croí
Fox-tí Nicky-tí Bobby- tí Pa
Is bhuaileamar Corcaigh le hiomlán naoi bpointí
Fox-tí Nicky-tí Bobby- tí Pa

Bhí daoine 'na mílte ag faire an lá san
Fox-tí Nicky-tí Bobby- tí Pa
Agus scata go ciúin ann ag faire na bpócaí
Fox-tí Nicky-tí Bobby- tí Pa
Nuair a chríocnaigh an chluiche bhíos déanach don Greyhound
Fox-tí Nicky-tí Bobby- tí Pa
Is d'fhilleas ar an gcathair i mbaclainn na traenach
Fox-tí Nicky-tí Bobby- tí Pa

Bhuaileamar Corcaigh i Luimneach an lá úd
Fox-tí Nicky-tí Bobby- tí Pa
Ach nuair shroicheamar Heuston bhí mo wallet ar iarraidh

Fox-tí Nicky-tí Bobby- tí Pa
An wallet nua zipeach ó Ghlaschú 's mo visa
Fox-tí Nicky-tí Bobby- tí Pa
'S bithiúnach ag baint as go gcuaidh sé as dáta
Fox-tí Nicky-tí Bobby- tí Pa
I dtús mhí na Samhna nó I nDeireadh an Fhómhair
Fox-tí Nicky-tí Bobby- tí Pa

Tháinig mo thicéad chugam maidin Dé Luain
Fox-tí Nicky-tí Bobby- tí Pa
'S bhuaileamar Gaillimh an bhliain a bhí chugainn
Le Fox-tí Nicky-tí Bobby- tí Pa

Tipp's Twenty Third 1989

By John O'Connell, Killenaule
Source: Received from Liam Ó Donnchú, Ballymoreen, Littleton, Thurles.

The famine is finally over; the long years of waiting have passed—
Forget all the tears and the heartbreak, it's time to start cheering at
last.
Liam McCarthy's come home to Tipperary, we've missed him, we
won't say a word,
But we'll carry him down, through famed Thurles Town,
With the boys that won Tipp's Twenty Third.

With big Ken Hogan from Lorrha, John Heffernan, O'Donovan too,
Noel Sheehy and young Conal Bonnar, all staunch Tipperary men
true.
Paul Delaney, Dick Stakelum, John Kennedy, Bobby Ryan, Colm
Bonnar, Joe Hayes,
They all had a say, they showed Tipp the way
Left the great Antrim team in a daze.

Chorus:

It's a team for your record books, that won league and championship
too—
A team all blessed with good looks, and all of them single bar two.
They said they'd do it for Babs, you know he was just one of the
lads,
We'll hang them on the wall; they're the greatest of them all,
The boys that won Tipp's Twenty Third.

The third of the Bonnar's from Cashel, John Leahy, John Cormack
as well,
And the cute little Fox in the corner as John Leamy from Golden can
tell.
On the wing was young Cleary from Nenagh, Aidan Ryan, if he were
in need

255

When we wanted a score, Declan Ryan tossed them o'er,
To put Babs' young babes in the lead.
When we come to O'Connell from that famed little place in the
south,
With English, the genius from Lattin—the greatest, there was no
doubt.
Pat McGrath, Declan Carr and John Madden made up the rest of the
side,
They'll forever remain in Tipp's hall of fame, they brushed all of
Ireland aside.

All-Ireland Hurling Final played at Croke Park, Sept. 3, 1989: Tipperary, 4-24,
Antrim 3-9.

Team—K. Hogan (goal), J. Hefferman, C. O'Donovan, N. Sheehy, Conal Bonnar, B.
Ryan (capt), J. Kennedy, Colm Bonnar, D. Carr, J. Leahy, D. Ryan, M. Cleary,
P. Fox, Cormac Bonnar, N. English. Subs: J. Hayes for Cormac Bonnar, D. O'Connell
for J. Leahy, A. Ryan for M. Cleary.

The author is a brother of Donie O'Connell, who played for many years with
Tipperary and who came on as a sub in this game.

Tipperary-All Ireland Champions 1989

By Gerard Ryan, Inch, Bouladuff, Thurles.
Source: Liam Ó Donnchú, Ballymoreen, Littleton.
Air: The Wearing of the Green. Chorus after second and last verse.

I will sing a song of a hurling team, who all others did outshine,
Tipperary was their birthplace and the year was eighty-nine.
Their grand display on final day was a joy for all to see,
At the end they were the champions and we shouted —victory.

Great teams have won on final day like Mackey and his men,
Kilkenny, Cork and Dublin and the gallant Slaney men.
But when hurling scribes are writing, great moments in our time,
They will have to give a mention to the men of eighty-nine.

Chorus:

Tipperary men around the world
Would like their hands to join,
And sing and sing the praises
Of the men of eighty-nine

All through the year they played so well, they were fit and fast and
clear,
Old timers looked at them in awe, their likes they had seldom seen.
For skill and flair, they could compare with any other time,
They beat the cream and realised our dream in the year of eighty-
nine.

For years and years, we were denied a win on final day,
Defeat upon defeat each time, left our exiles in dismay.
So in New York and Camden Town that September day so fine,
Tipperary men were dewy eyed with the men of eighty –nine.

All-Ireland Hurling Final played at Croke Park, Sept. 3, 1989: Tipperary, 4-24,
Antrim 3-9.

Team—K. Hogan (goal), J. Heffernan, C. O'Donovan, N. Sheehy, Conal Bonnar, B. Ryan (capt), J. Kennedy, Colm Bonnar, D. Carr, J. Leahy, D. Ryan, M. Cleary, P. Fox, Cormac Bonnar, N. English. Subs: J. Hayes for Cormac Bonnar, D. O'Connell for J. Leahy, A. Ryan for M. Cleary.

All-Ireland Champions 1989

By Frank ShanahanCeltic Park, Ave, Dublin.

The weather was good and the sun it did shine
As we won back the cup in nineteen-eighty –nine.
Our opponents were fearless and some were quite bold,
But none could compare with the blue and the gold.

First match was in Cork and Limerick were keen,
We were slightly too good for the boys in the green.
The Decies were next and we'll never forget
That we never succeeded in rattling the net.

Now we marched on to meet the brave men from the West—
The match was supreme but another real test.
We had Galway in trouble and soon in their place
As onwards we swept in the All-Ireland race.

The final was played on the third of September—
We played against Antrim—a day to remember.
The honour was ours with some joy and some tears—
Oh, the joy of it all after so many years.

I'll name all those heroes who played in this game
Who brought to the county such glory and fame.
Ken Hogan in goal was so strong and so brave
Had the eye of a hawk as he brought off each save.

We had Heffernan, Donovan, Sheehy, so true,
A line that was steady and equalled by few.
And Bobby our captain so steady and sure
With the hands of a craftsman and skills that were pure.

To complete our half-back line, two men from the west,
Conal Bonnar and Kennedy stood up to the test.
And young Colm Bonnar with tall Declan Carr
Were masters at mid-field and each one a star.
The skill of our forwards all backlines do fear,
They've speed and have style and are known far and near.
With Cleary and Ryan and young Leahy in flight
A trio of wonder, a hurler's delight.

A full-forward from Cashel, a hero as strong
As the famed Rock itself which has stood for so long.
It's the same clan again—a Bonnar holds sway,
And like old king Cormac he led all the way.

Pat Fox in the corner, another great star,
The power of his play is known near and far.
He darts from his minder—another great score
Reminding us all of the forwards of yore.

Nick English an 'All Star' with style and with flair
A talented star and with skills that were rare.
He dodged and he danced as he weaved on his way,
A master at work and a master at play.

Roscrea's Paul Delaney had quite a big say
In the honour and glory that now came our way.
Our subs. they were part of the team and the fold
That brought all Tipperary right in from the cold.

The deeds of our trainers, there's no need to tell
Donie Nealon and ' Babs' and brave Theo as well.
Three cheers for our hurlers, cheer each one and all
We can never forget but we'll ever recall.

May they long play together in many a game,
For the honour and glory of Tipp'rary's great name;
And when the great reaper will call us away—
May we all meet in heaven on some distant day.

All-Ireland Hurling Final played at Croke Park, Sept. 3, 1989: Tipperary, 4-24, Antrim 3-9.

Team—K. Hogan (goal), J. Heffernan, C. O'Donovan, N. Sheehy, Conal Bonnar, B. Ryan (capt), J. Kennedy, Colm Bonnar, D. Carr, J. Leahy, D. Ryan, M. Cleary, P. Fox, Cormac Bonnar, N. English. Subs: J. Hayes for Cormac Bonnar, D. O'Connell for J. Leahy, A. Ryan for M. Cleary.

The Gallant Tipperary Boys 1989

By Davy Cormack, Killenaule
Source: Received from Liam Ó Donnchú, Ballymoreen, Littleton, Thurles

Some say that the 'premier days are gone
And that Knocknagow lived only in song
But we're hungry no more,'cos the famine is o'er
We're there again sounder than Slievenamon.
So hurrah! For the gallant Tipp'rary boys,
Whose sound of the clash of the ash never dies,
After eighteen long years, we can dry up our tears—
The McCarthy is back in Tipp'rary boys.

To fearless Ken Hogan the net we entrust,
To guard with his life and he knows that he must.
Sheehy, Conor and Heffo, who'd face the Gestapo
Made many a forward line bite the dust.
Centre-half Bobby Ryan proudly captains our men
And he's flanked by young Bonnar and Kennedy John.
And if they're to be bet! Then we'll have to get
Langton, Mackey and Ringey to rise again.

And from the centre-field, Declan Carr so tall,
Straight over the bar, he can send the ball.
When they see Colm's worth, he'll be called to the North
To teach them the art up in Donegal.
Declan Ryan is a striker of brawn and bone,
All over the pitch, you can see him roam.
And beside him two giants, for picking off points
Young Cleary and Leahy from Mullinahone.

Up front we've the boys to bamboozle the backs,
As they palm to each other, when in round the box.
All three have scored shoals of magnificent goals—
Nick English, King Bonnar and sly Pat Fox.
Madden, Cormack and Leamy all answered the call,

Pat McGrath, Aidan Ryan and we can't leave out Paul.
Richard Stakelum, so fair and Joe Hayes debonair
And our own dashing Donie from Killenaule.

And there on the bench were the Three Wise Men—
Yes! They brought us back cross the desert again.
The joy from despair, so we'll end with this prayer,
Babs, Theo and Donie, 'God bless you' amen.'
So hurrah for the gallant Tipp'rary boys
Whose sound of the clash of the ash never dies.
After eighteen long years, we can dry up our tears—
The McCarthy is back in Tipp'rary boys.

Last Verse: Babs, Theo and Donie, refer to the selectors, Michael Keating, Theo
English, and Donie Nealon. All three were legendary Tipperary hurlers.

Ó Muircheartaigh's Miracle

By Garry .Fitzgerald, Tipperary Town.
Received from Liam Ó Donnchú, Balymoreen, Littleton.

Far away from Thurles town on Munster Final day
The wireless was our only hope of joining in the fray.
Le Harve is a long way off across the foaming sea
But Micheál Ó Muircheartaigh was there along with R.T.E.

We switched her on at throw in time to hear the self-same man—
But all we got was static, like rashers on a pan.
We turned knobs and aerials and did our best to clear it
And Micheál Ó Muircheartaigh sure we couldn't hear it.

At half past five, that's French time, the rashers quietened down,
Our joy at getting R.T.E. became a dreadful frown.
'O God, I don't believe it, are they selling us a pup'?
Micheál Ó Muircheartaigh had said that Cork were nine points up.

With higher mathematics we analysed this figure,
And came to the conclusion 'twas no smaller nor no bigger.
No matter how you looked at it, in France or Thurles town,
Than if Ó Muircheartaigh had said that Tipp. were nine points down.

The brilliant Gallic sunshine was soon replaced by rain,
And holidaying Carrick men were jumping in the Seine
The French police, the Gendarmes had never seen the likes
As Micheál Ó Muircheartaigh just said that Cork were on their bikes.

An old boy from Tipperary town took up the kitchen knife,
To plunge it in his saddened heart to end this hopeless life,
But first a pint in Corny's, he did things by the book,
As Micheál Ó Muircheartaigh now said, 'Poor Tipp. are looking
shook'.

A Bansha farmer kissed his wife, said goodbye to his dear daughters,
And headed slowly out the door and towards the foaming waters.
His last words to his missus were, 'I'll never stick it out',
As Micheál Ó Muircheartaigh then said, 'Tis looking like a rout'.

As if it wasn't bad enough that Nicky wasn't playing,
Auld ones from Clogheen took their beads and then they started
praying.
Their sons were drinking poison some time before they died,
To the tune of Muirceartaigh's refrain, 'They'll never stem the tide'.

That Cork would win and do us in, there seemed to be no doubt,
The red and white now rampant and the bookies paying out.
And not a sound from Tipp men, the county in a daze,
'Begod now', says Ó Muircheartaigh, 'They're bringing in Joe
Hayes'.

Ryans and Dwyers and Gleesons, the Heffernans, O'Mearas,
Were swept away in France that day, so far from Toomevara.
In Thurles town some men with guns were heading for the gate,
'Whisht now', says Ó Muircheartaigh, 'Pat Fox has made it eight'.

Saint Wedger Meagher in Paradise Bar, of this had gotten weary,
The Lord above looked down with love on Babs and Michael Cleary.
The saint slipped one to Declan Ryan—a point, a gift from heaven
Micheál Ó Muircheartaigh then said, 'And now 'tis only seven'.

The skies came clear, the sun spun round, we heard the angels play
The sweetest kind of music—another on the way.
A voice cried out from Thurles, 'Good man Pat Fox you whore'
Micheál Ó Muircheartaigh then said that six was now the score.

Divine in-ter-vention in hurling isn't rare,
And its use in Munster finals is deemed to be quite fair.
The Fox then scored that magic goal, designed celestially,
Micheál Ó Muircheartaigh then said, 'And now 'tis only three'.

The light that came from up above found Carr from Holycross,
Who saw his hurley lengthen and broaden at the bas.
He goaled from higher altitude, 'Take that and shame the devil'
Micheál Ó Muircheartaigh then said, 'And now the sides are level'.

Bobby Ryan and Delaney, Mick Ryan and Sheedy thundered,
The Bonnars drove out everything, the forwards struck and
plundered.
Hogan's saves were epic as Joe Hayes gave it his all,
And then we heard Ó Muircheartaigh sing, 'The Hills of Killenaule'.

The rest you know, as our great foe were burnt in Leahy's fire,
Through Cleary, Ryan and Bonnar, our tally mounted higher.
Said Aidan Ryan of Borrisoleigh; 'You ain't seen nothing yet'
Micheál Ó Muircheartaigh then roared, 'Sin cúl and Cork are bet'

The lads who went for drowning found the tide it wasn't in–
The knives were blunt, the bullets blank, the poison only gin.
The widows from Clogheen had reached the second joyful mystery,
As Micheál Ó Muircheartaigh told of Tipp men making history.

Many famous victories for Tipp one can recall,
And each man has his special one that's greater than them all.
One day we heard a miracle like Fatima or Knock,
From Micheál Ó Muircheartaigh–'Fair play to you auld stock'.

Munster Hurling Final replay at Semple Stadium on July 21, 1991. Tipperary 4-19,
Cork 4-15. Nicky English was out due to hamstring trouble.
Team: Ken Hogan, Paul Delaney, Noel Sheehy, Michael Ryan, John Madden, Bobby
Ryan, Conal Bonnar, Declar Carr (capt), Colm Bonnar, Declan Ryan, Donie
O'Connell, John Leahy, Pat Fox, Cormac Bonnar, Michael Cleary. Subs: Aidan Ryan,
Joe Hayes.

All-Ireland Hurling Final 1997

By Cathal O'Reilly, 211 Woodpark, Ballinteer Ave, Dundrum, Dublin 16
Air: 'Are Ye Right There Michael?

You may talk of Art Foley's great save boys
From the late, great, lamented Chris. Ring.
Last Sunday we peeped in the grave, boys
It's of Davy Fitzgerald I sing.
Our hero in blue guards his charge , boys
As Daly in dark days of yore,
On the high windy hilltop of Tulla,
He can rest peaceful for evermore.

In the sixty-ninth minute of time, boys
The Mullinahone men combined.
O'Meara picked out Johnny Leahy,
Remember they're one point behind.!
Then Johnny unleashed a fierce shot, boys
With GOAL!!! stamped all over the ball
But picked up again it just read, boys
O'Neills, made in Dublin, that's all.

Oh many a year by the Shannon,
The Fergus, The Bridge and Cratloe,
You'll hear how young Davy Fitzgerald
Helped the Banner to slay the old foe.
Victory is sweeter when hard won
And won on the double as well
As on the lush greensward of "Croker"
The Galway and Tipp lads all fell.

Verses to commemorate a remarkable save in the 69th minute of the All-Ireland
hurling final 1997, Clare v Tipperary by David Fitzgerald, Clare's goalkeeper.

We Believe in Hurling

Paul Durcan: 'We Believe in Hurling' from Greetings to Our Friends in Brazil.
First published in Great Britain in 1999 by Harvill. © Paul Durcan, 1999.
Reproduced by permission of the Harvill Press.

I have such a craving for thee, O Donal Óg
Because you praise my days with hurling deeds;
When you make leaps with your back to the goals
Plucking high balls out of teeming skies
To hurl them low between the posts;
Deeds alone are certain good.

3.15p.m. Sunday afternoon
In the bar of the Slievemore Hotel
On the side of the flapping mountain
Pegged down in cloud.
Red-eyed with grief, perched
On a high stool at the bar
I am staring up into a blank screen

Will nobody switch it on-
The TV up there on its black bracket?
Have I come out in vain
In the gale and the rain?
Do none of you here believe
In the All Ireland Hurling final
Between Tipperary and Clare?

If I ask-if I ask
The man behind the bar
To switch on the television
Will he? My scepticism
Whispers. Maybe he will not.
He smiles a barman's Japanese smile.
Pictures alight on the screen

Like birds on the bough.
The woods of Croke Park are alive!
The hurlers of Tipperary and Clare
Are warming up in the goals.
Like young fillies at Ascot
At the starting gate prancing;
All halters, all helmets.

For seventy deluged minutes
I do not budge from my stool.
 I roost on my stool
Making faces at the screen;
Big faces, little faces
At each orbit of the earth trajectory of the ball;
Catch, cut, puck, double, solo, hop.

These are the boys who were born
To sweeten and delight;
To bejewel and beautify.
I laugh, I gasp, I frown.
At the final whistle
I jump down to my feet,
Hug myself.

I stride over to the TV.
I stand under its black bracket
Gazing up at the Great Loughnane
Being interrogated about the game.
Tears alight in my eyes
As I listen to him rhapsodize
That it was the game that won the game.

He cries: 'The game of hurling
Is pure poetry.
Pure inspiration. Pure technique.
Hurling won the game today.
Not Tipperary, not Clare.

Today we saw the greatest game
Of hurling we will ever see'

I stride out of the bar
Into the gale and the rain
And I hasten off up into the mountain
Bareheaded, open-necked
Into the fuchsia, into the montbretia;
Into the stick-boss solitudes:
As free as a man can ever be.

Hurling is the father of freedom
When Jamesie O'Connor with a minute to go
At full tilt in the middle of the park
Pointed for Clare
Spacemen on *Mir* saw Planet Earth
Fly up out of its tree.
The hurler strikes, and man is free.

I have such a craving for thee, O Donal Óg
Because you praise my days with hurling deeds;
When you make leaps with your back to the goals
Plucking high balls out of teeming skies
To hurl them low between the posts;
Deeds alone are certain good.

All Ireland Senior Hurling Final, Clare (0-20), Tipperary (2-13) at Croke Park, 14
September 1997.

Camogie Champions '99

By Paddy Arrigan, Galway (formerly Tipperary)
Source: Received from Liam Ó Donnchú, Ballymoreen, Littleton.

Let history record what the country has seen
The O'Duffy Cup won by a gallant fifteen
They played for their county with honour and pride
And carried the cup to the sunny Suir side

The fifth of September in the year ninety-nine
Is a day to remember forever in time
When the girls appeared in the blue and the gold
And outshone all the heroines of Erin of old.

There was Gaynor the bold and Nealon the brave
With Stokes as their captain had many a save
Delaney a stalwart, she guarded the goal
And played the full game with stout heart and great soul.

Siobhán Kelly was mighty and O'Dwyer was so true
And Madden was crafty and knew what to do.
Hayden, McDermott and Brophy were sound
And Kiely, no doubt, helped as well to hold ground.

Where would we be without Deirdre Hughes?
She dummied and skipped and she tried every ruse.
And when at the finish, they tallied her score
Four points to her credit and with luck would have more.

Kennedy pointed with style and panache
One look at the goal and she'd give it a lash.
She put five to the total—her name will go down
In the annals of sport in Tipp'rary town.

Kiely was off and young Fogarty on
And Hennessy subbed when Harkin was gone

Stokes rallied the team—'we'll never give up
Till we master Kilkenny and bring home the cup'.

Hennessys two and McDonnells one
Made up the twelve and Tipp'rary had won.
Their names will be chiselled in song and in story
For they won for their county more honour and glory.

EPILOGUE

As the sunbeams still shine on the lovely Suir stream
There's a name that inspired this victorious team
With her wisdom and knowledge of playing the ball
The bold Biddy Phillips, mother of them all.

This was Tipperary's first senior camogie All-Ireland win. Tipperary, 0-12, Kilkenny, 1-8. Played at Croke Park on the 5th September 1999.

Team: Jovita Delaney, Suzanne Kelly, Una O'Dwyer, Claire Madden, Méadhbh Stokes (Capt), Ciara Gaynor, Sinéad Nealon, Emily Hayden, Angela McDermott, Noelle Kennedy, Therese Brophy, Helen Kiely, Emer McDonnell, Deirdre Hughes Niamh Harkin. Subs: Louise Ryan, Caitríona Hennessy, Philomena Fogarty, Sheena Howard, Maria Harkin.

Team Manager: Biddy Phillips.

272

PART THREE

Club Victories
and Rivalries

ALL-IRELAND MEDAL
1945

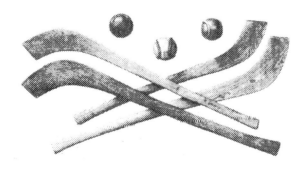

Toor v Templederry

By Tom O'Brien
Source: By the Mulcaire Banks—The Story of the GAA in the parish of Newport by
Michael Collins and Denis Floyd.

You manly sons of famed Newport
Come listen to my rural sport
A football team we will support
From Keeper, Toor and Blane.
It was of late we did arrive
From schoolboy chaps to men and boys
And now the county we defy
For a fair do on the plain.

It being upon the first of March
Our Gaelic sons in numbers large
Opposed the North Tipperary charge
In the Templederry shade.
We left our homes at half-past nine
To hire a brake from Henry Ryan
And made a coachman of Tom Brien
To drive the bold brigade.

'Twas Lanty Ryan and Luke McQuaid
Who went with me to hire the brake
But Luke got nervous for to spake
And soon made for the door.
So I took up the tender job
I spoke to Henry at the hob
Saying,'I'll go and harness up the cob
And make our business sure'.

We steered our coach as smooth as glass
To be in line for Reamore mass
Pat Hanlon rode Dan Duggan's ass
As far as Mick the Mowers.

'Twas there the rider loudly bawled
'Be cripes, says he, ''tis a woeful scald
I'm just beginning for to gall
My gable end is sore'.

So then the jock dismounted there
And walked with me to the cross of Rea
To congregate with members there
Who had lately joined our corps.
They all admired our pack of boys
All from one mountainside to rise
They'll surely burst the galvanise
Today in famed Reamore

We did our duty there alright
Then buckled up the harness tight
And used the whip both left and right.
'Till we landed on the scene.
The day of sport being rather rough
Our own cool boys jumped in their buff
And showed Lower Ormond play enough
Before they left the green.

The first half-hour they played the ball
Lower Ormond took the wind and fall
Though they had nothing for the call
When they reached the change of ground.
But when they changed you'd hear the strain
Of shouts for Keeper, Toor and Blane
Each man declared they'd beat them clean
On Toor I'd stake a pound.

This was a well-contested fight
The odds on either side were light
Though it was the Templederry's might
That day to lead the van.
Their shouts soon changed to awful howls

274

As our Toor boys gave them woeful scowls
And made black saucepans of their bowels
Though they had man for man.

'Twas near Kilcommon this went on
The cheers were heard on Foilnamon
And every Harry, Dick and Tom
Went to view the gas.
By Curreeney then we drove them out
The Curreeney boys they raised the shout
And we drank a pint of Adam's stout
Going down by Garryglass.

So now my feeble pen I'll sink
Being scarce in paper and in ink
That Templederry hung a link
For triumph they were late.
I own they fought like gallant men
But still to Toor they should give in
With the Union brand upon their shin
Which ends the whole debate.

A football game played in Kilcommon, (Above Rearcross, between Toor and
Templederry) in the early years of the Association . The author later emigrated to
Chicago where he became a policeman.

The Famous De Wets 1906

By Michael Mackey, Nenagh
Source:Kilruane MacDonaghs and Lahorna De Wets 1878-1916
Received from Seamus J. King, Boherclough, Cashel
Air: The Connaught Ranger. Chorus after each verse:

There is a team with gallant men
When playing you'd like to see them!
None can stand with that noble band
That loves the cause of freedom.
The name De Wet, victorious yet
With staunch determination,
With honour bold they mean to hold
The county's reputation.

Chorus.

Unconquered yet are you De Wet
Oh may you never vary,
The magic name that gained such fame
For gallant Tipperary.

Just see them when they place their men
With tactics like Napoleon:
And famous Brewer, whose stroke is sure,
To drive a point or goal in.
From far and near you'll ever hear,
The people sound the praises
Of brave De Wet, that will be yet
Renowned in history's pages.

The Clare men came and tried to gain
The medal prize so glorious
The Limerick team, they were I ween
Quite sure of being victorious.
To see that day De Wets' display

It filled the crowds with rapture
And now they wear the medals rare
Of Irish manufacture.

Oh may that team forever feel
Good strength to strike the leather:
And may they stand hand in hand
United well together.
May every game be crowned in fame
And may they never weary
But still remain the honoured name
In gallant Tipperary.

By 1900 hurling was played in every area of Cloughjordan parish. It was then decided to enter a team from the Lahorna area, which would embrace the whole parish of Cloughjordan for the newly formed North Tipperary championship for the year 1901. The team was called Lahorna De Wets in memory of the famous South African general De Wet, who had given the British forces such a rough time in the Boer War (1899-1902)

In February 1906.the Nenagh GAA club held a church tournament for seventeen medals. The teams were to be De Wets v Tulla (Co. Clare), Castleconnell (Limerick) and Coolderry (Offaly). The score in the final was De Wets, 5-10, Castleconnell, 2-6. Lahorna De Wets'team—J. Dwan, (capt), M. Conway, C. Brewer, D. Whelan, M & J Darcy, Tom Ryan, P. Kennedy, M. Maher, Dan Ryan, D. Hogan, J. Meara, P. Williams, M. McLoughney, T. Ryan, M. Walsh, Mick Reddan.

Lamogue v Grangemockler 1912
(Also entitled the Mocklers)

By George E.Glendon
Source: Received from Liam Ó Donnchú, Ballymoreen, Littleton

'Twas a glorious fine morning the thirteenth of May
To sweet Carrick town we all started away
With horses and donkeys and good old shanks mare
We travelled to witness a great contest there.

That Lamogue and Grangemockler each other defied
Was settled in Carrick, all bluff to decide
With plenty of money in country and town
Was plunged on those heroes of such great renown.

That Lamogue were the favourites there seemed no denying
The Mocklers were backed as they toed the line
John Power held the whistle to show them fair play
And right well he used it upon that great day.

About four o'clock he the ball to them threw
And at it like bulldogs around it they flew
They were scrambling and tearing, heels high in the air
And men flying like matches about everywhere.

Like demons and Trojans the both teams then fought
And attacked and repelled each successive onslaught
In less than ten minutes Lamogue a point scored
'Another', 'Another' their backers encored.

And yet with another their fame did renew
For those chicken hearted it looked rather blue
'They're winning', 'They're winning' Kilkenny did roar
Little dreaming for them their surprise was in store.

In the midst of the cheering Grangemockler then stole
And quickly registered a point and a goal.

'Ha'. said the Tipps, ' Our time has now come'
Lamogue were dismayed and their backer struck numb.

For they never suspected to see such a score
That made both teams level and the onlookers roar
But the Mocklers were heroes who never gave in
They had one thought that day and that was to score.

The Mocklers fresh mettle put into their work
Not a man on that team for a second did shirk.
They worked like good fellows and upheld the name
That crowned old Grangemockler with laurels of fame.

Grangemockler were County Senior Football Champions in 1907 beating Cashel.
Grangemockler were also one of the best football sides around in the county in 1912
and they played challenges and tournaments against a team called Lamogue, next door
neighbours on the Kilkenny side. The club is now known as Windgap. Lamogue had
one of the best football sides in Leinster at a certain period, benefiting from
employment in the slate quarries.

The Templemore Young Irelands 1913

Anon:
Source: G.A.A. History of Clonmore, Killea and Templemore, 1884-1988 by Martin
Bourke. Received from Seamus J. King, Boherclough, Cashel.
Air: The wearing of the Green
Chorus after each verse

On the seventeenth of August, in Thurles town so fair
Our Templemore young heroes went with hearts as light as air
To meet the Arravale Rovers, it's the third time they did meet,
But captain Connolly's gallant men soon ran them off their feet.

Then hurrah for the boys of Templemore may your banners never
fail
You beat the Arravale Rovers by two goals two points to nil.
You're a credit to your country, better match was never seen
For you're the boys know how to score in your colours white and
green.

For some years past you have not played, not through causes of your
own
For good men from Templemore now in foreign lands do roam
But they just got up another team as good as the one of yore
And called them brave Young Irelands from the town of
Templemore.

Success to Kelly and McGrath, Maher, Jack Carroll too–
Gleeson, Shelly and Dot Wright, Fogarty and Paddy Newe.
For the whistle it has blown, you are off just at the sound
And the ball it flies in front of ye like a hare before the hounds.

Give three cheers for Paddy Davern, that hero tried and true.
Grant, Dwyer and Arthur Carroll, they are the boys know what to do.
And likewise Jeffrey Garvan between the posts he stands
And if it was a cannon ball, he'd stop it with his hands.

Now to conclude my little song I bid you all adieu
You'd show'd the Arravale Rovers what the Young Ireland boys can
do.
Once you were defeated, it's plain for to be seen
So three cheers for the boys from Templemore in their colours white
and green.

Arravale Rovers won the first game but a replay was ordered after an objection by
Templemore. Templemore won the second game and a replay was again ordered after
an objection by Arravale Rovers. This second replay took place on the 17th August.
Templemore won by 2-2 to 0-2.

Team: W. Grant (capt), John Dwyer, Jim Shelly, J. Garvey, Jack O'Dea, W. Fogarty,
W. Maher, J. O'Connell, A. Carroll, M. Carroll (goal), F. Bermingham, J. Connolly,
W. McGrath, Paddy Davoren, P. Newe.

The Mullinahone 'Fifteen' 1916

Anon:
Source: Dan Herlihy and received from Liam Ó Donnchú, Ballymoreen, Littleton

The championship they entered in nineteen and sixteen
Where're you go, you'll easily know the Mullinahone 'fifteen'
They bet Clonmel and Fethard and Bansha they put down
And the Commons got a bad knock- out from the boys of Kickham's town.

They marched on to the field—by their captain they were led
Their splendid jerseys shining–'twas the green above the red.
They shook hands with their opponents before they tossed the coin
And the order was to 'line up boys' and then they toed the line.

The referee's whistle sounded and the ball went into play
Like thunder from the clouds above, big Magner tore away.
He passed the ball to 'Boggan'—you all know that big giant
Who lashed it o'er the crossbar for Mullinahone's first point.

The Commons forced it back again; Ned Egan was too quick
He raced on to the sideline, where he passed it to Jack Kick,
Who let the ball to Crotty, when Bill Vaughan let a roar
And the ball went in between the posts and we had a major score.

God rest you now Ned Egan, you were never known to slack
You were known throughout the county as the Mullinahone fullback.
You played on many a Gaelic field and never let us down
You were our gallant captain who lived near Kickham's town.

Chorus:

And when those boys win the day
Old women from their beds
Will raise the latch up to the thatch
And shout—'Come on the Reds'.

282

There was never such excitement when Bill Barrett began to run
Like a lightning flash, there came a dash, from the famous 'Bugler Dunne'
Before the game was finished, there was never seen such rain
Pad Egan tore across the field for Denny's aeroplane.

Going home through Grangemockler, they frightened all the cows
And scattered Mrs. Freaney's hens going in by Nine-Mile-House.
They whistled at Mickey Denny saying, 'try and keep her going,
For we must attend a fowl market in a place called Mullinahone.

Junior Football County Champions 1916. 'In 1916, a year of great struggle and strife in Ireland, Mullinahone had another year of glory. The football team of that year from Kickham's Town were described as unstoppable. They beat Clonmel in Grangemockler by 2-2 to 0-3 and followed that victory by beating Fethard 1-3 to 1-1. The final, which was delayed, resulted in a great win for Mullinahone over Bansha by 1-2 to 1-1. A feature of the Mullinahone team of those times was the appearance of five brothers on the side, the Egan brothers from Poulacapple, Ned, Jim, Paddy, Martin and Peter. At one period seven of the Egan brothers played on the C.J.Kickham team. They were sons of John Egan a great supporter of Maurice Davin and Michael Cusack in the early days of the Association.' (*Slievenamon in Song and Story* —Editor, Sean Nugent 1996)

Hurler on the Ditch

By Francis Phillips: Source: Cashel and Rosgreen GAA History
(by Séamus J. King, Boherclough, Cashel) 1985

I'd like to see Boherlahan knocked out
And reeled and wheeled and pitched about,
And their complete defeat and rout,
Today in Littleton.

I'd like to see them vanquished all,
Both back and front and sticks and ball
And then their pride would get a fall
Today at Littleton.

I'd like to see their flag hauled down,
Their name and fame and great renown
Swept onward into Thurles town
Today in Littleton.

I'd like to see each boasted son
In aimless fight and breathless run
Subdued as if by Mauser gun
Today in Littleton.

I'd like to hear the cheering throng
Cry out, 'They're bet' both loud and long
There give some bard a theme for song
Today in Littleton.

And every victory in the past,
Be changed to grief, quick, thick and fast,
So all could say, 'They've played their last'
Today at Littleton

In spite of all my froth and foam,
Boherlahan unrivalled, stands alone,
While on the ditch I cry ochone!
Today in Littleton.

Written on the occasion of the 1917 mid-championship final between Boherlahan and Thurles played on Sunday July 22nd at Littleton.

Shamrock Hurling Team 1917

By Michael Bourke
Source: Newport in Song and Poetry
Published by the Michael Bourke Festival Committee

At the foot of Keeper mountain
In a vale of verdant green
Stands the little town of Newport,
By the Mulcaire's sparkling stream.
There dwells as brave a lot of lads
As ever donned the green,
They're the pride of North Tipperary,
The Shamrock hurling team.

Chorus:
Then go to the good old Shamrocks,
Draw your camáns strong and keen,
You're the cream of Ireland's hurling men
The Shamrock hurling team.

God speed the brave O'Carrolls,
Dan Troy and Paddy Ryan,
Bill Kennedy and Benton
In future days will shine.
The Coffeys and Aherns,
Scotty Berkery and Jack Mack,
Are all determined home to bring
Our long lost laurels back.

When I see them on the hurling field
My old heart thrills with pride,
It reminds me of my boyhood days
Down by the Mulcaire's side.

They're tall and straight with manly gait,
Their faces tanned and brown,
They are loved by all the colleen's fair
Round lovely Newport town.

Give a cheer for bold Con Coffey,
To him all honour's due,
Well may the Gaels of Newport
Be proud of men like you.
We'll sing your praise in simple lays,
O'er mountain, glen and stream
May God guard that fearless little band,
The Shamrock hurling team.

In 1917 there was a divergence of views in the Newport club. The result was the emergence of a second team called Newport Shamrocks. Newport and Newport Shamrocks were drawn against each other in the first round of the junior championship. The North Board felt that the draw was unsatisfactory and so accepted late affiliations from Birdhill and Garrykennedy and the draw was then re-arranged.

Shannon Rovers v the Pike 1919

By Joe Ruttledge
Source: Lorrha and Dorrha GAA by Séamus J. King, Boherclough, Cashel

The anxious crowd is gathering fast
And as the hour draws near,
The Major steps up to his men,
They greet him with a cheer.

'Be quick me lads take off your coats
You cannot now delay,
For the honour of old Redwood,
Lies in your hands today'

Will Oakmore dressed in colours green
He caught the Major's eye,
'We cannot let you hurl today
But we'll let you by and by'

Poor Willie turned, his heart was sad,
'Ye told me to prepare
Why did ye make me wash meself?
And to shave and cut me hair?'

'Hold your tongue', says Mrs.Lang,
'Did you ever hear such stuff?
How can I make the bloomers?
When you didn't bring the stuff?'

Fleet as deer they make the field,
And look at such a crowd,
All Redwood felt triumphant,
And of their team felt proud.

The whistle sounds, the match begins,
The ball travels fast and slow.

Willie Tracy guards the Redwood goals,
And on the wing is Cos-tello.

O'Brien he gets the ball and shoots
Into the Redwood goals.
Willie tries to save and miss,
The Pikemen have a goal.

Three times the Pikemen score a goal,
Each Redwood face is pale,
By fierce attacks on Kaffir's men,
They try to turn the scale.

'What can I do to stop the ball?'
Poor Willie Treacy cried,
'The Major is so big and broad,
He's always in the light'

Dinny Brett, a man of four foot six,
Some say he's not so tall,
His eyes were on the girls fixed,
And he heeded not the ball.

For Din he was an umpire bold,
Who had to hoist the green flag,
Whenever Redwood scored a goal,
And not to act the gag.

There was a lovely maid there,
With eyes of charming blue,
He could not resist her smile,
O Denis boy, not you.

The match continued furiously,
And the ball travelled to and fro.
Old Redwood were defeated,
When the long whistle blew.

The hurling was over, the boys were dry
Right merrily they drank,
While Tony in the bar he sold,
His counter was a plank.

They crowded round and called for more,
He served without delay,
The flyboys in the crowd made sure,
They did not pay their way.

Never more a barman can he
Be on a hurling day,
For fifty bob and two half barrels,
I think it would not pay.

Revenge is sweet and soon again
Redwood will strike the ball,
Then you shall hear, the cry shall be
Old Redwood over all.

The words had been lost but many were rediscovered through the good work of Tom Lambe.

Football Memories of Kilsheelan

By Bill O'Keeffe
Source: Cill Sioláin-100 Years and More of Gaelic Games in the Parish of Kilsheelan
and Kilcash 1884-1988. Received from Seamus J. King, Boherclough, Cashel.
Air: The Boys from the County Cork

Full twenty years my thoughts go back to times of long ago
When as a carefree boy I roved where Suir and Anner flow
And clear against the skyline stood out lordly Slievenamon
To guard with pride a valley fair as ere the sun shone on.

Where often in the evening when the day's hard work was done
We gathered into Christy's for a chat, or bit of fun.
We played 'fifteen' or 'twenty five' to help us pass the night
And trees we felled and cut in logs to keep the home fires bright.

'Twas here a thought was born to have a football club.
So we talked and talked at Christy's and sometimes in the pub.
Bill Cummins, Andy, Christy, 'The Bunk' and Michaleen Burke,
Jim Fleming, Larkins, Coadys, all helped in the good work.

A team we strung together and to Ballyneale we went
A victory to our credit, then for honours we were bent.
At Clonmel, Fethard, Carrick, Cloneen, and Templemore,
The 'Blues' raised high their standards and added to their score.

Mick Doyle a man of judgment, stood then between the sticks,
He saved our bacon often, this little man of tricks.
And then in front stood Michael Strappe, a stonewall stout and
strong,
His fifties saved us more than once and seldom he did wrong.

Pat Larkin and Bill Reilly then flanked him on each side,
Their speed and clever footwork oft filled our hearts with pride.
Tom Kennedy from Ballydine at centre-half was game—
He caught and kicked some lengthy balls and always played the
same.

291

Jack Commins and Bill Larkin were dashing stringy men:
Faith you wouldn't find their equal then in mountain-home or glen.
The Cahills, Will and Tommy, who inches perhaps did lack,
But when the knocks came good and hard, Tom always gave one
back.

Jack Cullinane and bold 'Ebby' were men to do and dare,
And when the ball came high to Jack, he fisted in the air.
Jim Fleming and Jim Mitten were swift and clean and neat,
They drove the leather smoothly on, for both had lovely feet.

'Sticky' Reilly was a trier and when the game was done
Looked fresh as a new-born daisy just opened to the sun.
The 'Rajah' for his cuteness was famous far and wide,
As the goalman sought the leather, 'Rajah' slipped it past his side.

The lad from Toper was hard to beat; he feared not friend or foe,
And when he rose to field the ball the shout was 'style Cho'.
The Keeffes who led the forwards were quick and crafty too,
And Jerry's left was deadly as he banged the leather through.

The 'Mot' was then a nipper, not big, and yet not small,
In later years he proved to be the daddy of them all.
Con Lonergan, God rest him, was as good a man and bold
As ere travelled with the village to don the blue and gold.

We didn't travel swanky in those golden far-off days,
We had just Jack Culley's lorry with rough seats and wooden stays.
Dick Cahill was proud to take the wheel and as we rode along,
We talked about our prospects or broke into rousing song.

My thoughts roam now to training days when nights fall dark and
chill,
As we cantered past Jack Daniel's Cross and down the Chapel Hill.
Then later on we sprinted down a stretch of Dick Bourke's land
With two carbide lamps to guide us, for you couldn't see your hand.

Now 'Shackleton' our trainer kept us fit as men could be,
And he prided in our conquests for a sterling Gael was he.
The chairman too, Jim Coffey, kept a strict and careful watch,
While Bill Toole with Holy Water blessed the boys before a match.

I feel I must remember to those men of older days,
Who never failed to give support and cheer us on our ways.
'Mauk' Cahill with his merry laugh, John Coady and Jim Strappe,
The 'Dee' from Kilsheelan, Tommy Kelly in his trap.

We won the county championship and Fr. Synott's league.
We played matches oft in mid-week but ne'er suffered from fatigue.
I think of all the teams we met to combat in those days,
The gallant men of Powerstown were our worthiest foes always.

Now some of those old stalwarts never left their native home;
While some have wandered far away and some have crossed the foam.
Some too, have found an early grave in mother Erin's breast,
May God have mercy on their souls and grant eternal rest.

1924 was an historic year for GAA activities in the parish of Kilsheelan/Kilcash. A great revival began with the forming of a new club with a proper administration structure, officers and the appointment of a committee. The subject of forming of a club had been discussed many times. Eventually a meeting was held in Christy Connolly's, Kilsheelan, and amongst those who attended were, C. Connolly, J. Coffey, W. Cummins, J. Strappe, W. O'Toole, P. Larkin, W. Larkin, J. Cody, J. J. Cody, W. O'Keeffe, D. Burke, M. Burke, A. Doherty.-Kilsheelan are credited with winning the county junior football titles in 1924 and 1925. In 1925 they be the Mid Tipp selection by 1-1 too 0-1.
1925 team: P.Larkin (capt), M. Doyle (goal), W. Larkin, M. Strappe, W. O'Reilly, C. Lonergan, J. Cullinane, E. Butler, J. Fleming, M. Kehoe, J. Cody, J. O'Reilly, W. O'Keeffe, J. O'Keeffe, J. Mitten; Sub: T. Cahill.
The author Bill O'Keeffe was born in Kilsheelan. He wrote poems on many subjects including ones on his native Kilsheelan and the valley of Slievenamon. He died in 1984 and is buried in Newry, Co. Down.He was educated at Kilsheelan N.S, St. Mary's C.B.S. and St. Patrick's Training College. He was first secretary of the Kilsheelan club, which was formed in 1924. He taught for a while in St. Mary's C.B.S. He later became principal of Loughbrickland National School, County Down and assisted the local Glenn GAA club for many years.

The Hostile Hurling Team (Clonmore) 1922

Anon:

Source: G.A.A. History of Clonmore, Killea and Templemore, 1884-1988 by Martin Bourke. Received from Seamus J. King, Boherclough, Cashel.

Come on ye Gaels and sporting blades come listen for a while
To hear of our great hurling team, you can't suppress a smile.
For being as fine a type of men that ever greased the green
We are the ladies' pride and joy, though called the hostile team.

To see us when we're practising, the people come in mobs
And lassies all admire us from the hills of Mikes and Bobs.
We sport our little knickers and our jerseys on the green
To see us play you'd never think we were a hostile team.

We first became affiliated in the year of twenty-two
With energy and extra strength some teams we did subdue.
For we can use those grained camáns in the grand old style that wins
Though we scarcely ever hit the ball , we seldom miss the shins.

We first came into prominence in the year of twenty-four
When we beat the Griffin seniors by the margin of a score.
They played a well-contested game though minus style or dash
And there is no need to tell you boys, they went down before our
ash.

We towed the line with sweet Killea a team of great renown
With grim determination we pulled their credit down.
As our dauntless men their task began, the hurleys they did wield
The spectators thought we were insane and sprinted from the field.

To Templetuohy we did go to play a friendly match
We were just centred on the pitch when we found it was a catch.
Politics were introduced that made the camáns clash
And the brave withstood that fierce onslaught while the wise for
home did dash.

294

Across the Ballysorrell bog our heroes quickly flew
They dashed into a quagmire and quickly sank from view.
They baffled their pursuers who by them could not be seen
That eventful day came to a close with our hostile hurling team.

Now for these set of medals our captain he did cry
To gain such glory and renown we will fight to win or die.
The boys did cheer and drank their beer and homewards they were
bore
We will be up against Clonakenny in the park in Templemore.

The day being fine the sun did shine on that eventful day
When thousands of spectators came to witness our display.
The whistle blew and the camáns flew and the ball danced round the
goal
And to quit our fighting attitude we were disallowed a goal.

'We are bet' our noble captain cried as he did rage in foam;
'I am sick this day of such foul play, so show me the way home'
If we played against a ladies' team I'm sure we'd have a chance
And if we could not play them square we could do the ragtime
dance.

So hurrah for all those brave fellows who failed to win renown
And to all their gay supporters in country and in town.
We'll be juniors and old spooners until the end of time 'twould seem
So lets cheer once more for old Clonmore and our hostile hurling
team.

Inch and Borrisoleigh 1926

*Believed to be by Pat Mahon. Words received from Thomas Kinnane
Source:A Century of G.A.A. in Borris-Ileigh. Received from Seamus J. King,
Boherclough, Cashel.*

All on a drear and wintry day,
We sallied forth into the fray
The Borris boys, hip, hip, hurrah!
 We'll all remember.

No smiling sunshine met us there,
The Jockey was all bleak and bare,
With warm hearts what did we care,
Even though 't was November.

The Harriers from Templemore,
All trained into the very core,
Romped round the field—the match before,
Showing rare form.

The Borris boys did all inspire
With highest hopes and keen desire,
As they went forth with hearts afire,
Facing the storm.

The goalie stood between the sticks,
The pigskin rolled, Oh! What a mix,
The Harriers played a bag of tricks,
Borris knew one better.

The half-time whistle pierced the air,
The scores were low, did Borris care,
Ah! No, we have never known despair,
Their hopes to fetter.

The play resumed, then like a flash,
Delaney met the ball then crash,
Pat Harty passed to Shea and slash
Andy sent it soaring.

Tom Harty now showed judgement rare
Young Mack the ball kept in the air
Kennedy fed up with style and care
Whilst Long kept scoring.

Loughnane and Barry did their part
Joe Ryan outmatched his man from start
Lanigan's play gave all a heart
Smith smiled serene.

Pakie Flynn as fleet as hare
Captain Kenny too was there,
Coaching from goalpost in the rear
His flash fifteen.

Ned's training now began to tell
The Harriers knew their fate full well
The goals that now went in pell-mell,
And kept the flagman busy.

The medals won, now all is o'er,
The curtain falls for Templemore,
The victors stand a mighty roar,
Hails Borris champions.

Three ringing cheers and three time three,
Tis oft they'll county champions be,
Brave men of Inch and Borrisoleigh.

Mid Tipperary Junior Hurling Championship v Templederry. At the Horse and Jockey. Inch and Borrisoleigh, 6-1, Templederry 4-3.

Team—Jack Kenny, Andy Ryan (Boula), Pat Loughnane, Tom Delaney, Conn Kennedy, Tom Ryan-Lannigan, Jim Devanney, Pakie Finn, Mick Mack, Joe Ryan, (Farmer), Tom Harty, Din Shea, Mick Smyth, Pat Harty, Ned Long, Martin (Sper) Barry.

Sweet Old Toomevara

By Patrick Brett, Nenagh
Source: Toomevara G.A.A. 1885-1985.
Received from Seamus J. King, Boherclough, Cashel.

Proudly they undressed that day at Nenagh
Showgrounds for the fray
And knew right well they'd bring the sway
To sweet old Toomevara.

From the Devil's bit to Cashel rock
And back to Connemara
There is no team that I have seen
Can equal Toomevara.

There are no hurlers in the land
That ever took a ball in hand
Could place it to the net so grand
As sweet old Toomevara.

I travelled creation o'er and o'er
The like I never saw before
To win the crown by such a score
As sweet old Toomevara.

They are the Premier champs again
And will the laurels still maintain
A stream of memories remain
Of sweet old Toomevara.

I need not tell to you their names
On many fields they played their games
'Gainst men of no unworthy fame
Yes! Sweet old Toomevara.

Long live our men to conquer still
And play the game with right good will

Till pages of a history fill
In praise of Toomevara.

In praise of the 1930 winning team

Team: J. O'Meara, S. Hackett, D. Kelly, P. Ryan, G. Howard, Sgt. Gleeson, B. O'Meara, P. Collison, M. Kennedy, J. Gleeson, T. Gleeson, M. Collison, J. Burns, P. O'Meara, J. Kennedy.

Toomevara Greyhounds 1930

By Sapling
Source: Toomevara G.A.A. 1885-1985. Received from Seamus J. King,
Boherclough, Cashel.

Toomevara's fame is on the scale
On Sunday next in Nenagh town.
Old Boherlahan they must face to meet
And see who'll wear the crown.
Each man is trained; there's youth and speed,
And veterans like old wartime steed.
Advice in plenty has been let,
Remember 'Wedger' —never fret.
And when the leather is let go
Get at your work, don't mind a blow.
Right thro' the lines of Boher men
Each Gael in Toome his faith will pin
On you who wear the green and gold
To homeward bound, to cheers untold.
One flying hour shall all decide,
Uncertain is that greasy hide.
Now, boys be ready,
Don't look down,
'Will 'Johnnie's mile or will he frown'

Written prior to the 1930 Senior Hurling County Final, Toomevara v Boherlahan. The
game was a draw 5-5 to 6-2 and the game was replayed on December 10, at the
Showgrounds, Nenagh. Toomevara won the replay by 4-1 to 1-0.

Team: J. O'Meara, S. Hackett, D. Kelly, P. Ryan, G. Howard, Sgt. Gleeson, B.
O'Meara, P. Collison, M. Kennedy, J. Gleeson, T. Gleeson, M. Collison, J. Burns, P.
O'Meara, J. Kennedy.

'Johnnie' mentioned in the last line is Johnnie Leahy of Boherlahan fame.

Toomevara v Clonoulty 1930

Anon
Source: *Toomevara GAA 1885-1985*
Received from Seamus J. King, Boherclough, Cashel.

I never shall forget the day Clonoulty's pride went down
Beneath the skill of Kennedy's men in gay old Borris town.
Both teams lined up strict to time, with colours green and gold
With strong, brave hearts determined, past honours for to hold.

Chorus:

Then hurrrah for Toomevara, may their banner never fall
The beat Galway and Clonoulty and they burst in Clare's stone wall.
They're our coming county champions, they're true sons of the Gael,
A credit to Tipperary and to dear old Granuaile.

From Slieve na mBan to the Devil's Bit the Gaels come crawling in
As the autumn sun shone out on high, their cry went out, 'who'd
win'.
Tho' the Toom boys were favourites, yet I heard an old Gael say,
'It's only just two years ago, Clonoulty won the day'.

As now my lines are ending, let us toast their health with pride,
That they may bring the laurels green, safe home from Liffey's tide.
Then Tipperary's hearts will greet them with cheers both loud and
high,
Oh, God bless the Gaels of gallant Tipp, may their spirit never die.

1930 County Hurling semi-final at Borrisoleigh

The Gaels of Kilcommon 1931

By Johnny Conway
Source: Received from Liam Ó Donnchú, Ballymoreen, Littleton.

On the second day of brilliant May in nineteen-thirty-one,
Kilcommon's junior hurling team a glorious victory won.
Against the Gaels of sweet Rossmore in Annacarty Town,
Our mountain boys have won esteem in fame and high renown.

On that brilliant summer's maiden day, our boys in blue and gold,
Accompanied by the Hollyford band, sped forward through and bold.
In first-class cheer and warlike gear to conquer without fail,
That powerful team of old Rossmore in the spirit of the Gael.

A light refreshment on the field, they readied for the fight.
The whistle blew, our boys all drew their hurleys to the right.
In first class sport rotation, each man went to his place,
Both right and left, centre-back and front, in warlike shining face.

The days of old were soon recalled by old spectators there,
When the ball went forth from centrefield to Rossmore's goalposts
fair
It was gallant Matt McLoughlin scored from position on right
wing—
Ned Hayes, Ned Connell and Ger Toole made Rossmore blackbirds
sing.

Bold Rody Kennedy, Thomas Hayes, Tim Billy and Jack Keane,
Showed game on earth in blissful light, with physical force and
brain.
The Raider made his hurley tell as sure as you're alive
And Jack Benton active, flight and fierce into Rossmore did dive.

Mick Cleary, sure we'll ne'er forget and gallant Mick Spillane.
Their hurling blows were heard to sound in the taverns of Drombane.
And Matty Carey, here and there, where're a ball went forth,
Both Denis Ryan and Pat O'Toole proved Gaelic sons of sport.

Three goals, two points, Kilcommon scored to Rossmore's stubborn nil,
Our selectors, Mick Collins and Mick Rody—their memories linger still.
Athletic and Dark Rosaleens will crown each mountain glen
And may freedom's joy and victory's light, e'er shine on those young men

Newport v Ahane 1933

By Michael Bourke
Source: Newport in Song and Poetry
Published by the Michael Bourke Festival Committee.
Chorus after each verse

About the hurling final, a few lines I will pen down,
Played on the fourth of August near far-famed Newport town:
Between the Limerick champions to their county ever true—
And the dashing Gaels from Newport in their colours gold and blue.

Hurrah for good old Newport, Tipperary's pride and joy
They went that day determined to win the match or die.
They beat the ball right through them all and gave the backs the slip,
And brought fresh victory back once more to the hills of gallant
Tipp.

Tipperary's scroll of heroes bold is packed deeds of fame,
Moycarkey, Thurles, Boherlahan, may the heavens bless you name.
Horse and Jockey, 'Borris, Holycross and the brave men from Suir
View,
But we have men today to take your place, the boys in gold and blue.

Give a cheer for the bold Gleeson, O'Connors, Coffeys, Ryan,
Ahern, Close and Rainsford, in future days will shine.
Delaney, Lee and Boland, in the front were always seen,
Their splendid shots from mid-field oft raised that flag of green.

At three o'clock the teams lined up, the ball it was thrown in—
'I'll bet a quid' says Joe McGrath, 'our Limerick boys will win'.
The crowd was shouting 'Up Ahane'—they made tremendous noise,
But quickly they were silenced by our rattling Newport boys.

Cheer up Ahane and do not fret, what if your boys go down—
We will keep your memory evergreen in village, glen and town.
Give three ringing cheers for Newport and the boys that toed the line
And a cheer for Ireland's noblest Gael, our leader Fr. Ryan.

Final Score: Newport 5-4, Ahane 3-4.

Castleconnell and Ahane played their part in raising money for Newport's new church in 1933. Many players who took part in this match went on to win glory on the hurling field. Mick and John Mackey, Paddy Scanlon, Mick and Pat Ryan, Timmy Ryan, Jimmy, Jack and Mickey Coffey, Jim Close and Mick Boland.

Team—John Ryan, Tom Connors, Ned Rainsford, Tom Rainsford, Mick Lee, Martin Ahearne, Mick Ryan, Jack Coffey, Ned Gleeson, Jim Close, Martin Rainsford, Jimmy Coffey, Mick Crowe, Pat Ryan, Neddy Delaney. Subs: Mick Coffey for John Ryan and Mick Ahearne for Mick Crowe.

Borrisokane v Moycarkey 1933

By Jim Molloy (Postman)
Source: Commemorative Programme for opening of
Seamus Gardiner, Memorial Park in Borrisokane, May 14th 1978.

The championship is over; our Borris boys went down—
But one and all to play the ball, they're a credit to the town.
Paddy Ryan and Murt O 'Meara, those two I can't forget—
O'Meara passed the ball to Ryan, who smashed it to the net.

Dan Cunningham and Malachy Lambe, oh boys did they attack,
Against that great All-Ireland man, Phil Purcell at half-back.
Jim Kelly got a finger broken and the ball he could not send
It caused the poor chap awful pain, but he stuck it to the end.

The two McKennas, Jack and Frank, to no foe would they yield.
They got it hard but played right well—two heroes at mid-field.
Guilfoyle and Tierney both played well, but got no room to shine,
For they were marked by two good men, Kennedy and Sweeper
Ryan.

Martin Kennedy and Tim McKenna, they played in gallant style—
A word of praise is also due to that young man Guilfoyle.
Jack Brien at left hand corner back, Jack Kearney on the right,
With grim determination, they made a gallant fight.

To Paul McKenna goes the palm, heroic at full-back—
And every time they tried to score, he broke up their attack.
The coolness of Willie Meara, I never will forget,
Shots came from every angle and he bravely held the net.

Billy Donoghue and Jim Meara too, to Borris were a loss
But the man who beat them on the field was Phil from Holycross.
Ye have no regrets to offer for ye played a manly game—
Ye gave hard knocks and took them according as they came.

Moycarkey Borris 1-7, Borrisokane 1-0

A tribute to the Borrisokane team that lost to Moycarkey in the county final, 1933.
The Phil mentioned in the last verse was Phil Cahill, Holycross.

Borris Builds on Glory 1933

By P.J.Doyle, Borrisokane.
Source: Commemorative Programme for opening of
Seamus Gardiner, Memorial Park in Borrisokane, May 14th 1978.

Let other Gaels their songs recite, to shield, perhaps, their name,
So I will take my pen and tell how Borris played the game.
The right to win is not to all or else life has no story
Whilst some have risen by strange ways, Borris builds on glory.

As others cheer their comrades on, I see no harm why mine
Should not be given their applause, they have a right to shine.
So here's to them, brave yet and true, their flag not stained or gory
They'll play the game as good men do, for Borris builds on glory.

Last Sunday on the hurling pitch, their hurlers there did clash,
'Gainst strong men of the country nigh, who lacked no fighting dash.
Yet not that I should ever speak, that day still holds a story,
Yet courage talks and tells the tale how Borris builds on glory.

With Paul McKenna to the rear, 'twas a noble sight to see
The stalwart of a hundred fights still hold the backline free.
With Brien and Guilfoyle to his aid and McKenna brothers two
And Kearney linked with Meara, there's nothing could go through.

As on the flying ball did shoot and there swept throu' and throu'
The deadly volleys from the guns of the brothers Donoghue.
And like a flash the shattering hail at Lorrha's foremost line
There laid to rest another score from never failing Ryan.

Down the field the issue tugged a test of grit and grain
With strength for strength the battle waged, a trial of blood and
brain.
Whilst Tierney lodged with Kelly and foremost in the jamb
A deadly volley sped its way from hard repeating Lambe.

Around the goal the tension rose with Meara and Hennessy,
Who looked to find that Cunningham knew where the posts could be.
And so they won as now is told and so they'll hold their story
When Toomevara will hear the cry—Old Borris builds on glory.

Borrisokane won its first North Senior Title in 1933 by defeating Lorrha.

Team—Willie O'Meara, Jack Kearney, Paul McKenna, Lad Meara, Willie Donoghue,
Martin Kennedy, Jack McKenna (capt), Frank McKenna, Jim Kelly, Malachy Lambe,
Jack O'Brien, Dan Cunningham, Joe Guilfoyle, Malachy Guilfoyle, Jim Tierney.
Subs: Mick Hennessy, Pat Noonan and Pat Ryan.

Lines to the Bawnmore Hurlers 1933

Anon
Source: Commemorative Programme for opening of
Seamus Gardiner, Memorial Park in Borrisokane, May 14th 1978.

There's a spot in North Tipperary; it's a place of great renown,
The old folks called it Bawnmore, just a mile from Borris town.
It has produced a hurling team that lacks no fighting dash
And when they take the field to play, those lads can use the ash.

To Lower Ormond they brought fame by winning all the way,
Outclassing many crafty teams, who were favourites in the fray.
Their name in history will go down for centuries I'm sure,
For miles around there can't be found a team to beat Bawnmore.

The personnel I'll try to spell—five Kellys and O'Brien,
With combination on the field they can get there in time.
With Reddan Mick and Keevy Bill, they're always to the fore,
When they send the ball to Torpey, he is waiting there to score.

The brothers Burke and Brennan, their play is fast and sound—
They take the day for what its worth, their equals can't be found.
The Brophys and Pat Kennedy are swift lads on a ball
And if Noonan gets possession, the net will surely fall.

A last word for the trainer—the veteran, Kelly Din,
Who showed them how to use their sticks, in short he trained them in.
I'll end my song ere it gets too long, I've annoyed you much I'm sure,
So fill up once more and drink a toast to the lads from old Bawnmore.

Borrisokane won its first North Tipp senior hurling title in 1933, while Bawnmore, which is also in the Borrisokane parish took junior honours in the same year. This was also the first year of Bawnmore's existence as a club.

Moycarkey's Young Fifteen 1937

By George Ely
Source: Moycarkey Borris GAA Story 1984

Oh, you sportsmen of this parish and you winners of the Gael,
To see them for the final, not one of you should fail.
'Ere ye sons of old King Cormacks in many a field have been, *1
You will find your hearts contented when you meet our young
fifteen.

Chorus:

Then hurrah for Moycarkey, may your banners never fall—
You beat Boherlahan and Fethard and we levelled Kickham's
wall.   *2
But I never will forget the day that Cashel's pride went down
Before the skill of Sweeper's men in dear old Thurles town.   *3

Oh, God bless you Hayes and Kelly, Mutt and Cusack too,   *4
And brave young Balty Maher, you were always sound and true.
Give one cheer for Sweeper, that hero tried and true,
Young Clohogue and Dempsey, you all know what to do.   *5

Our hero Martin Healy, you are the lad can fly,
Not forgetting Hayes and Willie Ryan, the Two-Mile Borris boys.
There is Alex, Keeffe and Willie Ryan, your feats I will recall
But our 'Jockey Hero' Thomas Keeffe would hole a four foot wall.

Oh, 'twas shortly after three o'clock this famous match began—
To hurl for the championship, each champion faced his man.
They fought like tyrants tried and true, while on the ball did roll
And from a pass from young Bill Keeffe sure Alex scored a goal.*6

Now the game is fast and furious, it's a game you won't forget—
The Cashel boys are on the ball and still undaunted yet.
And Mickey Burke, he takes a free and he makes no mistake,
The ball did soar, 'twas seen no more, 'till Kelly's net did shake.

Now the game is over, we'll now join hand in hand,
For in thirty-eight my boys, we'll make a gallant stand.
We'll bring credit to this county unless it's unforeseen,
And we'll capture the blue riband with a dashing young fifteen.

There is still one name unmentioned, I will not let him down,
'Twas tall Moll Maher with his motor car, who brought us from the town.
When we arrived at Littleton, 'twas well gone closing time,
But we filled that cup and drank it up with health to 'Sweeper' Ryan.

A celebration of Moycarkey's win on the 19th Sept. 1937. Moycarkey 7 - 6 , Cashel 6 –2 , in the County Championship Final. Gate takings £297.

Moycarkey Team—Paddy Ryan (capt), Tommy Kelly, Tommy Hayes, Johnny Ryan, Martin Healy, Thomas O'Keeffe, Mattie Ryan, Paddy Maher, Michael Dempsey, Tom Kennedy, Tom Hayes, James Maher, Mutt Ryan, Willie O'Keeffe , Willie Ryan. Referee: J. O'Loughlin, Thurles.

*1	Cashel Hurling Club
*2	Thurles Kickhams GAA Club.
*3	Sweeper was Paddy Ryan, brother of Johnny and Mutt.
*4	Tom Hayes, Tommy Kelly, Mutt Ryan. Johnny Ryan was called 'Cusack'after Michael Cusack. who died in November 1906. Johnny was born on the 16th Aug. 1914. As Johnny writes, 'It was around that time that Michael Cusack died. That was the man I was called after. I have it from one of the hurlers, Jimmy Bourke, who marched to Glasnevin as a mark of respect to the great man Cusack'
*5	Clohogue, Jimmy Maher. Mick Dempsey.
*6	Alex—Matt Ryan

O'Neills v St. Mary's 1939

By David O'Riordan?
Source:St Mary's Hurling club, Clonmel, 1929-89.
Received from Seamus J. King, Boherclough, Cashel.

On the sixteenth of April nineteen thirty-nine
The O'Neills and St. Mary's marched out to the line.
Lar Power led the Mary's; they looked quite serene,
Says one big spectator; 'The Saints are the team'

Behind him stepped Tony a Bannerman true,
Who said through the O'Neills his way he would hew.
'Brave words', says Jim Williams, they call for a drink,
But ere one hour is o'er, his hopes I will sink.

Ned Ryan and young Kennedy with Bill from Moyglass
Were up on their toes, the O'Neills to outclass.
Joe Power and Dag Hogan, Wuz Brien and the Thatch,
All hurled like heroes to win this great match.

Ryan, Condon, Mackey and Byrne so true,
With O'Riordan and Marshall, they gave all they knew.
They broke the fast rushes of Power and O'Keeffe
And when danger was threatened, Bill Hayes brought relief.

Dick Power and Dag Hahessy well flanked by Speed Maher
Sent many a high one right over the bar.
Pat Condon and Morris who drove dead and true,
Showed Tobin and Cleary what small men could do.

Bob Walsh and young Gavin, they donned white and blue
For they thought that St. Mary's the O'Neills would subdue.
Had they thought of Jim Byrne and Purcell's wild dash,
They would seek glory elsewhere in wielding the ash.

O'Neills Club (Clonmel) were a breakaway group from St. Mary's (Clonmel). In this
new club were long standing members of St. Mary's and many of the younger players

who had played in the St. Mary's street leagues and on the minor teams since 1936. The new club lasted until 1942, and while it did there was intense rivalry between it and St. Mary's. Efforts were made to resolve the differences but O'Neills decided unanimously not to amalgamate with St. Mary's. The battle now shifted to the County Board meeting of 12 February when the transfer of twelve more St. Mary's players to the O'Neills was sanctioned and the affiliation of two O'Neills teams for the forthcoming junior championship was accepted. Then the first round draw was announced. The O'Neills' first team, in the club's first ever-competitive match, was drawn against St. Mary's. The game was fixed for the Sportsfield on the 16 April and the Nationalist sensing the public interest and in a way worthy of a Munster hurling final announced the two line outs as follows:

O'Neills—Bill Hayes, Willie Condon, David O'Riordan, Mick Ryan, Paddy Marshall, Joe Mackey, (capt) Dick Power, Jim Byrne, Tommy Hahessy, Paddy Condon, Jim Williams, Dinny Byrne, Gus Morris, Joe Purcell, Willie Maher.
St. Mary's—Bob Walsh, Jack Tobin, Mick Flynn, Tom Power, Billy Gavin, Tony Nealon, Willie Cleary, Tommy O'Keeffe, Ned Ryan, Larry Power (capt), Willie Boland, Tommy O'Brien, Andy Hogan, Sean Kennedy, Joe Power.

O'Neills won by 2-2 to 1-0. This victory of the O'Neills was the finest hour of the new club. They even burst into verse and the above ballad was the outcome. It became the standard party piece of the more zealous followers for years to come. But the celebrations proved to be premature. St. Mary's lodged an objection. The South Board ordered a replay. This time St. Mary's won and this time O'Neills objected. Again the South Board ordered a replay. The third meeting of the two sides was at the end of October. St. Mary's won but were beaten in the second round by Ballybacon.

Kilruane v Kildangan 1940

Anon:
Source: Kilruane McDonaghs and Lahorna De Wets 1878-1916 (the Story of the GAA in Cloughjordan Parish). Received from Seamus J. King, Boherclough, Cashel

Sit down all my friends now and listen
I will give you a sweet little poem
It's all about good men and true men
I promise I won't keep you long.

The year it was nineteen and forty
To build up our team we began
It was a team of good men and true men,
Led on by the great Iron man.

Our backs they would stop an invasion
Our midfield—a wonderful pair
Our forwards—I wish you could see them,
With them there were none to compare.

First we met the old boys of Nenagh
On a beautiful Sunday in May.
Although they fought hard to defeat us,
Still to MacDonaghs they had to give way.

Next we met Roscrea and we conquered
In a game that was glorious to see,
In Nenagh's old town sure we lowered
The colours of Borrisoleigh.

The sun in the west it was sinking
'Twas the eve of a bright harvest day,
When we met Kiladangan in Borris,
The final of North Tipp. to play.

The play it was skilful and glorious
But the game that we played was no fun
But when the long whistle has sounded
The cheers said MacDonaghs had won.

Tho' all the bright dreams that we cherished
Were scattered in Templemore town
Still those men of the good fighting spirit
Those boys in the green and the gold
Will one day be the champs of Tipperary
Like De Wets our heroes of old.

Kilruane MacDonaghs won the North Tipperary Senior Hurling Championship on the 11th August at Borrisokane in 1940. This was the first senior championship won since -De Wets were North Tipperary champions in 1908. Kilruane 2-5, Kildangan 3-1. In the semi-final of the Tipperary county championship Kilruane were beaten by Cashel King Cormacks at Templemore on the 15th Sept, with Phil Purcell as referee. The jerseys were green with a gold sash over the shoulders and going down under the left arm.

KilruaneMacDonaghs Selection—Michael (Micksey) O'Meara, Jack Dunne, Des Dwan, Con Heffernan, Jack O'Meara (capt), Mick O'Meara, Tommy Williams, Jack Reddan, Pat Peters, Din Bevans, Paddy Williams, R. Skehan, Jim Rohan, Jack Dwan, Martin McLoughney, Jim Spain, John Kennedy, Mick Heffernan, Francie Darcy, Jim Waters, Tom Darcy.

The Hurlers of Coolmoyne 1941

Paddy Leahy, Annesgift
Source: Fethard, Coolmoyne and Killusty—Centenary G.A.A. Story 1887-1987:
Received from Seamus J. King, Boherclough, Cshel

I am an honest working man and humble is my station
I never boasted high degrees or college education
But to our hurlers ever true, I'm forced to pen this line
In answer to the poet who wrote, 'The Downfall of Coolmoyne'.

Now Mr. Poet and Gaels likewise, I'll have you all to know
Since first I hurled with Coolmoyne, 'tis eighteen years ago
And hanging from my walk-chair still, that medal bright you'll see
Since we won South County honours in nineteen twenty-three,

On the first day of September to Drangan we went down
To fight for hurling honours 'gainst the boys from Kickham's town.
In the field outside the village as the clock was striking three
The game was set in motion by John Ryan the referee
Soon the homes of Tipperary were vibrating every one
As the clash of ash re-echoed round the slopes of Slievenamon.

Ned Walsh of well known hurling stock, our captain on that day
Led forth his men to battle and was foremost in the fray
Full eighty yards he drove that ball with every powerful drive
As his father did before him in the days of ninety-five.
Sure Ned can hurl with camán fine or simple wooden spoon
And beside him 'Matt the Thrasher would look like a mere Gorsoon.

The Hayes' two in Gaelic fields, their merit is well known
Their native club for medals fought, they never would disown.
To rise and strike a hurling ball they showed the Kickhams how
And they're envied by that jealous poet who is gone from hurling
now.

The brothers Ryan with Tommy and John were stalwarts in the fray
Their stickwork, speed and fieldcraft were a sight to see that day.

The Kickhams' net they oftimes found with many a well placed shot
That swept the goalie off his feet and staggered Waltzie Scott.

Mick Treacy too, proved loyal and true and never funked a Kickham
With courage steeled he ploughed the field and said , 'Come on,
we'll lick 'em'.
Each man he met went down and out and at the count of nine
They were raving in their sleep about those hurlers from Colmoyne.

Those rugged men from Kickhams den 'oft josselled ' but in vain
For German tanks would fail to shake Dick Wall from Tullamaine.
With good old ash in every clash he fought with courage fine
He soon convinced the Kickhams he was hurling with Coolmoyne.

The brothers Flynn both Tom and Aust. with stout ash from the glen
They proved that day in Drangan too, a match for Kickham's men.
Their efforts strong the whole hour long together did combine
To enfold the flag of victory in favour of Coolmoyne.

Bill Crean from sweet Ardsallagh, he hurled like a boy
We knew he would not fail us when our hour of trial was nigh.
Sure his polished style of hurling you could class as quite unique
As he kept the Kickham's guessing, in manner so to speak.

Now lads a cheer for Peter Walsh, the hero of the day
The Drangan Gaels will ne'er forget his grand old style of play
As he bottled up the Kickhams, there was victory in his smile
To go crashing through the goalposts in the real Tipperary style.
Since the days of famed Tom Semple such a hurler was not seen
He's the pride of Tipperary and his native Carrigeen.

With excitement reaching fever pitch, the thousands on the stand
Saw Kickhams' hostile bombers near our goalmouth tryin' to land.
Joe Ahearne, Lee and Leahy, they quickly sent them flying
With a burst of anti-aircraft fire, from the hills of sweet Coolmoyne.

When at last the battle ended and the final whistle blown
The Kickhams headed sadly towards their native Mullinahone
Our followers a thousand strong came rushing o'er the line
To congratulate their hurling heroes from the hills of sweet
Coolmoyne.

Now Mr. Poet please take note, don't at our hurlers sneer
When next you go to see a game, don't wallow deep in beer.
For if you do, you know my boy, you'll see things upside down
As you did that day in Drangan when the Kickham boys went down.

Had Charles Kickham lived today, long cherished be his name
He'd swiftly be in Drangan for to witness this great game.
His learned pen he'd wield again and there in every line
He'd say the gallant phrases of the hurlers from Coolmoyne.

So let fly Coolmoyne forever and may fortune on you smile
And add further to your laurels on the day you're meeting Foyle.
Stick together for the game's sake and I'll lay an even bet
In the years that lie ahead boys, you'll win the county yet.

Coolmoyne were one of the earliest clubs in South Tipperary and in 1923 won the
South junior hurling championship. But this ballad apparently refers to the semi-final
of the south Tipperary junior hurling championship in 1941. Even though the ballad
writes about a victory, Coolmoyne were defeated in this game. (according to Joe
Aherne of Fethard). However, they won the South junior title in 1942.

A difference of opinion with their Fethard counterparts caused the Coolmoyne hurlers
to split from the Fethard camp in 1941 and 1942 and form a team of their own. A
Fethard supporter wrote to the local paper stating that Coolmoyne would never be able
'to go it alone' and that the split from Fethard would prove to be the downfall of
Coolmoyne. Coolmoyne, according to the author beat Mullinahone in Drangan and
this victory prompted a Coolmoyne follower to answer the Fethard man who had
written the original letter. The reply was in poetic form and it is attributed to the late
Paddy Leahy, Annesgift. The split was very short lived and very soon Coolmoyne and
Fethard were re-united.

Anacarty Abú 1943

By Patrick B. Ryan, New Line, Dundrum
Source: Éire Óg, Anacarty-Donohill GAA History: 1886-1986 by Eileen O'Carroll.
Received from Seamus J. King, Boherclough, Cashel.

The cup has come West! The cup has come West!
Anacarty leads proudly the way.
For her fine hurling men from the plain hill and glen
Are the great county champions today.
Like their sires in the past, again to the mast
Their flag they have nailed white and blue
Never to yield, fighting hard on the field
With the cry Anacarty Abú!

Peerless and bold with the grand dash of old
The victory is yours gallant men.
Fling the news far and wide; with the winds let it glide
O'er valley and mountain and glen.
Luck be yours—All the best—Sturdy men of the West—
We now look with pride unto you.
To add further fame to Tipperary's fair name,
With the cry Anacarty Abú!

Brave men and true, fearless hurlers are you—
Your gallant forefathers won fame:
In the dark bitter past they upheld to the last
Far famed Anacarty's good name.
Their soul with the blessed now peacefully rest
Their honour's entrusted to you.
This trust to the end is yours to defend,
With the cry Anacarty Abú!

Brave hurling men, proudly onward again
Bring you back steady Tipp's old renown.
Pick well our fifteen dashing hurlers and clean
Fit to conquer the All-Ireland crown.

Together and loyal be yours the old style
Traditional, skilful and true
And still greater fame to Tipperary's fair name
With the cry Anacarty Abú!

Anacarty Glory 1943

By Anon
Source:Éire Óg, Anacarty-Donohill GAA History: 1886-1986 by Eileen O'Carroll.

Here's a health to Éire Óg, may your banners never fall—
You beat Cappawhite in Cashel and your feared not Killenaule.
On the third day of October nineteen and forty three
You beat Moycarkey champions and gained the victory.

Long life to Fr. Meagher and in glory may he shine—
Likewise his gallant parish team, all in their youth and prime.
With his good advice and training he has surely done his best
And succeeded in the final to bring honours to the West.

From the strong Moycarkey tactics our backs did never yield,
The ball went down like lightning to the goal from centre-field.
Our forwards now were ready; they too were trained and fit,
And with style and combination, they seldom missed the net.

The training now has told its tale, it suppled every limb
For this we must pay tribute to our old Tipperary Tim.
Now Gaels all o'er the county to victory you'll advance
If you loyally keep together and give Éire Óg the chance.

So loyally work together and soon we'll see the day,
We'll bring back the golden glories of our Gaels beneath the clay.
All youth now pay attention and wield the native ash
And cheer once more to victory, Tipperary's famous dash.

County Final 1943 played on the 3rd October 1943. Éire Óg, Anacarty, 4-3,
Moycarkey –Borris2 -4. Fr. Meagher mentioned in verse two was parish priest of
Anacarty and Donohill and was a prominent member of the County Board. Tipperary
Tim mentioned in verse four was Tim Crowe (champion athlete).

Team—Jim O'Donnell, Jim Hanly, Jack Dee, Patrick Ryan (R), Patrick Hanly, Phil
Ryan , Johnny Ryan (W), George Ryan, Tom Ryan (C) (Reilly) Tom Burke, Bill
O'Donnell, Jerry Ryan, Jerry Ryan (W), Tom Joy, Denis Condon, John Carroll, Jackie
Cooney.

Tales of the Gael

Anon
Source:*Éire Óg, Anacarty-Donohill GAA History: 1886-1986 by Eileen O'Carroll.*

We sang the praises of the West
In nineteen forty-three
When captain Thomas Ryan
Brought home the cup of victory.
The bonfires blazed all o'er the West,
It was a glorious year,
Each Annacarty man today
Doth hold their memory dear.

Big Tom was captain of the team,
Playing centre-back was Phil
And Michael in the forward line,
Showed courage speed and skill.
Now Tom has left Annacarty's fields,
Ballysheedy and those boys,
Who played with Philly, Michael, John
Where the castle lonely sighs.

Farewell to you great captain true,
Big Tom of the Castle fame
While hurlers play old men will pray
And revere that well-known name.
Moycarkey men will salute again
Bill O'Donnell, Bourke and Ryan
When the men of the West
Proved they were best
And Annacarty's flag did shine.

Tom Ryan (C) captained Anacarty, when they won the county hurling championship
in 1943. He was better known as 'Reilly'. He was central to the Éire Óg team, which
took the four-in-a-row West championships from 1941-1944. The family nickname
'Castle' or sometimes mispronounced as 'Cashel' comes from the fact that

Ballysheedy Castle is beside the home. Tom died on the 10th Jan. 1987 at the age of 69. Friends and foes of many a sterling hurling battle came to pay their respects to a man who had led the parish of Anacarty and Donohill in their finest moment on the hurling field. The surviving members of the 1943 team carried the blue and white flag draped coffin.

Team—Jim O'Donnell, Jim Hanly, Jack Dee, Patrick Ryan (R), Patrick Hanly, Phil Ryan , Johnny Ryan (W), George Ryan, Tom Ryan (C) (Reilly) Tom Burke, Bill O'Donnell, Jerry Ryan, Jerry Ryan (W), Tom Joy, Denis Condon, John Carroll, Jackie Cooney.

The Sunday when Toomevara beat Roscrea 1946

Anon:

Source: Toomevara G.A.A. 1885-1985.
Received from Seamus J. King, Boherclough, Cashel.

On the twenty- fifth day of August in the year of nineteen forty-six
When thousands of sportsmen assembled and views of the outcome
were mixed.
They came from each end of the county to see thirty champions at
play
With hopes of a great game rewarded on the Sunday when Toome
beat Roscrea.

It was at the Sportsfield at Nenagh—Fr. Cosgrave; he led out his
men
For the honour of great North Tipperary, these teams were in action
again.
The champions with confidence were ready to beat the young
Greyhounds that day
But they had a great rude awakening on the Sunday when Toome
beat Roscrea.

So here's to your skill Rody Nealon and to you for your courage
Sean Ryan,
O'Meara, Young and Devanney who will keep green and gold
colours flying.
Billy Shanahan too, we'll remember and for Buster we'll shout 'Hip
Hurrah'
And we'll still recall Casey and Cawley on the Sunday that Toome
beat Roscrea.

Martin Bourke, he was playing like a wizard and Tom Dunne took
the place of a giant—
Not forgetting our own Dinny Kennedy, who chalked up a goal and a
point.

For Harty and Guerins and Gleeson for most meritorious play
And McCarthy was one of the stalwarts on the Sunday when Toome
beat Roscrea.

So here's to you men of Ballymackey, Ballinamona and likewise
Lismore
Greanastown and Gurtagarry, whose fame we have heard of before.
Ballybeg, Curraheen and Coolderry were each represented that day
And cheered for the new North Tipp. champions on the Sunday
when Toome beat Roscrea.
So here's to you old Toomevara, where Tipperary's great hurlers
bloom
And when in Croke Park for the final, give three cheers for the
champions from Toome.

North Tipperary Hurling Championship Final played at Nenagh on the 25th August.
1946. Toomevara 6 -7, Roscrea 2 - 4.

Team: Rody Nealon, Mick McCarthy, Sean Ryan, Billy Shanahan, Willie O'Meara,
Paddy Shanahan, Paddy Guerin, Patrick Young, Tom Dunne, Paddy Devaney, Jack
Gleeson, Martin Bourke, Dan Casey, Tom Cawley, Willie Harty. **Subs**: Denis
Kennedy, Phil Shanahan, Matt Nolan, Jim Morrissey, Mick Duff, Thomas Duff, Rody
Ryan, Ger Devaney. Referee: Denis Costelloe ,Shannon Rovers

The Boys in Black and Red 1947

By Dick Britton, Copper.
Source:Ballingarry 1887-1987—100Years of Gaelic Games.
Received from Seamus J. King, Boherclough, Cashel.

I am proud of Ballingarry's team no matter where I roam
It broke my heart last Sunday when I had to stay at home.
But sure we were delighted when the news it did come in
That Ballingarry won the day, we were told by Father Quinn.

To see them stepping on the bus, their seats for to secure
To conquer Ballybacon at Kilsheelan by the Suir.
They walked out boldly on the field, each man was out to win
And they blessed with holy water by that same priest Father Quinn.

They conquered Ballyneale's great team where Kickham's heart
grew pale
The Carrick Davins too likewise and the Swans at Ballyneale.
We heard of Ballybacon then, great noise they did create
But to conquer our great junior team they found they were too late.

From the backline to the forward line, I'll give you each man's
name.
We had Hayden's Jim and Connell's Bill and Molloy now of great
fame.
We had Dalton's Luke, God rest his soul, who's now beneath the sod
But we know his soul forever more is safe above with God.

We had Carey from Ballintaggart, who was always sound and still
Not forgetting Richard Ivors, who comes from Boulea Hill.
At centrefield they will not yield, that great man James Molloy
With Richard Maher he is a star, on him you can rely.

With Dalton, Hayes and Carey—they'll score, you need not fret
Nor forgetting Paddy Mullally or that nippy boy De Wett.

We had the army man, they call him Dan, and never will he talk,
But to see him flying with the wind like that great dog Ausprey
Hawk.
With Richard Butler in the goal and nothing will him shock.
We are proud of him in the village and his native home Tinnock.
Ballybacon bold he did uphold and we'll give him now three cheers
With his minor and his junior medals and he only sixteen years.

And to conclude and finish I have one more word to say
That unless we're dead with the black and red we'll fight another
day.

In 1947, the junior hurling South Tipp. Final was played at Kilsheelan between
Ballingarry and Ballybacon. Ballingarry won by 3-4 to 1-1.

Memories 1947

By Jim Armshaw: Received from Liam Ó Donnchú, Ballymoreen, Littleton
Air: Martin Sharey's Ball

This little song I'll dedicate to the Rearcross team who went of late
To hurl, to conquer and defeat the boys from Pallasgreen.
'Twas a day of great concussion and excitable discussion,
For the Pallas boys 'twas bruising as they yielded in defeat.

Our heroes without worry, started out in Flannery's lorry
And they caused an awful flurry when they landed down in Doon.
Oh the people got excited as these mountaineers alighted
And the Pallas hopes were blighted for they knew it was their doom.

Then the signal to get ready, sure our boys looked brave and steady,
Though they knew that many a bloody rag, they would wear before
'twas o'er.
Yet in grim determination without any hesitation
They advanced in good rotation like a well-trained army corps.

When the ball was set in motion and the crowd was all commotion,
Yet our boys were all devotion to their duty on the field.
And they kept their heads together, concentrating on the leather
And they never hurled better—their opponent's doom was sealed.

Christy Ryan (Keown) was our brave goalie and he used both head
and hurley,
Though the forwards were unruly and they did their best to score.
He encountered opposition with a cheerful disposition.
He accomplished his ambition and could any man do more.

In the back, Pat Lynch defending, where the pressure was unending,
Against three or more contending, sure he never budged an inch.
He upheld his reputation and our shouts of acclamation
Nearly shattered all creation—on all sides 'twas, 'come on Lynch'.

And captain Danny Heffernan, played the game where're he ran.
He didn't care two hoots about any man from Pallas or Dromkeen.
He saved the situation in this memorial occasion—
In a sudden altercation boys, 'twas then his worth was seen.

The Careys from fair Shanbally, were everything that men should be.
They never stopped or turned to flee, but upheld that good old name.
The Hayes brothers too from Foilnadrough, they were as steady as a rock
And gave those Pallas boys a shock—those hurlers of great fame.

Jack Quigley and the two Jack Ryans; they were as vicious as three lions.
Where're a ball or hurley joins, you'll find them in the fore.
Pat Quinlan and Pat Ryan and Mick Keogh with speed were flying
And they kept their men from trying to even up the score.

There's one man left to mention and he hurled with distinction
And it's my whole intention to sing of him in praise.
Jimmy Nolan, but a minor; sure his deeds could be no finer—
He outclassed a good old-timer and he just did what he pleased.

My vocabulary is diminished and my song is almost finished
And may it long remain unblemished, be my one and only praise.
Here's a bumper to those hurling men, who rallied forth from field and glen
And may they never fail to win fresh honours for Old Rea.

Back in the 'forties' teams from Rearcross and Kilcommon always drew the crowds to Doon for the Clanwilliam Cup hurling competition, which was run by the Doon club. There were great clashes against Doon, Cappamore and Pallas. This song celebrates a win in one of these games by Rearcross against Pallas in 1947.

Our New Champions 1947

By Jimmy Roche, Ballinard, Cloneen
Source: Michael Hall, Drangan. Also received from Seamus J. King, Boherclough,
Cashel. First published in Clonmel Nationalist 1947

Come Gaels of the County Tipp'rary
And honour our champions with me
The black and the amber is waving
Raised above us in victory.
Drangan to night is rejoicing
Excitement is high in Cloneen
On the hilltops the bonfires are blazing
To honour our gallant fifteen.

They galloped their way to the final
Through the ranks of past champions they tore
Disregarding the efforts of Fethard
Killenaule, Ballyneale and Loughmore.
The attacks of the great Galtee Rovers
They soon had them under control
Those lines of cute forwards from Bansha
Never tested Phil Shea in our goal.

With Tom Keane, Billy Hickey and Stevens,
John Nash, Mickie Ryan and young Hall
Time and again they've been tested
And have earned the title 'Stonewall'.
With Phil Ryan and Pat Sugrue at 'centre'
I have praises galore for that twain
Wherever there's Gaels there's a longing
To see them in action again.

Jimmy Hickey the pride of our forwards,
Harry Connors and Fleming so small,
The Mahers and Mickey McGarry,
They battled their way through them all.

332

Drink the health of the gallant St. Patricks,
May they wear their laurels in state,
And we hope to lustily cheer them
In the coming nineteen forty-eight.

Commemorating St. Patrick's (Cloneen and Drangan), victories in the South Tipp and County Tipperary Senior Football Championships and also the Tipperary Men's Cup in 1947. County final score: St. Patrick's 0-6, Galtee Rovers 0-3. St. Patricks defeated Galtee Rovers (Bansha) in the County Senior Football Final at Clonmel. St Patricks 0-6, Galtee Rovers 0-3.Tipp's Men Cup Final. St Patricks 4-6, Clonmel Commercials 2-3.

Team: Phil O'Shea (capt), John Nash, Tom Keane, Mick Ryan, Brud Stephens, Billy Hickey, Ml.Hall, Philly Ryan, Pat Sugrue, Paddy Meagher, Jimmy Hickey, Ml.McGarry, Henry O'Connor, Patsy Maher, Dick Fleming. Subs: -Ned O'Connor, Thomas Mullally, Sean Keane, Eamonn O'Halloran, John Fleming, Eamonn Cunningham.

The 1948 Lorrha Hurling Song

Anon|:
Source: Lorrha and Dorrha GAA, 1884-1984 by Seamus J. King.

I've been to hurlings lately but there's one I shall recall,
Of all the jewels in dear old Tipp, it's the diamond of them all.
When those dazzling lads from Lorrha that sprang a great surprise
In the county semi-final, when they beat the Cashel boys.

On the nineteenth of September it was a gloomy autumn day
When those two conquering parish teams got ready for the fray.
To decorate old Thurles town came those thirty stalwarts bold,
Lorrha in their blue and white and Cashel red and gold

Spectators in their thousands came from counties far and near
To see those senior champions and to give each side a cheer.
The game was fairly handled as I'm sure you'll all agree
By Moycarkey's 'Sweeper' Ryan, the appointed referee.

So long this game awaited at last they came in view,
Those lads like young All-Irelanders about the task to do
For the O'Mearas and the O'Donoghues starred on the Lorrha side
While the Devitts and Billy Hickey were surely Cashel's pride.

Sullivan, Lambe and Brophy, those backs a real stone wall
While Reddan in between the sticks shone brightly over all.
Ryan, Guinan and Hogan, a terrific pace they set
With raids upon the goalmouth that shook the Cashel net.

So the Lorrha lights still shining as the game came to an end—
That grand old style of hurling was coming back again.
The ash that went in splinters, the ball soared like a lark—
Supporters rose up to their toes throughout old Thurles Park.

The next big undertaking after countless years of loss
To capture crown and glory by defeating Holycross.

So all ye lads together, stand like brothers loyal and true—
Three cheers for good old Lorrha, the lads in white and blue.

There's a fair spot in Ireland where the sun shines near upon,
Where Tipperary meets old Offaly and the Shannon rolls along.
We'll drink down now our glasses and get a fresh refill,
It's hard luck on you Cashel boys but it's up old Lorrha still.

Lorrha won this county championship semi-final by 2-4 to 2-3. There were beaten in
the county final by Holycross on Oct. 3, at McDonagh Park by 4-10 to 2-4.

Team—T. Reddin, P. O'Sullivan, D. O'Donoghue, M.O'Meara, T. Lambe, M.
Brophy, J.O'Meara, E.O'Meara, P. Guinan, D.O'Meara (capt), T.Ryan, M.O'Meara,
B.O'Donoghue, M.O'Meara, B.Hogan, Hubie Hogan.

St Patrick's v Fethard 1948

By James Kennedy, Ballinard, Fethard.
Source: Received from Liam Ó Donnchú, Ballymoreen, Littleton

Ho! Boys of St. Patrick's make merry
You have won and with plenty to spare
From Knockroe to the mountains of Kerry
Your victory will float in the air.
You have silenced the braggards of Fethard
Henceforth they'll be meek and demure
If only in passing you'll mention
The game by the banks of the Suir.

Then here's to the boys around Drangan
Rathkenny, Knockroe and Kyle,
With Newtown, Knockeno and Magoury
And a portion of old Shanakyle
And what of the boys from the heather
And the banks of the Anner so pure
Whose imprint you'll find on the leather
That was played by the banks of the Suir.

James Kennedy, Ballinard, Fethard was born in 1864. The above poem was written in his eighty fourth year to celebrate St. Patrick's victory over Fethard in the South SF Final 1948. The game was played on October 5th 1948. He died at the age of 94 in 1958. St. Patrick's represented Drangan-Cloneen. (Source: Sean Nugent, Kilsheelan)

Up Borris-Ileigh '49

By Pat Mahon
Source: A Century of G.A.A. in Borris-Ileigh
Received from Seamus J. King, Boherclough, Cashel.
Air: Kelly the boy from Killane. Chorus after each verse.

I'll sing you a song of the brave young fifteen
Who went forth in the year forty-nine
To gain honour and fame in the grand hurling game
And all the great champions outshine.

Chorus:

So here's to the boys of Borris-Ileigh,
The pride and the joy of our land,
May they keep fit and strong till they're led to Croke Park,
With the 'soggart' aroon in command.

Tipperary's great hurlers they put to the test,
Boherlahan, Holycross and Roscrea.
The pick of the North, the South, Mid and West,
Fell before their onslaught in dismay.

Up Borris-Ileigh, may their hearts never fail
With hands always steady and true,
As they march on the field, all opponents must yield
To the gallant old white and blue.   *

Knockavilla were last to draw up for the fray
On the showgrounds in old Thurles town.
They had hoped for the best but just like the rest,
Before better men they went down.

Commemorates the senior hurling final played at Thurles on the 30th October 1949.
Borrisoleigh 4-6, Knockvilla-Donaskeigh 2-1.
Team—Ned Finn (goal), Phil Maher, Mick Joe Dwyer, Hugh Bourke, Phil Crowley, Billy Stapleton, Jimmy Finn, Phibbie Kenny, Philly Ryan, Ned Ryan, Seán Kenny, Jim Quinn, Paddy Kenny, Johnston Hackett, Tom Ryan. Subs: Donal Meagher, Michael Shanahan, Jimmy Coffey, Joe Ryan, Martin Ryan, and Paddy Ryan.

* Borris-Ileigh colours at that time were blue and white

Borris-Ileigh v Boherlahan 1949

By Pat Mahon
Source: A Century of G.A.A. In Borris-Ileigh.

Oh, 'twas in the year of forty-nine on a fine October day,
When Borris and Boherlahan met in a championship replay;
The pitch was like a carpet green, 'oul' Tipp was there in strength
And famous Boherlahan came on victory intent.

With Jimmy Maher in the goal and Flor at centre-back
They swore that no combination spoil their strong attack.
And now the ball is flying, as ball ne'er flew before,
And ash with ash is clashing in a dour attempt to score.

Luck favours Boherlahan when a hard won point they get
And they dance an Indian war dance when a major finds the net.
Are our Borris boys downhearted? —Oh! Not the smallest bit,
For they very soon show Boherlahan their hurling skill and grit.

And point by point up goes their score, 'till Boherlahan sighs
And when right soon they take the lead Johnny Leahy rubs his eyes.
'There's something-wrong' bould Johnny cries, 'this surely cannot be
That Boherlahan's walloped by Borris and Ileigh'.

But shout and bawl as Johnny will, the truth sinks in at last,
That Boherlahan's hurling men can boast but of their past.
For when the final whistle went and foiled their final bid
The boys of Borris proudly stood—The Champions of the Mid.

Replay of the Mid Senior Hurling Final on the 2nd October 1949. Borris-Ileigh 1-9, Boherlahan 2-3. This was Borris-Ileigh's first divisional senior hurling title.

Team—Ned Finn (goal), Phil Maher, Mick Joe Dwyer, Hugh Bourke, Jimmy Finn, Billy Stapleton, Phil Crowley, Seán Kenny (capt), Phibbie Kenny, Ned Ryan, Philly Ryan, Paddy Kenny, Jim Quinn, Johnston Hackett, Tom Ryan.. Subs: Ralph Ryan for J. Hackett, James Coffey for Tom Ryan, Joe Ryan for Jimmy Coffey.

Champions Again 1953

By Jimmy Roche, Ballinard, Cloneen
Source: Received from Seamus J. King, Boherclough, Cashel

The Anner banks are ringing, with shouts of, 'boys well done'
Merry hearts are singing, 'they're back; they're here; they've won'
Ballingarry's boys are beaten, though valiantly they tried.
They couldn't foil the challenge of the boys from Annerside.

'Gainst backs like Tom and Teddy Keane, they could not pierce the line,
Where Mackey, Lawless and St.John, stood guard by goalman Ryan.
Paddy Gleeson was outstanding; Mick O'Connor helped him well
And gallant Quirke was truly great, when the pace began to tell.

Forwards Maher, Connor, Ryan, withstood the final test;
And Holohan, McGrath and St John gave of their very best.
If I had space, I'd spare no praise of stalwart Dinny Roche,
The hero of a hectic hour—Tipperary's worthy coach.

Bravo, Ballingarry! What a pity you should fail:
Next time you will uphold your fame and make the critics quail.
Your sportsmanship was really grand—your football too, was fine;
A credit to your county and the home of Smith-O-Brien.

Celebrating the win of St. Patricks (Cloneen) in the South and County Senior Football
Championships 1953. St. Patricks, 0-5, Ballingarry, 0-4.

Team: Mick Ryan, Tom Keane, Teddy Keane, John Mackey, Charlie Lawless, Percy
St. John, Paddy Gleeson, Ml. O'Connor, Ml. Quirke, Paddy Meagher, Henry
O'Connor, Philly Ryan (capt) Rody Holohan, Ml. McGrath, Philly St. John. Subs:
John Clancy, Eamonn O'Halloran, Dick St.John, Eamonn O'Connor, Lo.Lo. Clancy.

Silvermines v Gurtygarry 1955

By Tom Shanahan

Source: Received from Seamus J. King, Boherclough, Cashel.
Air: The Wild Colonial boy

The twenty-fifth of September in the year of fifty-five
The Mines and Gurtygarry for the championship did strive
In Nenagh's famous sportsfield where thousands came to cheer
Those teams of junior hurling for honours did appear.

When the referee from Moneygall the two teams set in play
The Gurtygarry forward line began their great display.
And each stout Mines defender was working like a giant
When the flying Thomas Tierney sent over our first point.

When the boys from Toomevara added to the score
And Rody Nealon's goal and point increased the margin more.
Helped on by Austin Martin of Gurtygarry fame
It now was easy to forecast the winners of the game.

Here's health to Tony Ryan, may he guard the post for long—
To Frank Kennedy of Bredagh a fullback tried and strong.
And here's to Matt O'Gara of county minor fame
To Tierney and McDonnell who come from Blakefield Lane.

Rody Nealon and Chris Ryan would be a much-felt loss,
With Cummins, Ryan and Meagher who come from Curraheen
Cross.
Pake Fitzpatrick, Austin Martin, recalls Gurtygarry's fame
And Toomevara's Donovan brings old memories back again.

Here' success unto the Mines, they did their best I'm sure
But the craft of Gurtygarry, their boys could not endure.
May we always have such sportsmen and for honours they will strive
As they did to win the championship in nineteen fifty-five.

North Tipperary Junior Hurling Final 1955

Newport v Cappawhite 1957

By Mick Ryan L
Source: By the Mulcaire Banks by Michael Collins and Denis Floyd.

God rest your kindly soul Mick Bourke, I wish I had your wit,
To pen those lines that come to mind as by the fire I sit—
To sing in praise of hurling men of honour and renown
A good and homely ballad like your 'Dear Old Newport Town'

Then let me tell how Newport won the county junior crown—
Let me tell you of the boys that won that honour for the town—
Let me tell you of the teams we played in sunshine and in hail
And of our trainer Mick Ryan, who would not let us fail.

In May or June I don't know which, we met the boys from Rea
And victory came easy way down in Cragg that day.
Templederry were the next to fall though hurling with a will
They could not match the Newport lads in hurling, speed and skill.

The Silvermines next challenged us and put us a real good fight
Although we won by just a point we got an awful fright.
Mick Ryan discussed it with us and he made it fairly plain
That we'd have to train severely to conquer Borrisokane.

So every evening all the boys would come to Lacken Park
Dinny Brien, Ted Hackett and Mick Ryan would keep us there till dark.
The training told, for fit and bold, as anyone can tell
The lads from Lower Ormond before our onslaught fell.

The North Tipperary champions returned home that night
And on the cross a bonfire blazed and shed its victory light.
The schoolboys' band played clear and sweet, its strains I oft hear yet
And the boys around the bonfire danced a Ballycommon Set.

Next the county semi-final with St. Luke's of old Clonmel
Was played in Boherlahan where they know their hurling well.

St. Luke's were rough, but we were tough and so we earned a right
To play that great and final game against brave Cappawhite.

When I think of how that game was won, my heart just fills with
pride
And our dauntless foes from Cappa we never will deride.
And now to mention all the boys, you know them one and all—
Long, long, may we remember them and now their names I'll call.

Liam Keown our captain served us well, his hurling it was grand—
Bill 'Jim' would never lift the ball but kept it on the land.
Galway's Brendan Lohan did not seem to care a rap
While he held opposing forwards out and 'Jimmo' manned the gap.

The youthful Jim Joe Nicholas a lad from Gortnanoe
With brother Bill and Danno Fitz. were fearsome to the foe.
Rarely were they beaten, they were never at a loss
And many a foe in trembling will remember Molly's Cross.

Mick Caplis, Paddy Óg and Ned—a trio bold from Cragg—
They were my inspiration; they never seemed to lag.
But each and everyone of them was solid as a rock—
Michael Ryan as tough as teak, a chip off the old block.

Now to the boys who raised the flags, the white ones and the green—
Gay Rainsford, 'heaven help us' his likes are rarely seen.
Donal Kennedy sped along the wing as fast as any fawn—
The umpire stooped the raise the flag when he passed it to Noel
Bawn.

Mick Lacken and Joe Malachy, God bless his fine red head—
'Twas due to Joe, I know it so, we never once were led.
When out he dashed his blade would flash and friends you well may
bet
The goalie sadly looked behind for the ball was in the net.

Strike O'Leary, Mattie Farrell, Davey Egan and Pake Jones
Were reliable replacements, should we break any bones.
So keep hurling boys for Newport—all for one and one for all,
In the game of life, in joy and strife, may you always play the ball.

Junior Hurling Final, Thurles, Dec. 8, 1957. Newport, (5-1), Cappawhite, (2-2)
Team—Jim Fitzgerald, Brendan Lohan, Ned Ryan, Bill Ryan, Mick Caplis, Willie
Nicholas, Paddy Ryan, Mick Ryan (C), Danno Fitzgerald, J.J. Nicholas, Martin
Rainsford, Donal Kennedy, Mick Ryan (L), Joe Ryan, Noel Ryan. Subs: Mattie
Farrell, Matthew O'Leary.

Fethard 1957

Anon
Source: Fethard, Coolmoyne and Killusty—
Centenary G.A.A. Story 1887-1987, by Seamus King

You have heard about the Fethard team of thirty years ago
Their fame throughout the land sure everyone did know.
Their deeds I do boast manfully and hope I'll be forgiven
If I sing the praises of the champs of nineteen fifty-seven.

This gallant team was organised by a selection committee
That left no stone unturned for the best has got to be.
They trained up in the barrack field prepared to do or die
For the honour and the glory of our famous Fethard blue.

First they played Kilsheelan in the Sportsfield of Clonmel
The village lads fought bravely but speed was bound to tell.
Commercials, that year's champions, they hadn't got a clue
They were baffled by the combination of our boys in blue.

On to the South Final we thought it mighty quare
The opponents were not Old Bridge but a faster team from Cahir.
But whether Cahir or Old Bridge it didn't matter much
Fethard was the form team and proved themselves as such.

In the County Semi-Final we opposed a North fifteen
Who were to prove that they had been an under-rated team.
We were leading by eighteen points and we thought that we were there
But at the final whistle there was just a goal to spare.

On to the county final our opponents were once more
The standard bearers of the Mid—the gallant foes Loughmore.
Beside the City of the Kings as the clock was striking three
The game was set in motion by Seán Hayes the referee.

345

Loughmore now had two Connellys, they thought would see them through
But they forgot that Fethard had some Connellys playing too.
With Mick Byrne, Seán Moloney and Cly Mullins to the fore
We won the County Final by four-ten to five goals-four.

Celebrating Fethard's win in the county football final at Cashel on 6 Oct. 1957. Fethard, 4-10, Loughmore 5-4. At half time the score was Fethard 4-9, Loughmore 0-3. (A lead of six goals)

Team—Tony Newport (goal and capt), E. Butler, J. Williams, E. Casey, J. O'Shea, Ned Sheehan, Gus Danagher, Leo English, M. O'Riordan, Joe Hannon, Cyl Mullins, Liam Connolly, Seán Connolly, Seán Moloney, P. McCarthy, Gus Neville, Pat Woodcock.

Solohead's Fighting Men

By Donie Nolan, Monard
Source: Seamus J. King, Boherclough, Cashel
Air: Slattery's Mounted Fut.

You have heard of Solohead's fighting men Sean Treacy and Dan
Breen
Have you heard of their mighty hurlers, the finest ever seen?
How they went up to Thurles town the final there to play
And thrill at the way we saw the boys perform there that day.

We had the 'Yank' between the posts as safe as Ollie Walsh
We had fullback Jim Stapleton who many a spark did quench.
Joe Stapleton at corner-back as strong as any horse
And Phil Quinlan on the other side, who many a raid did stop.

Michael Cunningham at centre-back, too clever for his man
And Bertie on the right of him with 'pass me if you can'
Phil Verdon at left halfback did his duty cool and fine
And this half-line, they were just fine and the sun for us did shine.

Our captain who was Con Aherne we played at centre-field.
He played a captain's part that day and not an inch did yield.
Long side of him young Morgan Sharp was like a rubber ball
They outhurled their men right up and down and made no mistakes
at all.

On the 'forty' we had Rooky Ryan who was like a streak of light
Long side of him was Aidan Dwyer who made all the wrong things
right.
And Oliver Ryan (Darby) was always in the fray
They made the ball do all the work and never did delay.

Full forward we had 'Chicken'Ryan he scored a goal or two
Long side of him Ned Donovan, couldn't be stopped by me or you.

Now we come the 'Chucky' Gorman, he scored goals and points galore
He aggravated all the backs; they were lucky he didn't score more.

Here's a health to dear old Solohead, so famous, tried and true
And here's to four loyal fans who loved you true and true.
We'll tell our kids in future years how men were men that day
So remember Thurles town me boys and say a mighty big hurrah.

The county junior hurling final 1959. Solohead 4-7, Coolmoyne 2-4.

Solohead: Jim Crowe, Joe Stapleton, Jim Stapleton, Philip Quinlan, Bertie Cunningham, Michael Cunningham, Philip Verdon, Con Ahern, Moggie Sharpe, Aidan O'Dwyer, Jimmy Ryan, Oliver Ryan, Ned Donovan, John Ryan, Thomas O'Gorman.

Verse 2- The Yank=Jim Crowe
Verse 3 Bertie=Bertie Cunningham

Dan Breen was born in Donohill in 1894. In 1913, he joined the Irish volunteers with Sean Treacy. He began drilling volunteers after the 1916 rising and by 1919 he had participated in the ambush at Soloheadbeg. This was the beginning of an illustrious career during the war of independence and the civil war. He was a Dail deputy for South Tipperary for many years.

The first mention of the Dan Breen Cup is on page 316 of Canon P. Fogarty's book, 'Tipperary's G.A.A. Story'. The Tipperary Senior Hurling Final for 1931 was not concluded until February 1932 (delay due to Tipperary's tour in Autumn of 1931), Toomevara v Moycarkey- won by Toomevara. Dan Breen, who presented a valuable perpetual cup, started the game. Toomevara were the first winners. The cup, in existence since then had come to the end of its days in 1972. The new Dan Breen cup, with the design of an ancient Irish drinking vessel—the Mether—is similar to, though slighty smaller than the Liam McCarthy Cup. It is of solid silver with an unique base in that the conventional type base is abandoned and in its place is a two-tiered mahogany plinth manufactured specially by a Moneygall craftsman. Roscrea were the first winners of the new Dan Breen Cup (1972).

Toomevara v Thurles Sarsfields 1960

Anon
Source:Toomevara G.A.A. 1885-1985
Received from Seamus J. King, Boherclough, Cashel.

Hurrah for the gallant Greyhounds, hurrah for the men of Toome
Hurrah for the North Tipperary boys, from Keeper to Sliabh Bloom
By the home fireside, we'll tell with pride of that day in Templemore
When they took the crown from Thurles Town and the cup they
homeward bore.

The bonfires blazed in Toome that night, they raised the victors high
And the hills around gave back the sound and bright flames lit the
sky.
But old men sighed as they thought with pride of great deeds they
had done
Of that gallant band that took their stand in nineteen thirty-one.

But let us sing of our daring side, of O'Donovan and his men
Of Jimmy and brave captain Bill, we'll hear of them again.
In goal was Roger Mounsey, right in the Reddan mould
Well covered by Matt Hassett, who wears the blue and gold.

McCormack was a great fullback, McDonnell, stout and brave,
Neil Williams shone at centre-back; no forward could get through.
Phil Shanahan and brother Tom, lion hearted Matt O'Gara
Courageous John and Gerry Hough the pride of Toomevara.

Quick and keen over the green roamed Knockhaunna star
Frank and Con came sweeping on and sent them over the bar.
The subs. too were always true, Cummins, Tierney, Bevans, Browne
The Cuddys, Galvin, Hennessy, they too have won renown.

To those who trained the gallant teams, to supporters loyal and true
We say 'well done' great Toomevara men, Toomevara Boys Abú
Then hurrah for Toomevara whether you win or draw or lose,
Hurrah for the gallant Greyhounds who beat the Thurles Blues.

See notes included with the Boys in Green and Gold 1960

The Boys in Green and Gold 1960

By Tom Shanahan
Source:Toomevara GAA 1885-1985.
Received from Seamus J. King, Boherclough, Cashel.

The month it was October and 'sixty' was the year
Toomevara men were there again with supporters round to cheer.
Again a county final between teams of great renown
Toomevara's famed old 'Greyhounds' and the boys from Thurles
Town.

The groundsman had his work well done and the sward was neat and
clean.
Our lads were fit and ready in their colours gold and green.
The boys from Thurles did their best their trophy to retain
For in five long years they fought and won but the sixth year fought
in vain.

Our lads they played like champions and were first to every ball
And with first time hurling on the ground old-timers could recall
The cherished days of long ago, the Greyhound days of old
The dash and daring, skill and craft of the boys in the green and gold.

Here's to Mounsey and McCormack, McDonnell, Hassett too
O'Gara, Williams, Shanahan, all back men good and true.
There was young Tom Ryan, stout-hearted and Hough a man so rare
With Donovan, Ryan and Shanahan they had hurling skills to spare.

There was Frankie Ryan and Jerry Hough; they'd never miss a ball
And captain Willie Donovan, the sweetest of them all.
So here's to Toomevara from Ballinree to Oilatrim
We hail you and acclaim you county champions once again.

Senior Hurling Championship Final at Templemore, Oct. 16th, 1960. Toomevara 3-15, Thurles Sarsfields 2-8.
Toomevara Team: R.Mounsey, M.Hassett, J.J.McCormack, J.McDonnell, M.O'Gara, N.Williams, T.Shanahan, J.Hough, Tom Ryan, C.Ryan, Phil Shanahan, W.O'Donovan, J.Donovan, J.Hough, F.Ryan. Subs: P.Cummins, D.Tierney, T.Cuddy, M.Bevans, D.Galvin, D.Cuddy, P.Hennessy, S.Maxwell, M.Brien.

Verse 2: Thurles Sarsfields had won this championship five years in a row, 1955-1959 (incl).

Famed Borrisoleigh

By a number of local scribes

Source: A Century of G.A.A. in Borris-Ileigh
Received from Seamus J. King, Boherclough, Cashel.

Borrisoleigh is famed in story
Its name resounding in poem and rann.
It bore brave men who died for Ireland
And holy saints like the monk, Culann.
Since Sighle's arrow sped down the hillside   *
And Sassanach's massed in the glen below,
Her sons have stood in the gap of danger,
Fearless of cell, or sneer or blow.

'Tis but two weeks since Devanney's Ceili,
When we thronged the floor and thronged the door,
With tune and dancing, with talk and laughter,
To honour our champion, Liam asthore.
The neighbour who set Ireland cheering
In old Croke Park with his brilliancy,
The quiet lad who walks amongst us,
In the little streets of Borrisoleigh.

Two more weeks pass and again we gather
With songs and bonfire in glad array
Waiting to welcome the Kenny brothers
Who, in Clounanna have won the day.
For them Croke Park cheers today re-echo
When Ireland's sportsmen thronged to see
And cheer their dog, whose speed and brilliance
Brought the Irish Cup to Borrisoleigh.

In early 1962 Liam Devaney, Borrisoleigh. was named 'Hurler of the Year in 1961'. Liam is also holder of All Ireland medals for the years, 1958,1961, 1962, 1964, (sub) 1965, and was on the Tipperary teams beaten in 1960, 1967, and 1968. In February 1962, the club held a reception, which is still referred to as 'Devaney's Ceili' at which, a presentation was made to Liam. Greyhounds and hurling are synonymous in the parish of Borrisoleigh. Shortly after 'Devaney's Ceili' Jimmy and Joe Kenny's dog 'Simply Terrific' won the Irish Cup at Clounanna, one of the most coveted cups in greyhound coursing. A reception was held for the return of this famous greyhound to Borrisoleigh and another night of celebrations was held.

- Sighle Ní Guira lived in Cullohill Castle, Borrisoleigh—a not too pleasant lady, who used put people into barrels with nails in the sides and roll them down the hill.

Newport v Mullinahone 1965

By Jimmy Power, Drangan
Source: By the Mulcaire Banks by Michael Collins and Denis Floyd.

You have heard of the men from the kingdom of Kerry,
The wizard of Cloyne and the Bould Thady Quill   *1
But in Newport to night, they honour their heroes
The boys who play football around Keeper Hill.

Near the town by the Rock, they tackled the champions,
The rest of the county had failed to dethrone.
But the men in the green had other ideas
Of Kickham's ball-kickers from Mullinahone.   *2

'Twas hard to get scores 'gainst men like Mick Collins
Mick Lacken, Noel Gorman and sturdy Ned Óg.
The goalie Dinny Ryan and his young brother Jack
Sure you couldn't get the end of a Ryan or a rogue.

At mid-field young Carroll and Mahoney lorded
Centre-back Gleeson was out on his own.
He played so much ball 'gainst all opposition
You'd think he had friends around Mullinahone.

Seamus Shinnors, Noel Shea, Joe O'Brien and 'Neighbour'
Willie Nicholas and Durack would not let them down.
They got some fine scores and Dinny Brien the trainer
Made a cute switch and the boys went to town.

Warrior Mahoney moved to corner-forward—
Pulled down a high ball—paused and let fly.
The green flag is waving, the crowd jubilating
Supporters around him are dancing with joy.

With pride dear old Newport can look to the future—
Her youth ever true to the cause of the Gael.

These green-jerseyed boys are a sporting example
Of honest endeavour that never could fail.

By the silvery Mulcaire, by Clare Glens and the Shannon—
Rejoicing to night and enjoying their fill.
They're drinking black porter and praising their heroes
The boys who play football around Keeper Hill.

This was the county junior football final at Cashel on July 3, 1965. Newport
2-7, Mullinahone 1-4.

Team, substitutes and officials—Denis O'Brien, Noel O'Gorman, Joe O'Brien,
Michael Jones, Austin Durack, Jimmy O'Brien, Paddy Gleeson, Seamus Shinners,
Michael Ryan (L), Noel O'Shea, John Ryan, Martin Courtney, Jack Ryan, Pakie
Jones, William Nicholas, Bill O'Mahoney, Michael Carroll, Denis Ryan (D), Denis
Ryan (B), Ned Ryan, Michael Collins, Jim Coffey, Christy Heffernan, Harry Ryan.

*1   *The wizard of Cloyne*—Christy Ring, Cork.
The Bould 'Thady' Quill is a famous song written by John Thomas (Johnny Tom)
Gleeson. Timothy 'Thady' Quill (c 1860-1932) was a real person but it is generally
agreed that Johnny Tom was lampooning Thady. Thady was an itinerant labourer, and
an occasional 'jobber'. Because of his strength, he often used to lift bog oak out of a
depleted bog and was known as a human hydraulic lift. He was also in demand for
man-versus horse pulling contests—it usually took eight men to hold back an Irish
draft horse, but with Thady in the group it only took seven. Thady never had the time,
opportunity, or inclination to become a hurler or track man but was known as a very
good bowl-player. No one remembers him as being a ladies' man- a bachelor he
remained until the end. *Seanachas Duthalla Vol IX 1993* tells us that this version was
provided by Denis McSweeney, whose father housed Thady on many occasions. A
slightly different version can be found in James N. Healy's book 'Ballads from the
Pubs of Ireland.Mercier Press, 1965

*2 **Kickham**: John Devoy regarded by Padraig Pearse as the greatest of the Fenians
wrote: 'Kickham was born in Mullinahone, on the 9th May 1828. His mother's maiden
name was O'Mahony and she was a cousin of John O'Mahony, the founder of the
Fenian movement. He came of a very well-to-do family and received the training of
an Irish boy of his class up to fourteen years of age, when the accident happened
which changed the whole course of his life. He was holding a flask of powder near a
fire to dry and it ands it exploded with the result that he was rendered nearly blind
and almost completely deaf. Kickham had great literary ability and a wide knowledge
of modern litreature. His principal stories are '*Knocknagow*', '*Sally Kavanagh* or the
Untenanted Graves, For the Old land and *Tales ofTipperary*. Kickham was one of the
four most prominent men in the old movement, and as chairman of the supreme
council for several years before he died was the unchallenged leader of the
reorganised I.R.B. Kickham's ability is not to be measured by his writings although

356

they give him a place. He displayed knowledge of men that was remarkable on account of the paucity of his information about them and his inability to see and hear them but his estimates of their character and ability were all correct. It was the same with public events and foreign affairs. He was the master of Irish politics. His reading had to be done with his spectacles lifted up on his forehead, his hand shading his eyes and the book, paper or letter held within a couple of inches from them. Conversation with him for many years had to be carried on by the aid of an ear trumpet and for a long time before he died by means of the deaf and dumb alphabet. When Kickham died in 1882 there was a great funeral procession in Dublin, which the Freeman said exceeded in numbers that which followed the remains of John O'Mahony, the American Fenian leader, to Glasnevin in 1877. The IRB was then 35,000 strong and the members came from all over Ireland and from England and Scotland to pay their respects to the chairman of the supreme council.

William O'Brien in an editorial in the United Ireland 1882 wrote: Charles Kickham possessed the soul of a hero, free as virgin gold from fear or stain. A dreamer by the Anner, a child with merry children in the cabin of Phil Lahy, his darkened sight could flash with pride in the dock, and his soldier heart grow none the fainter for being buried in an English felon-tomb. A nation that can produce such sons and return their love with passionate increase cannot fail in the destiny whose vision illumined Charles Kickham's years of penal suffering and brightened his dying eyes. His works and his example will be a precious legacy long after Death in his chilly chamber has left nothing of the mortal part of the poet, novelist, and patriot, except the 'bare ruin'd choir where late a sweet bird sang'.

And John O'Leary wrote:'but there was another kind of knowledge, beside that of books, possessed by Kickham, and in this I have never met with anyone who excelled him. He knew the Irish people thoroughly, but especially the middle and so-called lower classes, and from thoroughness of knowledge came thoroughness of sympathy. It was not that he at all ignored the faults or shortcomings of the people, but he was convinced that these were far more than counterbalanced by their virtues, and anyway, whatever merits or demerits they might have, they were *his* people, to whom he was bound to cling, through life unto death, and this he did with a strength and force excelled by no man of his generation, if equalled by any.'

(The above information was extracted from '*The Valley near Slievenamon*, a Kickham Anthology, edited by James Maher, 1941.)

> I love you Tipperary dear, for sake of him who told
> The tale of homely 'Knocknagow' —its hearts as true as gold—
> For sake of 'Mat the Thresher's strength, and Nora Lahy's grace,
> I love you Tipperary, tho' I never saw your face.
>
> (Brian O'Higgins)

The Boys in Blue and White 1966

Anon
Source: The Lorrha and Dorrha GAA club History1884-1984
By Seamus J. King, Boherclough, Cashel.

'Twas on the fourteenth day of August in the year of sixty-six,
When Lorrha gained this victory with Moylan between the sticks.
Sure there were many times we faulted him but who there now could say,
That the goalie failed the Lorrha team on that victorious day.

'Twas on that lovely autumns' day our heroes names were made
No sun shone for old Kilruane, they failed to make the grade,
The Moloughneys and McCarthy were held by a rallying side,
The Gibsons and the Gaynors sure failed to stem the tide.

To single out one hurler is a thing we would not do,
For every man there played his part for Lorrha tried and true.
But we'll long remember Gleeson and the gallant game he played
And young Kennedy from the Castle and the golden point he made.

There was Morris, King and Liffey too all artists in their part,
With the Lanes and O'Meara brothers brought joy to every heart.
We've watched them play for many years and they never failed to show,
That our trust in them was not in vain no matter where we go.

We'll remember Paddy Madden too, that fair-haired veteran—
Moran, Larkin and Mick Doyle each proved he was a man.
Mick Lack and Peadar Hogan, who were never known to flinch
And that hero Fennor Ryan who came to us from Inch.

'Twas in the dying moments when a cheer shook Borrisokane,
The ball was in the rival's net, 'twas a goal scored by Noel Lane.

Sure the hats and caps flew in the air and our heads and ribs were sore,
Our hurlers hearts were happy, they had done their best and more.

And now as we march forward to the North Tipp. Championship,
We'll meet the green clad team from Toom; we'll meet them hip to hip.
And when we have them conquered and the greyhounds in full flight,
We'll prove our boast and we'll drink a toast to the men in blue and white.

All praise and thanks to Lorrha and before my story's told,
The subs who are not mentioned and who played a major role
Kennedy, Gorman, Coughlan, their hearts were made of gold,
They were watching from the sideline, just waiting to be told.

With Patsy Carroll trainer, and Paddy O'Sullivan,
O'Meara , Duffy ,Hogan and our Reverend chairman.
So we'll all drink down our glasses and we'll get them freshly filled,
It was hard luck on the Toom boys but its 'Up Old Lorrha still'.

This is mainly an account of the North Senior Hurling Semi-Final, Lorrha v Kilruane MacDonaghs which Lorrha won by 3-6 to 2-7 at Borrisokane. Lorrha followed this up on August 28th by winning the North Tipp Senior Hurling Championship Final by beating Toomevara by 3-11 to 2-13.This was the first occasion the Frank McGrath Cup was won by Lorrha.

Lorrha Team—Gerry Moylan, Michael Liffey, Paddy O'Meara, Seamus O'Meara, Liam King, Sean O'Meara, Michael Gleeson, Wilsy Morris, Jim Lane, Noel Lane, Jim Ryan, Peter Hogan, Paddy Madden, Michael Doyle, Michael O'Meara..

Roscrea's Hurling Men 1968

By Pat Joe Whelan
Source: Roscrea Hurling Club Commemorative Programme,
St Cronan's Park, 1ˢᵗ June 1980.

On the thirteenth of October in the year of sixty-eight,
The story of a hurling game, to you I will relate.
It was the county final and all hurling hearts were gay,
When fifteen gallant hurlers brought the title to Roscrea.

Long life to Tadhgie Murphy, may he guard the posts for long,
To far-famed Kieran Carey, a full-back brave and strong
And the gallant Michael Hogan, who gave a great display—
Sure hooray for brave John Dillon, the captain of Roscrea.

Pat Rowland so brave and true and Brendan Maher too,
And the stylish Tadhg O'Connor, whose equals they are few.
Well we'll not forget Pat Dynan, the hero of the day—
His hurling power for half an hour carved victory for Roscrea.

And Mick Minogue at centre-field was always to the fore,
With the one and only Frank Loughnane who got the vital scores.
When hurling men will gather for to talk of this great day,
They will speak with pride of Frankie boy—the idol of Roscrea.

Now with the men in the attack, I will spend a little while,
To meet the youthful Tynan who has hurling skill and style.
With Mick Nolan and Liam Spooner, their stickwork paved the way
And that famous name of Brussels laid victory for Roscrea.

So here's to Barney Hogan, in the corner he played fine—
And likewise Jackie Hannon who always kept on trying.
Sure we'll raise our glass to Har Loughnane whose vital goal that
day
Was the one that made the bonfires blaze in good old sweet Roscrea.

Well here's a health to John Joe Maher, a leader loyal and true,
And the evergreen Martin Loughnane to mention only two.
But to all the men who did command we'll drink a health today,
For we're proud to see the Dan Breen cup at last in sweet Roscrea.

This ballad recalls Roscrea's first Senior Hurling Title. Roscrea, 2-13, Thurles
Sarsfields, 3-4. Referee: John Moloney.

Roscrea; Tadhg Murphy, Mick Hogan, Kieran Carey, John Dillon (capt), Patsy
Roland, Tadhg O'Connor, Brendan Maher, Mick Minogue, Francis Loughnane, Joe
Tynan, Mick Nolan, Liam Brussels, Barney Hogan, Jackie Hannon, Harry Loughnane.
Subs: Pat Dynan, Liam Spooner.

Shannon Rovers 1968

By May O'Meara, Gurteen
Received from Liam Ó Donnchú, Ballymoreen, Littleton, Thurles
Air: The Men of the West

We honour Tipp's sixty-eight
The Rovers who came from the north.
And beat the brave south men at Thurles,
On November the great twenty-fourth.
They came from Slevoyre and from Roran,
Bellevue, Ballinderry, Coolbawn—
The Burkes of Kylebeg and Jim Horan
And the pride of the Cahalan's, Sean.

They came from the farm and the cottage,
Magicians at scoring a goal,
From the carpenter's bench and the counter
And even from Gárda Patrol.
The forwards were sturdy and fearless,
The backs they were eager and brave
And many's the rally they halted,
Many goals did Sean Cahalan save.

The fleet footed Guests and the Horans,
Brave brothers, as everyone knew:
But the bravest of brothers at Thurles
Were Jim Bourke and Ailbie so true.
For Jim was the captain undaunted,
In years of defeat he fought well
And so did Joe Hogan and Ailbie,
With Matt Fogarty running pell-mell.

At centre-field Matt is a winner,
 Anselm Walsh has the brains and the skill.
Mickie Cahalan too and Joe Hogan,
Back them up with a heart and a will.

Jim Egan a stout-hearted forward,
Timmy Tierney a hurler of grace—
Tony Hogan is ever a danger,
They have stamina, courage and pace.

Cyril Darcy, the greatest of heroes,
That day with the title at stake.
Forever and always his sallies,
The south men's back-line they did break.
So hail to the sixty-eight champions,
All hail to the deed they have done.
Their names will be always remembered
And the glorious victory they won.

Their names will live on in Kilbarron,
Terryglass will remember them too,
And now I will finish my rhyming
And bid these great heroes adieu.

Celebrates the county junior hurling title of 1968 played on the 24th November.
Shannon Rovers 6-3, Lattin-Cullen, 2-5.
Team: - Sean Cahalan (goal), Jim Bourke (capt), Seamus Horan, Tom Bourke,
Raymond Guest, Willie John Hogan, Michael Cahalan, Matt Fogarty, Anselm Walsh,
Martin Guest, Tim Tierney, Cyril Darcy, Martin Horan, Jim Egan, Tony Hogan.

Drom-Inch 1970

By Gerard Ryan, Inch, Bouladuff, Thurles
Source: Liam Ó Donnchú, Ballymoreen, Littleton

From regal Cashel they brought home
The coveted county crown
The vanquished have retreated,
The victors won renown.
But all combined in sportsmanship,
A heritage to unfold
A Gaelic pleasure to renew,
The pleasures to unfold.

In the final of the Mid
By the 'Church they were opposed.
A classical exhibition
And their rivals were exposed.
The tradition 'church' spirit
Seemed missing on that day
A contributory factor
In a one-sided affray.

The county semi-final
In Nenagh Town was played
The conditions there prevailing
Left the participants dismayed.
Burgess hopes of victory
In the second half were dashed
When against superior hurling skill
Those vain hopes were smashed.

Then onwards to Cashel
For the county final grand;
Ballingarry were opponents
And made a hectic stand.
A keenly fought encounter

For fifty minutes ensued,
At the end Drom-Inch were champions,
Ballingarry were subdued.

The spirit of the Butlers
A credit to their race;
Such spirit gets results
Whatever odds we face.
Their do or die efforts
For their team throughout the year
Four stalwarts and a captain
So gentle, so sincere.

This celebrates the 1970 victory of Drom Inch in the County Junior Hurling Final at
Cashel. Drom Inch, 2-9, Ballingarry 2-2.

'Church' in second verse refers to Upperchurch/Drombane.

Moyne-Templetuohy 1971

By Gerard Ryan, Inch, Bouladuff, Thurles
Source: Liam Ó Donnchú, Ballymoreen, Littleton.

To Semple Stadium they came with spirit rare
Spirit born of adversity through the years.
True grit depicts their effort on that day,
An exhibition that stirred the heart of every Gael.
A do or die display reminiscent of Kickham's passage.
All for the sake of the combined villages
What a renewal of this celtic craft we saw?
This treasure of a thousand years—
The result of a fitting climax to a supreme parish effort—
A final to rank with the epics of the Premier County stage—
Long may such Gaelic spectacles flourish!
Europe could make our great occasions small.

County Senior Hurling Final at Semple Stadium, Thurles, on Oct. 31, 1971. Moyne-Templetuohy 2-8, Roscrea 0-6. This was their first success in the competition. Winning Team: P.Russell, Tom Grady, Jim Fogarty, Tom Fogarty, Martin Esmonde, Jim Fogarty, Michael Coen, Michael Grady, Martin Grady, Willie Fogarty, Tom Egan, Murty Troy, Willie Grady, Tom Quinlan, P.Sweeney.

Arravale Rovers v Lattin-Cullen 1972

By Dick Meagher
Source: The Arravale Rovers Story by Tom O'Donoghue .
Air: The Irish Rover

In the year of Our Lord
Nineteen seachtó –dó
We set out for St. Ailbe's Emly.
Our buses and cars
Were laden with stars
We're the best we're the Arravale Rovers.

We'd an elegant team
It was plain to be seen
When adorned in the black and amber.
Our hope they ran high,
Our flags kissed the sky
We're the best, we're the Arravale Rovers.

We had talent galore,
When we put to the floor,
The champions Lattin-Cullen.
In case things went wrong
We had gallant subs in the throng
We're the best wer're the Arravale Rovers.

We had Davy O'Ryan,
Fresh and young in his prime,
We had Tom Kinane from the clover.
We had Seamus O'D,
In jersey number three,
We're the best we're the Arravale Rovers.

We had brilliant captain Tom,
His famous brother John
We had Kelly and Crosse quite sober.

We had Maher in attack,
We had Shanahan half-back,
We're the best we're the Arravale Rovers.

We'd a Horse, we'd a Mouse
We'd those terrible twins,
Who roamed the pitch all over.
We'd Phoebe there too,
To see that we'd get through,
We're the best we're the Arravale Rovers.

When Jim Crowley took a shot
What a volley he got,
The net it heaved way over.
We all leaped up from the ground,
Arravale were crowned,
King-pins of West Tipperary

The West Senior Football Final was played at Emly on Nov. 19: Arrravale Rovers 1-6,
Lattin-Cullen 0-4.
Arravale Rovers: D. Ryan (goal),, T. Kinane, S. O'Donoghue, M. O'Dwyer, T.
Crowley, J. O'Donoghue, J. Shanahan, T. O'Donoghue, (capt), T. Flynn, M.
McCarthy, P. Kelly, M. Crowley, W. Crosse, J. Crowley, P. Maher.
Verse 6: *Horse*=Michael O'Dwyer, Main St. Tipp. *Mouse*= Tommy Flynn N.T.
Ballydrehid. *Terrible Twins*=Crowleys, Mick and Ted, Bansha Rd. Tipp.
Phoebe=Comdt. Michael McCarthy, Dillon St. Tipp.

Castleiney and Loughmore 1973

By William Comerford and Sean Ryan
Source: Received from Liam Ó Donnchú, Ballymoreen, Littleton.

We're in the Munster final now, I heard the boys declare
Our opponents are from rebel Cork, so well we can prepare.
We're Tipperary's football champions, we have men of county fame;
Again Loughmore is to the front and well-deserved acclaim.
So raise our banners to the breeze in nineteen-seventy-four
A future great must now await Castleiney and Loughmore.

I remember hearing round the fire of the mighty and the bold;
And of the great achievements of the famous men of old.
I heard of Patrick Barry and with pride I now recall
No equal in all Ireland for his long kick of the ball.
I claim that we have great men still as we had in days of yore
To bring that record back again to Castleiney and Loughmore.

Our task, it won't be easy now, but it's fitting to recall
The men we met in seventy-three and conquered one and all.
In rapture I have watched them when they overcame Clonmel—
Then how my spirits heightened the day Moyle Rovers fell.
In the Mid. Tipperary final our boys were to the fore
And brought the medals once again to Castleiney and Loughmore.

On the twenty-first day of October, a game that will go down
In Tipperary's football history was played in Cashel town.
Our players looked resplendent, athletic, young and tall
To meet Ardfinnan's power and strength, undaunted one and all.
I had yearned for that hour to come to cheer our boys once more
And proudly wear the colours of Castleiney and Loughmore.

Ardfinnan looked so confident, so eager and so keen—
But unshaken stood the fearless men, who wore the red and green.
Now for the first ten minutes, 'twas almost point for point,
Until our rivals forged ahead led by their towering giant.

But only for that sound defence I'll praise for evermore—
The margin would be greater 'gainst Castleiney and Loughmore.

Now soon the second half was on, our score still under par—
But 'twas not long till Kearney sent directly o'er the bar.
Hayes, Maher, Kiely, Stapleton, abandoned every care
Sean Kearney and Tom Laha Maher were lords in midfield air.
Young Healy got possession now to level up the score
And prove that we had forwards still in Castleiney and Loughmore.

The tempo now had risen high, 'twas exciting to be there—
To see Stapleton, young Treacy and Johnsie on the square.
Brave Healy, Hynes and Jackie Walsh displayed their fitness too,
While goalie Michael Maher was sound and staunch and true.
But 'twas Eddie Webster's mighty kick from sixty yards and four,
That brought the County Final to Castleiney and Loughmore.

Oh how our pride did heighten and our spirit did inflame
To see our son's victorious when that great climax came.
High praise to all our mentors: may their glory ne'er go down
They upheld the proud tradition that can wear a Munster crown.
Yet that clarion cry on the four winds fly from Slieve Bloom to
Galteemore
No boundary to our onward march, Castleiney and Loughmore.

Loughmore Castleiney won the 1973 Tipperary Senior Football Final. Loughmore
Castleiney 2-10, Ardfinnan 0-7. This was their first victory since 1955. In the Munster
Club Championship of that year they won their way to the final but were beaten by
U.C.C.

Team Panel: Pat Quinn,Martin Walsh, Sean Kiely, Jack Walsh, Eddie Stapleton,Tom
Treacy, Tom Hayes (capt),Tom Maher, Martin Hynes, Jim Healy, Pat Healy, Mick
Webster, John Brennan,Tom Kiely, John Treacy, Paddy Stapleton, Tom Maher, Sean
Kearney, Mick Maher, Martin Kiely, Eddie Webster, Derry Stapleton,John Bourke,
Pat Dwyer, Pat Kiely.

Sean Treacys v Éire Óg 1973

By Bill O'Brien
Source: Source: Éire Óg, Anacarty-Donohill GAA History: 1886-1986 by Eileen O'Carroll. Received from Seamus J. King, Boherclough, Cashel.

On a damp and dreary November day the hurling heroes came
To Leahy Park in the Golden Vale to play the national game.
Sean Treacys from the mountains high, Éire Óg from further down
'Twas a West Tipperary final that day in Cashel town.

The ball went in on a sodden soil; the Rock looked kindly out
From end to end the leather flew, the spectators loud did shout.
Come Éire Óg, Come Treacys, the whistle no one did drown
For the first blood came to Treacys, a point in Cashel town.

A second and a third came too, with Treacys three to one
When a lofted point to Éire Óg was cheered both loud and long.
Young Caplis soon had a high one in as Din came charging down
John Carey's shot put the goal flag high that day in Cashel town.

The second half was keenly fought, the skin and hair did fly:
Came score for score above the lath as Caplis shot them high.
The final whistle came at last, Éire Óg were three points down
The hilly men were the champions proud that day in Cashel town.

The 1973 West Senior Hurling Final played at Cashel. Sean Treacys 1-8, Éire Óg, Anacarthy 0-8.

Éire Óg, Anacarty—E. O'Loughlin, T.J.Ryan, J. Hanly, J. Hogan, P. Corbett, D.J.Gleeson, S. Hanly, T.O'Dwyer, E. Morrissey, S. Fox, J. O'Brien, J. Morrissey, J. Carew, R. Shanahan, T. O'Rourke.
Sean Treacys: Philip Berkerry, James Nolan, Christy O'Dwyer, Paddy Ryan (C), Frank Lysacht, Phil Ryan, John Quigley, Jack Berkerry, Frank Berkerry, Paddy McLoughlin, Billy Berkerry, P.J. Caplis, John Carey (capt), Mick Ryan (W), Dinny Ryan.

Sean Treacy's, Kilcommon v Golden-Kilfeacle 1974

Anon
Source: *Kilcommon My Home—Mountainy People at Play (1978) by Bill O'Brien*
(Reisc). Received from Seamus J. King, Boherclough, Cashel.

Down from the top of Curreeney,
Along by the hillsides fair,
From Foileen, Coolmore, Cummer Judy
The neighbours were gathered there.
In spite of the wind and the weather
At Dundrum by the Multeens shore,
To cheer Sean Treacy's to victory,
In nineteen seventy-four.

From the moate of Kilfeacle and Golden,
Where the Suir flows gently down,
Came the lads to strive for the honours
And wear the victory's crown.
But they had to give best to the hill men,
Steeped in the hurling lore,
The camán game was easy for Treacy's
In nineteen and seventy-four.

(Extract from Golden-Kilfeacle: the Parish and its People by Senator Willie Ryan, p294) The senior championship was played on a league system in two groups. The club was in B group along with Treacys, Arravale Rovers and Cappawhite. Their first game was against Cappawhite and the final score was Cappawhite 2-8, Golden/Kilfeacle 2-6.

On July 14th at Dundrum, they met and defeated Sean Treacys on the score 2-6 to 1-6. This was a surprise as Treacys were champions. In the play-off their first game was against Cappawhite at Sean Treacy Park on September 19th. Final score: Golden/Kilfeacle 2-8, Cappawhite 1-7. On October the 6th in the semi-final at Emly, golden Kilfeacle were again victorious, this time over Kickhams on the score 2-6 to 1-7, and met Sean Treacys who won the other semi-final, but this final was a most disappointing affair as far as Golden Kilfeacle was concerned as the final score read Sean Treacys 4-10, Golden Kilfeacle 0-6.

Sean Treacy, (3rd Tipperary Brigade) after whom the club Sean Treacy's is called, was born in Solohead, Tipperary on the 14th February, 1895. The entry in Solohead church Register says simply: 'John Treacy born February 14, 1895, child of Denis Treacy and Bridget Allis. Baptised at Solohead, February 16, 1895, by Rev. J. Murphy, C.C. Sponsors, Michael Allis and Kate Allis'. His father died three years later. Sean and his mother then went to live at Lackenacreena, Hollyford, (approx. seven miles away) with his Uncle Jim Allis. Until his eleventh year he passed his boyhood at Hollyford. He attended national school there until after the marriage of his uncle Jim Allis, he returned to Solohead with his mother. He subsequently attended the Monastery Secondary School in Tipperary run by the Christian Brothers. He was living at Solohead at that time. He made his first communion at Hollyford and was confirmed at Solohead. At Solohead, Sean Treacy the youth was often seen serving mass and then again hurling with the boys of the townland. He finished school in 1911. (*Sean Treacy by Desmond Ryan, 1945*)

Sean was a man of athletic frame, who loved the national games, but bad sight compelled him to wear glasses from childhood. This prevented active participation. However, he devoted his time to learning history and Irish, in which he became fluent. He loved the Irish language and the music and songs of the Irish countryside that he learned as a child among the Slieve Felim Hills above Hollyford. He was tireless and fearless in his work to win independence and freedom for Ireland.

He was arrested on the 21st August 1917 and imprisoned, went on hunger strike and was eventually released. On 21st January 1919, Sean Treacy organised the Soloheadbeg ambush, the first active engagement since the 1916 rising. This decisive action began the War of Independence. Sean Treacy and his comrades were involved in numerous engagements against Crown forces following the Soloheadbeg ambush. He was killed in action by British troops in Talbot St, Dublin on the 14th October 1920.

'The funeral took place on Monday, October 18, to Kilfeacle.... all business houses including banks, were closed...as the coffin reached the graveside at Kilfeacle, the last of the funeral procession was then only leaving Solohead, some five miles away'.

Drom Inch 1974

By Gerard Ryan, Inch, Bouladuff, Thurles
Source: Liam Ó Donnchú, Ballymoreen, Littleton

Mid Tipperary hurling champions,
From Semple home they brought
The coveted Mid senior crown.
The champions were unseated,
The victors won renown.

The Sarsfields started favourites,
But as the game progressed,
It left no doubt in any mind,
Which team was the best

John Dwyer, the captain,
Between the posts did shine;
In front Costelloe, Doherty and McGrath
Comprised a formidable line.

In the half-line Connolly played it cool,
As only he can play;
Backed by the Butler brothers,
Who were always in the fray.

At centre-field two Butler boys,
Enhanced their claim to fame,
In that vital sector they held sway,
For most of this fine game.

Martin and Eamon Butler,
In the half-forward line played well
And wonder points by John Harkin,
At the final whistle tell.

The full-forward line of Kennedy,
Brennan and Paschal Ryan,
All played their part in winning,
The Mid for the first time.

Drom Inch won their first ever Tipperary senior hurling final in 1974 by defeating Thurles Sarsfields at Semple Stadium on Sunday Sept. 8, 1974. Drom Inch 3-9, Thurles Sarsfields 3-6.

Drom Inch: John Dwyer (capt), Michael Costelloe, Larry Doherty, John McGrath, Pat Connolly, Seamus Butler, Michael Butler, Paudie Butler, Tommy Butler, Martin Butler, Eamonn Butler, Johnny Harkin, John Kennedy, John Brennan, Paschal Ryan.

The Heroes of Silvermines 1974

By J.G.S.
Received from Liam Ó Donnchú, Ballymoreen, Littleton.

On the eight day of September nineteen seventy-four
History was made in Nenagh town to a devastating roar.
The chips were down, the fight was on, two sides would not give up
And Silvermines it was who won, the title and the cup.

No sweeter victory than this one could any team achieve
To beat Roscrea on a final day was difficult to believe.
But spirit, strength and a will to win and flair with these combined
To make that day a signal one for the heroes from the 'Mines.

Just two years old as seniors, their tasks was great indeed
They weathered set backs, braced themselves and to mentors gave
their heed.
Borris, Burgess, Newport and the men from Moneygall
Bowed the knee to these great lads and like sportsmen true did fall.

In lining out against Roscrea, those hurling giants to fear
They knew it would be difficult but 'defeat' they would not hear.
All flags and banners swayed around to the crowd's exultant roars
The men from the 'Mines were doing their stuff and notching up the
scores.

The blue and white was everywhere, the children came and cheered
And women also, young and old, as those longed for moments
neared.
And when the clock had just passed five and the scoreboard told its
tale
The victory was proclaimed throughout in every hill and dale.

Tom Kennedy between the posts as brave as any man—
With Michael Maher and Jim Keogh—nephew of the famous Dan.

And in the corner Jim O'Brien, the captain of the team
He led his men to victory and achieved his life long dream.

Also Mike Fitzgibbon—yes, heroes that great day
Not to mention Pat and Jack with the surname of Dunlea.
John Sherlock and Mick Hanley like greyhounds at midfield
As to an awe struck gathering their prowess they revealed.

The Ros. defence was thought to be as as sturdy as a board
But even it could not contain the wiles of Johnny Forde.
Also Eamon Dillon, John Kennedy and Jim Ryan,
Pat Quinlan, Maurice Daffy—each one always tryin'.

'A team's as good as all its subs' —and togged out on the line
Were men of equal standing led by Mike O'Brien.
The brothers John and Denis Quirke all fit to last the pace
As well as Eddie Kennedy, John and Danny Grace.

Paddy Collins guides the club and helped to pick the team—
Rody Kennedy, Paddy Quinlan those knowing men supreme.
Not to mention proud Tom Gleeson the pride of Ballinaclough
Four shrewd men of knowledge that none would dare to mock.

But players need more than hurling, they too need craft and guile—
And who better to supply it than the legendary John Doyle.
Presiding over all of them the Canon staunch and true,
How proud he was to see the feats of the boys in white and blue.

They're celebrating in the village, in Dolla and Shallee,
In Lissenhall and Ballinaclough it's such a sight to see.
And in future years when they recall the feats of days of yore
They'll speak in awe and wonder of the 'Mines of seventy-four.

Silvermines: T.Kennedy, J.O'Brien, J.Keogh, M.Maher, P.Dunlea, M.Fitzgibbon, J.Dunlea, J.Sherlock, M.Hanley, J.Forde, E.Dillon, J.Kennedy, J.Ryan, P.Quinlan, M.Daffy. Subs: J.Grace, M.O'Brien.

The Moneygall Men of Seventy-Five

By Diarmuid Ryan, Moneygall

Through countless days without much praise, our gallant lads hurled on.
Each played his part and showed great heart in matches lost and won.
Year in, year out you'd hear them shout, 'you'll never win', they said.
They should have seen how sharp and keen were the men in black and red.

'Twas clear to all in Moneygall these lads could match the best
The time was ripe and full of fight, they faced the opening test.
Killadangan fell; we beat them well with speed and combination;
With brilliant play we beat Roscrea —a cause for celebration

As spirit grew the players knew the cup was now in sight.
The Lorrha Blues were next to lose but gave us quite a fright.
And then to Clough the crowds did flock and loudly did we cheer,
The 'Mines went down we took their crown in the showpiece of the year.

We had our eyes on the biggest prize and aiming for the double.
With final day not far away, we found ourselves in trouble.
The County Board was given word, we told them of our plight
But sad to say we had to play our prospects far from bright.

But fighting heart now played its part we readied for the fray,
Though some were ill they had the will to line out on the day.
When things looked bleak though legs were weak and muscles ached with pain
Each gallant lad gave all he had and lived to fight again.

The second day I'm glad to say we had a fit fifteen
With skill and style and craft and guile they played it hard but clean.

With every score we cheered them more and when the hour had passed
The job was done, the cup was won and Kilruane outclassed.

Let's hail with pride this champion side and drink their health to night;
There's none so brave to make a save as goalie sound Noel White.
He's shown his style since juvenile —a cut above the rest,
He's made his name and staked his claim to rank among the best.

To guard the square and take good care of any team's attack,
In give and take there's none can shake, John Gleeson at fullback.
And on his right so full of fight is Joe McCormack bold
And at left full, Mick Doherty's pull is in the classic mould.

The steel and style of Dan Guilfoyle shone brightly on the wing
There's many a foe who feared a blow from Billy Fanning's swing.
And Eugene Ryan completes the line, so good to clear a ball;
Mick Nolan too was brave and true each time he got the ball.

Our centre-field would never yield, they held the upperhand.
They won new fame in every game, the finest in the land.
Jack Ryan so fast from first to last, no foe did him surpass;
For power and flair none could compare with Philip Fanning's class.

Our forwards all were on the ball and took each chance they got.
In every clash Sean Doughan's dash set up a scoring shot.
And Seamus Ryan with skill so fine, none better on his day;
And on his right the sheer delight of Donal Kennedy's play.

There cannot be another three to match our inside line,
For ball control in front of goal, there's none like Philip Ryan.
Pat Sheedy's stick was sure and quick, he played a captain's role
And none could reach the bould McLeish when Billy raced for goal.

And let's hail too the faithful few, the men behind the scene
The selectors and the mentors, the finest we have seen

And let's salute each substitute —the trainer most of all;
All won renown and brought the crown to gallant Moneygall.

Moneygall won the 1975 Tipperary Senior Hurling County Final. This was their first victory in the competition. Moneygall 3-13, Kilruane MacDonagh 0-5. (Replay)

Moneygall Panel 1975: Pat Sheedy (capt), Jimmy Treacy, Billy Fanning, Séamus Ryan, Joe Mc Cormack, Sean Doughan, Donal Kennedy, Noel White, Donal Fanning, Mike Nolan, Phil Sheedy, Philip Ryan, Jim Guilfoyle, John Joe Comerford, Seamus Doherty, Dan Guilfoyle, John Gleeson, Billy McLeish, Mick Doherty , Philip Fanning, Eugene Ryan, Jack Ryan, Bobby Jones.
Trainer: Mick Minogue: Masseur: Pat Cleary.

The championships in Tipperary have been conducted on different lines from time to time. In the 70's the county championship was an open draw among the senior clubs in the county and was entirely divorced from the divisional championships. The ballad deals almost exclusively with the divisional championship of North Tipperary for the Frank McGrath Cup. The four games played by Moneygall to win the championship were against Killadangan, Roscrea, Lorrha and the final v Silvermines (the holders). In the meantime the open draw county championship was progressing. Moneygall defeated the following on the way to the county final for the Dan Breen Cup— Ballingarry South, Toomevara, Lorrha and Moycarkey-Borris. KilruaneMcDonagh also won their way to the county final which was fixed for Thurles on the second Sunday after the North final. The North Board dinner after the final caused a crisis for Moneygall club (verse 5) as many of those attending suffered food poisoning and the appeal for postponement of the county final for a week was turned down. So, they had to play and the game ended in a draw. In the replay, Moneygall won easily. The mention of a double (verse 4) refers to the North final and later the county final.

Clonmore's Ballad of '75

Anon
Source:G.A.A. History of Clonmore, Killea and Templemore, 1884-1988 by Martin
Bourke.Received from Seamus J. King, Boherclough, Cashel.
Air: Master McGrath

It was late in October, a day of renown
Clonmore took the field for the Mid junior crown
To beat Gortnahoe, to die or to do
And to bring back the laurels in the sash and the blue.

At the Sportsfield in Thurles the final was played
For some unknown reason the start was delayed.
Some said the referee had gone down with the flu
And both teams agreed to appoint someone new.

The teams took the field with a roar from the stand.
They were played round the pitch by the Moycarkey pipe band.
The sun it shone down on that colourful scene
As they stood to attention for Amhrán na bhFiann.

The whistle was blown and the ball was thrown in
Gortnahoe were both certain and sure they would win.
They had captured the title at least twice before
And now for the third at the expense of Clonmore.

The first half was played at a very great pace
With both teams in turn taking over the lead.
Such lashing and clashing was ne'er heard before
As Gortnahoe faded before the skills of Clonmore.

Jack Quinn's reputation continues to grow
He was ably assisted by George D'Estelle Roe.
The star corner forward once more failed to shine
He was completely outplayed by hard tackling Tom Ryan.

Andy the manager played well on the wing
Though lacking in weight, every stroke it had sting.
The sound Michael Doyle like a wall of limestone
Was forced to retire with a cracked collarbone.

The princely Bourke brothers, in all there were five
As backs and as forwards they did manfully strive
While Fitzpatrick and Larkin from old Knockinroe,
Made both their opponents look weary and slow.

The teams they were level with some minutes to spare
It was fever pitch tension to quote Michael O' Hehir.
Seamus Bourke sent one over after playing great stuff
And the cheers from the stand could be heard in Lisduff.

The Gortnahoe forwards tried hard to score
They were flatly denied by the backs of Clonmore.
The long whistle sounded, a cheer it went up
As Fitzpatrick advanced for the Mid junior cup.

The captain he spoke on behalf of the team
Saying they had now achieved what was once like a dream.
Now that the dream was a reality
Three cheers for the trainer from Borrisoleigh.

It will often be said at De Lacy Byrnes
How Bourke and Mick Maher both scored in their turn.
How Delaney, Doyle, Egan and Doherty too
Were others to shine in the sash and the blue.

Junior No. 1 Hurling Mid -Final.

Team—J. Quinn, T.Ryan, T. Bourke, G.D'Estelle Roe, A. Maher, P.Bourke, M.Doyle,
T. Larkin, J.Egan, J. Fitzpatrick, (capt) S. Bourke, J. Fitzpatrick, M. Maher, J.Bourke,
J.Meade.

The Men in Red and Green 1977

By Cis Riordan
Source: Seamus J. King, , Boherclough, Cashel
Air: Sean South from Garryowen.

All roads lead to Sean Treacy Park, near the slopes of Galtee More
To meet and beat the Bansha boys as we did in days of yore
Our stalwart men in red and green they kicked the football high
And they took the pride from the Bansha boys beneath a dreary sky.

In the early minutes of the game our boys they scored a point
To be followed by the Bansha boys who got two on the sly.
Our opponent's thought they had us then, they were in glory high
When a shocker goal was stuck in the net by the gallant Solohead
boys.

To prove the ball was in the net they waved the green flag high
It spurred again one brave young man and showed them how to try.
Our supporters too it was their day, sure it was their pride and joy
To wave the red and green of Solohead beneath a darkened sky.

The second half was yet to come be that as it may
We battled on for our senior crown, as it was West Final day.
Our fine subs too like soldiers stood; they were our loyal support
They waited there those gallant men while the lead was held at four.

On the stopwatch of the referee the minutes ticked away
They ticked away to our success, as it was West Final day.
And when the final whistle blew, sure it was our pride and joy
To bring back the cup to Solohead on a cold November night.

So here's to brave young Solohead, in glory may they shine
Likewise our gallant hurling team all in their youth and prime.
With the good advice on training, sure they surely did their best
And nearly did succeed again to bring back another West.

S.F. West Final played at Sean Treacy Park, Tipperary on Dec. 3, 1977. Solohead 1-6, Galtee Rovers 0-5.

Solohead: James Hourigan, Paul Lynch, Michael Kennedy, Pat English (capt), Jimmy Ryan C, Pat Ryan S, David Ryan R, Thomas Hanley, Michael Ryan S, Timmy O'Dwyer, Pat Hadnett, T.J.Riordan, Danny O'Dwyer, Liam Greensmyth, John Ryan S.

Dinny Cahill's Men 1977

By Con Heffernan, Ardcroney
Source: Received from Liam Ó Donnchú, Ballymoreen, Littleton
Air: She lived beside the Anner

They tell in song and story of the mighty men of old
How they fought for fame and glory in Tipp'rary's blue and gold
Tony Wall and Tony Reddan, there was John and Jimmy Doyle
Tom Mc Loughney and Len Gaynor, Jimmy Finn and 'Sweeper'
Ryan.

Now alas their reign is ended and their day is past and gone
But their memory we will cherish and forever 'twill live on
And dear old Tipperary, she will soon be 'tops' again,
She can trust in Dinny Cahill and his bold MacDonagh men.

Chorus

Oh God bless the great MacDonaghs, may their name and fame live
on—
Cloughjordan and Ardcroney too, and dear old Kilruane.
Hand in hand we march together on to victory again—
Give three cheers for Dinny Cahill and his bold McDonagh men.

'Twas in glorious seventy-seven, that our heroes took the field
And to Dinny Cahill and his men, all others had to yield
There was Lorrha, Toome and Newport and we saw their colours
fall,
Then in Borris town we routed county champions— Moneygall.

On the fourteenth day of August, we flocked to Nenagh town
To meet O'Dwyer's men, who wore the North Tipp crown.
Old Kilruane went marching on, our banners waved again
And the cheers rang out in victory for Dinny Cahill's men.

Repeat Chorus

Then on to Semple Stadium one bright September day,
From Carrig town came mighty Swans who failed to bar our way.
Sean Treacy's true, they came there too—their colours fell again,
For none could halt the onward march of Dinny Cahill's men.

Oh I never will forget the day, below in Thurles town,
We played again O'Dwyer's men and won the county crown.
The Old De Wets from heaven came back to cheer again
And the Dan Breen Cup, they filled it up, for Dinny Cahill's men.

Repeat Chorus

Senior Hurling Final 1977 at Thurles on Oct 2, 1977. Kilruane 1-11, Borrisoleigh 2-8
(a draw). Replay on Oct. 30, 1977 at Thurles. Kilruane 1-5, Borrisoleigh 0-5.

Kilruane MacDonagh Team: Tony Sheppard, Sean Hyland, Denis O'Meara, Enda
Hogan, Jim O'Meara, Paddy Williams, Dinny Cahill (capt), Seamus Hennessy,
Mackey Keogh, Liam O'Shea, Len Gaynor, Gilbert Williams, Jim Williams, Sean
O'Meara, Jim Reddan. Subs: Eamonn O'Shea for Reddan, Mackey Waters for Sean
O'Meara.

Fethard Tradition 1982

By Micheál McCormack
Source: Fethard, Coolmoyne and Killusty—Centenary G.A.A. Story 1887-1987:
Seamus King, Boherclough, Cashel

Grass will grow and rivers flow
Day will follow night.
Tradition in the Friary town
Is to wear the blue and white.

For weeks on end, for summer long
The thoughts of boys are bright
I wish I'll get the chance to wear
The glorious blue and white.

On to Bansha town they went
The quest to take a crown
The boys from Hospital the foe,
The challenge was laid down.

And when the team came on the field
A sight so rare to see
Were the boys in white dressed up in blue
So happy and so free.

In the goal stood Liam Dwyer
A giant at five foot one,
With Colm Kehoe and Mullins Paul
And Kane from Slievenamon.

John O'Connor on the half
Wore the seven with a grin
And Willie backed by Fergus
Said, 'there is nothing going in'

Captain Hayes and big boy Brian
Hold the centre like a castle
While Dermot Chris and Eddie said
'There won't be any hassle'.

Up in front Big M.O.R.
Was ragin' like a lion
And Gerry said to Davy,
'I'm nearly killed from trying.

With time slowly passing
A change we'll have to make
Hayes into the back-line
And Metha for a place.

The move was good, the day was won
The crowd cheered with delight
Oh, how it must be lovely
To wear the blue and white.

Munster (under 15) Colleges Final for McGrath Cup at Bansha on March 5, 1982.
Ref: John Moloney, Currana, Bansha. Fethard P.B.S. 4-2, Hospital C.B.S. 1-2.

Team-Fethard P.B.S. L.O'Dwyer, R.Keane, C.Kehoe, P.Mullins, F.McCormack,
P.Hayes (capt), J.O'Connor, B.Burke, W.O'Meara, D.Hackett, C.Coen, E.Casey,
D.Hogan, M.Riordan, C.Horan. Sub: R.Metha for Horan.

Champions '82

By Jack Doherty
Source: Moycarkey-Borris GAA Story 1984
Received from Seamus J. King Boherclough, Cashel.

In the year of eighty-two, we've won trophies, quite a few,
InTipperary and in Munster we're supreme.
After forty-two years down, we returned to Thurles town
And Roscrea's hurlers in the final tamed.

It is no idle boast in this month of fog and frost—
This month when Santy down the chimney comes.
We won Munster's hurling prize 'neath Ormond's frosty skies
Our hearts beat proud in our Tipp'rary homes.

For two and forty years, no sound of victory cheers,
No county final won and no 'Dan Breen'.
Then that red and yellow roar was heard louder than before—
Forgotten then the lean years in between.

We beat Roscrea in Thurles town, the second time around—
The county final we'd been dreaming of.
And celebrations were still on, with music and with song
But our hurling skills once more we had to prove.

The singing then did stop, to get our men in shape
To Lismore town we then did make our way.
Ballyduff club felt secure they beat us double scores
But Moycarkey-Borris hurlers won the day.

By seven points we won that game, the Decies men we tamed—
One more step and then the Munster crown.
For the men from Patrickswell with hurling pride did swell—
But our prescription would bring their 'swelling' down.

They had a hard day's work against Finbarrs there from Cork
And in the end then had one point to spare.
The 'Papers' praise them high, Munster champions they would be
From Tipperary hurling —no need to fear.

We've been a long time down, no All-Ireland senior crown
Since John Flanagan graced the scene in seventy-one—
But we showed the experts all, this time we would not fall
Charles Kickham's cry, remember Slievenamon.

So in frosty air we went on Nenagh road so bent—
In Gaelic tongue that means of course *go dona*—
And in Nenagh town so neat, parked in a quiet street,
Then to the field named after brave MacDonagh.

With hurling swift and clean, no better game was seen—
It charmed the hearts of friend and foe alike.
With points both teams did score, 'a goal we want', we roared
That thirst our forwards very soon did slake.

Then our forwards so cool did score a vital goal—
At half time we were three points out in front.
With the second half now on, the 'Well' fought might and main
But our hurlers in the back-line bore the brunt.

The pressure now was on, our three points lead near gone
We hung on grimly with a point to spare.
But just when all seemed lost, Tom Doran the sliotar grasped
With pride and admiration how we cheered.

With thirty minutes gone, the game still carried on—
Then a throw-in near the half-way line,
Then the ref did give a free; Patrickswell then jumped with glee,
A point would equal our one goal and nine.

Like Thurles seventy-three, Richie Bennis took the free,
A hush descended on spectators all.

Off balance when he struck, Patrickswell were out of luck
Moycarkey-Borris hurling did prevail

With our heroes shouldered high, 'neath the frosty Ormond sky,
A victory for Tipp'rarys hurling men.
Like our heroes gone before, Tipp'rary's pride restored
By Moycarkey and brave Borris hurling men.

Moycarkey-Borris v Roscrea in the county final v Roscrea on Sept. 27th. Final Score: Moycarkey-Borris, 3-9. Roscrea, 1-15. The replay was on the following Sunday at Semple Stadium, October 3rd. Final Score: Moycarkey 2-12, Roscrea, 0-11. It was Moycarkey's first county final win for forty-two years. Moycarkey then went on to win the Munster club championship but were beaten by Loughgiel in the All-Ireland club semi final at Casement Park. Loughgiel won the All-Ireland final.

Teams for the first game:

Moycarkey-Borris—Tom Doran, Eddie Clancy, Willie Ryan, Robert Hayes, Eamonn Darmody, Jack Bergin (capt), Tom Mullins, Bill Gooney, Liam Bergin, Tommy Quigley, John McCormack, David Fogarty, Jack Caesar, Dick Quigley, John Flanagan. Subs: -John Hackett, Jimmy Leahy and Matty Bourke. For the replay Moycarkey had Tom Mullins at corner-back, Jimmy Leahy, wing-back and Jim Flanagan at midfield.

Roscrea—J. Rowland, K. Brady, B. Maher, E. Hogan, K. O'Connor, T. O'Connor, J. Spooner, R. Dunne, P. Loughnane, G. O'Connor, P. Queally, L. Spooner, P. O'Connor, F. Loughnane, J. Butler.
Referee: George Ryan

County Final 1982

By Danny Fanning
Received from Liam Ó Donnchú, Ballymoreen, Littleton.
Air: The Stone outside Dan Murphy's Door

Now people of Moycarkey and Borris
Just gather around in a throng.
And if you will pay good attention
I will sing you a verse of a song.
It's about the final in Thurles
A game that was honest and true.
Moycarkey they brought home the honours
In the year of nineteen-eighty-two.

The clash of the ash was exciting.
The crowds they were shouting for more.
A game that was played in good spirit,
The likes I have ne'er seen before.
Our backline was under hard pressure
But everything seemed to work fine.
Our captain Jack Bergin, rock steady,
And also fullback Willie Ryan.

The goalie Tom Doran was brilliant,
He brought off some marvellous saves.
There was help from John Hackett and Darmody,
Not forgetting Tom Mullins and Hayes.
The mid-fielders hurled demons,
Liam Bergin, Jim Flanagan and Bourke.
Likewise the men on the forwards—
It was here that Roscrea met their fate.

Young Fogarty, Tom Quigley, McCormack,
They're men that shone out like the stars.
Roscrea did not know what was happening
When they tipped the ball over the bar.

Fair play to Dick Quigley and Caesar—
Those boys sure I cannot forget.
The whole team was really outstanding,
Their target being always the net.

Bill Gooney, Eddie Clancy, Jimmy Leahy,
Our three injured heroes were down.
But still in the hearts of our parish,
We hold them in greatest renown.
Last of all is an Old Faithful hurler,
I cannot but mention his name.
He's John Flanagan our full forward,
A great man of All-Ireland fame.

Now that my song is all over,
Let you give another good cheer.
That the boys of Moycarkey and Borris,
Will win another final next year.

See *Champions '82* for teams and notes on the games.

Moycarkey 1982

By Paddy Power, Drangan
Received from Liam Ó Donnchú, Ballymoreen, Littleton.
Air: Where the Mulcaire river flows

Come gather round me hurling fans and I'll sing a verse to you
It's about the county final, in the year of eighty-two.
'Twas in Thurles town of high renown on a bleak October's day,
When those heroes from Moycarkey beat the stalwarts from Roscrea.

Here's a health to you Tom Doran; you kept your goal line clear—
And likewise stalwart Willie Ryan, sure you're praised both far and
near.
With Mullins, Hayes and Darmody and Leahy, strong and tall
And your captain brave Jack Bergin, he lorded over all.

The blonde head of Jim Flanagan, round the centre oft was seen
With the neat touch of Liam Bergin; what an asset to the team. —
The Quigleys and young Fogarty, with Caesar brave and bold
They fought like lions for every ball, those boys in the red and gold.

'Twas a pity on you Cormac lad, that you did not see it through—
You were caught up in that incident and some blame was laid on
you.
You did your best like all the rest, for to keep your temper cool
But the referee who're he may be, has to apply the rule.

Now here's to you John Flanagan, your hour at last has come
That you'd win that county final, was the wish of everyone.
Down through the years, we gave long cheers, you were held in high
esteem
And please God next year, you might reappear for to lead the county
team.

Moycarkey-Borris v Roscrea in the county final v Roscrea on Sept. 27th. Final Score:
Moycarkey-Borris, 3-9. Roscrea, 1-15. The replay was on the following Sunday. Final
Score: Moycarkey 2-5, Roscrea, 0-6. It was Moycarkey's first county final win for
forty-two years. See Champions '82 for teams and notes on the games

Moycarkey-Borris County Champions, S.H. 1982

By Bro. J. Perkins, C.B.S. Thurles.
Source—Moycarkey–Borris GAA Story, 1984

Mighty men of Moycarkey marching merrily on their way,

Ormond's brightest offspring, never outclassed in the fray:

Yet still with young hearts yearning, never yielding as of yore,

Champions worthy of their county, they've been always to the fore.

All accomplished, able athletes, always adroit with the ash—

Rise up, be ready to respond, recoil not from the clash.

King Corc's great kith and kin knew well the worth of this kind
land—

Endowed, esteemed throughout the earth, extolled by every band.

Yellow and red: 'Squeeze 'em up', 'tis said, with strong and skilful
hand.

By Borris' banks and braes they boast of boys both brave and
bold—

Old honourable ex hurlers, who have donned the blue and gold.

React and rally to the cause, come strike the parish drum.

Rejoice ye rural, rebel sons, your hour of joy has come.

Industrious men, from hill and glen, made strong by work and
tillage—

Strike up the band and take your stand, 'for sake of the little
village'.

See Champions 82 for teams and notes on the games

Moycarkey—Borris Juveniles 1983

Anon
Source: *Moycarkey-Borris GAA Story, 1984*

They have studied all the finer skill
As their fathers did of yore
Since O'Grady led his mighty men
Way back in eighty-four.

These young heroes quickly learn
From those men of former days
They, too, are quite determined
To win honour, fame and praise.

They've brought credit to the village
We are proud of them by now
They're the pride of Tipperary
And the homes of Knocknagow.

They've got men from Horse and Jockey
Two-Mile Borris and Littleton—
Moycarkey's mighty hurlers
Are well known to everyone.

We will sing of all those victors
Who won the county crown,
They're a credit to their parish
For they never let us down.

In their colours red and yellow
They come running on the field—
We are proud of each brave fellow
For they never once did yield.

In the under fourteen final,
Like your ancestors of yore,
You beat the great Toom greyhounds
That wet day in Templemore.

You play with skill and courage
And the boys of Toom did yield—
Brave captain Brian, played like a lion
And brought home the Harty shield.

Moycarkey-Borris u 14 Mid and County Tipperary Rural Hurling Champions 1983.
County Final was played at Templemore on Oct 8, 1983. Moycarkey-Borris 4-8,
Toomevara 2-8.

Team: Pat Buckley, Kevin Fallon, Thomas Flanagan, Andreas Maher, Henry Bourke,
Billy Lanigan, Michael Hayes, Dermot Maher, Brian Maher, John Corcoran,
J.J.Maher, Declan Gleeson, Ken Ralph, Dan Kavanagh, John Ryan.

Moycarkey—Borris Minor Hurlers 1983

By Bro. J. Perkins, C.B.S. Thurles
Source: Moycarkey-Borris GAA Story, 1984,

Magnificient Moycarkey,
And Borris famed of old,
Your victory in eighty three
Has shown you're true as gold.

You too were great in sixty-eight,
And again in seventy-two
You proved again great hurling
To your parish you were true.

Your captain, Mike McKenna,
Proudly wore the blue and gold,
And brother Mark, and Morris,
Were with Cooney brave and bold.

Joe Bracken and Frank Gleeson
Were true heroes on the wing,
But the famous name of Bergin
All round Grallagh we shall sing.

Tom Noonan was our hero now,
It was his greatest game—
And as long as hurling games are played
We'll sing Phil Cahill's name.

The Clearys, Shaw and Commins
And Dec Kirwan strong as steel,
With Darmody and Byrnes
No shyness they'll reveal.

To help their gallant comrades,
Croke, Bracken, Gleeson, Quinn,

With Kelly, Cahill, Doherty,
They were ready to come in.

To their trainer bold, Tom Harold
Paddy Maher we'll combine
With the other two selectors,
Great Bill and Eddie Ryan.

Moycarkey-Borris County Minor Champions 1983. County Final replay at Cashel, Nov. 13, 1983. Moycarkey-Borris 2-5, Roscrea 1-5.

Team: Michael Cooney, Mark McKenna, Michael McKenna (capt), Seamus Morris, Jimmy Bergin, Joe Bracken, Frankie Gleeson, Phil Cahill, Tommy Noonan, Milo Cleary, Johnny Clancy, Declan Kirwan, John Commins, Mark Shaw, Declan Byrnes. Sub: Timmy Darmody.

Borrisoleigh—Champions of '83

By Gerard Ryan, Inch, Bouladuff, Thurles:
Source: Liam Ó Donnchú, Ballymorreen, Littleton.

Once more the premier trophy returns to Borris town
The vanquished have retreated, the victors won renown.
But all combined in sportsmanship, a heritage to uphold—
A Gaelic pastime to renew, its pleasures to unfold.
The county all applaud now the men of Borris—Ileigh,
Who sought and brought the trophy home in the year of eighty-three.
The best of thirty teams or so, a real hectic campaign,
Victory after victory, in sunshine or in rain.
Onward, Onwards, men of Borris—Ileigh, to the year of eighty-four,
Help restore Tipp to its rightful place, standard bearers as before.

Celebrating the county final, played at Leahy Park, Cashel on Oct.30, 1983.
Borrisoleigh 0 17, Loughmore Castleiney, 1 11.

Team: Owen Walsh, Mick Ryan, T.F.Stapleton, Timmy Delaney, Richard Stakelum,
Gerry Stapleton, Francis Spillane (capt), Timmy Ryan, Pat (F) Ryan, Philip Kenny,
Bobby Ryan, Aidan Ryan, Mick Coen, Timmy Stapleton, Noel O'Dwyer. Subs:
W.Maher, J.McGrath, T.O'Dwyer, B.Kenny, P.Tynan, F.Collins, P.Kavanagh,
T.Ryan, J.Treacy, A.Kelly.

Moycarkey-Borris v Lorrha 1984

By Mary Cashin and Rita Barry
Received from Liam Ó Donnchú, Ballymoreen, Littleton
Air: By the Bright Silvery Light of the Moon.

Sure the boys have won the day
They have finished making hay
They have come and conquered all before.
The tyres are rolled in sight
And the fires will burn bright
When the county final champions will come home.

It was in Thurles town
In that stadium of renown
That Moycarkey-Borris hurlers won the day.
With spirits running high
They went out to do or die
And not show the Lorrha boys the light of day.

Sure they played as ne'er before,
Just like the men of yore;
And their followers shook the stadium with a roar.
And the flags were raised on high-
They knew that victory was nigh,
When Borris man Ned Slattery scored a goal.

There was Darmody from Gaile;
He never seemed to fail;
He ran a ring-a –rosy round them all.
And who could forget
The blonde within the net,
Tom Doran, the Galbertstown stone wall.

There was Flanagan and Ryan,
Who some thought were past their prime
And swore that the team they would ruin.

But it has been said before
I repeat it now once more,
The oldest fiddle plays the sweetest tune.

There was Tom and Liam and Jack
And guts they did not lack;
They proved themselves as stalwarts of the game.
There was Hayes and Hackett too
And Dempsey from Coolcroo.
And Fogarty and Leahy, young and tall.

And the smallest of them all
Sure when he grabbed the ball
Sent it flying high, 'twas nearly lost from view.
And the Count was in a blaze and Cullagh did amaze,
It was only then the final whistle blew.

County Hurling Final   Final Score: Moyoarkey Borris, 2-8, Lorrha 0-9 Played at
Semple Stadium , Thurles on the 21st October 1984.
Team: T.Doran, J. Hackett, W.Ryan, T.Mullins, E.Darmody, J.Bergin, J.Leahy,
L.Bergin, L.Dempsey, T.Cullagh, J.McCormack, D.Fogarty, N.Slattery, D.Quigley,
John Flanagan. Subs: R.Hayes, Jim Flanagan.

Newport v Carrick Swans 1985

Anon:
Source: By the Mulcaire Banks
By Michael Collins and Denis Floyd.

'Twas a cold and bitter afternoon on a grey November day
To Leahy Park in Cashel, we went to join the fray.
On a bare and rock like surface as a wintry sun shone down
We face the Swans of Carrick for the intermediate crown.

God bless the men of Carrick, they showed bravery and skill
They played the game both hard and fair and battled with a will.
My poor old heart was thumping and I thought that we were bet
When midway through the second half they shook the Newport net.

Yet 'twas this goal sent up the spark that set the game alight
And Newport warmed to their task now conscious of their plight.
They powered it down the centre and flashed along the wings
And the cheers reverberated 'round famed Cashel of the kings.

They breached the walls of Carrick and shattered that vain claim
That only South Tipperary can boast of football fame.
They laid the ghosts of latter years that haunted our proud past
And brought the Barrett cup to rest in Newport town at last.

So Carrick for a horse or dog—now this we'll not dispute
But if you're looking for a man to lace a football boot,
A man who'll clutch the greasy ball, whose hands will not let slip
Go seek him in the high terrain on the hilly slopes of Tipp.

Where flows the Mulcaire river and where ageless Keeper Hill
Stands guardian o'er the countryside from Knockfune to Birdhill.
Where barren mountain towers high o'er Lackamore
And the winding road thro' Newport sweeps down to Shannon's
shore.

I'll call out the roll of honour and give credit where 'tis due—
No team in North Tipperary could stick the pace with you.
Moycarkey thought they had it won, but then they let it slip
Before the final onslaught of the champions from North Tipp.

There's our captain bold Pat Shinnors, the man they called 'the Mouse'
He has a pair of powerful hands as safe as any house.
Murt Moloney and Ned Quigley who played on either side
You'll not find a finer trio to front brave Gerard Floyd.

Big Lar McGrath at number six, his motto none shall pass—
He'll tackle everything that moves above a blade of grass.
Flanked by cool D.J.O'Brien and that other sturdy lad
I have never seen him beaten—the eager fearless Brad.

Midfied is manned by two O'Briens, a fast elusive pair—
Both Sean and John are noted for their energy and flair.
They roamed around the centre and the soaring balls pulled down—
Set up the moves that made the scores that won for us the crown.

The wingers tall John Keating who so often found the net
And speedy Seanie Shinnors like a super-sonic jet
Zoomed along the touch-line and careered from side to side
As he drew the central marker to make room for Timmy Floyd.

There's power-packed Connie Keating who has rattled many bones
And the bearer of a famous name is Cully's Timmy Jones.
The maker of so many scores was veteran Dinny Floyd—
He kept the ball in motion and he seldom let it wide.

Let's not forget the great reserves—they made the winning side
And we'd be not celebrating were it not for Floyd.
It was his scores—no doubting that—that brought us to the fore
His name shall be for e'er enshrined in Newport's football lore.

And the others too who played their parts in league and
championship—
They well deserve the honour—be their names on every lip.
John Hogan and John Coffey and Young Pat Keating too,
Peter Coleman and Terry O'Brien—all trusted tried and true.

Now what lies in the future, well I've got no crystal ball,
But I'll wager they'll be heard of, those heroes one and all.
They will keep the flag a-flying, keep our Gaelic games alive—
So lets toast the brave Mick Larkin and his men of eighty-five.

Intermediate Football Final at Cashel on November 24[th]1985: Newport 1-5, Carrick
Swans 1-3.

Team—Ger Floyd, Martin Moloney, Pat Shinners, Ed. Quigley, D.J.O'Brien, Larry
McGrath, Ger Bradley, John O'Brien, Sean O'Brien, Sean Shinners, Tim Floyd, John
Keating, Timmy Jones, Denis Floyd, Con Keating.

Borris-Ileigh —All-Ireland Champions 1987

By Gerard Ryan, Inch, Bouladuff, Thurles.
Source: Liam Ó Donnchú, Ballymorreen, Littleton.

The club hurling cup of Ireland
Now rests in Borris-Ileigh
Their grand display on St. Patrick's Day
Was a joy for all to see.

The speed of youth, the guile of age
A unit to the core
Brought exultations from the stands
As each score followed score.

The best of Tipperary
Could not match their skill and flair
In North, South, Mid and West
Nothing could compare.

The provinces fell before them
And when victory came to be
The cheer in Borris was heard
In that lofty place Ileigh.

By training late and early
Their work was not in vain
Each man played his own part
In a hectic campaign.

When hurling men speak hurling
Borris-Ileigh are to the fore
The players that were, the ones that are
Part of the hurling lore.

The All-Ireland club championship hurling final played at Croke Park on St. Patrick's Day 1987. Borris-Ileigh 2-9, Rathnure 0-9.

Team: N.Maher, F.Spillane, T.Stapleton, M.Ryan (capt), R.Stakelum, G.Stapleton, B.Ryan, T.Ryan, F.Collins, C.Stakelum, N.O'Dwyer, J.McGrath, M.Coen, P.Kenny, A.Ryan. Sub: B.Kenny for T.Ryan.

The Hurlers of Clonmore 1987

Anon
Source: G.A.A. History of Clonmore, Killea and Templemore, 1884-1988 by Martin
Bourke. Received from Seamus J. King, Boherclough, Cashel.
Air: Carden's Wild Domain

There's joy to night where bonfires bright light up the verdant plain
And hurling men play games again round Carden's Wild Domain.
The blue and gold as in days of old will forever proudly soar
To recall the names and the gallant games of the men of sweet
Clonmore.

Though beaten by the Fennellys, they conquered Gortnahoe
And then Moycarkey Borris went down before the gold and blue.
Tommy Treacy's name on that cup of fame in the Mid they proudly
bore
Friends from Killea were proud that day of the men of sweet
Clonmore.

Then bowed the boys of Solohead the champions of the West.
In the Borris field the Mines did yield; Clonmore proved they were
best.
The eighty-seven intermediate team, the Millar cup now bore
There's rejoicing still round Shanakill and the homes of sweet
Clonmore.

Captain John Lee played manfully, Brendan Bane his class did show
The Larkins and Delaneys are the pride of Knockinroe.
Dromard's Delaneys, John and Pa, who got many a smashing score
To win the day with a great display for lovely sweet Clonmore.

John Fitzpatrick came from Graffin and another from Dareens.
And James and Michael Cahill are the boys of Ballyheen.
Mick of the Hill is remembered still for his Harty feats of yore;
John Costigan's dream and the Harty team were honoured by sweet
Clonmore.

We'll ne'er forget the brave Bourke boys beneath Dromard's fair hill.
There was Martin, Tommy, Seamus, Joe, with brave Paddy, Johnny, Phil.
Martin was the captain bold in seventy-eight who bore
The famous Dr. Harty cup to his school in Templemore.

'Tis true Clonboo we're proud of you with Butler, Deegan, Clarke;
Mick Doyle, Jim Meehan, Declan Bourke, you all have made your mark.
Laherty, Foley, Purcell, Morris, Madden, Pat Bergin to the fore,
Who played the game brought honour and fame to the homes of sweet Clonmore.

Selectors, trainers and masseur, Thady Maher and Francis Bourke;
Francis O'Meara, Billy Sweeney and Danny Moloney did their work.
The hurrah for eighty-seven and those boys who proudly bore
The victorious Intermediate cup to the homes of sweet Clonmore.

County Intermediate Hurling Final. Clonmore 2-10, Silvermines 1-11.

Team—B. Bane, M.Delaney, P.Bourke, M.Doyle, J.Lee, M.Bourke, P.Bergin, M.Larkin, J. Fitzpatrick (D), J. Fitzpatrick (G), M.Ryan, J.Cahill, J.Meehan, P.Delaney, S. Bourke. Subs: D.Bourke, T.Bourke, T.Clarke, R.Morris, S.Madden, M.Fitzpatrick, S.Delaney, B.Larkin, M.Cahill, J.Butler, P.Laherty.

The Ballad of Cappawhite 1987

By Rev. Bro. Perkins, C.B.S. Thurles Source: The Cappawhite GAA Story 1886-1989.
Received from Seamus J.King, Boherclough, Cashel.
Air: The West's Awake

Arise, Arise, your hurleys take,
The West's Awake, the West's Awake.
Rejoice, rejoice, your banners shake,
Sing loud and long for Cappa's sake.
'Tis four and forty years ago
Since Annacarty's boys did show
A county title they could take
And prove to all 'the west's Awake'.

Now Cappawhite boys take your stand
As champions of this glorious land;
Your hurlers now are in command
Forever honoured, proud and grand.
And eighty-seven shall ever be
Remembered long and faithfully;
For Cappawhite that year did see
Their first great senior victory.

In the championship they did contest
'Gainst Golden and the Kickham's best
With Clonoulty then, they stood the test
To win the title of the West.
By Boherlahan's broad famed way
They met and 'bet' the North's Roscrea;
And on county semi-final day
They beat the Sars with a fine display.

Against Loughmore's famed red and green
In as fine a match as e'er was seen
They won the cup of great Dan Breen
And score one seventeen to two thirteen.

Then here's to the Buckleys, Ryans, O'Neills,
The Coughlans, Barrys, each prevails;
Quirke, Hennessy, Maguire, true Gaels
And brave McDermott never fails.

Then rise and sing with all your might
And raise those colours blue and white.
With Creedon, Treacy, Keane unite
And play for lovely Cappawhite.
Hark! I can feel Slieve Phelim shake;
The West's Awake, The West's Awake
My heart with pure delight will break
But we'll gladly die for Cappa's sake.

Commemorates the county senior hurling final win (1-17 to 2-13) v
Loughmore/Castleiney on November 1ˢᵗ at Thurles.

Cappawhite—Dan O'Neill, Myles Coughlan, Michael Buckley, Dan Ryan (P),
Deasun Hennessy, Anthony O'Neill, Ger Ryan, Eamon Ryan (B), Simon Ryan (L),
Austin Buckley, Conor Ryan (H), Pa O'Neill, John O'Neill, Ger O'Neill, Martin
McDermott. Subs: John Ryan (P), Eugene Maguire.

Emly's Centenary Glory 1987

By Jackie Lonergan, Emly.
Received from Seamus King, Boherclough, Cashel.
Air: The Men of the West.

We honour in song and in story
The names of our great sporting men
Whose valour has covered in glory
The mountain, the field and the glen.
Forget not the boys of St. Ailbe's
Who rallied our bravest and best
When winning a South senior title
Then booked a new home in the West.

The homesteads of Emly were glowing
'Twas the eve of a great Gaelic day
Our founders had gathered and chartered
Our prospects, our hopes and our way.
The story went over our parish
To stir and arouse every breast
And the great Gaelic fire of our people
In the last great outpost of the West.

The crackers and blues had their innings
The seeds of dissension did grow
But the priest with his verve and his blessing
Anointed each wail and each woe.
The West it was there for the taking
When Father Ned Ryan beat the drum
Our footballers took up the anthem
A County was there to be won.

We are proud to announce that at this time
Two Emly men Hennessy and Joye
Gave their skills and their talents in forming
The West Board's new born baby boy.

The Crowleys and Daly and Carrolls
The Hennessys, Crowleys were best
And brought home to Emly the County
A first for the new born West.

We had good teams and bad teams in plenty
But we never went into decline
And thanks to the men of the 'fortys'
Father Tim, Ger Birrane and Sean Brien.
In the 'fifty's' the Ryans and the Frawleys
O'Donnells and Clancys so true
In the 'sixty's' the West senior title
The Dawsons the pick of the crew.
Nineteen sixty-eight down in Thurles

A special year for special men
When Lorrha were first to be taken
We praise Emly again and again.
With our neighbours the Glen as our allies
Patsy Dawson was there to the fore
Lattin-Cullen they vanquished in earnest
To win the West title once more.

The prize that we always had cherished
And from which we could never renege
Intermediate the grade was the treasure
Had avoided our boys like the plague.
Clonoulty, Newcastle and Rockwell
Were all left behind in the past
We hoisted our old black and amber
And nailed them at last to the mast.

We are blessed with the Park called St. Ailbes
New players were needed and planned
It began in the schoolyard at Emly
Sean McManus the teacher at hand.
This nursery gave us young players

413

And trophies and titles galore
The future looks good for our parish
And honour for Emly once more.

The fruits of our labour has blossomed
We look on with joy and with pride
At the men who have played for the county
We surely have nothing to hide.
We had Cunningham stately and noble
And Corcoran surely a treat
Who have set up a standard forever
For the young men of Emly to meet.

We had Malachy brave— an O'Brien
And no man or foe would he shun.
And he played at a time when the going was tough
And the teams, they comprised twenty-one.
With Limerick, he faced his opponents
In a game that was hard and no fun,
He brought honour to Emly and homeland,
With the first football crown ever won.

In eighteen eighty -seven we started
By men who were brave and were bold
We thank them for their dedication
We now are a hundred years old
With confidence now we will follow
And retrace all their steps to a man
And the old black and amber will flourish—
This great unforgettable clan.

Verse 10, Malachy *O'Brien*: - Emly man, Malachy O'Brien, was a member of the
Limerick (Commercials) team that won the first All-Ireland Football Final (1887) v
Louth (Dundalk Young Irelands) at Clonskeagh, Dublin, on Apr.29th, 1888.

Loughmore '88

By Gerard Ryan, Inch, Bouladuff, Thurles
Source: Liam Ó Donnchú, Ballymoreen, Littleton

The Dan Breen cup rests at last
In Purcell country, Loughmore,
Where oft the football cup was brought
In heady days of yore.

In the dying minutes 'twas swept away
From the men of famed Ileigh.
A grand display in the replay
Was a treat for all to see.

That classy man Philly Gleeson
Would quietly relish the replay
Though his body rests in chapel yard
His spirit was not far away.

Our tormentors are all banished
Forever from our shore
Fine people amid fine homesteads
Abound now in Loughmore.

Onwards! Onwards! Now dual winners
To the year of eight-nine
With Pat McGrath overdue the helm
The Tipps should do just fine.

County Senior Hurling Final Replay, Oct 8th 1988 at Semple Stadium. Loughmore Castleiney 2-7, Borrisoleigh 1-8. Referee Willie Barrett.

Verse 3 Philly Gleeson—Philly Gleeson was a former Loughmore club officer and footballer of note who died Oct 1, 1987.

Last Verse-' dual winners'—As Loughmore Castleiney had won the '87 Tipperary football championship, they were dual champions at the time of the '88 hurling final win.

Loughmore Castleiney: F. McGrath, P.Cormack, P.Brennan, E.Brennan, P.McGrath. J.Maher, E.Sweeney (capt), N.Ryan, T.McGrath, M.McGrath, P.Treacy, S.Bohan, L.Cormack, J.Cormack, T.Larkin.

Fethard County Champions '88

By Denis Bourke
Source: Received from Liam Ó Donnchú, Ballymoreen, Littleton, Thurles

In the last week of September, the sun did surely shine,
As Fethard and Commercials, in sporting fray did join,
In Kilsheelan's lovely village where thousands came to cheer,
The boys in blue and green and gold, who for honour did appear.

Kilsheelan's Tommy Lonergan soon set the teams at play.
'Twas then the Fethard forward line began their great display.
Though each Clonmel defender was toiling like a giant,
The deadly left foot of Joe Kane, flashed over a great point.

Our thoughts were now a lead to build and set a scorching pace,
Against the second moiety and the stiffish breeze we'd face.
For moments we were just inclined Commercials to forget,
Till in a flash, a rasping drive, had found Pat Kenrick's net.

When half-time break, it did arrive, our plight was plain to see,
To face the wind without a lead, the scores at parity.
Could our young team face wind and foe was the thought on every mind?,
In thirty more short minutes, the answer we would find.

The second half display that day was the greatest ever seen,
As the boys in blue, made railroads through, the ranks of gold and green.
A mighty roar rose to the sky and shook the very grounds,
When a mighty drive found Commercials net from the boot of Michael Downes.

The final whistle sounded and the prize we sought was won,
Though the margin of our victory, in the end was only one.
Like knights of old, our gallant lads, the Commercial giant slew,
The County Crown, came to the town, well known for royal blue.

Here's health to Paddy Kerwick, may he guard the net for long
And Buddy Fitz. in front of him, a half-back, brave and strong.
The Ryans, —Shay and Michael were heroes on that day,
Hackett, Morrissey and O'Meara, all gave a great display.

Of Brian Burke, our captain, you've heard of him before,
His prowess at the ancient game, is known from shore to shore.
His partner was Liam Connolly, a famous name round here,
Tommy Sheehan's skill and blinding pace, caused panic, pain and
fear.

The Riordans and Eoin Cummins could be proud of their display
And minor Micheál Broderick, when called into the game.
Wacky Healy too, when he came on, showed the speed of winter
rain,
And when they fouled to keep us out, they were punished by Joe
Kane.

The trainer of this fine young team is known as Jimmy Shea.
'No sympathy, you'll get from me, we often heard him say'.
He works them hard in sun and rain, till they're ready to fall down,
But without his help, they would not wear, Tipperary's county
Crown.

So well done, we say, to this fine young team, your fame will surely
grow,
And in many years ahead, more victories you'll know.
Stand up and play a manly game against every team you meet,
And bring honour too to the jersey blue, in victory or defeat.

A celebration of Fethard's South and County Senior Football Championships in 1988

County Senior Football Final at Kilsheelan, Sat. 25, 1988. Fethard 1-11, Clonmel
Commercials, 1-10.

418

Remember '88

By Rev. Br. J. Perkins, C.B.S. Thurles
Received from Liam Ó Donnchú, Ballymoreen, Littleton.

Long we'll remember eighty-eight and the county final game
When Loughmore-Castleiney boys won everlasting fame;
'Twas the eight day of October when the Borris boys did yield
In a great replay, they won the day in the famous Thurles field.

When captain Eamon Sweeney raised the cup of great Dan Breen,
There were tears of joy as the flags flew high, with their colours red
and green.
There were bonfires bright throughout the night and lights by the
Castle tower,
By Cuguilla's side they cheered with pride for this their greatest
hour.

Young boys were seen in red and green and cheered with sheer
delight;
And ladies fair, without a care, danced round the fires that night.
But old men wept as they homewards crept and thought of days of
yore,
Of many a son, who played and won, with Castleiney and
Loughmore.

We've got men yet, do not forget, brave men of might and brawn,
We have courage still, with strength and skill, to wield the grand
camán.
Other games they'll play, but this great day for long they'll celebrate,
For they won renown and the county crown in nineteen eighty-eight.

Celebrates Loughmore-Castleiney's first ever victory in the Tipperary Senior Hurling
Championship.
Loughmore Castleiney 2-7, Borrisoleigh, 1-8. (Replay)
Panel: Tom Mc Grath, Frank McGrath, Liam Cormack, Eamonn Sweeney (capt),
Michael McGrath, Eamonn Brennan, Seamus Bohan, Tom Larkin, Ned Ryan, Jim
Maher, Pat Cormack, Pat McGrath, John Cormack, Peter Brennan, Pat Treacy.
Coach: Jackie Walsh.

Gortnahoe-Glengoole v Arravale Rovers 1988

By Billy Barnaville
Source: Received from Liam Ó Donnchú, Ballymoreen, Littleton

Come all ye young hurlers, who are fond of the game,
I'll tell you a story that brought us great fame.
At Boherlahan Sportsfield on a November day,
Gurtnahoe-Glengoole, sure they came out to play.
The inter-county was the prize now at stake
Against Arravale Rovers, it was now make or break.
Now a great crowd had gathered and we got a great thrill
As they fought with great heart and great spirit and skill.
The Rovers from Arravale were a grand sporting team
But our stout-hearted boys soon shattered their dream.
Canon Lambe said, 'it's great they are tackling so fast'
Father Tony dragged his pipe, said, 'the cup's won at last'.

Denis Laffan in goal gave a faultless display
Our backs they were gallant on a very cold day.
With the wily Noel Barnaville, we couldn't go wrong
With Purcell and Webster so sure and so strong.
Jim Lanigan and Martin with the nice curly hair
Are as good a midfield as you'll get anywhere.
Kevin Moriarty, Michael Egan, P.J. Fogarty too,
Kept the flags flying often for Gortnahoe.
Michael Lyons took his points well and so passed the test
Kevin Laffan played great and is now at his best.

Eamonn Lanigan, the captain, he played a big part—
With his courage and skill and mighty big heart.
To the men who were subs, we say congrats to you,
For no team can manage without one or two.
Blackie Lanigan was injured and so could not play
But we'll see his great talent on another big day.
Justin Norton, P.J. Walsh, they're coming on quick
Conor Egan has shown us, he's sweet with his stick.
Brendan Teehan, Eamonn Egan had done battle before

And the lethal O'Brien is so sound for a score.
Christy Walsh and Pat Lanigan were always at hand
John Kenny had moved to a far distant land.

Delaney and Broderick, two more of our players,
They were ready to go if we got in arrears.
When you want hurleys or drinks or some kind of care,
The great clubman Andy Gorman, sure he's always there.
For the trainer Bill Martin we raise glasses up
For he trained these lads to win our first cup.
And the selectors too, we must give them great praise,
For they plotted and schemed in their own little ways.
The soft spoke Teehan, a hurler well known,
Jimmy Meighan, our chairman, his great work is now shown.
Tom O'Hara works hard for his county and club,
So we'll toast them all when we get to the pub.

Fair play to our supporters, who make lots of noise
When they shout for their heroes, Father Fogarty's boys.
Joe Dufficey, John Laffan said, 'it's great all the same
To see that George Webster recorded the game'
Danny Ryan, Tommy Teehan and Mick Doheny as well
Were seen jumping and cheering and shouting like hell.
And Willie Fitzgerald, his spirit was there
With the club that he loved and took such good care.
In Gortnahoe-Glengoole, the people I bet
Nineteen eighty- eight, sure they'll never forget.
God bless all the hurlers, present and past
May they keep the flag flying to the very last.

Celebrates the historic victory of Gortnahoe-Glengoole in the County Intermediate
Hurling Championship Final 1988. Played at Boherlahan, November 20, 1988.
Gortnahoe-Glengoole 2-8, Arravale Rovers 1-7.
Panel: Denis Laffan, Noel Barnville, Eamonn Purcell, Spencer Webster, Michael
Lanigan, John Stokes, Jim Lanigan, Jimmy Lanigan, Martin Lanigan C, Michael
Egan, P.J. Fogarty, Kevin Moriarty, Martin Lanigan (B), Kevin Laffan, Eamonn
Lanigan (capt), Conor Egan, Paudie Delaney, P.J. Walsh, Michael O'Brien, Michael
Lyons, Justin Norton, Brendan Teehan, Eamonn Egan.

The Tipp 21 — 1989

By Paddy Power, Drangan
Source: Received from Liam Ó Donnchú, Ballymoreen, Littleton.
Air: The Tipp 23rds

Come listen you Gaels of Tipperary
And hear those few words that I'll say
It's in praise of our gallant young hurlers,
Who won a great victory that day.
The last twenty years have been lean ones,
But that's all forgotten right now
Up in famed Holycross with John Leahy as boss,
They brought honour to old Knocknagow.

We'll start with Liam Connors the goalie
A lad who is destined for fame.
Not forgetting the brave Martin Kennedy
Thomas Cahill and that star Michael Skehan.
Then those five sturdy boys up from Drangan
Colm Duggan, the Ryans, Michael Nash
And we'll never forget you Paul Halloran
How you cut through those backs like a flash.

Jim O'Neill he commanded the centre—
Noel Leahy kept battling away.
On the wing there's the stylish Brian Meara
He was there in the thick of the fray.
Philip Skehan—sure your goal was a beauty
Gerry Bolger—you're as tough as they come
Now those are their names, sure they all played great games
For to win us the Tipp 21.

To the subs and selectors we thank you
You all played your part on the day.
And that band of gallant supporters·
Who cheered every inch of the way.

They said that they'd do it for Jimsey
And they surely did not let him down.
In Drangan we have Michael Cusack
Jim Egan in old Kickham's town.

Cross the hillsides, the cheers are still ringing
From Crohane to old Carraigmoclear
Now I'll lay down my pen
And just say 'well done men'
Please God we'll be with you next year.

Mullinahone under 21 hurling champions 1989. Mullinahone 3-7, Clonoulty
Rossmore 2-8

Mullinahone panel: P. Costello, M.Nash, B.O'Meara, S.O'Connor, C.Duggan,
J.O'Neill, E.O'Keeffe, J.White, F.Morrissey, N.Leahy, P.O'Halloran, J.Ryan,
K.Morrissey, E.Duggan, D.McNamara, T.Cahill, P.Skehan, M.Skehan, J.Leahy,
G.Bolger, M.Kennedy, J.Ryan.

The Green and White 1990

By Johnny Dwyer, Ballacuragh.
Source: Gaelic Games in Holycross Ballycahill 1884-1990 by Bob Stakelum.
Received from Seamus J. King, Boherclough, Cashel.
Air: Master McGrath

The fourteenth of October was the date of the year
Two teams from the county once more did appear
Holycross Ballycahill, a great team of renown
Met Cashel to fight for the county's true crown.

There was stonewall Pat Slattery and his young brother Paul
Who helped to make sure of old Cashel's downfall.
Pat in the goal blocked all shots left and right
And kept colours flying, the green and the white.

There was Stephen and Paddy and Ruairi Dwan
Who were worthy successors to the men that passed on.
The pace was a cracker how the fans they did roar
And we re-lived again nineteen fifty-four.

There was speedy and skilful young hurler Paul Maher
And that captain, so fearless, the brave Declan Carr.
With Pat Joe he wrapped it all up centre-field
With encouraging words such as 'never to yield'.

A foul on Phil Cahill gave our lads a free
And the ball it was placed by an apt referee.
Dwan lifted and struck, Lord how it did soar,
Straight over the bar for a beautiful score.

Tipperary is full of the hurling name Doyle
We had Michael and John who played it with style.
There was Tommy Dwyer and his skilled brother Phil
With courage and craft they gave many a thrill.

There was then Robert Stakelum a most famous name
In great games of the past they always won fame.
His passes were timely and always went right
And kept colours flying, the green and the white.

A beautiful pass from that shrewd Declan Carr
Was snapped up by Tonto and sent over the bar.
Tonto ran round those famed Cashel giants
And in six minutes flat had scored three winning points.

A game of true grit it was plain to be seen
Three cheers for our heroes, that gallant fifteen
We dream of Tipperary and her hurlers supreme
Holycross- Ballycahill is part of this dream.

Commemorates the senior county hurling final. Holycross-Ballycahill, 0-13, Cashel 0-10.

Team—Pat Slattery, J. Doyle, T. Dwyer, B. Browne, Phil Cahill, M.Doyle, R.Dwan, D.Carr, P.J.Lannigan, Paul Maher, S.Dwan, Tony Lannigan, Paul Slattery, Donal Ryan, Ciaran Carroll.

Boherlahan v Toomevara 1996

Anon:
Received from Liam Ó Donnchú, Ballymoreen, Thurles.
Air: The Wearing of the Green. Chorus after each verse.

In Ireland's hurling history
Tipperary holds first place,
For many a glorious victory
Has been won by Kickham's race.
And whilst we give due credit
To each team and to each man,
We now must sing the praises
Of the boys from Boherlahan.

Chorus:

Up the boys from Boherlahan,
Gallant hurlers every man,
Ireland's choice and Ireland's champions
Are the boys from Boherlahan!

Then here's to Tippperary,
To her hurlers bold and brave,
To her homesteads bright and cheery,
Where they never reared a slave.
And now a toast I give you,
And let each one fill a can,
'Here's many more All-Irelands
To the boys of Boherlahan'

'Twas a damp October evening
When we came to Thurles town
Faced up to Toomevara
To wrestle for the crown.
The 'Hounds were firm favourites
All deft with the camán

426

But they clean forgot the pride and grit
Of the boys from Boherlahan.

There were Ryans, O'Dwyers and Hickeys
Conor Gleeson and Liam Maher,
The Flanagans could put the ball
A sailing o'er the bar.
Murphy, Ferncombe, McGrath
You're the first since forty-one,
To bring the Dan Breen trophy back
Again to Boherlahan.

County Hurling Final at Semple Stadium, Thurles, on Oct.27, 1996. Boherlahan-Dualla 1- 16, Toomevara 2 - 12

Boherlahan: P.Ryan (capt), W.Hickey, T.J.O'Dwyer, T.Dwyer, S.Hickey, C.Gleeson (capt), D.Ryan, M.Ferncombe, J.J.McGrath, G.Flanagan, M.Murphy, B.O'Dwyer, P.O'Dwyer, L.Maher, A.Flanagan.

Newport's Hurling Men 1996

By Michael Collins, Newport
Source: Liam Ó Donnchú, Ballymoreen, Littleton.
Air: Seán South of Garryowen

It was on a bright September day as the evening sun shone down
Hordes of North Tipp's hurling fans converged on Nenagh town.
The blue and white of Lorrha on the sideline did unfold
But the stand was saturated with the purple and the gold.

The cheers that rose for Newport as they marched behind the band
Were heard for miles and miles around, resounding from the stands.
The mast on Keeper trembled and the old hill shook with pride
As the cheers of 'Come on Newport', they rang down the
mountainside.

Mid the colour and the atmosphere, the tension that was there
Strong hearts were now a fluttering, with excitement hard to bear.
But the boys who conquered bold Portroe, with Toome and
Moneygall,
Were all prepared for battle when T.F. threw in the ball.

Well I'll not describe the action, suffice it now to say,
When T.F's whistle blew full time, Newport had won the day.
For they played with passion in their hearts, commitment, pride and
flair,
And brought the Frank McGrath Cup back to the banks of the
Mulcaire.

Now let us toast our heroes, write their names in letters bold.
Proud champions of Tipperary North in the purple and the gold.
They shall never be forgotten while the Mulcaire waters flow,
From the hillsides of Sliabh Phelim, to the lovely Ballymackeogh.

Ger Floyd, our stalwart goalman, great guardian of the net,
Has kept his cool against the odds and many a fierce onset.

428

And the brothers Liam and Timmy Jones, who formed the famed last line
Beside the stout defender, D.J. or 'Cha' O'Brien.

Young O'Gorman held the centre as his father did of yore.
McCabe and Barry Gleeson were always to the fore.
Pat Keating's move to midfield proved the trump card in the pack
For himself and Tommy Moylan kept the harness on the 'Lak'.

The captain bold big Con McGrath, his likes you'll never meet.
Like the Trojan warriors of old, he does not know defeat.
Ger Bradley, champion of the frees, great forward staunch and true
And John Ryan, with dash and spirit played a hero's game all through.

Ger Moloney and John Mahony are in the firing line.
There's a buzz of expectation when the ball's with Dinny Ryan.
The Cooper's jinking side-steps; well you can safely bet,
When he passes to John Mahony, he'll plant it in the net.

Peter Coleman, Kieran Buckley, P.J.O'Rourke and Ken O'Brien,
With Eoin Bonfield and John Keating and 'Blondie' Paddy Ryan.
Ger Carey, David Hickey and the Coffey's Mike and Brian
Are all ready to do battle as they're waiting on the line.

Now a word in praise of the backroom boys, the men behind the team,
Who worked right hard with might and main, for to fulfil their dream
Timmy Floyd and his selectors, Eddie Quigley, Martin Ryan
With the shrewd, astute Len Gaynor, asisting on the line.

The coaches Paudie Butler, and Colm Honan too,
Kept concentrating on the skills as all good coaches do.
They raised to fame, the proud old name, of Newport once again,
So let's raise our glass and drink a toast, to Newport's hurling men.

Newport v Lorrha 8th Sept. 1996. Newport 1-9: Lorrha 0-12. Replay 15th Sept. 1996:
Newport 2-13, Lorrha 3-6.
Verse 3—T.F. Stapleton, Borrisoleigh
Verse 7—The Lak—Declan O'Meara, Lorrha
Verse 9-The Cooper—Dinny Ryan

Knockavilla—Under 14 B County Camogie Champions 1997

By Eamonn de Brún, Kilenure, Dundrum

'Twas in the year of ninety-seven, the final day of May
We reached the Ragg Camogie pitch and the final there did play.
The opposition came from Cashel, the city of the Rock
And at the end most people felt the result was quite a shock.

But those in charge were not surprised our girls came out on top,
Because we knew, for sure they would pull out all the stops.
The way this team went out and played, it made us all so glad
And surprised a fancied Cashel team and many more I'll add.

Our supporters came in numbers and this was very good
To shout and cheer along the girls as well they really should.
The team responded very well and sure surprised us all
And very soon the signs were there as they chased for every ball.

They were intent to win this game despite what others thought
And reputations though already made, counted then for nought.
The nights spent in the hurling field in building up morale
Were now about to bear some fruit, though tough at times they were.

Between the posts was Valerie Horgan, so cool and so secure.
At fullback, Sarah Murphy, so strong and yet so sure.
A star was born at wingback, her name was Dervla Keane,
Beside her was our captain, the stalwart Helen Breen.

Helen played a captain's part and by example led.
A team of stars in all our eyes, despite what others said.
We never did have any doubts and always felt we'd win.
Our hopes and aspirations too, we kept them all within.

What can one say of Linda Breen, so brilliant and so fair?
She dealt so well with every ball on the ground and in the air.
At centre-field we had our stars, who really showed their class
Lorraine McGrath and Mary Horgan—no others did surpass.

Paula Butler in her second game gave of her level best,
While K. McGrath on Cashel's star, was put to quite a test.
She passed with flying colours, keeping Philly very quiet,
While we got an honest effort from C.Taylor on the right.

Amanda Green has rarely played a game as good as this.
And E.English at full forward did not many chances miss.
Ronwyn Murphy then emerged and played a vital part
And likewise Teresa O'Dwyer, who really has great heart.

And we had girls on our bench, so vital to our team—
E.Hayes, A.Ryan, M.Carroll, were any coaches dream.
M,Keane, S.Cranley, C O'Brien, were vital to our cause
And really did enjoy, I know, the praises and applause.

S. Ryan and Marguerite Alley, as well as all the rest,
Would not I know have left us down, if put on to the test
They put in an honest effort, thro' all the summer nights
And really were delighted that their team-mates reached such
heights.

We thank the girls sincerely for the efforts which they gave.
And though they played in searing heat, no effort did they save.
There was one thing surely on their minds—to beat the opposition,
Which early on in Dundrum field had won the first edition.

When Marie Lacey joined the group we'd no one to assist
Her interest in the team was such, she couldn't well resist.
We worked so well in this great cause, the two of us together,
In wind or rain, in hail or sun, in every kind of weather.

Again to all concerned my thanks—my thanks a thousand times
And I hope your worth is captured in these special little rhymes.
But your deeds will live in memory for many years to come,
In Knockavilla-Donaskeigh and also in Dundrum.

Final Score: Knockavilla 1-3, Cashel 0-2.

A Song for the Toomevara Hurlers

By Anon
Source: Tomevara G.A.A. 1885-1985.
Received from Seamus J. King, Boherclough, Cashel.

There's good boys and true in Killarney
They're hurlers in Leix to a man
Kilkenny's bold talk was no blarney
Before they met Boherlahan.
But take me from Wexford to Clara
From Cork down through Wexford and Clare
Then come home to our own Toomevara
For you won't get the likes of them there.

Chorus:

Here's luck to our own Toomevara boys,
Here's luck to their muscles and brawn,
Old Ireland is still to the fore boys,
While they wield a Tipperary camán.

They say the old spirit is dead, boys
That we're not like our fathers of yore
That old customs and manners are fled, boys
And that soon we'll be Irish no more.
But I know they are sadly mistaken
When I see gallant Toome 'on the ball'
And hear the wild cheers that are breaking
From Clash to sweet Moneygall.

Chorus:

Here's luck to our own Toomevara boys,
God prosper their muscles and brawn,
Old Ireland is still to the fore boys,
While they wield a Tipperary camán.

Our hurlers are true to the core, boys
They were always the flower of the flock
We've strong hardy fellows in store, boys
True chips off the old Irish block.
In work and in play none are bolder
We know that for both there is room
And our motto is 'shoulder to shoulder'
For God and for Ireland and Toome.

Chorus:

Here's luck to our own Toomevara boys,
Here's luck to your muscles and brawn,
Old Ireland's not finished with yet, boys
While they wield a Tipperary camán.

Lovely Fair Ileigh

Anon
Source: A Century of G.A.A. in Borris-Ileigh.
Received from Seamus J.King, Boherclough, Cashel.

I know a little winding road
So beautiful to stray,
When the wild perfume of hawthorn's bloom
And the woodbine skirts the way.
The heather brown upon the hill
And the wild flowers in the lea,
The shady road winds on between
To Lovely Fair Ileigh.

Ileigh it is a beauty spot
Down in a shady dell
The green hills fair they rise above
Where many a brave man fell.
Here the trees are evergreen,
The flowers you'll always see,
The roses' perfume scents the air
'Round Lovely fair Ileigh.

If you wander up the green hill slopes
Midst the pure and balmy air,
You can view the rolling plains below,
So lovely and so fair.
There nature gives her richest garb
To every bush and tree,
And spreads the wild flowers o'er the vale,
'Round Lovely Fair Ileigh.

At evening time in the old kiln field,
You can see the boys so bold,
'Twould remind you of old Knocknagow,
In Kickham's story told.

To see them wield their camáns,
So brave and manfully,
There's many a Matt the Thresher
'Mongst the lads of Fair Ileigh.

Yonder stands the little church
And the graveyard all around,
Where three of Ireland's noble dead,
Rest in that holy ground.
There are three green graves; sad I ween,
No monument have they
Where rest in peace the ashes
Of young Russell, Bourke and Shea.

But the day is not far distant
And we hope it may not be,
When we'll raise a monument o'er their graves
In Lovely Fair Ileigh.

Regarded as the Borris-Ileigh Anthem.

Hail Gallant Toomevara

By Anon

Source: Toomevara G.A.A. 1885-1985
Received from Seamus J. King, Boherclough, Cashel

Hail! Gallant Toomevara,
Scion of a noble race
Home of 'Wedger' and O'Meara
Ready any foe to face.
You've upheld the county's honour,
Never were you known to fail,
When you country asked for soldiers,
You bravely manned the Bearna Baoil.

When your county wanted hurlers
You again were to the fore;
Sweeping onward came those Greyhounds,
Like the winds down Galteemore.
See those banners proudly waving
The bon-fires glow, the hills illume
For the credit of the village,
And the hurlers of great Toome.

You have won the final honour!
You have won the county crown!
To the homes of Toomevara
You—their hurlers brought renown.
Kilruane, Burgess, and Nenagh
Kildangan and Roscrea,
Moneygall, Borris and Lorrha
They cheered you on that day.

Keep the flag of victory flying;
Uphold the North's great dash and name:
Toomevara's gallant Greyhounds
And Tipperary's dauntless fame.

Toomevara down the years

By Rev. Bro. J. Perkins, C.B.S. Thurles
Source: Toomevara GAA 1885-1985
Received from Seamus J. King, Boherclough, Cashel

You have heard of 'Wedger Meagher and the O'Mearas too of old
And many another hurler brave who wore the green and gold.
Their names rang out through Ireland on numerous hurling grounds
And 'Wedger's ' men were known even then as Toomevara's famed
'Greyhounds'.

Long, long before eighteen eighty-four, their hurlers could be seen
Round Carraway and Clonalea, Stuick, Coole and Blakefield Green.
By Ballinveny, Bunacum Park, Ballybeg and Clash,
Garnafarna, Greanstown; they heard the sound of ash.

In nineteen-ten, arose those men with 'Wedger' in command:
Like greyhounds dashing o'er the sod they won fame throughout the
land.
In nineteen-thirteen, their worth was seen, the 'Greyhounds' did not
yield,
They won the Croke Memorial cup in famed Dan Fraher's field.

In nineteen-fifteen and 'sixteen' too, further honours did they seek:
They won once more the armlets wore in memory of Easter Week.
The Gaelic League gave the Thomond Shield to have it as their own
Twice they shone and twice they won against Cork, Clare and
Garryowen.

From nineteen-twelve to twenty-three, Boherlahan felt their steel:
Five times they won, five times each shone, their (true) worth they
did reveal.
In twenty-seven 'Wedger' sailed to the shores of Americay:
He said: 'I always loved old Tipp. for her honour did I play'.

Tipperary's great full-forward, Martin Kennedy of renown
In nineteen-thirty led great Toom to win the county crown.
With Jack Donovan, Tom O'Meara, who in the All-Ireland had
shone
They beat Moycarkey-Borris in nineteen thirty-one.

Nineteen-sixty was the historic year we saw Toom come again
To take the Dan Breen trophy from the Sarsfield's stylish men.
Matt Hassett took the McCarthy cup from the Dubs in sixty-one
And with him Matt O'Gara, John Hough and Mounsey shone.

And still great Toom goes marching on their juveniles to the fore:
It won't be long, they'll be as strong and as powerful as of yore.
Come! Raise the green and gold again and let us proudly say:
'Three cheers for the gallant 'Greyhounds', Toomevara boys, hurrah!

The Boys of Newport Town

By Michael Bourke
Source: Newport in Song and Poetry
Published by: Michael Bourke Festival Committee.

Tipp'rary men, attention pay I'll sing a verse or two,
In praise of those brave heroes, the boys in gold and blue.
They conquered all, from Monegall, right down to Knockmealdown,
They are now the champions of the North, the boys of Newport
town.

Chorus:

Tipp'rary's fame and peerless name
Will never be let down,
For victory's flag shall be kept flying
By the boys of Newport town.

Moycarkey, Thurles, gallant Toom, Kildangan, Cappawhite,
Ahane, Young Irelands and Claughaun went down before their
might.
They conquered all both great and small from Roscrea to Shannon's
side,
Tipp'rary men in years to come will think of them with pride.

Then fetch around the whiskey and we'll give those men a toast—
For of those dashing hurlers Tipp'rary now can boast.
To see them march through Nenagh town, it would fill you heart
with pride,
They will bring All-Ireland's final to the sparkling Mulcair's side.

Then success to those brave heroes, hurlers true and grand—
You could not find their equal if you searched all Ireland.
Give one cheer for Tommy Coffey and Michael Rainsford too
And a cheer for Father Ryan and the boys in gold and blue.

My Old Home Town

By Michael Schofield

I'll toast to night my old home town,
Built by the Ara's side,
Beneath the lordly Galtees crown
Where friends of mine abide.

Tipperary of the Gaelic men—
Great John O'Leary's town,
And gentle Ellen—whose proud pen
Wrote ballads of renown.

The fame of sweet Tipperary shines
On Gaelic records yet,
I'll toast you here in these few lines
The teams we shan't forget.

Old Bohercrowe! Great Bohercrowe!
That made the 'eighties ring'
Old Bohercorwe whose records show
Great was that Gaelic spring.

And Arravale, sweet Arravale,
Where hast thy glory gone
Are there no lips to tell the tale
How gloriously it shone?

Rosanna! Sound again the lyre,
Mount Sion stands beside,
Where ardent hearts it should inspire
To Gaelic feats of pride.

A parting toast ye exiles then
From out that old home town
We'll toast the famous Gaelic men
That bore the victor's crown.

442

Bohercrowe and Rosanna were former G.A.A. clubs in Tipperary town. Bohercrowe won the All-Ireland football final in 1889.

The present club is Arravale Rovers

John O'Leary was a Fenian leader and G.A.A. patron.

Ellen O'Leary was a sister of John O'Leary. Her poems have been described as 'simple field flowers which blossomed above the subterranean workings of a grim conspiracy'

Ara (Arra) —The river that flows through Tipperary town from which the town and county takes its name.

Mount Sion—Christian Brothers' Schools, Tipperary.

Shall I Ever See Them More?

By Sister Mary Alberta Meagher, Boulea.
Source:Ballingarry 1887-1987- 100 Years of Gaelic Games.
Received from Seamus J. King, Boherclough, Cashel.

O my mind is ever wandering, wandering far across the foam,
To the dear old hills of Boulea, where in childhood I did roam.
And my heart is ever yearning, yearning for the friends of yore,
So in anguish I keep asking, shall I ever see them more?

Shall I see the hills and valleys, more dear to me than all?
Shall I see the boys upon the bridge, gathering for a game of ball?
Shall I hear the hurleys clashing, hear the shouts and cheers galore?
Oh acushla won't you tell me, shall I ever hear them more?

Shall I see those fine smart fellows, of the Commons football team?
The dashing sons of Smith O'Brien, for real to me they seem.
Shall I see them march to victory, with the pipers on before?
Oh, tell me, won't you tell me, shall I ever see them more?

Ah, those days are gone forever; they were too good for to last,
The friends I once did cherish, around the world are cast.
Each day before God's altar, with fervour I implore,
God bless you all and keep you, should I never see you more.

Composed for the members of the Commons Smith O'Brien's team of some years
ago.

Thurles C.B.S and the Moycarkey-Borris Connection

By Bro. J. Perkins
Source—Moycarkey-Borris GAA Story 1984

Through winding streets and country roads,
They come in haste to join
Drombane, Clonoulty, Inch, Loughmore,
Holycross, Ballycahill and Moyne.

Fennellys, Sarsfields, Kickham's boys,
With Gortnahoe, Glengoole,
And famed Moycarkey-Borris play
In the Christian Brothers school.

At the gate I stood, warm grew my blood
As I watched those young men dash
O'er the hard black ground, I heard the sound
The sweet music of the ash.

I had seen it all before I'm sure,
In spite of war and woe
When their fathers played the self-same game
Forty years ago.

The same deep fire is in their veins
Their spirits still the same—
They love the skills and the treasured thrills
Of that grand old hurling game.

Brother Perkins writing in 1984 says: 'it would be difficult to think of Thurles C.B.S. without a Moycarkey Borris boy in it' Since the brothers came to Thurles in 1816, long before the GAA was founded, the names of those hardy boys from Moycarkey-Borris are to be seen on the roll-books. Hurling was their game then, and hurling is their game now. Space does not permit to give the names of the Harty Cup winners in 1933, 1938, 1939, 1950, 1951 and 1956. Six times they brought back the Harty but how many more times were they beaten by only a point? They always put up a good show and the young boys were always proud to gain a place on the Harty team.....

The work done by the Primary schools in Moycarkey-Borris must never be forgotten. In their grand rural schools they had learned the basic skills of hurling, and more important still, they had been imbued with a love for hurling that remained with them for life.

Thurles C.B.S. did not forget the mighty men of Moycarkey-Borris. They could depend on them on any team and were prepared to give everything for the sake of their school and for the honour of their former parish...

The spirit of Moycarkey-Borris and the names of the hurling heroes shall live for ever, 'so long as Slievenamon holds memories of Knocknagow the Rock of Cashel stands guard o'er the smiling fields of Magh Coirce and the friendly homes of Two-Mile Borris'.

~ PART FOUR ~

Hurling

The Old Hurler

By Winifred Letts
Source: Vincent O'Dea, Ennis.

'When you are old', she said 'grown old and grey…'
I laughed to hear her say it, till the cold
Strange thought came afterwards: you will be old someday
And give your hurley stick away
For someone else to play.

It seemed a foolish word yet she spoke true,
That you must be like other men and trail
Your dragging feet and tell a twice-told tale,
Rubbing dry wrinkled hands as old men do—
And yet it will be you.

Young men will praise new heroes of the game,
This one's endurance, that one's flying feet.
How will they know how strong you were and fleet—
You who were once a storm wind and flame?
They will forget your name.

They will not dream, the careless and uncouth,
That you who wag an old man's tedious tongue
Were once splendour, tawny-haired and young.
But I shall laugh at them who doubt the truth
Of your immortal youth.

The author was born in Dublin and contributed several plays to the early Abbey
repertoire. Her best remembered poem is 'A Soft Day'.

The Old Hurler

By Dáithí Fitzgerald, C.B.S. Thurles
Received from Liam Ó Donnchú, Ballymoreen, Littleton.

I lost my heart to hurling, ah 'tis seventy years ago.
My pitch was then the cobbled yard before the kitchen door,
But the hens kept getting in my way and I found it hard to score.
But I thought my heart would burst the day that I was picked to play
For the honour of our little school, in a strange town miles away,
I tremble still when I recall the glory of that day.

My summer evenings all were spent with hurling men, you know
As we pucked the ball to them in Barry's field below
And wondered why they never flinched before the fiercest blows.
Until, one fine September day, the parish lads and I
Gave battle for the county cup; and not an eye was dry
When we wound up a point in front; I watched the old men cry.

And so the years just melted by, and every where I'd be,
I seemed to meet with hurling men; they seemed to follow me.
There's some mystery or magic in the game that we can't see.
From the fertile fields of Munster to Antrim's hurling glens
And every little place between that knows the hurling men.
My blessing on the men I've seen; may we see their likes again.

When God created this auld world He had courage left to spare
Along with grace and beauty and a dash of devil-may-care.
He saved it for the hurlers; He said, 'twont be wasted there'.
Now I know that where I'm going, to the land beyond the clay
There's hurlers waiting there for me, and God will let me play
And his good Mother will come out and call us in for tay.

The Hurler

By Rev. J. B. Dollard
Source: History of the GAA, 1910-1930 by Phil O'Neill.

Upon his native sward the hurler stands
To play the ancient pastime of the Gael
And all the heroes famed of Innisfail
Are typified in him—I see the bands
Of the Craobh Ruadh applauding with their hands,
The Fianna shouting over Clíu Máil,
Oisín and Finn with eager faces pale
Caoilte and Goll are there from fairylands.

And fierce Cú Chulainn comes, his godlike face
With yearning wild to grip in hand once more
The lithe camán and drive the hurtling ball
In Walsh's, Kelleher's and Semple's grace.
He sees again his glorious youth of yore,
And mourns his dead compeers and Ferdia's fall.

A sonnet dedicated to three legendary hurlers, 'Drug' Walsh, Kilkenny, Tom Semple, Thurles, and Jim (Jamesy) Kelleher, Cork. Tom Semple, according to Raymond Smith, in *Decades of Glory,* 1966, p62, was born to lead. A towering figure of a man, he immediately commanded respect and his example and enthusiasm inspired the players around him with the desire for victory. He led the Thurles Blues selection to All-Ireland successes in 1906 and 1908. After his retirement he became a noted administrator. When the old Thurles Blues met Dungourney in the Munster final of 1909, the Cork supporters were already letting off the pigeons. Pat Fitzgerald recalled the towering captain, pointing to the disappearing pigeons as he addressed the men in the centre of the field (no dressing rooms) rousing his men with the words, 'There they go; Cork think it is all over. These chaps cannot beat us if they do not get the ball. They must not get possession in this half.' There were no half measures with him. Individual glory was secondary to the benefit of the team as a whole.

'What is your fear boys while Semple is with you,
That gallant old captain who leads in the fray?
Why should you doubt when you think of the past boys
That one word 'Dungourney' ought all trouble allay.
Forward to victory then; on to the Leinster men,
Let Erin see what the 'blue' boys can do—

Practise at dawn and noon, train hard and train soon.
On! On! The battle cry is Thurles Aboo.'

Seamus J. King in his *History of Hurling* (1996) writes about an article in the *Cork Examiner*, by Carbery (J.D.Mehigan) December 1908: 'Few men playing the game in Ireland have achieved the fame that the Thurles captain-Tom Semple- has known. As an organiser and a player he deserves a high place in any story of the progress of hurling during the infancy of the 20th century. Tom is a conspicuous man-there is no chance of mistaking another player for Semple...In build Semple is one of the tall, sinewy type, more of a thoroughbred than a hunter, if I may so express myself. He is well over six feet in his 'vamps'. And. Like most Tipperarymen, square cut and as hard as nails. Considering his great height he is light all over him particularly at the waist and limbs...

Semple's career stretched from 1897 to 1911, and its height coincided with the success of the Thurles Blues. He led his club to county championship victories in 1904, 1906, 1907, 1908, 1909 and 1911. He was a regular on the county team for many years and led the Blues to all-Ireland victories in 1906 and 1908. In 1906 also he won the All-Ireland long puck championship, sending the nine-ounce ball 96 yards. He was also captain of the Tipperary team that travelled to the Continent in 1910 and played exhibition games at Brussels and Fontenoy.'

Suir View Rangers 1895-1898-a History also record that Tom Semple was the most famous player ever to wear the Suir View colours. He was first selected for the Tipperary team in 1898 and won the first all-Ireland with Two-Mile-Borris in 1900. He was on the first interprovincial teams to contest the Railway Shields in 1906, 1907 and 1909. He was on the original committee formed in 1910 to take over the running of what was then Thurles Showgrounds and which now bears the name Semple Stadium. He was chairman of the Tipperary County Board in 1915 and 1916 and was Tipperary's representative on the Munster Council from 1911 to 1915. He served one term as treasurer of the central council of the GAA. Tom died on the 11th April 1943 aged 64 and is buried in St. Mary's (C.Of I) churchyard in Thurles.

Innisfail—A poetic name for Ireland. -the island of prosperity, The word Fál has been interpreted in various ways e.g. destiny, enclosure etc but the original word seems to have been prosperity. The word Fál is discussed by C-J Guyonvarch in Ogam, vol. 16 pp436-440 and by An Dr.. Dáithí Ó hÓgáin, U.C.D. in a forthcoming book.

Craobh Ruadh—the palace of the legendary king of the Ulaid, Conchobhar mac Neasa was called by mediaeval writers 'an Chraobhruadh', which means the red-branched or red-poled edifice. *(Myth, legend and Romance* by Dr. Dáithí Ó hÓgáin, Ryan Publishing Co. Ltd., London, 1990.

Fianna—the word 'fianna' was used in early times for young hunter-warriors. Such groups of young men were a social reality in many early societies, as it was part of a warrior's training to live for a period in the wilderness in order to learn how to hunt and fight. *(Myth, Legend and Romance* by Dr. Dáithí Ó hÓgáin, Ryan Publishing Co. Ltd., London, 1990.

Clíu Máil—An area in East Limerick surrounding Knockainey, near Hospital in County Limerick. Clíu in Old Irish is a term applied to some kind of territory and Máil in Old Irish denotes a champion. Clíu Máil, therefore, denotes 'the range of champions'.

Oisín—a leading character in the Fianna cycle. He was son of the celebrated Fionn Mac Cumhaill. His name means 'little fawn' and was a common one in early Ireland. Its application to him, however, reflects the hunting imagery of the Fianna. *(Myth, Legend and Romance* by Dr. Dáithí Ó hÓgáin, Ryan Publishing Co. Ltd., London, 1990.

Finn—A celebrated hero in Irish litreature and folklore. Stories concerning him are continuous in the litreature for well over a thousand years. In the earliest texts his name occurs in the Old Irish form Find, in Middle Irish it is written Finn, and in Modern Irish Fionn. . *(Myth, Legend and Romance* by Dr. Dáithí Ó hÓgáin, Ryan Publishing Co. Ltd., London, 1990.

Caoilte—As great athlete and faithful comrade of Fionn Mac Cumhaill in the Fianna Cycle. His full name is Caoilte Mac Rónáin and he figures prominently in the stories of Fionn in both litreature and folklore. . *(Myth, Legend and Romance* by Dr. Dáithí Ó hÓgáin, Ryan Publishing Co. Ltd., London, 1990.

Goll—Goll Mac Morna was a leading rival of the hero Fionn Mac Cumhaill in the cycle of stories concerning the Fianna. Goll himself was a heroic character and a great warrior, and the leader of the Morna clan. . *(Myth, Legend and Romance* by Dr. Dáithí Ó hÓgáin, Ryan Publishing Co. Ltd., London, 1990.

Ferdia The first mention of the warrior Fear Diadh is in a text written in or about the 9c. He is there described as son of Fearghus mac Róich and slayer of Ceithearn mac Fionntain. And was so associated with the Ulster Cycle. As that cycle developed and its characters became synchronised, Cú Chulainn and Fear Diadh were represented as having as youths trained in arms together. *(Myth, Legend and Romance* by Dr. Dáithí Ó hÓgáin, Ryan Publishing Co. Ltd., London, 1990.

Fr. Dollard, (later Monsg.) the author, born 30th August 1872 was a Kilkennyman from Ballytarsney, Mooncoin. He wrote numerous poems and articles about hurling. In Carberry's Annual 1946/47 Carberry writes, 'Dear kindly Mooncoin man who loved the hurling and the hurlers with an abiding love…Fr. Dollard's book of sacred poems, written in exile has won him a high place in church litreature. His droll tales of Myles n gCamán, his ballad of The Little Villages; his beautiful translation of Donnaca Rhua's Bán-Cnuic-Éireann-Ó; his beautiful poems perfectly balanced and brimful of Celtic imagery, on the fairies, sports, romances of his homeland; his descriptive verses of Suirside and Clontarf, all endeared him to our hearts'. He died in Toronto in 1946. (*History of the GAA,* 1910-1930, Phil O'Neill, (Sliabh Ruadh).

Edward O'Keeffe, Mooncoin writes, 'Very early in life Fr. Dollard became a student of the mystery and folklore of Ireland. With his great talents and gifts of expression he developed a love for poetry, drama and short stories. His many literary works in later life reflected that love. Having completed his classical studies in Ireland he left for Canada in 1890 going to New Brunswick..... He immediately began his studies in the Grand Seminary in Montreal......Fr Dollard was ordained to the priesthood in 1896; he served successively as curate at St. Mary's and St. Luke's churches in Toronto. For nine years he served as P.P. at Uppergrove where he erected a new church. He later served at St. Monica's and Our Lady of Lourdes parishes.

While devoting his life to the spiritual well being of his parishioners, Fr. Dollard found time to carry on his writings. At least four volumes of his poems were published in Canada. His books *Irish Ballads and Lyrics*, *Irish Mist and Sunshine* were some of his most popular and best known works. In *The Gaels of Moondarrig*, a volume of short stories chiefly describing Mooncoin hurlers, it also depicts a way of rural life over a hundred years ago. As well as following the fortunes of the Mooncoin and Kilkenny teams, several of his poems of that period (1904-13 were written in praise of the hurlers of Cork, Kilkenny and Tipperary, and his writings under the pen name 'Slievenamon' were widely read.

The Hurler

By Paddy Whelan, Ballymacarbry, Co. Waterford.

When the buachaill óg is born, all relations come to see
With gushing admiration full, what name now will it be?
But the sire is not too worried, could be Jack or Bill or Mick,
The problem is much different—Now, will he swing a stick?

He creeps and crawls then stands and walks and learns to take a
tumble
As he wobbles round the kitchen floor, he causes many a rumble;
He fastens on to wooden spoon midst cutlery and delph,
With glint in eye, he swings it high, a proper hurling elf!

Time passes as it always does and then his first camán,
He raps his mother on the shins, 'Now get out on the lawn!'
Dad has a lot of patience for the proper grip and swing
We could have here a genius now like Mackey, Keane or Ring.

Then to the schoolyard hurly burly and exciting lunchtime game,
As he braces for the clash of ash his teammates shout his name;
His hands and body feel the sting of ash from stronger fellow,
But in his heart he makes a vow—I never will be yellow!

With tennis ball against the wall he fine hones down the skill
That will in heat of battle shine and loyal supporters thrill.
The lift and strike from left or right, the sideline cut and flick—
He will always thank the gable for many a hurling trick.

He goes into his bed at night still slighty 'fraid of dark
But his dreams they are all happy ones of playing in Croke Park;
Of dashing forward in the fray to score that vital goal—
He wakes up hoping that in life he'll realise that role.

His first time in club colours is a day he won't forget,
He wouldn't have more butterflies for the first trip on a jet.

As he pulls on numbered jersey he is part of hurling lore
And share the pride and spirit of all who went before.

And when in battle muscles ache, lungs hammer on chest wall–
He really cannot give up; he has to chase that ball.
He senses old club heroes are there above the fray,
Urging on this present lot, 'Bring home that cup to day!'

He loses many games in life a lot more than he wins
And always takes the blame himself for some foolish hurling sins.
He forms many friendships new from within the GAA
And they blossom with maturity until that final day.

And when the ref. blows full-time and the game of life is o'er
His pals and teammates gather round to see him from the shore.
They wrap him in club colours and they wish him bon voyage
And through the mists of mourning they see a bright mirage

Of a youthful hurler in his prime and he dashing o'er the sward
Going for to make a score then back to help rearguard.
Urging on his teammates for that little extra spurt
And he always spoke encouragement; he was never mean or curt.

As the clods fall on his coffin they remember his great joy
To always turn out for his club since he was just a boy.
Though his body has gone back to earth his spirit it will stay
To lift the parish players for many a long long day.

And when they field out loyally from passing year to year
They'll always give their utmost, supporters they will cheer.
And when the going it gets tough they hear above the fray,
A voice recast from hurling's past, 'Bring home that cup today'.

The Hurlers

By Rev. James B. Dollard
Source: New York-Irish Independent,1910

On Erin's sward the hurlers stand
Swinging the lithe camán in hand.
Their game is racy of the soil
And welcome after days of toil
The game beloved in Erin old
When Fergus, Finn and Oisín bold
Made the wild echoes ring afar
With stormy clash of mimic war.
When Diarmuid , to the king's surprise,
Struck the swift liathróid to the skies!.
When young Cuchulainn on his track,
Drove the wild goal-ball forth and back!
When on the wide Tailteann plain
Great champions strove with might and main
To wrest the laurels for their own
In Desmond, Ormond or Tyr-Owen.
Oh, yet, thank God, in Ireland still
Are hurlers who their place can fill;
In old Moondarrig by the Suir,
Or where the Lee runs silver pure!
Or where Tipperary's fearless band
Stand steadfast for their native land.
Or Clare, where western tempest blows;
Or Limerick, where the Shannon flows;
Or Dublin by the Liffey side;
Or Wexford where proud heroes died.
O'er all the land where're they be,
Dear are the hurling men to me.
Long may they live in each green vale
To be the pride of Innisfail.
And long be heard in field and bawn
The clashing of the sweet camán
Till Erin once again be free
Bright crowned with radiant liberty.

Hurlers and All

By Dermot Kelly, Limerick
Received from Dermot Kelly. Also published in Legends of the Ash by Brendan Fullam
(Wolfound Press Ltd., 68 Mountjoy Square, Dublin 1

He gently tugs his father's coat, Mam said, 'Keep close now Pat',
You're goin' to a hurling match, your first—remember that.
Don't get lost in that big crowd, bless yourself when goin'out,
And after in the pub be quiet—let Daddy drink his stout.

And so I saw the mighty game and traced the sliotar's flight,
The flashing ash, the roaring crowd, the colours all about.
I pinched myself, looked up at Dad, so proud that I was there.
Such drama, action, music, laughter— splendour everywhere.

The years rolled on and, oh the joy of balancing the ball
On the bos and then a toss, against the gable wall.
My first day on the Claughaun team—a boy, but I was proud
To be a hurler—I could have cried or shouted it aloud.

Then to the Brothers, Harty Cup—the Brother's name was Tynan,
A Tipperary man for sure and one you could rely on.
At Physics, Maths and Latin, a genius at his station,
But hurling was his burning love, an Irish celebration.

The county team then beckoned on, an honourable promotion.
With hurling games in Munster, such passion and emotion.
Limerick, Cork, Tipperary, Clare—the proud men of the Decies,
The ebb and flow of luck and woe—the hope one never reaches.

And through the crowd the calls come loud, some good and many
strange sounds,
'Get the lead out of your arses', boys,' 'Come on ye Mackey
greyhounds.'

'Doubt ya boy'—there goes the cry, Ringey has awoken,
He's won the match with lightning dash, all Limerick hearts are broken.

And so the hurlers come and go, to day's lads are much faster,
With helmets, shin guards, rubs and pills that make the ball go farther.
Names come tumbling through my mind: Mick Mackey, Power and Ringey,
The Rackards, Bobbie, Nick and Bill and who'd forget bould Youngie.

The 'Rattler'. 'Diamond', 'Goggles', 'Fox', Con Murphy, Connolly brothers,
Smyth, Hayes of Clare, McKenna, Keher, Doyle, Stakelum and others.
The writers John D., Raymond Smith, Fullam, Paddy Downey,
Norman Allen, Austin Flynn, and singing Joe McDonagh.

O'Hehir, Ó Muircheartaigh, Ó Siocháin, Ó Dúlaing, Tynan, Cregan,
Herbert, Hartigan—I could go on, but you'd be here all evenin'.
The shadows stalk the gable wall—there's no-one left to shout,
Pull the door as you cross the floor, and bless when goin' out.

The author Dermot Kelly played in the backs and the forwards for Limerick for many years. He was captain of Munster in 1956 when they failed to Leinster in the Railway cup final. His decade in the top time yielded few rewards in the form of major trophies: a Munster title in 1955, Railway Cup honours in 1957 and 1960, two county titles in 1957 and 1958.

Hurlers of Éire

By Celt
Source: Muiris de Prionnbhiol Blanchardstown and Gaelic Echo Sept 5, 1942

There's a lilt in the heart of the hurler
A sparkle of light in his eye;
And his spirit takes flight
With a condor's might
Through the ambient sheen of the sky.

There's a joy in the stride of the hurler
O'er the sward where his feet scarce press;
And his camán swing
Makes the echoes ring
With its carefree joyousness.

When the dun ball flies like a bird aloft
And whirling forms press on—
Mark his tensing frame
And the brightening flame
And the poise of that lithe camán.

In the throes of a goal endangered,
See his rush to the Bearna Baoil;
List the stinging stroke
Midst the ranks that broke
And that cry like a battle peal.

Or mark him again in the vanguard
With goal and glory in sight;
Note the wary stance
And the eagle glance
And the flash of the ball in flight.

A thousand thrills of the ages
Are compressed in this hour of life

The fame of his sires
His soul inspires
In this game of god-like strife.

When ye cheer on the eager hurler
Ye echo the song of his heart
That beats to the strains
Of the blood in his veins
And becomes of his spirit a part.

Oh: hurlers of Éire the envied
The flower and pith of our kin
May your manhood prevail
For the hopes of the Gael
And the crown of the field you would win.

To ye, heirs of the contests of heroes
Who fashioned the frame of our race—
Is committed the fire
Of a nation's desire
Strength, Chivalry, Freedom and Grace.

Where Hurlers All Are Heroes

Anon
Source: Limerick Heroes by Séamus Ó Ceallaigh.

Here's to each Gael from the Golden Vale
And their hurling records grand.
Their deathless fame at that Tailteann game
Sheds glory all over the land.
Swift passes too and an eye that's true
And a dash to do or die,
While sliotars ring to the camán's swing
Sends the green flag soaring high.

How memories come from the year agone
Of where famed teams used to be—
Dungourney's might and the records bright
Of the *Rockies* by the Lee—
Of Moycarkey and Boherlahan lads,
Yes, Tallow and Irelands's Own,
And of Tulla's thrills and O'Callaghan's Mills
Three Castles and Tullaroan.

I'm thinking of Dublin's wondrous teams
And of Boys of Wexford fame
And of Galway's sons and of Cavan men
All past masters of the game.
Ah, Louth and Kildare played fair and square
In Croke Park by Liffeyside
Against that classic team o'er which glory gleams,
Laune Rangers, the Kingdom's pride.

May God bless each Gael from the Golden Vale,
All true sons of Garryowen,
From the borders down to the grand old town
That treasures the Treaty Stone.

Where hurlers all are heroes
In Tailteann game so grand,
We hail them and proclaim them
The glory of the land.

The Greatest Game of All

By John Duggan, Longford

One evening I went into town to buy a bag of flour
And a mile or two from 'Comer' I caught up with Jimmy Power.
I stopped and offered him a lift, he was going to buy some grub
But before we did the shoppin', well! —We dropped into a pub.
And as we sat here talkin' I could see around the bar
There were pictures of great hurlers like Paddy Larkin and Lory Meagher.
And right above the fireplace in a frame for all to see
Was the team in black and amber and the year was sixty-three.

Well we started reminiscing just to pass the time away
And comparing all these former greats with the hurlers of today.
We mentioned Ring and Mackey, Jimmy Langton , Eddie Keher
And we wondered how our present hurling heroes would compare.
An old man in the corner then left down his glass of beer
He'd been watchin' games for sixty years and had travelled far and near.
Says he, 'I've seen the greatest, but I think it's fair to say
That we still have got their equals in the young lads of today.

In Wexford and Kilkenny, in Tipperary Cork and Clare
In Offaly and Galway there are talents that are rare.
The Dubs are fairly handy and the Limerick men in green–
And I'd swear that D. J. Carey is the best I've ever seen.
I never make comparisons, I think it's out of place–
Who can say if Nicky English would get scores off Paddy Grace?
And every dog will have his day and the memories will abide
Of so many famous hurlers, I remember them with pride.

The first time that I saw Croke Park was September thirty-nine
We travelled in an early train and the weather it was fine.
I remember the excitement when we got to Dublin town
As we left the railway station ,sure the rain was falling down.

Well we belted up our overcoats; it wouldn't spoil our fun
Then we heard the news by shoutin' out—'The war has just begun'
I felt a sense of horror which I never will forget
'Till a man in black and amber roared, 'The Corkmen must be bet'.

With Kilkenny's Paddy Larkin, Paddy Phelan, Paddy Grace
And a teenage Jimmy Langton who so well deserved his place.
They were leading at the interval, but Corkmen never flinch
They got back on level terms captained bravely by Jack Lynch.
Then the lightnin' flashed and the thunder roared and the rain came pourin' down
But the players never faltered in that final of renown.
'Twas a point from Jimmy Kelly filled Kilkenny's hearts with glee
They had bet the mighty Corkmen by two-seven to three-three.

I went back in nineteen-forty to the final once again
This time our brave Kilkenny met Mick Mackey and his men.
With mighty Paddy Clohessy and midfield Timmy Ryan
Sure Kilkenny couldn't match them and wound up two goals behind.
Jack Mulcahy and Jim Langton were the black and amber's best
But the Mackeys, Stokes and Power were the men who stood the test.
The old man reached to lift his glass and he made this proud remark
I'm glad that I was there to see Mick Mackey in Croke Park.

The years that followed after saw the Corkmen come alive
And of six all-Ireland championships the rebel men won five.
It all began in forty-one the beginning of a dream
When the one and only Christy Ring arrived upon the scene.
Three times they beat brave Dublin and enjoyed a scoring spree.
Then Antrim was their victim back in nineteen forty-three
Antrim won the semi-final and Kevin Armstrong was a giant
Against Galway they scored seven goals but not a single point.

And then in nineteen forty-five the Corkmen let it slip
They were beaten down in Munster by John Maher's men from Tipp.
But back they came in forty-six and loud the Banks did sing

When they bet a great Kilkenny team they were led by Christy Ring.
So Ring and the O'Riordans and Con Murphy got reward
Although Leahy, Grace and Kelly and Jim Langton tried so hard.
For the men in black and amber forty-seven proved a treat
When again they met the Corkmen and avenged that last defeat.

And then came nineteen forty-eight and history was made
When a team from County Waterford their hurling skills displayed.
Defeating Cork in Munster and then Galway from the West
Against Dublin in the final they were easily the best.
With John Keane and Andy Fleming, Bastion, Moylan and Carew
They were masters over Dublin by six-seven to four-two.
Dublin's goalie Kevin Matthews was a star who played his best
And that man Seán Óg O'Callaghan was the pick of all the rest.

I didn't go in forty-nine 'twas the day before a fair
And I had cattle to bring out so I listened to O'hEithir.
Tipperary bet the Laoismen and the game was dull and slow
And I sold my bullocks Monday and was glad I didn't go.
I remember Tony Reddan, Mickey Byrne and young John Doyle
Tony Brennan was a stalwart, Jimmy Kennedy had style.
Pat Stakelum was the captain, he was only twenty-one
We didn't realise that a new era had begun.

Ah the Ryans and the Kennys, Tommy Doyle and Sonny Maher,
With Finn and Hough and Shanahan—aye and Bannon was a star.
They won again in 'fifty' when the black and amber fell
With Shem Downey, Jack Mulcahy, Diamond Hayden, Mark
Marnell.
Again in nineteen fifty-one we saw the Tippmen shine
When they bet the men from Wexford by seven-seven to three-nine.
But that was such a special day when we heard the Wexford cheers
For they hadn't won a Leinster crown for thirty-three long years.

The next three years were won by Cork, that team was really great,
Beating Galway, Dublin, Wexford, Christy Ring had won his eight.
Dave Creedon—'What a goalie'! with O'Shaughnessy and Lyons

The O'Riordans and the Twomeys, Mattie Fuohy and O'Brien.
Johnny Clifford and Paddy Barry were the scourge of any back
With the great Willie John Daly in the centre of attack.
Willie Griffin, Abbernethy, and Josie Hartnett—they could swing
Gerry Murphy, Hayes and Goulding and that legend Christy Ring.

But the 50's are remembered best when stories are revived
Of the mighty men from Wexford who had certainly arrived.
Art Foley, Nick O'Donnell, with Ned Wheeler and Tim Flood,
Jim English and the Morrisseys and Kehoes were really good.
O'Hanlon, Ryan and Hearne were always on the ball
And the three great Rackard brothers were the greatest of them all.
In fifty-five and fifty-six they won the hurling crown
When Jimmy Duggan's Galway and the Corkmen both went down.

I wasn't there in fifty-six—do you know it was a shame?
For listnin' to the radio it was a most outstandin' game.
The Wexfordmen were at their best and hurlin' mighty fine
But the Corkmen were determined to win Ring his number nine.
From twenty-five yards out the field bould Christy he let fly
But Art Foley saw it comin' with that brilliant eagle eye.
He saved the day for Wexford and he bravely cleared his line
And the first man in the shake his hand was the mighty man from
Cloyne.

I remember goin' in fifty-nine the bus was almost late
Kilkenny met with Waterford who were goin' really great
The Decies men were brilliant 'twas the best I ever saw
But a great display by Ollie Walsh had earned the 'Cats' a draw.
It was early that October when these giants clashed again
And Waterford were winners by three-twelve to one goal- ten.
Frankie Walsh and Seamus Power, Larry Guinan, Philly Grimes
And that mighty man Tom Cheasty were the heroes of the time.

Tipperary ruled the 60's when the titles won were four
With the men in black and amber winning three All-Irelands more.

One for Cork and two for Wexford four great teams had won their
share
'Twas the era of two legends, Jimmy Doyle and Eddie Keher.
John Doyle had eight All-Irelands won in nineteen sixty-five
And Devanney, Roche and Keating were the finest men alive.
Tony Wall , Kieran Carey, Theo English and Michael Maher
With McKenna, Burns and Nealon, every one of them a star.

Kilkenny in the 60's were possessed of skill and flair
The Walshs, Billy Dwyer, Paddy Larkin, Eddie Keher
Ted Carroll and Martin Coogan, Paddy Moran, Seamus Cleere
And the one and only Ollie Walsh the man who knew no fear.
Sean Clohessy, Jim Treacy, Denis Heaslip and Claus Dunne
Frank Cummins and Pa Dillon, mighty hurlers every one
Tommy Murphy was a flyer; Johnny McGovern was the best
With the towering Pat Henderson, Martin Brennan and all the rest.

I'm vague about the 70's, I was gettin old you see
But Limerick beat Kilkenny, that was nineteen seventy-three.
'Twas back in nineteen-forty when the men from Shannon side
Had won their last McCarthy cup and Mick Mackey was their pride.
The Bennis's and Hartigans, Eamon Cregan, Rea and Grimes
With Moore, McKenna, Foley, O'Donoghue and O'Brien.
Frankie Nolan, Mossie Dowling, they all played a vital role–
I remember Seamus Horgan had a mighty game in goal.

September nineteen-eighty saw proud Galway make their mark
When they beat the men from Limerick, 'twas my last time in Croke
Park
As they lifted the McCarthy cup there were tears for all to see
They had failed to win nine finals since their last in twenty-three.
Yes they waited fifty-six long years but now their hour had come
Amid scenes of great emotion they would take the trophy home.
And as cheers went up in Galway, Castlegar and Athenry
The Tribesmen in the Capital had raised their heroes high.

There was never such excitement by the wild Atlantic waves
Mike Conneally was the goalie who made many brilliant saves.
Conor Hayes, Niall McInerney, Jimmy Cooney held their men
With Sean Silke and Seamus Coen and the bould Sylvie Linnane.
The Connollys from Castlegar, there was Michael and big John
And Joe, he was the captain, how he urged his heroes on.
Frank Burke and Stevie Mahon, Bernie Forde, P.J. Molloy
And Noel Lane at corner forward–shure his shootin' was a joy.

Then came September eighty-one and history was made
The Galway men were back again but they failed to make the grade.
For Padraig Horan's Offaly became new hurling giants
By defeating gallant Galway by two-twelve to fifteen points.
'Twas their first All-Ireland final in the history of the game
But their class and dedication had at long last brought them fame.
A late goal from Johnny Flaherty caused western hearts to stop
And Offaly had their name inscribed on the Liam McCarthy cup.

The Tribesmen though were rampant then and they hadn't long to
wait
They were back All-Ireland champions in eighty-seven and eighty-
eight.
And our thoughts went back some thirty years to another famous
side
Which didn't win All-Irelands but they played the game with pride.
The Duggans and the Sweeneys, Tommy Kelly, Jim Fives
And the brilliance of Joe Salmon brought excitement to our lives.
The Burkes and P.J.Lally, Fergus Benson and Joe Young
With O'Neill, Spillane and Corless—now their praises were being
sung.

Yes we had some famous county teams which failed to make their
mark
And many famous hurling men who failed to reach Croke Park.
When I think back on all these years and ye can check it up
Only eight of all our counties won the Liam Mc Carthy cup.
Yes, so many brilliant hurling men have played throughout the years

But never won a final like so many of their peers.
However good your talent is, it saves a lot of work
To be born in Tipperary or Kilkenny or in Cork.

There were many well-known Dublin men with talent to admire
The Bootmans and Mick Bermingham, the Foleys and Jim Prior.
And goalie Kevin Matthews, I've mentioned him before
Noel Drumgoole and Norman Allen, aye, and many many more.
I remember Snitchie Ferguson as sound as any bell
And I still remember Harry Grey who played with Laois as well.
Laois had Styles and Tom Fitzpatrick and Paddy Lalor we all know
And their captain had a funny name, 'twas Paddy Rustchitzko.

The famous Wexford Dorans and the Quigleys strong and fit
And don't forget Mick Jacob, aye, and Clare had Jimmy Smyth.
The great Dan McInerney, Seamus Durack and Sean Stack
And in Galway Josie Gallagher was their hero in attack.
Frank Burke and P.J. Qualter, these lads were really great
And before them Inky Flaherty his likes was hard to bate.
Sean Herbert starred for Limerick and Noel Gallagher for Cork
And Westmeath produced the Jobber—what a brilliant piece of
work.

The old man then got up to go but he stopped inside the door
He says, 'these are just some memories but I've many many more'.
I leave ye with a question and a hurler ye must name
Who has **ten** All-Ireland medals for this ancient hurling game.
And you'll wonder when I tell you; twenty-one long years have
passed
From the day he won the first one till the day he won the last?.
I looked across at Jimmy and Jimmy looked at me
I didn't have the answer nor did Jimmy I could see.

We turned to this rare ould man admittin' our defeat
But he had quietly slipped outside and was shufflin' down the street.
So if you have the answer you deserve a rousing cheer
For there is no doubt about it that the question was sincere.

Meself and Jimmy left the pub and then we got a shock
For with all the conversation we forgot about the clock.
The grocery shops in Comer had been closed for half an hour
So he went home without the grub and I without the flour.

Ireland's Dashing Hurling Men

Anon
Source: Story of the GAA by Séamus Ó Ceallaigh.
Air: Clare's Dragoons

Rise up. We'll drink another toast
To Éire's pride—a gallant host.
What nation upon earth can boast
Such sons as Ireland's hurling men?

When terror reigned o'er mount and plain:
When death stalked grim on road and lane;
Then Éire looked—nor looked in vain—
For aid from her brave hurling men.

Who boldy manned the Bearna Baoil?
Who faced the foreign fire and steel?
Before whose charge did foemen reel?
'Twas Ireland's dashing hurling men.

And as the years glide slowly on,
Who'll guard our freedom dearly won
And hand that trust from sire to son?
Why—Ireland's trusty hurling men.

And by the graves of those who fell,
Who wait in peace the final knell?
Glory, to guard their ashes well,
Knees watch o'er fallen hurling men.

Ireland's Hurling Men

By Brian na Banban (Brian O'Higgins)
Source: History of the GAA 1910-1930 by Sliabh Ruadh (Phil O'Neill)
Air: Clare's Dragoons.Chorus after each verse.

Who say our country's heart is dead?
Come; let them hear the marching tread
Who say our country's soul has fled?
Of twice five thousand hurling men.
They hold the hopes of bye-gone years,
They hold its past—its smiles and tears,
But quavering doubts and shrinking fears
Are far from Ireland's hurling men.

Hurrah! Hurrah! The stout camán,
No English steel can match its blow.
Hurrah! The arms of might and brawn,
And hearts with freedom's light aglow.

On Irish fields when brave men died,
And foemen thronged on every side,
Our leader's joy—their hope and pride,
Were gleaming pikes and hurling men.
And if God wills that war's red train
Shall sweep once more o'er hill and plain,
Our land shall call and not in vain,
For fighting lines of hurling men.

When comes the day as come it must,
When England's rule of greed and lust
Shall all be broken in the dust,
We'll still have Irish hurling men.
Then here's to her, the land we love,
Each grand old hill and glen and grove,
Her plains below, her skies above,
But best of all—her hurling men.

471

Ireland's Hurling Men

By Ros Cairbre
Source: An Camán, Iúl, 1931

Let us hear a song be it short or long,
Of great men struggling for hurling sway,
Of the clans of Munster at whose deeds you'd wonder,
Their feats are famous, full many a day.

Down in Aughabullogue some great men struggled
With ashen blades I'd have you know,
While Dungourney's story is crowned in glory
From the Cove of Cork to far Dungloe.

Blackrock and Mallow 'twould beat you hollow
On Ireland's ground their match to find—
Whilst Midleton and Carrig the foe oft harried,
Ne'er did those hurlers lag far behind.

In gallant Tipperary 'twould be quite contrary
Should I not make mention of honours won—
In famed Moycarkey, the Horse and Jockey
With Boherlahan and Toom well in the run.

Down by the Noreside, upper and lower side,
The old hurling game is well to the fore—
With the great Moondarrig who oft victory carried,
Likewise Mooncoin and old Tullaroan.

Loch Garman storied, who never worried
If laurels they have not often won—
Castlebridge and Oulart and men of stout heart,
From Blackwater district did often come.

Then give me a song be it short or long,
Of great men struggling for hurling sway,
On the fields of Éirinn where deeds are daring
Are sure to live full many a day.

The Lass that Loves a Hurler

P. D. Mehigan, Cork.
Source: The Gaelic Echo, St. Patrick's Day Number, 1942
Air: The Lass-á-gowrie
Chorus after each verse

I know a maid with sparkling eye,
She looks so sweet, she seems so shy-
But she smiled at me as she passed by,
Going down to mass last Sunday.
She's Irish too both kith and kin,
I'm sure she's pure and free from sin,
But I'd like to tie her apron's pin-
When she keeps house on Monday.

Chorus: -

Come fill your glasses to the brim,
We'll toast that maid so neat and trim;
Her step is light, her waist is slim-
The lass that loves a Hurler.

At last night's Céilidhe down in Keel
I saw her dance an Irish reel,
Her dainty glance of toe and heel,
Sent my poor senses storming.
She joined in chorus with the best,
Her voice was soft as thrush on nest,
I longed to press her to my breast-
And keep her there 'till morning.

Her deep blue eyes and neck of snow,
Her breasts like billow soft below,
Her hips in easy numbers flow,
Going to the well for water.
She cheers our team, her eyes aflame!
And after Sunday's final game,

I'll meet her in a glen I'll name-
And ask her to the altar.

P.D.Mehigan, the author, was born in Ardfield, Co. Cork, and wrote under the pen names of "Carberry" and Pat O in the Irish Times, the Kerryman, the Cork Weekly Examiner and others. He wrote from about 1920 until his death in 1965. He wrote novels and the history of both hurling and Gaelic football. He was deeply interested in Irish wild life, athletic prowess, step dancing, coursing, music making and everything that touched on the Irish life style. He gave his first open-air games broadcast to Europe and the Western World, Kilkenny v Galway in August 1926. He played with the London Irish v Cork and lost in 1902. He then played with Cork v Kilkenny in 1905, won, but an objection by Kilkenny was upheld. Kilkenny won the replay. He won the Irish title in the hop step and jump. He was also an Irish champion step dancer and an accomplished bowl player. As Sean Kilfeather says in his book *Vintage Carberry*, "Carberry was a remarkable man and his writing to-day is as lively and evocative as when first penned".

The Hurler's Dream

By D. Ó Longaigh, Bendemeer, Corcaigh
Source: Gaelic Weekly, Sat. Apr.4, 1959

Who is the boy with the golden hair
And why is his smile so sweet
As he lies in the shade of an old oak tree
With a hurley and ball at his feet?
You know him not and you never will,
For famous he'll never be;
And yet, he is happy and even now
In his dreams he can surely see
Another field where the grass is green,
Where the crowds in their thousands sway;
And surely he's there in the midst of it all
In Croke Park on All-Ireland day.
Not on the terrace, or Hill Sixteen,
Or up in the Cusack Stand,
But leading his county on the field
With his trusty camán in his hand.

The whistle, the throw in, the game is on!
The drama! the thrill of the fray!
Fighting it out for one golden hour-
Can they triumph and carry the day?
Ah yes! for the thousands are cheering now-
What frenzy and fire they bring!
Roaring as often they roared before-
For Mackey and Rackard and Ring.
The others are leading- they always are
Two points- and a minute to go!
'Tis the age old dream of an Irish boy,
And the ending you all must know.

He's fighting hard for possession now,
And the sliotar is in his hand:

Seventy yards from the Railway goal-
And his chances are far from grand.
He's running, he's running, while thousands cheer,
And opponents are tossed aside:
But what if he's beaten or hooked or robbed,
Or the ball is sent inches wide?
Forty yards, thirty left to go,
Beating them, fooling them yet:
Rounding the backs with a final burst
To bury the ball in the net!

The whistle is gone and the game is won,
His county has carried the prize,
They're chairing him off with the cup aloft
And the tears of delight in his eyes.
The dream is over, the picture fades,
And yet, while it lived 'twas fun;
And he'll play again in another dream
The match that is always won!

A Hurler's Prayer

Grant me, O Lord a hurler's skill
With strength of arm and speed of limb;
Unerring eye for the flying ball
And courage to match them what're befall.
May my aim be steady, my stroke be true,
My actions manly, my misses few;
And no matter what way the game may go,
May I rest in friendship with every foe.
When the final whistle for me is blown
And I stand at last at God's judgment throne,
May the Great Referee when He calls my name,
Say, 'You hurled like a man, you played the game'

A Hurler's Wish

By Jack Ryan,Greystones, Limerick,(formerly Newport)

Oh God! Please grant that when this life I'll yield
That in heaven you'll have a hurling field;
With goalposts white and a green field grand
And sunny days and a grand pipe band.
And maybe, God, a singer or two
To lilt a ballad for me and you.
Then all I'd wish is to spend each day
Watching all the great hurlers play.
With Ring and Mackey and Rackard too   *1
And Semple and Lory to name a few.   *2
To watch Scanlan or Daly mind the net.   *3
You'll promise too it won't be wet.
Ten year tickets, they will not be.   *4
Your ones will be for eternity.
No corporate funding you'll require   *5
For who was it said, "God loves a trier".
Where every one is the same to you
In red or white or gold or blue.
Your field, dear Lord will have a mighty stand
To hold the people from every land:
Jew and Gentile, Pole and Moor,
For the kings and queens and the humble poor.
Put St. Patrick on the gate
For the new arrivals might be late.
So line the field and cut the grass,
I know some day it will come to pass
When all will go to the final game
Where rich and poor will be the same.

*1   Christy Ring, Cork, Mick Mackey, Limerick, Nicky Rackard, Wexford.
*2   Tom Semple, Tipperary, Lory Meagher, Kilkenny.
*3   Paddy Scanlan, Limerick, Dr. Tommy Daly, Clare.
*4   A scheme, which allowed tickets to be purchased for a period of ten years
             in order to provide capital for development.

*5   Corporate funding is a reference to finance provided by the corporate
    sector for the building of the New Cusack Stand, at Croke Park, in return
    for which they were entitled to avail of premium seating for All-Ireland
    finals.

The Camogie Player

Anon:
Source: *Our Games Annual 1962*

Soaring sliotar and joy-choked cries
Wind-wafted the white-flecked skies.
In flashing ark like the snipe at dawn,
Go the swing and swoop of the lithe camán
One who is fair with an emerald stood,
Model of Irish womanhood.
Graceful of step, glides here glides there,
And strikes with delight in the heat-hazed air.
So Princess Eithne the sagas say,
On Connaght's plains was wont to play.
At the veiled cloister bent in prayer,
Still the limbs of the camogie -player.
The head that danced now in fervour bowed,
While from the shadows the angel crowd
Watch with the referee unseen
With a heavenly hush such as must have been.
At Cruachan when, in the days long dead,
St. Patrick blessed fair Eithne's head.

The Game of the Gaels

By Sliabh Ruadh
Source: History of the GAA 1910-1930 by Sliabh Ruadh (Phil O 'Neill)
Air: Top of the Cork Road.

Of late they are giving a deal of attention
To physical culture with every invention;
Without being too bold I would just like to mention
That hurling's the manliest art of them all.
A tonic for all 'tis surest and best;
Good for the arms, the legs and the chest:
If you're nausey or needy or sickly or seedy,
A cure that is speedy- the ash and the ball.

The shoneens all swear that the game is nefarious:
Others declare that 'tis very precarious:
Still, I adhere there is nought so hilarious
As pucking a ball with a tidy camán:
Here you have work that will do you no harm,
'Twill straighten your back, too, and strengthen your arm:
Something with 'bis' in it, always a "fizz" in it,
Plenty of "gizz" in it- muscle and brawn!

Don't talk about soccer or rugby or cricket,
Or such foreign games for they're not on my ticket:
With our old-fashioned pastime, their best we can lick it,
For all their amusements are lazy and lame.
What we want here is some frolic and fun
For Irishmen all and for everyone.
Sport with a dash in it, clitter and clash in it,
Something with ash in it, surely a game.

Hurling's a sport with a genuine swing in it:
Rhythm and reason and plenty of ring in it:
Faith, an' the taste of an old Irish sting in it,
Racing and chasing the stout leather ball.

Here's then a health to our forefather's game,
With the changes of time, sure 'tis ever the same.
For dashing and daring, for tumbling and tearing,
And devil-may-caring, the game of them all.

The Grand Old Game

By Joseph S. Considine, Dublin (Formerly Ennis, Co. Clare)
Source: Mrs Valerie Byrne,(niece of author)

Give me the grand old hurling game
For there's naught on earth I ween
To match two well-trained balanced sides
When the ball flies fast between,
The air like wine, the sun aslant,
O'er the light sod's velvet sheen.

Give me the primal urge to win,
Youth's call with its verve and dash.
The lusty cheers impartial given,
As the well-matched athletes clash
With pulses high and soul a thrill
To the music of the ash.

Give me the mighty back-line drives
And the fast play overhead.
The lightning turns, the "doubling" strokes
That will keep the forwards "fed".
The tumult at the goal-line's mouth,
And the sward with bodies spread.

Give me the cute culbáire tough,
Keen-eyed and with muscles taut,
Who pucks each ball to some man unmarked
And is cool when things are not;
Who senses danger when it comes,
And "draws" on each lightning shot.

Give me the final minutes tense
Of some grand All-Ireland clash,
With level play, each side on edge,
As the heaving bodies clash,

And the ball is sailing pointwards
From a wizard forward flash.

Give me the men, who've lustre shed,
On old Ireland's hurling game,
And helped to light that quench'less fire
That burns in freedom's name.
For long we'll treasure in our hearts
Their memory and their fame.

The author Joseph S. Considine is brother to Tull and "Dodger" (Willie) and Brendan
Considine who played senior hurling with Clare. The "Dodger" and Brendan won an
All-Ireland with Clare in 1914 while Tull played in the football All-Ireland with Clare
v Wexford in 1917 and in the hurling All-Ireland v Kilkenny in 1932. The Considines
were a legendary Ennis and Clare family.

Convent Camogie

Source: GAA History of Cashel and Rosegreen 1884-1984
By Seamus J. King, Boherclough, Cashel.
Air: Y Viva Espania

We are pupils from Cashel don't you see now
We have some team now
With bonfires all ablaze.
You know every time we play a team we stitch them
We even teach them
Brilliant camogie ways.
Do you know that St. Paul's will feel the strain?
For we'll beat them, be it sunshine or in rain.

For this year we'll win great fame again.
Y Viva Scoil Mhuire.
St. Paul's will try but all in vain,
Y Viva Scoil Mhuire.
If you'd like to cheer us and to roar,
We're some school, Scoil Mhuire
And we have supporters by the score
Scoil Mhuire here we come.

In the course of time the Presentation Convent Cashel built up a repertoire of sixteen songs. The above song was the most popular. The gamesmaster Willie Prendergast put great emphasis on the value of song. Cheer leaders were appointed to get the supporters organised. On the morning of a match they went around the classrooms getting the girls in voice and sufficiently motivated for the task ahead.

Cashel defeated Athenry in the senior camogie final in 1977 by 2-2 to 1-3 and beat Athenry in the final again in 1979 by 3-3 to 1-3.

1977 Team—Nuala Bonnar, Mary Hayes, Eleanor Brennan, Cora Hennessy, Eithne Bonnar, Claire Bargary, Mary Luby, Mary Ryan, Majella Hallinan, Kathleen Ryan, Regina Mulligan, Kathleen Ryan-Hennessy.

1979 Team—Ursula Cummins, Aileen Anglim, Margaret Maher, Caroline Kelly, Kay Maxwell, Elaine Lawrence, Eithne Bonnar, Ann Fitzgerald, Michelle Fogarty, Sheila Morrissey, Regina Mulligan, Majella Hallinan.

An Chamóg

Le Tórna
Foinse: Muiris de Prionnbhíol
Fonn: The Rocky Road to Dublin

Cíoram cíoram ó,
Cíoram ó, agus canaimís,
Cíoram cíoram dóibh
An rí-chamóg 's a leanann dí

Graidhin mo chroidhe go deó,
Graighin gach óigfhir chalma
Buidheanta riaghbhan óg
Suídhte I gcóir ar machaire
Cíoram agus rl.

Radharc nách faghfaidhe a shórd
Choidhche i bfódaibh eachtarann:
Flíop do dhruim chamóg
Is sírrith ród don leabhar úd
Cíoram agus rl.

Firinnighe 'na mbeóil,
Lí agus rós 'na leaconaibh,
Croidhe agus duibhe gan dóghadh
Agus fírshliocht mordha maith ortha
Cíoram agus rl.

Guidhimse is guidhidhse fós
Rí agus ró gach rath ortha,
Sinsiridheacht 'na dtreo
Agus claoidhe le nósa Banba
Cíoram agus rl.

Hurling

By JimmySmyth, Ruan, County Clare

Hurling is special, the body and soul
Of a people surviving to speak
Of a past that is noble distinctive and proud
With a game that is surely unique.
Of a land that survives in a classical way
From the Lagan right down to the Lee.
Hurling is special, a language and crest
Of a nation, instinctively free.

The ball as it travels with speed is controlled
By an uncanny balance and play
And the hurler will take any tackle and stress
That the game will demand on the way.
Each man has to challenge the swing of the ash
If he is to play any part
Then bridle the ripple of blood on the boil
With a burst of exuberant art.

Those players are best who have finish and craft
A feeling, a touch and a dash.
A little flick here or a little swerve there
Will enjoy all the challenge of ash,
And are men who expect that a player with class
Can withstand any strain or upset
And continue to fashion through hassle and stress
A reward at the back of the net.

Hurling is old, as old as the hills
And tough as the rocks that lie under.
Hard as the metals that smoulder within
A simmer of passion and wonder.
Hurling is part of the soil and the land
A mixture more polished than gold
And comes to the surface expressive and free
As a skill that is daring and bold.

488

Hurling

By Gerard Ryan, Inch, Bouladuff, Thurles.

Something racy of the soil
That the foe could not erase—
Loved by young and old alike
Our ancient game—hurling.

Though a man be low in ways
There is a tonic that will not fail
It lifts the spirit of the Gael
A victory in this game of games—hurling.

An exile returning from afar
Telling the things he misses the most—
Music, dance and loyal friends
But above all—hurling.

When our finest hour was nigh
We saw the bravest of our race
March with hurley sticks held high
They revelled in that splendid game—hurling.

The Hurling

By Frank Doran, Waterford
Source: Clonakilty GAA 1887-1987

Have you seen this grand old hurling game
With its glamour, its glory and its dash.
Handed down from bye-gone ages, yet the same;
Have you listened to the music of the ash?
Have you seen the teams parading with the piper on before?
Have you felt the hot blood coursing through your veins?
Have you chafed and grown impatient for the coming treat in store
As you listened to the piper's stirring strains?
Have you stood there fascinated as the ball is thrown between?
They pull, and someone near you cries, 'Well Done'
As a player hits a beauty, see the forwards now are fleeing;
You can scarcely realise the game's begun.

Have you marvelled at the daring, the feat of skill you see?
Have you wondered as they crash and sway and fall?
Yet, they're up again and going, hear the thousands shout in glee;
It takes a man to play it after all!
Have you watched the wingers speeding?
The lightning shot and save;
The struggle in the goalmouth has it thrilled you to the core?
The forwards inwards surging like the angry ocean wave;
The whistle now has sounded and the flag goes up—a score.

Have you seen the tide of battle, have you watched its ebb and flow;
Have you wondered at the grandeur and the beauty of it too?
When the teams are running level and the scoring list is low,
Then your pulses throb with gladness and the game appeals to you.
Have you seen this fine Old Irish game?
Have you never heard the clashing of the camáns in the strife?
You haven't. Now I wonder, 'tis a pity all the same;
You've really lost the pleasure of something fine in life.

Iomáint

Le Liam Ó Donnchú, Ballymoreen, Littleton

Ar pháirc an chatha, is beag nach bhfuil ráite
Ar éachtanna móra agus dortadh folla,
Ach focal a chara ar gníomhartha is gaisce
I dtaobh fhir na gcamán ag buaileadh báire.

Is bródúil and radharc é an sliotar a fheiceáil
Mar shaighead as bogha, nó eas ar sileadh,
Ag fágáil bas, nó ag árdú chun spéire,
Ar ghort na hiomána, an slua i rabharta.

Tá an taoide ag casadh le neart na beirbe,
Na madaí ag luascadh le fuinneamh an leoin,
An leathar ag seoladh ó chúl go chéile,
Na súile go beacht, an toradh sa mheá.

Is aosta an spórt í, ó Setanta aniar,
Bascadh í faoi Rí ach d'éirigh in áirde,
Seachtar le brí, a árdaigh an bratach,
In Ostán Uí Aodha i nDúrlas Eile.

491

Camán

By Séamus Ó Riain, Moneygall (Iar Uachtarán ,Cumann Luthchleas Gael.)

Fashioned from ash
Root-toughened in the hungry earth
For lasting bas,
And supple-stemmed for handle spring,
The measured shape is spoke-shaved
By a craft of ancient lineage
For balanced swing.
The root is bedded in the Red Branch of Setanta,
And heart strings stretch in pride
When wedded to the wrists of Roche and Keher
The strokes of grace excite
To consciousness of heritage.

Hurling Music

(The Camán tells its story)

By Jack Ryan, Beechwood Drive, Greystones, Limerick (formerly Newport)

They've all played my music these great hurling men
In city and town, and in valley and glen
And oft with a craft that is rare and unique
They have brought me to life and have taught me to speak.
They have shaped my ash body with spokeshave and plane
And have carefully nurtured my balance and grain.
They have banded my boss for the height of the fray
And have held me aloft when winning the day.

The young lads have carried me off to the school
With a pride and delight, and with pencil and rule.
I have filled men with passion, with spirit and pride
As they traced the great finals by open firesides.
My music has lifted the old and alone
From the green Glens of Antrim to the famed Treaty Stone.
With them I made music so sweet to recall
And my favourite music was 'After the Ball'.

My solos with Mackey, I'll never forget
As we planted the sliotar secure in the net
I teamed up with Ring when the weather was fine
He brought out my best, this hero from Cloyne
I stood in the goalposts with Reddan and Daly
In Thurles and Cork and in Birr and Killarney.
I have played in the backline with Stakelum and Doyle
With Henderson too, with courage and style.

I have travelled to Wexford; I'll have you to know
With O'Donnell, the Rackards, Tim Flood and Kehoe.
And I'm well known in Dublin from Rush to Rathcoole
My friends were the Foleys, Seán Óg and Drumgoole.
There's a village near Ennis; its name is Ruan

And from that dear place came a great hurling man
His name Jimmy Smyth, of great skill and flair
'Twas with him that we played hurling music for Clare.

I have partnered great stickmen in the middle of the park
As the sliotar soared skywards in flight like the lark.
With Jack Lynch, Lory Meagher, Frank Cummins, Tim Ryan—
In those long summer days—oh, the music was fine.
With John Joe Doyle of Newmarket and Cork's Josie Hartnett
The Jobber McGrath and Galway's Mick Gill
With hurlers like these and the soft summer breeze
Of the real hurling music you could take your fill.

In Tipperary I partnered great men I must say
From Borris and Toome, Kilruane and Roscrea;
Holycross and Moycarkey, the best in the county
From Carrick and Thurles, Boherlahan, Clonoulty.
From Lattin and Nenagh and Cashel also
And Lorrha and Newport, Ballina and Portroe.
Oh! Great was the music we played one and all
Myself and the hurler and the auld sliotar ball.

In Tipp. the hurlers I've been with are many
Mick Roche, Jimmy Doyle, Jimmy Finn, Liam Devaney
James Cooney, Tom Treacy, who came from Killea
Mick Ryan and Jack—true sons of Roscrea.
From Moycarkey, more Ryans— 'Mutt', Johnny and 'Sweeper'
Reddan from Lorrha our famous goalkeeper.
Phil Cahill, Phil Purcell, Tom Semple and all
Martin Kennedy, James Coffey, John Maher and Wall.

In the 'eighties' when Galway came into their own
No more would they linger unproven alone.
Joe Connolly lifted the cup with great pride—
I was there too—I was just by his side.
When they burst into song, the stand it did shake
The crowd all joined in, faith, the 'West was Awake'.

The Tribesmen all gathered on the pitch with delight
And waved their famed banners, the maroon and the white.

'Twas a day for the West and they proved they were best
And captured the trophy of hurling's great test.
The old folk at home with rapture did cry
In Tuam, Castlegar and famed Athenry
In Spiddal and Barna there was great commotion
The cheering nigh silenced the Atlantic's big ocean.
Oh! The music of hurling was playing that day
'Twas heard quite distinctly 'round Galway Bay.

Of the county of Clare, oh what can I say?
It played second fiddle for many a day.
It was loyal to its culture and true to its name
And never gave up but kept playing the game.
But in nineteen ninety-five, what a day in Croke Park!
The Banner at last emerged from the dark.
Those heartlands of hurling from the 'Bridge to the 'Mills,
Newmarket, and Barefield and round its fair hills.

From Ennis, Clarecastle so famed long ago,
Whitegate and Scariff where the Graney doth flow.
All cheered on their heroes with fervour and might
As the bonfires blazed skywards all through the night.
I was there on that field with Loughnane there's no doubt
When all through the land was heard the Clare Shout.
The music of hurling was mighty that day
And on that hillside at Tulla I'm sure it did play.

My memories of Limerick are wonderful too—
By the Shannon, the Maigue and famed Croom Abu.
They had hurlers there, the best to be seen
Togged out in those colours, the white and the green.
The Mackeys, the Herberts, Tim Ryan, Pat and Mick,
Jackie Power, Pat McMahon, oh boys! What a pick!

The Clohessys, Cregans, Mick Kennedy too
And remember Jimmy Humphries from lovely Murroe.

Paddy Scanlon, Mick Hickey Jim Close and Ned Chawke
Mickey Cross, Garret Howard—of them I can talk.
Jim Roche, Willie Gleeson and Knockaney's Tom Cooke,
Willie Hough and Dick Stokes—too quick for to hook.
I played with them all throughout this fair land—
Their skills unsurpassed, their spirit so grand.
They made wondrous music of hurling supreme
May they long be remembered by the Shannon's fair stream.

Oh, great were the days I spent 'round the Nore
In Kilkenny where they have great hurlers galore
With Langton and Blanchfield, Walsh and Delaney
With the 'Diamond' and Larkin 'gainst the men from the Slaney.
Eddie Keher, Denis Heaslip, and famed Paddy Grace
Paddy Buggy and Carey of wristwork and pace.
Paddy Phelan, Jack Mulcahy, the Brennans and Cleere
Faith they made hurling music, the best you could hear.

In Offaly also I've played with the best,
With Pilkington, Delaney, Troy and the rest.
Damien Martin and Horan with Duignan and Fleury
Not forgetting young Carroll and three of the Dooleys.
They brought hurling music to Birr and Coolderry—
'By heavens 'twas lovely and sure it was merry.
They took the famed trophy where the Brosna flows bright
The Faithful camán men in gold, green and white.

Fair land of Bould Thady by the banks of the Lee,
'Twas there I met hurlers the finest you'd see.
Men from the Rockies, Glen Rovers and Barrs
From Carrigtwohill and Midleton and also the Sars.
They were there in their hundreds the greatest of men
And to mention them now where can I begin?

They had Jack Lynch and Jim Young and Batt Thornhill too
The Ahearne's and Riordans — all these men I knew.

Paddy Donovan, Con Murphy, and Willie John Daly
Mick Kenefick, Sean Condon, Buckley and Healy.
Paddy Barry, Con Cottrell and 'Mika' also
And a fellow called Ring—'God be with long ago'.
These were the men who made hurling music
In the footsteps of Davin, Paddy O'Keeffe and Mick Cusack.
Sure many have left us, ah, 'tis sad they are gone—
But while there's a camán, their music lives on.

'Twas down in the Decies I met hurling men
From Mount Sion, Portlaw and famed Cappoquin.
Their skill on the field is known far and wide
At home in Dungarvan and famed Abbeyside.
And from Ballygunner to the town of Lismore
To Fraher's famed field in legend and lore.
Jim Ware, Seamus Power, Austin Flynn, Philly Grimes
John Keane and Vin Bastion, great men of their times.

Martin Óg, Jackie Goode, Frankie Walshe, Larry Guinan
Fleming and Galvin, Ned Power, Christy Moylan.
Flannelly, Curran, with Barron, O'Connor
All these mighty men to their county brought honour.
I was with them in Dublin in famed forty-eight
Oh, their deeds were remembered I'm glad to relate.
I'll never forget them, with them I did shine
And we thrilled all the people in nineteen fifty-nine.

I've a big day to morrow, now let it be said,
I'm standing right here by a young hurler's bed.
'Tis his first competition at under fourteen
He has painted me brightly in claret and green.
His helmet hangs proudly on a peg by the door
All part of this culture, the great hurling lore.

His stockings and boots are under the chair
And when he takes the field, sure I will be there.

It's honoured I'll be when I'm held in his hand
With the team marching proudly behind the school band.
Like his father before him he knows the position
He'll play in the game of our country's tradition.
He will never forget this wonderful day
And I'm there with him now as our anthem is played.
On the flagpole our tricolour is waving and curling
And soon we will have the sweet music of hurling.

So that is my story as far as it goes
Where I'm going next sure nobody knows.
I'm sure I'll be busy in the forthcoming days
In the hands of the hurler while the music still plays.
So a big *bualadh bos* for the players I knew
Who brought pleasure and sunshine to me and to you.
Farewell one and all, *beannacht agus slán*
Best wishes to all from an Irish camán.

The Crooked Ash

By Brud White, Scariff
Source:- Scariff Club History 1986

Crooked sapling, I grew o'er the bend of a stream
'Longside big brothers tall and straight.
Haunt of young truants with crippled camáns.
Ah, in each hungering eye I read my fate
When I came of age—'twas one windy night
A young guest with a gapped-tooth saw and soap
With conquest as his mad right crept by;
Around his waist a ragged rope
He cut me down the barefoot whelp
His soapy saw it made no noise.
And he hummed to himself in the dead of the night
Sure, as the schoolmaster says, 'boys will be boys'.
Dismembered in a vacant wheel-less hearse,
I was butchered- God help me, planed and planed.
No more to be choir loft for linnet and finch
Or to rejoice with the eels when it rained.
Next I lashed an oul ball to the left and to right
Rebellious on soft wet threadbare grass.
'Too damn heavy'—from my freckled devil's limb,
Mercy, planed again with broken glass!
On a blazing Sunday late in June
Oh how fiercely came my baptismal clash!
Ah, splinters showered the sky that torrid noon
Not mine, oh no, but from big brother ash!

When the long whistle shrills to end the fray
How a bouchal revels in man's rugged part!
Oh bashed, bloodied, blessed crooked ash
Long long will you reign in a hurler's heart!

Cutting The Ash in Moycarkey-Borris.

By Rev. Bro. J. Perkins, C.B.S. Thurles
Received from Liam Ó Donnchú, Ballymoreen, Littleton.

Last year to John Joe's fields they came
Where tall ash trees were looming:
They passed the lovely level lawn
Where daffofils were blooming.

For twenty years he watched with joy
Those fair young ash trees growing;
In sorrow he went, but he did not resent
The wind of change then blowing.

He knew that in the years to come
Moycarkey's sons would need them;
Alas, alas, it came to pass,
His own would never heed them.

By Ballyerk I sadly sighed,
As I walked through field and fallow,
Past Borris, Jockey, Maxfort House,
Towards Ashills groves and Grallagh.

The groaning chain saw filled the air;
A fair ash-tree was falling;
There was joy all round, as it struck the ground,
I could hear young voices calling.

The 'meitheal' then set to their task;
Strong hands began to hew it;
Its fair light limbs were torn off
As steely teeth tore through it.

In triumph from the field they trod;
They were proud of their rich 'takings';

On a future day, we'd see them play
With all those lovely 'makings'.

While men can toil and sow the soil
The spirit ne'er will vary;
We've got the dash and we'll cut the ash
For the hurlers of Tipperary.

Line 1 John Joe Hayes

A Well-Grained Ash Camán

Anon

Received from Muiris de Prionnbhiol,Blanchardstown, Dublin (formerly Cork)

Some sportsmen love the dog and gun
Some like the coursing hound,
And others when the day is done,
Will seek the golfing ground:
My heart in haste would scorn to taste
The pleasures from such drawn,
In the sport I toast is a hurler's boast
A well-grained ash camán.

In ancient days when Éire reigned
A nation great and grand,
When Oscar's and Cú Chulainn's fame
Was spread throughout the land:
On Tara's plain, with might and main   **
In contests fiercely drawn,
What else could grace the pride of place
But the well-grained ash camán?

In later days, when hope seemed dead
And bleeding lay our land,
At times to freedom's call came forth
A stout and stalwart band:
To man, to stride with gleaming pike
And died before they'd fawn,
Had known the swing and the gladsome ring
Of the well-grained ash camán.

Had I the gold of England's king
The wealth of France and Spain
Or all the jewels that big ships bring
From o'er the Eastern main;
I'd leave them all, the big and small

For a verdant Irish lawn
My comrades all, the flying ball,
And a well-grained-ash camán.

Chorus:

Then glasses clink and let us drink
This toast in cruiscín lán
Our nation's game, her hurler's fame
And the well-grained ash camán.

**Tara (in Irish, Teamhair, earlier Temuir): the centre of the high-kingship in early mediaeval Ireland, it is situated a few miles North West of Dunshaughlin, in County Meath. The anglicised form 'Tara' is based on the genitive 'Teamhrach'. The word itself meant 'spectacle', and the fine view of the centre of Ireland available from this vantagepoint must have been the original reason for the importance attached to the place. Archeology has shown that Tara was an important burial site from the second Millennium BC. After their arrival, probably around 500BC, the Gaelic people adopted it to their own culture, and made it a centre of a culture of a sacred king. The hill of Tara is central to most of the great drama in early Irish literature, but it was always regarded as the site of ancient rather than of contemporary glory. (*Myth, Legend and Romance* by Dr. Dáithi Ó hOgáin, Ryan Publishing, London, 1990)

Song of the Camán

By Peadar Kearney
Source: Story of the GAA , by Séamus Ó Ceallaigh, Limerick.
Air: The rare old mountain dew

There's joy for me in the old ash tree
I see in the fading light
For memory weaves in its whispering leaves
Brave thoughts for me to night.
And the ash is king of the song I sing,
A song of sinew and brawn;
A song for men- while men are men-
The song of the brave camán.

When the whistle's gone and the game is on,
Away with worry and care,
For the hopes and fears of a thousand years
Once more are pulsing there.
There's a rhythmic clash as ash meets ash.
Men fleeter than flying fawn-
'Tis the symphony of the old ash tree-
The song of the brave camán.

There's a glittering sheen in the changing scene
In the glory of manhood's glow;
In the steadied nerve and lightning swerve
To counter the friendly foe.
In the breathless dash and the challenging crash,
In the play of muscle and brawn,
'Till hearts are still with a glorious thrill-
The thrill of the old camán.

No need to mourn for a race out-worn,
No heed for the groundling's sneer,
Nor bell to toll for a nation's soul,
While the men and the ash are here.

And when the Gael in his strength shall hail
The coming of freedom's dawn,
Be his prayer and praise for the vanished days-
For the men and the brave camán.

The author born in Dublin in 1883 also wrote the national anthem, *"The Soldier's Song"* in 1907. Other compositions by him were *"Down by the Glenside"* and the *"Tri-coloured Ribbon"*

The Old Camán

By *Phil O'Neill (Sliabh Ruadh)*
Source: *Story of the GAA by Séamus Ó Ceallaigh, Luimneach*

One day a friend accosted me in the language of the Gael
He could tell of things that happened years ago in old Kinsale
And soon he started telling of days long past and gone
And how when he was but a lad, the "goal" was fought and won.

And if you'd like to have it, sure I'll give you my camán,
There's none to whom I'd give it but to you a bouchall bawn;
For I know you're Irish to the core and worthy of your race
There's Gaelic on your youthful tongue and pleasure in your face.

I answered my acceptance, and done day he brought the stick
Its one time smooth and greying face with soot and slime was thick.
And as he handed o'er the gift, his eyes with tears were blurred
You'd think it was a general surrendering his sword.

I gazed upon my souvenir, moth eaten, black with age,
It's slimy face more eloquent of the past than history's page;
And when I asked how old it was, he said amid his tears,
I think gorsoon just like myself, 'tis well o'er sixty years.

I am proud to own that hurley, and shall keep it safe and sound,
For the love of old time relics of my country is profound.
And when upon that blackened ash a glance at times I'll cast,
'Twill light the lamp of memory on a grand and glorious past.

The author, Phil O'Neill, who also wrote under the pen name Sliabh Ruadh, wrote the
History of the GAA, 1910-1930

The Song of a Hurl

By Crawford Neil
Source: Story of the GAA , by Séamus Ó Ceallaigh, Limerick.

Oh! cut me a hurl from the mountain ash,
That weathered many a gale,
And my stroke will be lithe as the lightning flash
That leaps from the thunder's flail.
Oh! my feet shall be swift as the white spindrift
On the bay in wintry weather,
As we run in line through the glad sunshine
On the trail of the whirling leather.

Oh! give me the field on a Sunday morn
When gay spring -winds are swinging
Thro' copse and lane to the merry tune
The lads from the South are singing.
Give a rose to a maid, or a silken braid
Give a singer his song's full measure,
But give to a lad whose heart is glad
The width of a field for his pleasure.

Oh! to dart to the wing, and twist again
With a puck that is swift and burning
Or to swing out the line in attack and strain
Every nerve till the tide is turning-
To weaken the swirl of a Wicklow hurl
With a good ash bred in Kerry,
And press for the goal with all your soul
Or lose with a heart as merry.

I have seen the children of other lands
Applauded by dames with delicate hands
In the mild, midsummer weather-
But such poor sport is a weary sort,
With never a thrill to quicken

Like the flash and flame of the Gaelic game
When the hot strokes warm and thicken.

So, fashion a hurl from a fine young tree,
And give it the grace of your blessing-
'Twill fare right glad in the whirl of play
When the southern lads are pressing;
And honour bestow on the dead below
The meadows our heels are spurning
Who fought for the fame of the Gaelic game
When the fire of their youth was burning.

The author was accidentally shot during the Easter Rising 1916 and died as a result of
the wound.

With a Hurley in his Hand

By Joseph S. Considine, Dublin and formerly Ennis, Co Clare)
Source: An Camán, Nollaig 17, 1932

The English play the hockey game, Canadians lacrosse:
The Yankees boast of baseball with its deadly pitcher's toss:
The Scotsmen shine at shinty, that they borrowed from our land,
But the Irish boy is born with a hurley in his hand.

What fairer sight could one desire upon a summer day
Than see our ashcraft wielders in a bout of thrilling play:
Their scientific skill and stroke our plaudits must command,
For the Irish boy is born with a hurley in his hand.

Hurling teaches manliness, endurance, self-control:
Our Gaelic land and mother tongue forever as its goal:
'Gainst foreign culture, language, games to take a noble stand:
Ev'ry Irish boy is born with a hurley in his hand.

And well have the traditions of the glorious GAA
Sustained Caitlín Ní Houlihan against all alien sway:
And history will record how a gallant patriot band
Could use the trusty rifle like a hurley in their hand.

Unite, Unite, my brothers, 'neath our national pastime's flag,
For Ireland's weal, her storied truth, each glen and towering crag.
'Gainst wielders of the stout camán no foreign force can stand,
For each boy controls her future like the hurley in his hand.

Hurling in the Bar

By John Ely, Wexford.
Source: Received from Paddy Berry, Wexford.
Air: I am a Roving Journeyman: Chorus after each verse.

We have a junior hurling team way down in Ballyvard
And every evening after work, the boys are training hard.
I've been to all their matches, but they play their best by far
At night-time drinking porter down in Nicksie Cullen's bar.

Chorus:

When they're hurling in the bar—yes, they're hurling in the bar,
They score points from every angle and hit points from near and far.
They pull left and right and centre and sure every man's a star
You'd want to wear a helmet when they're hurling in the bar.

An expert saw them play one day and said they would go far
Provided they had petrol for to drive their motor car.
And heroes like Mick Mackey, Christy Ring and Lory Meagher,
They wouldn't hold a candle to our hurlers in the bar.

Our captain scored a point one-day, the ball went very far
And it came down with snow on top, it had been near a star.
If you don't believe this story and you think it's fetched too far—
Well all the p (o)ints are white on top in Nicksie Cullen's bar.

Our forwards are ᴄharp shooters but they sometimes miss by yards,
And once from seven inches with the goalposts wide ajar.
And 'twenty-ones' have been hit wide with pain that leaves a scar,
But they never, never miss them when they're hurling in the bar.

Our goalie can be brilliant and you'd think he was a star,
To hear him stopping 'bullets' at night time in the bar.
One day he let in twenty goals—his worst display by far,
But that's a tale he'll never tell in Nicksie Cullen's bar.

All referees are villians and they've hearts as black as tar,
But I sometimes think, without them, that we'd often have a war.
And our men have got the sideline, when they started out to spar,
But no one blows the whistle when they're hurling in the bar.

Hurling of the Green

Source: Six hundred and seventeen Irish songs and ballads,
Wehman Bros. New York.

'Twas night. On Antietam's height
The weary warriors lay.
Tired where the long and bloody fight
Had tired their worth that day.
Darkness had stilled the strife's alarm,
Though streams of lifeblood yet were warm
Where the drowsy outpost sank,
And shook his sleeping comrade's arm:
"You're surely dreaming Frank".

The startled sleeper gazed toward
The camp- fire's waning glow;
"Where are we"? "Here on the sloping sward
And the beaten foe below"
"Thunder! I dreamed of Ireland lad,
And a hurling match". "Well our foes have had
Full plenty of what I ween".
"But I dreamed I tossed the ball like mad
On a fair broad Irish green."

"Ah Frank, full many a ball we've hurled,
And many a head today
The game we've played with our flag unfurled
Is the game I love to play:
When that glorious flag at our front floats out,
And with rifle clubbed and with ringing shout,
We spring 'neath its emerald sheen,
And scatter the foes like rabble-rout,
On the crimson dappled green"

"Shall we ever again see Ireland, Frank
And play upon Irish ground.
This glorious game where our brethern sank

In the death of the starved hound?
On our side Erin, our island mother,
Each hurler true as a sworn brother;
Blighter game had ne'er been seen
Than I hope to play some other day or other
To the goal of an Irish green!

The foe was gone with the morning's light,
And the flag of emerald hue
Waved proudly above the wooded height,
Begemmed with the morning's dew.
And o'er many a fight did that banner wave,
And o'er many an Irish warrior's grave
Its mourning folds were seen; -
But how many of all that phalanx brave
Will again see an Irish green?

The Battle of Antietam was fought on Sept.17, 1862. during the American civil War.
The verses depict an Irishman, after the battle, dreaming of home, a game of hurling
and the use of the skills of hurling to club and to rout the enemy. In an article by
Thomas J. Mullen, JR, K.M in *The Irish Sword*, Vol. 1969-1970, p52, the Journal of
the Military History of Ireland writes, " As they closed in on the 88th, the Tigers
noticed that their enemy had not had time to halt and fix bayonets, and when the 88th
had fired a volley the Tigers rushed upon them before they had time to reload. The
men of the 88th flipped their muskets, grabbed them by the muzzle and proceeded to
wield them like giant clubs. It was quickly shown that a hatchet or bowie knife in the
hands of the most fearless and experienced 'gut fighter'" was no match for a clubbed
gun". "A few days later when Gen Summer asked about the large number of broken
and bent rifles in the Brigade, Sgt.Grainger explained what had happened. "Them
rebels went for our boys with bowie knives and the men went for them the way they
knew best". It is possible that this item may be a reference to this engagement or
some such engagement in the Battle of Antietam. The 88th Irish Brigade was under
the command of Brigadier General Francis Meagher (1823-1867), born in Waterford,
a Young Irelander (1842-45), Secretary of Montana State 1865, and accidentally
drowned soon after being appointed temporary Governor.

The Brigade's Hurling Match

By Robert Dwyer Joyce
Source: Ballads of Irish Chivalry by Robert Dwyer Joyce
Air: The Game Played in Erin go Bragh

In the South's blooming valleys they sing and they play
By their vine shaded cots at the close of the day:
But a game like our own the Italians ne'er saw
The wild sweeping hurlings of Erin go Bragh.

Our tents they were pitched upon Lombardy's plain;
Ten days nigh the foemen our army had lain;
But ne'er through their walls made we passage or flaw
Till we showed them the game played in Erin go Bragh.

Our sabres were sharp and the forest was nigh;
There our hurleys we fashioned ere morning rose high;
With the goal-ball young Mahon had brought from Dunlawe,
We showed them the game played in Erin go Bragh.

Our captain stood out with the ball in his hand;
Our colonel he gave us the word of command;
Then we dashed it and chased it o'er esker and scragh,
While we showed them the game played in Erin go Bragh.

The enemy stood on their walls high and strong,
While we raced it and chased it and hurled it along;
And they opened their gate as we nearer did draw,
To see the old game played in Erin go Bragh.

On a sudden we turned from the ball's swift career;
And rushed through the gate with a grand ringing cheer;
Ah, they ne'er through our bright dauntless stratagem saw,
While we showed them the game played in Erin go Bragh.

Their swords clashed around us, their balls raked us sore,
But with hurleys we paid them with hard knocks galore;
For their bullets and sabres we cared not a straw,
While we showed them the game played in Erin go Bragh.

The fortress is taken! Our loud shouts arise;
For King Louis and Ireland they swell to the skies.
Ah, he laughed as he told us a game he ne'er saw
Like the wild sweeping hurlings of Erin go Bragh.

The original 'Irish Brigade' comprised regiments in the service of France after 1691.
In 1605 Spain formed a separate Irish regiment under the command of Hugh O'Neill's
sons. Spain created five more Irish regiments in the 1630s and recruited 30,000 ex-
soldiers of the Confederate Catholics. France first enlisted Irish troops in 1635 but its
Irish Brigade stemmed from the 16,000 'wild geese' migrating after the Williamite
War. Initially commanded by James 11, these regiments were later integrated into the
French Army still wearing their red coats. Replenished by an average of 1000 recruits
per year, mainly from Kilkenny and Munster counties, they earned fame at Fontenoy
in 1745. (*The Oxford Companion to Irish History* edited by S.J.Connolly, p202)

The Hurling Match

By Germaine Ryan
Source: Coaching News: Vol 3, No. 1. July '93

Happy spectators jostle at the turnstile
Some travelled far to share the magic hour;
"Quick, quick, get to your seats, " they must miss nothing-
All greedy for the coming thrills.

Quickly the field become surrounded
By tier on tier of kindred, neighbours, friends
All eyes fixed on the arena,
Some joke and laugh to ease the tension.

The band strikes up; players are on the field.
Young Adonis like contesters, idols everyone
Their counties' colours flashing in the sun,
Self contained, they seem, but are they uptight?

Gravely a coin is tossed, hush!
"Who's playing with the wind? It's ours, good luck!"
The whistle blows, a yell goes up, they're off!
Excitement mounts, some rise up in their seats.

The ball is pucked, tossed, caught,
Passed to fellow player, intercepted,
Hit again way up the field, the crowd is wild
"It's a goal! No, Yes," all eyes are on the board.

At each "free", puck out, point or goal
Adrenaline flows madly, advice is yelled
"Get it, you thick" or "More power to you, boy"
Best hurlers on the ditch, as always.

Swift players, focus of attention
Run, strike, hit, miss, intent on winning

Their supple bodies leap, struggle, and sweat.
For though the game's the thing, the crown is victory.

Hell-bent on being the heroes of the day
Our players in Blue press on,
They won't let down loyal Hill Sixteen
Or myriads who'll remember them in song.

The final whistle blows. the stands are emptied,
Handshakes, backslaps, contrast, on the field,
Weary, smiling heroes mount the platform
They must be seen- a duty to supporters.

The vanquished, heads down, slink away
They'll live to fight another day.
"You'll beat them next time, lads", shout well-wishers
Hurrying to seek solace in a Guinness.

A Hero's Troubles

By David P. Murphy
Source: Gaelic Echo, July 11, 1942
Kilkenny Journal Nov. 29, 1913.

'My arm is sore' said Walton,
'My arm is very lame.
The way it feels, I'll never play
Another all-Ireland game'

'Why, what's the trouble'said Dan O'Connell,
'What ails your good old arm?
I'm sure you haven't played enough
To do it any harm'.

'Oh no it wasn't playing Dan
That made my arm so lame;
It wasn't playing but I'll swear
It hurts me just the same'

'Just tell me' he continued
As he scratched his handsome chin,
'The total population
Of the crowds that we've been in'

'About five millions' said O'Connell
When he had made it out:
'About five millions', Simon said
And Dan replied, 'about'

'If that's correct' said Walton,
'Everytime we leave Kilkenny's climes,
I figure that I've shaken hands
About five million times'.

A tribute to Sim Walton, after Kilkenny had beaten Tipperary in the 1913 final.

A Score

By Celt
Source: Muiris de Prionnbhiol, Blanchardstown, Dublin (formerly Cork)

'Pass it to Tommy', and Matttie flies on
And the brown ball is flashed at the angle acute—
And Tommy's deft double the rearguard has drawn,
The Matt's in possession and Brian cries 'shoot'.

One glance at the posts, one flick of the wrist
And the ball o'er the sod takes wing like a hawk.
Vainly big Murty its flight would resist—
That ball has a mission no mortal can baulk.

Thrice in that hour Tom, Mattie and Brian
Conspired for the goal that would not be denied.
For the honour of Mumha, the game of the Fiann,
And the glory of Éire—their hope and their pride.

All Ireland

Author: James Lyons
Source: Our Games Annual 1963

Hurrah for Tipp! Shoulder to shoulder stand
The stalwart two—the dauntless blue and gold,
The sporting red—as many times of old,
And lead the hurlers of their native land.
Foes on the field, but friends when trials demand,
They win their honours against brave and bold
And, guardians of honour, proudly hold
Their hard-won laurels in a generous hand.

Hurrah for Tipp! Hurrah for Wexford too,
For Cork, Kilkenny, Waterford and Clare—
The vanquished and the victors—counties true
To Ireland's culture in the games they dare.
Hurrah for all who yet may wear a crown,
For they put loyalty above renown.

The Final

By Garry McMahon, Listowel.
Source: All-Ireland Programme, Cluichí Ceannais Iomána na hÉireann,
1 Meán Fómhair , 1996 Loch Garman v Luimneach

By cornfields lush, the fuschia bush, sheds tears of blood red down.
Hand crafted ash in sweet sounds clash o'er countryside and town.
It's hurling final time again, two teams line out to play,
Whichever side gains victory - let hurling win the day!

The atmosphere before the game I savour in the sun.
The banter, camaraderie, the laughter and the fun.
I stroll along to Jones's Road, drink a pint along the way,
While hoping in my heart of hearts, that hurling wins the day.

Cuchulainn played this ancient game in bygone days of yore,
His prowess now remembered, making pulses race once more.
We come each year to clap and cheer, to shout a loud hurray,
Whoever wins, we'll come again, while hurling wins the day.

Amhrán na bhFiann, I rise to hear, our anthem sung by all.
I face our flag, remembering, the stars of the camán,
Who thrilled me in my boyhood days, before my head was grey,
Caring not, whom won or lost, once hurling won the day.

Croke Park it looks so splendid now, its coat a verdant green.
Boys from Artane, with martial strain, parade the two fifteens.
Now proud they stand, in colours grand, tense, ready for the fray,
The ball is in; the game is on, let hurling win the day!

Lynch, Mackey, Smyth, the Rackards too, they made the sliotar sing:
Keher, Doyle, the Considines --but best of all was Ring.
The memory green of those I've seen will never fade away.
They all ensured while life endured that hurling won the day.

Another hurling final o'er, the cheers have all died down.
Cars, buses, trains dispersing now, once more from Dublin town.
A chirpy little traveller lad looks up at me to say,
"Who won", "I'll tell you now my boy", I said, "Twas hurling won
the day".

Arise Ye Gaels

By Rev. J. B. Dollard, Kilkenny
Source: History of the GAA, 1910-1930
By Phil O'Neill

On Tailteann plain, the Fenian men in friendly conflict met.
From far they came to play the game— the pride of Erin yet:
And many a fierce and well-fought field proved well their skill and
brawn,
For the hands behind the battle spears were trained at the camán.

Chorus:-

Arise, ye Gaels, through Erin's vales
From Foyle to Slievenamon-
By glen and hill let echoes thrill
To the clash of the camán.

At Benburb and the Yellow Ford our fathers faced the foe.
Their blows of hate with slashing weight the Sasanach ranks laid
low.
For land and faith, they courted death and still by field and bawn;
When war was o'er rang out once more to the clash of the camán.

Chorus:

Arise, ye Gaels, by Liffey's side and ye by Suir and Bann:
Wake and uphold that game of old that suits an Irishman!
The peal of Erin's victory shout, when chimes her freedom's dawn,
Will mingle with each joyous note to the clash of the camán.

Chorus:-

Benburb, battle of (5 June 1646), the largest engagement of the Confederate War,
between the 6,000 strong armies of Owen Roe O'Neill and the Scottish commander
Robert Munroe. Munroe's Scots, intending a rendezvous with the Lagan and
Coleraine armies, encountered the Irish near Benburb, Co. Tyrone. After O'Neill's

cavalry returned from defeating the Coleraine force, his pike advanced down Drumflugh hill. Munroe was forced back towards the Backwater River losing 2000 to 3000 men. O'Neill chased off the Lagan army but otherwise did not follow up the only pitched battle the Gaelic Irish ever won. (*The Oxford Companion to Irish History* edited by S.J. Connolly, Oxford University Press 1998)

Yellow Ford, battle of (14 Aug. 1598), the greatest single defeat suffered by English forces in 16c Ireland. The queen's army under Henry Bagenal taking supplies to the beleaguered Blackwater Fort was ambushed in difficult terrain north of Armagh by Hugh O'Neill. Bagenal and 800 of his men were killed and the Backwater and Armagh garrisons had to be abandoned. O'Neill gained unimpeded access to the midlands enabling in turn the overthrow of the Munster plantation. . (*The Oxford Companion to Irish History* edited by S.J. Connolly, Oxford University Press 1998)

Childhood Days

By P. D. Mehigan (Carbery)
Source; Catherine Leyden,(Dublin) Carbery's granddaughter.

'Cut me a hurl,' says the sturdy youth,
His limbs were straight and strong: ——
I liked his eyes of budding truth
Alight to right some wrong.
'My mates play other games,'— he said
I saw his proud lip curl;
'I'll play the game my granddad played,
—I want a hurl.

'Cut me a hurl,' says the winsome lass–
Her brown eyes smiled at me–
'For I can take a camóg pass,
Too fast for you to see;
I hold my left hand down like all,
I strike without a turn,
I love to hit a flying ball
—Cut me a hurl.'

'Tut me a hudle,' says the lisping boy,
Who climbed a weary knee;
My chain and medals were his joy–
'What are they Dad?' said he.
The light of God was in his face;
His head had many a curl,
With pleading eyes he pressed his case
— 'Tut me a hudle'

So I cut the hurls in the ashen lane,
When Christmas fires burnt clear,
I shaped them true with serried grain
When springtime days were near–
Mayhap in life's more serious play,

Or in some final's whirl,
We'll bless the hour the children say
–'Cut me a hurl.'

Hurling Beyond the Atlantic

By T.D.Shanahan, Port Costa, California. (formerly Monagee, Limerick)
Received from Liam Ó Donnchú, Ballymoreen, Littleton.

Oh, wouldn't Fionn Mac Cumhaill feel proud
Were he alive today,
And saw the games at Celtic Park,
When camán wielders play;
When bold Tipperary's gallant sons,
The boys who love the green,
Were fielded for a hurling match
'Gainst Limerick's seventeen.

Ho, Tubberadora, home of Gaels!
Moycarkey—bless the name!
Fair Toomevara, Bohercrowe,
And Templemore of fame.
Grangemockler and dear Thurles too,
Brave hearts and bold, I ween,
Immortalised Tipperary's home,
'Gainst Limerick's seventeen!

Can we forget dear Mainistir,
Where heroes bold abound,
Nor Croom so fair, nor Boher where
The Trojans true are found?
'Tis proud we are, dear land of thee,
Tho' countless leagues between—
Our hearts beat for Tipperary and
For Limerick's seventeen!

And where's the Gael from Innisfail,
Who would not bless the name
Of two such glorious hurling teams—
Exponents of the game,
Which Fionn —the Mighty—used to play

In Erin's fields of green?
Our hopes are in Tipperary yet,
And Limerick's seventeen!

Now victory's laurels deck the brows
Of sons of Slievenamon,
But hero-hearted foemen were
The boys of Garryowen.
And now we pray the Tipps. some day
'Neath flag of em'rald sheen
Will wage the fight for Ireland's rights
With Limerick's boys in green.

A hurling match played in California on the 14th July 1912 between Tipperary and Limerick.

Mud and Marriage

By Michael Ryan, Bawnreagh, Askeaton
*Source: An Anthology published by Askeaton Civic Trust and edited by Patrick J.
Cronin 1998.*
Air: Master McGrath.

Of a handsome young maiden I tell you a tale
This maiden did marry a gallant young Gael,
Who often went hurling as gallant Gaels should
And brought home in his kit-bag a fair share of mud.

There was mud from Tipperary , from Cork and from Clare
And the local fields too did contribute their share;
There was earth from Croke Park, when Limerick were beaten
But most fertile of all was the soil from Askeaton.

Now things were all right in the honeymoon year
And oft midst the flowers, herself would appear.
And mud that she scraped from his boots, shorts and gansey
Did nourish the dahlia and strengthen the pansy.

But after a while the love faded in patches
The pity was, she never went to the matches;
'Till her mother advised her with the wisdom of mother
'Go follow him round or he'll look for another.'

So they drove to the final the next Sunday evening
And nobody spoke but their own little Stephen:
The rain-clouds had passed but had wept for their troubles
And the fields and the goal-mouths were covered in puddle.

The ball was thrown in and the flags started waving
She was proper disgusted at the ranting and raving,
Of respectable women in wild jubilation
Most improper behaviour for ladies of station.

Then Stephen cried, 'Mammy, hey Mammy look quick.
There's Daddy off with the ball on his stick'.
And there sure enough he was gone like a demon
The green flag was waving and she found herself screaming.

Aye, lepping and screaming as loud as them all-
'Come on Paddy me darling, will you pull on the ball;
Stand down on him you there, no use being too tender
Every man a man! give 'em timber boys timber.'

When the long whistle sounded they gave Paddy the cup
And her heart with great lumps of emotion filled up.
She was proud of her man with brown mud covered over
And they courted that night like two honeymoon lovers.

So now as they scrape off the mud from his boots
And places it round the chrysanthemum roots,
She smiles at the red rose, its soft petals curling
Saying 'Thanks be to God for the mud and the hurling'

The Old Sport

By J.J.Finan, (Myles)
Source: The Patriotic Songs and Poems of 1865-1912

I love to see two rival teams
Upon a 'sporting ground,'
Beneath the mellow Autumn beams
With eager crowds around.
Prepared with might and main to vie,
Until the game is won—
For I would make the leather fly
When I was 'twenty-one'.

I love to see our young athletes,
With clean and healthy frames,
Display their strength in manly feats,
Their nerve and skill in games.
And not like drones to sit or lie
Supinely in the sun—
For I could make the leather fly
When I was 'twenty-one'.

Your fathers, boys, had lots of snap
Which some call nerve or vim;
Your ginger you must keep on tap
To be the peers of them.
Then fame and honour were the prize
The victors sought and won—
For sports were never worldly wise
When I was 'twenty-one'.

I know young fellows always hate
To hear an old man brag.
But those you now deem 'up-to-date',
Will soon begin to lag.
O, once I could with Semple vie

531

Or emulate Bob Quane—
For I could make the leather fly
When I was 'twenty-one'.

Then, hurrah for him who makes a goal,
And him who scores a point,
And may their lives be always whole
And never out of joint.
I see them play with many a sigh
For happy days long gone—
When I could make the leather fly
And I was 'twenty-one'.

Then each should in some game engage,
If games with them agree,
Or else he'll croak when half my age—
And I am sixty-three.
Enough— I see it in your eye,
You're sceptical, my son—
That I could make the leather fly
When I was' twenty-one'.

The Tipperary Hurlers

By Gerard Ryan, Inch, Bouladuff, Thurles
Source: Gaelic Weekly, Jan. 9, 1965

From Gaeldom's birthplace they went forth
A tried and trusted band
Of gallant Tipperarymen
They were our hurlers grand.
How well they played that September day
In the twilight of the year
Will be spoken of for many a day
In counties far and near.

Tipperary! O Tipperary!
What pride rings in your name
In Ireland's turbulent history
You never brought her shame.
From Carrick town to Ormond
In battle or in play
Your sons have carved a niche for you
That leaves others in dismay.

The county of bold Treacy
Of Lacey and Dan Breen
Of Tisdall, McGrath, Kiely, Davin
In the forefront all have been.
When you see the Hogan Stand
Tipperary strikes you too
Not forgetting brave MacDonagh
Who was 'mongst the faithful few.

The 'showmen ' of Ireland
On our hurlers was conferred
The 'cradle' is a familiar name
Which everyone has heard.

Onwards! Onwards! Tipperary men
And keep your rightful place
Leaders in almost every field
And standard bearers of our race!

Tipperary Hurlers in Exile 1910

By M. O Dwyer, Ballagh
Source: The Tipperary Star 1910
Received from Liam Ó Donnchú, Ballymoreen, Littleton.

Through the long roll of ages since Patrick first blessed
The shamrocks and fountains, loved isle of the West.
Thy sons and thy daughters at home and abroad,
Have cherished the memories of Érin go Bragh.

And the youths of Australia, the pride of our race,
How they marched in our ranks with a smile on each face;
Prepared by their training for work and for play
As our war pipes strike up on St. Patrick's day.

When Perth and Freemantle lined up on the ground,
With hurleys all crossed —then away with a bound,
You'd think 'twas the Tipps, 'aginst' the boys of Mooncoin
With Munster and Leinster wild cheering each line.

There was Maher and Murray, Moroney and Ryan
And Crowley and Cranley for Perth did combine;
With Tobin, Mulcahy, Mick Ryan and O'Neill,
And more of the boys who for pluck did not fail.

For Freemantle, Jim Maher and Wallace and Shine
With Healy, young Cranly, O'Moore and O'Ryan.
Dwyer and O'Connell played fast on the ball
But the pride of Freemantle was brave Michael Wall.   **

How they played, how they struggled for medals and fame,
They acted throughout like the Gaels in the game.
May such games and such men in the West always stay,
To gladden our hearts on St. Patrick's day.

Crash, crash went the hurlers, away went the ball,
Don't wait to get up if you happen to fall.
Father Fahey was there right amidst the melee
All the boys say he made a first class referee.

Then here's to the Gaels from the hills to the coast
And on each Patrick's Day let it be their proud boast,
That for speed and agility, courage and brawn,
There's no game on earth like the Irish camán.

The above song was accompanied by the following note:-
'The folowing verses taken from the *West Australian Record* will be of interest to our readers as it describes a match in which many well-known Tipperary hurlers, now in exile, took a prominent part.
Captain Jim Maher is at home presently enjoying a brief holiday under the shadow of Killough. His old friends of the Jockey, Borris and Thurles will be pleased to hear that Mike Wall is doing well under the Southern Cross. His heart is at home here with the boys, and his earnest wish, in which he is joined by several fellow exiles, is that the Tipps will endeavour to win this year's All-Ireland'.
The following information on Mike Wall is extracted from *The Horse and Jockey 1899 Centenary Booklet*.
**   'Mike Wall from Grallagh lived next door to his cousins Tim and Mickey Condon. The turn on the road where his home stood was called 'Wall's Turn' and has survived to the present time. To this day, one can see a stone, which was part of the Wall residence, on which the initials, T.C. and M.W. are carved. Mike Wall like Tim Condon, won three All-Ireland medals. Mike won his medals with Tubberadora (1896), Horse and Jockey (1899) and Two-Mile Borris (1900). Mike emigrated to Australia in 1906 and there he continued to hurl with distinction. The following is a section of a song, which describes a famous hurling match played in Australia':

> When Perth and Freemantle lined up on the ground
> With hurleys all crossed, then away with a bound.
> You'd think it was Tipp against the boys of Mooncoin,
> With Munster and Leinster wild cheering each line.
> There was Meagher and Murray, Moroney and Ryan
> And Crowley and Cranley for Perth did combine:
> With Tobin, Mulcahy, Mike Ryan and O'Neill
> And more of the boys who for pluck did not fail.
> For Freemantle, Jim Maher and Wallace and Shine
> With Healy, young Cranley, O'Moore and O'Ryan;
> Dwyer and O'Connell played fast on the ball
> But the pride of Freemantle was brave Michael Wall.

Mike Wall died in Australia in 1918, the same year that Tim Condon died in Cashel: both men were in their early forties.

~ PART FIVE ~

Laments and Tributes

ALL-IRELAND MEDAL,
1920

CUMANN NA SCLEAS LUC USAOSOALAC
(GAELIC ATHLETIC ASSOCIATION)

GREAT CHALLENGE MATCH
(FOOTBALL)

Tipperary v. Dublin

AT CROKE PARK
On SUNDAY, NOVEMBER 21, 1920

MATCH AT 2.45 P.M.

ADMISSION   1/-

Bloody Sunday

Bloody Sunday

By Criostoir O'Flynn
Source: Centenary, F.N.T. Átha Cliath

One Sunday in the month of Samhain
The spies of England were cut down
In Dublin city by command
Of Michael Collins. That viper's band,
Shot in their beds, were men of blood
Who suffered the fate their spying brood
Had planned for Ireland patriot's sons.
When tyrant's armies feel what guns
Of freedom's fighters have to say
They let their violent vengeance play
On innocent civilians. Soon
The blood of Irish victims doomed
By cruel fate was spilt by guns
Of England's scum. The Black-and-Tans
Came to Croke Park on that same day,
Where Tipperary and Dublin were to play
A football challenge. A hail of death
Swept through the crowds, life's last breath
Sighed from the lips of young and old,
And on the field, caught in the cold
Rigidity of death, a young man lay
Who had been active in the play
As one of the Tipperary team.
The blood that poured in that vital stream
From Michael Hogan's heart has made
That green Croke Park a holy glade
Where Ireland's children, born free,
Can learn the price of liberty,
For Hogan and all who died
On Bloody Sunday our nation's pride
Has raised a mighty stand to bear
His name where gathered thousands hear
The Artane Boy's Band proudly play

In October 1920 came a sudden and brief revival of inter-county fixtures, which the next month was to have a tragic result. Early in October 5000 spectators, who had so far that year had little exciting fare, were entertained by a rousing challenge football match in Croke Park between Dublin and Kildare. Soon afterwards the Tippperary board issued a challenge to Dublin; a match was arranged for 2.45 p.m. on Sunday November 21, again in Croke Park. The events of that day, Bloody Sunday as it came to be called inside 24 hours at GAA Headquarters are now part of modern Irish history. Without advance warning from either side the Association found itself caught up in the grim military activities of both sides; more accurately, perhaps, the GAA became a convenient target for reprisal purposes by the British forces which that morning had suffered irreparable loss. Nothing more strikingly illustrates the close connections between 1916 and 1922 than Bloody Sunday.

Around 3p.m. when the crowd of under 10,000 was settling down to an entertaining game, a British military plane flew over and emitted a red signal-flare. Immediately Black-and-Tans began to climb over the walls at each end of the ground, some using ladders. At once a withering fire was directed straight into the crowd, first from small arms and then from machine-guns hastily set up on the ground just inside the main entrance. After about 10 minutes an RIC officer advanced across the pitch, announcing a proposed search of spectators. An initial stampede resulted; most of the crowd was detained, and it was some hours before the search was concluded. After the shooting and subsequent stampede 13 people lay dead around the ground; close on 100 were injured. The dead included the Tipperary captain Michael Hogan, a young Wexford man who had been rendering spiritual assistance to Hogan, a 26 year- old Dublin woman due to get married a few days later, and three Dublin boys, aged 10, 11 and 14 years.

The Croke Park shootings were, it soon transpired, only part of a series of events in Dublin that same day. Early in the morning, with the authority of the Dáil Cabinet and on express directions from Collins, the republican counter-espionage service had executed 14 British intelligence officers in their lodgings in the city centre, whose mission in Dublin had been the assassination of Sinn Fein leaders. Satisfied from his own efficient intelligence machines that it was a case of survival for whichever side was quicker to the draw., Collins in one carefully planned operation destroyed the centre of the whole British spy network in Ireland. Bloody Sunday proved to be the turning- point in the combined political and military struggle. It served notice on Britain that neither the IRA the underground Dáil Government would easily be broken. Once this vital message got through, there was no alternative to a compromise with Sinn Fein. Within weeks feelers went out for a truce.

At home and abroad the shootings in Croke Park were at once recognised as a savage reprisal for Collin's shattering blow to the British espionage machine. As the details of the afternoon's events were pierced together, all the evidence was seen to be against the official explanation. There were no IRA sentries around the ground, inside or outside; the firing was begun by the Black-and-Tans and not returned. Some of them and also some of the Auxiliaries were drunk: at least one indiscreetly admitted that they had come for revenge. From the pre-raid survey by the plane to the departure of the last military lorry (trailing along behind it the Tricolour always flown at Croke Park), the shootings could only be interpreted as a planned act of punishment by enraged and undisciplined troops for the loss of their leading officers that morning.

As for the GAA itself, like the rest of the community it was stunned by the outrage. Even before the game began Nowlan, O'Toole and McCarthy anxiously considered cancelling the match as if fearful of some counter-action by the British. McCarthy in particular, who worked closely with the Sinn Fein leaders, would have been fully aware of the significance of the shootings. None of the three can have been surprised at the discovery of some 30 revolvers scattered around the ground that evening; far from suggesting that some of Collin's men had come to escape detection, these weapons served only to confirm that the men of the GAA were in the forefront of the military struggle. After the shooting officials and players alike dispersed quietly. This time unlike 1916, there was no central council deliberation, no protest to the British, no contact whatever with Dublin Castle. The GAA was justly proud of the recognition by the British, implicit in the selection of the target for the reprisal, of the Association's identity with what one of the shrewdest of contemporary observers called' the underground nation'. (Extract from *The GAA: A History*, by Marcus de Burca published by Cumann Luthchleas Gael. (Pp 148-150)

Mick Hogan

Anon:
Received from Liam Ó Donnchú, Ballymoreen, Littleton.

Beneath the shadow of the chapel
At the foot of Slievenamon,
Lies Mick Hogan in his early grave,
Now fifty years have gone,
Since that Sunday in November,
When he donned the white and green,
And he strolled out on that Gaelic field,
With Tipperary's football team.

The match had scarcely started;
How the people sang and cheered,
Until John Bull's sons with their vengeful guns,
Brought death down on that field.
Mick Hogan fell in a hail of lead,
That swept across Croke Park—
He dyed the grass a crimson red,
With the young blood of his heart.

His comrade Egan saw him fall,
Upon that field of play
Undaunted he rushed to his side,
The final prayers to say.
The Saxon had his vengeance,
For his spies who died that day,
By shooting down Mick Hogan,
In this cowardly brutal way.

His mother! Oh God help her,
How those bullets pierced her breast,
And burning tears ran down her cheeks,
As they laid her boy to rest.

Now fifty years have passed away,
Since they laid her martyred son,
In Grangemockler's hallowed graveyard,
At the foot of Slievenamon.

Mick Hogan

Anon
Source: *Tommy Barrett, Iar Runai, Tipp. GAA, Thurles.*

In Croke Park one Sunday evening
Drunken forces of the Crown
Turned their guns upon the Irish
And like dogs they slayed them down.
A gallant Gael from Tipperary
As he played his native game
Was laid low by British bullets,
Michael Hogan was his name.

Take him home to Tipperary,
To his silent lonely grave,
Take him home to Tipperary,
There to rest among the brave.
Men like Hogan loved their country,
It was proved that fatal day,
When the mighty British Empire
Tried to smash the GAA.

Little known that Sunday evening
When the teams came out to play
That the murder gang from England
To Croke Park were on their way.
'Till an aeroplane it hovered,
O'er that quiet yet tranquil scene
And sent down a shower of bullets
On the crowd on Hill '16.

Then the Tans jumped from their lorries,
Scruff and scum of London town,
With their rifles at the ready,
Our young hero was gunned down.
Every year the Gaels assemble

At the site of that sad scene,
When the rosary was recited
For our one and only Queen.

While her martyrs gather round her
In that holy place above
There to rest with her forever,
Those young Gaels we Irish love.
And in memory of our martyr
Is the mighty Hogan Stand—
Where underneath they play the anthem,
Those grand boys of the Artane Band.

Now you Gaels from all o'er Ireland
When Croke Park you will attend,
Give a thought to Bloody Sunday
And let this little prayer ascend.
It's not much that I am asking,
Just one Pater and Ave,
For all those the British murdered
On that bleak November day.

Take him home to Tipperary,
To his silent lonely grave
Take him home to Old Grangemockler
There to rest among the brave.
Men like Hogan loved their country
It was proved that fatal day,
When the mighty British Empire
Tried to smash the GAA.

See the poem *Bloody Sunday* by Criostoir O'Flynn for an account of the massacre.

The Gael from Slievenamon

Anon
Source: M/s Áine Hogan Breanormore, Ninemilehouse, Carrick On Suir and Tommy Barrett, Iar-Runai GAA, Thurles.

'Twas not within his home he died nor 'mid the battle grim,
But when playing a grand Old Irish game British guns killed him.
When Croke Park grounds were crowded and leaden hail swept wide
Upon the sod he loved so well 'twas there Mick Hogan died.

His lifeblood trickled o'er the sward; his soul had flown on high—
Machine guns swept the playing pitch no comrade dares draw nigh.
But when the 'Amritsar' was o'er his comrades gazed upon   ***
The still and lifeless form of their Gael from Slievenamon.

It was not thus he'd wish to die a soldier of his land,
For he had answered duty's call when freedom's flame was fann'd.
But on that Bloody Sunday when England's work was done,
Another rebel heart lay still in the Gael from Slievenamon.

When Grangemockler will muster on the green sward once again
And the blood of Ireland's brave and best has not been shed in vain.
The memory of our martyred dead will in our hearts live on,
Ah, we won't forget Mick Hogan then who sleeps 'neath
Slievenamon.

When the flag of Irish freedom waves throughout the land we love,
The souls of those who died to save will guard it from above.
For they that bore their cross for Him have heard the words 'well
done',
And amongst the host of Ireland's best is a Gael from Slievenamon.

This song was kept alive by Ned Hanrahan, a singer from Mick Hogan's own parish.

*** **Amritsar** is a city in India. Great Britain was supported by the Indian people in
World War 1 (1914-1918) and for this support was promised a major role in its own

government.. The Montagu-Chelmsford Reforms in 1919 increased the powers of the provincial legislatures but the viceroy and the governors could still veto any bill. The Indians were not satisfied and believed that the reforms did not give them enough powers and so their violent protests continued. As a result the British government restricted their civil liberties, including trial by jury. The discontent of Indians reached a turning point after the **Amritsar Massacre** on April 13, 1919. A British general ordered troops to fire on an unsettled, unarmed crowd. Nearly 400 Indians were killed and at least 1200 persons were wounded. After the Amritsar Massacre, Indian history became an almost constant struggle for existence.

Verse 2— For the story of this tragic day, see the notes to the poem Bloody Sunday by Criostoir O'Flynn (*Centenary*, F.N.T. Átha Cliath)

Mr Thomas Walsh

By Francis Phillips
Source: GAA History of Cashel and Rosegreen 1884-1984 by Seamus J. King.

Into the great eternal home
Where lives the Living Light,
A patriotic noble soul
At last has taken flight,
And from our ranks God called away
As sound a heart as beat this day.

For many long and weary years
Through tempest and through shock,
He held the flag despite our fears,
His faith was like the 'Rock'.
And when the waves with fury roared,
The prouder still his spirit soared.

Out from his kind and generous heart
And from his genial face
There burst a beam 'twas more than art,
A beam of nature's grace,
That you might judge that fire did blaze,
That Fenians lit in byegone days.

He loved to talk of colleagues gone,
Of heroes who have been,
Forever with the faithful throng,
Those sons who loved the green.
And with him strove that 'She' might be,
A Nation rocked in Liberty.

And yet though death has still'd that heart,
His memory shall not fade,
With Spartan strength he played his part,
Such stuff are heroes made.

Some day when freedom's lights will burn.
Ere flickering ray may gild his urn.

When Mr. Thomas Walsh died in January 1913. No man's passing was more widely regretted. Thomas Walsh was a veteran Nationalist and an indefatigable worker in the National fight for freedom. In 1885 he launched the Cashel Sentinel as a weekly paper, which devoted its columns to the dissemination of the numerous grievances that actuated the founders of the Land League in their efforts to secure redress and reform. In one of the issues of the paper he was tried and convicted for daring to quote from a speech and spent three months in Clonmel jail.

His support for the GAA was enthusiastic from the beginning. Again and again he exhorted the Gaels of Cashel in the editorials to come together and get a strong club going in the town. He attended many GAA meetings and involved himself with the sportsfield committee and the establishment of a good field for Gaelic games in the town of Cashel. In his preface to the above poem, to the Tipperary Star, Francis Phillips wrote: 'The deceased was a patriot of the old school, a sterling and uncompromising Nationalist, and one who in the days now passed stood fearlessy and independently for the cause of Justice, Liberty and Right.

Sam Maguire

By Sean Morrison
Source: An Raithneachán,
The Gaelic Quarterly Review, No. 2 September 1936.

When Ireland bled at tyrant's heel and men were hunted down
And through each glen the rifle's peal oft answered Britain's frown.
You laughed to scorn the tyrant's wrath, your heart with love afire
And nobly trod the danger path, God rest you Sam Maguire.

The Irish heart refused to beat in foreign captive chains–
It never would admit defeat while life and love remained.
With high resolve, with courage bold and zeal that could not tire,
In life and death, in every breath, you were Irish Sam Maguire.

Perhaps some bard may frame a lay more fitting fair than mine–
When Ireland wakes, when dawns the day of liberty sublime
Then let me tell of one, who fell while toiling up still higher,
A patriot among the few, God rest you Sam Maguire.

Sam Maguire was born of Protestant parents about four miles north of Dunmanway,
townland of Maulabracka. He was a member of the London team defeated by
Tipperary (Clonmel Shamrocks) in the All-Ireland football final 1900. He was captain
of the London team and of the London team defeated by Dublin (Bray Emmets) in the
All-Ireland final in 1901. He was again captain of the London team defeated by Kerry
in 1903. Sam also interested himself in the legislative side of the Association's affairs.
In 1907 he was elected president of the London County Board of the GAA. There is
no record that Sam Maguire played football in Ireland.

Sam in London soon became associated with Irish Ireland organisations. He played an
active part in the war of independence. It was he introduced Michael Collins into the
I.R.B. They worked together in organising a system of gun-running and information.
His efforts led to his imprisonment and his removal from his post in the Civil Service.
After the Treaty of 1921 Sam Maguire lived for a time in Dublin. He returned to his
native Dunmanway in 1924 and died there in 1927.

The people of Dunmanway feeling that the memory of Sam Maguire should be
perpetuated decided to erect a monument to his memory and to secure a public park
that would be called after him. In May 1941 a Celtic Cross was unveiled at his grave
in St. Mary's Church of Ireland Cemetery in Dunmanway. In April 1974, the Sam

Maguire Park was officially opened by Dr. Donal Keenan, Uactarán Cumann Luthchleas Gael. In 1984 a memorial known as the Sam Maguire Memorial was erected by a special Memorial Committee near his birthplace at Maulabracka, Dunmanway.

His memory is also commemorated with the 'Sam Maguire Cup' the All-Ireland Football Final Trophy wrought by Hopkins and Hopkins, Dublin, to the design of the Ardagh Chalice. Kildare was the first county to inscribe its name on the Sam Maguire Cup when they defeated Cavan in the 1928 All-Ireland final. (*Sam Maguire Memorial Maulabracka, Dunmanway, 1984*)

Bill Kelly

Anon

Source: Toomevara G.A.A. 1885-1985:
Received from Seamus J. King, Boherclough, Cashel

You proudly wore the green and gold
In Toomevara's golden years:
Your craft and skill with Wedger's men
Adorned many a hurling field.

When the call of Ireland's freedom
Re-echoed round the glen,
You shared many a lonely vigil
With your gallant mountainy men.

Tipperary's fighting spirit
You sought forever to uphold
With men who proudly fought and died
In defence of the green and gold.

The caoin is heard 'neath the Devil's Bit
Where in childhood days of yore,
You roamed those hills and woodlands
Round Barnane and Templemore.

Your life of toil has ended
The soft green sod moistened with tears
May your soul we pray, be safe with God
Reprieved from all earthly fears.

Bill Kelly was a member of the famed Toomevara Greyhounds.

Bold Captain Hayes

Anon:
Source: *Moycarkey Borris GAA Story 1984.*

Arise, Captain Hayes, up and marshal your men
The Gaels of Moondarrig to conquer again
You met them before, on many a field,
The Gaels of Moondarrig, you forced them to yield.

Then hurrah for the Borris boys, who were never a craze,
When led out to battle by bold Captain Hayes,
All-Ireland they conquered—'tis well known their fame,
In defeat or in victory, they're always the same.

'Tis well I remember, for the shields they did play
Against famous Kilkenny, always first in the fray.
For the Gaels of Moondarrig, strong and stout in their ways,
But still they went under to bold Captain Hayes.

On Carrick's famed ground, where they lined up to play,
For forty-five minutes Kilkenny held sway.
But the last fifteen minutes, we rushed man and ball
When the long whistle sounded, 'twas eighteen points all.

The next time they played on that same field again,
Before the long whistle, dark night had set in.
Though Kilkenny had boasted—'twas premature,
For the onslaught of Borris, they couldn't endure.

The third famous match was on Jones' Road Ground,
When three times five thousand assembled around.
But the power of Tipperary on that day of days
Was led by the veteran, our bold Captain Hayes.

Two-Mile-Borris was formed some time in 1885. In senior hurling the Borris sides
won the All-Ireland of 1900, three Tipperary county championships in 1900, 1903 and
1905, and a Mid championship in 1910.Ned Hayes was a hurling stalwart for Borris
and Tipperary from the latter years in the 19c up to 1910 when he won the Mid Tipp.

551

championship. He captained the Borris team, which represented Tipperary winning team in the All-Ireland hurling championship in 1900. The Railway Shields were inaugurated for an inter-provincial championship, which was first played in 1906. Munster was represented by Two-Mile-Borris. Ned Hayes captained the team.

John Joe Hayes (Ballyerk)

By Br. J. Perkins, C.B.S. Thurles
Source: Morcarkey-Borris GAA Story, 1984

To 'Borris from famed Ballyerk
We took our hurler bold.
As selector, treasurer, player
He served the blue and gold.
Great John Joe's gone
But his name lives on
With men like Maher 'Best'
In a 'Borris grave
'Midst hurlers brave
We laid him down to rest.

John Joe won an all-Ireland in 1925 v Galway and was on the losing side v Kilkenny in 1922. He played with Moycarkey-Borris and was one of the parish's outstanding Gaels both as a player and administrator. Winner of county medals on four occasions, also four Munster medals, and one National League . Played in the Tailteann games. The old Two Mile-Borris hurlers trained.in his field. On retirement he officiated as a selector and was treasurer of the board for a number of years.

Johnny Leahy-In Memoriam

By Eamonn Fitzgerald (1949)
Received from Liam Ó Donnchú, Ballymoreen, Littleton.

When hurlers march again last rites to yield
Where many sleeping teamsmen wait the call,
I think I hear past voices from the field
Rouse many sleeping memories of them all.
Games earlier played; I see them play again
Till echoes the long whistle at the close;
I think I see long lines of hurling men
March out above dark clouds, strong winds and snows:
So musing on old names of morning time;
Remembering all in one, I mourn their loss,
While ash grows by the Suir, God's breeze will rime
Above one captain's grave in Holycross;
For deathless spirit sings no death could bow
And Tubberadora lives like Knocknagow.

Johnny Leahy's long association with the GAA made him known far and wide. He played his first hurling with Cashel in 1908 at the age of sixteen. There was no club in Boherlahan at the time. The junior championship at provincial level was inaugurated in 1910. Tipperary won this championship and repeated the victory in 1911. Johnny played both years.

He graduated to senior ranks in 1912 and continued to play until 1928, captaining two All-Ireland winning teams in 1916 and 1925. Soon after his retirement, he was elected county secretary, a position he held with distinction for twenty years. During that period he was a regular delegate to the Munster Council. He put Boherlahan so much on the hurling map during his playing days that the place became synonymous with all that was sturdiest and best in Tipperary hurling.

The title of 'Captain', which was usually given to him, was not only in recognition of having captained two All-Ireland teams but also because of the leadership, which he gave to the county for many years as a player, as a fighter in Ireland's cause and as a GAA administrator.

This poem re- echoes some of the thoughts of Dr. Bryan McMahon, Listowel, in his ballad, *Lament for Doctor Thomas Daly.*

Beyond this place of toil and tears
Beyond this plain of woe
There is a bourne in Paradise
Where all the hurlers go,
And there in prime they're goaling
And race across the sod
And thrill our dead forefathers
On the level lawns of God.

555

Martin Kennedy

Anon
Tomevara GAA 1885-1985.
Received from Seamus J. King, Boherclough, Cashel

'Twas four and eighty years ago he saw the light of day
The greatest Tipp full-forward that ever we say play
From Templederry's Kilnafinch, to Latteragh's school he came,
The lion of Kildangan and Toom's brightest star of fame.

The fastest foot that ever sped around the dusty square,
The flying ball he never missed on ground or in the air.
His steel like wrists and lightning twists, his goals we'll ne'er forget:
He beat the best fullbacks with ease as raspers shook the net.

The likes of Martin Kennedy will never more be seen—
So bold and brave in battle, so quiet spoken and serene.
Another Matt the Thrasher, before all hurlers bow,
The eagle of Tipperary, and the pride of Knocknagow.

Whenever forwards face the foe or fear the fretful prey
When Tipp. goes thundering towards the goal to bear the crown
away,
Remember Martin Kennedy that loved and gentle soul,
And the feather marking out the spot from where he scored the goal

Farewell to Castlesheela and to lovely Dromineer,
To Carrig, Kildangan, Kilnafinch and also Toom so dear.
In Monsea's mournful graveyard, he rests beneath the sod,
While his soul meets happy hurlers on the friendly fields of God.

Martin Kennedy was born on the border between Toomevara and Templederry in the
townland of Kilnafinch. Initially he played with Borrisoleigh and unsuccessfully
played in two county intermediate finals. The following year he transferred his
allegiance to Toomevara and travelled as a sub goalie to the famous Tom O'Meara
until one day their regular full-forward Major Collison missed a game and Martin took
his chance. He never looked back. He was 5'8" in height, sturdily built and used his
12st. to great effect. He had a good brain and was a good tackler. He joined the county

team in 1919 and became a regular in 1922 and for a period of fourteen years maintained his form as being the finest exponent of full-forward play in the country— until serious injury curtailed his county career. He won two all-Irelands, six Railway cup medals, two Thomond Shields, eleven North Tipperary medals and four county medals. He moved to Kildangan in 1932 and was soon responsible for bringing a county title to the shores of the Shannon. The last two lines of verse four point to one of his amazing plays. He placed a feather directly in front of the goal on the 21yd. line so that when in possession and with his back to the goal, he turned fast and shot accurately without looking for the posts.

The Hassett Brothers

Anon:
Source: Received from Matt Hassett,, St Conlan's Rd, Nenagh.

We sing of great men and the great deeds they have done
Of gallant Tipperary and her noble sons.
We sing our our hurlers with their backs to the wall,
Who brought honour and glory with every stroke of the ball.
Let us sing of our handball that game of renown
And the men who have played it from old Nenagh town.
McMahon, O'Gorman and Joe Bergin too,
But none could compare with Ned Hassett and Joe.

Chorus:

So here is to the men of old Silver Street,
Who were champions of Ireland no one could beat,
From the banks of the Shannon to the Gap of Dunloe,
None could compare with Ned Hassett and Joe.
There were other great men of handball fame,
Whose names are inscribed in that great book of fame.
Men from Kilkenny, Roscommon, Mayo,
But none could compare with Ned Hassett and Joe.

Chorus:

The Hassetts of Nenagh were champions supreme,
Who's skill in the alley will ne'er more be seen.
They won the All-Ireland five years in a row,
For none could compare with Ned Hassett and Joe

Extract from *Handball* by Tom McElligott: -'Travel Ireland and you will not find any
pair of ballplayers as popular as Ned (born 1908) and Joe Hassett! When I first knew
them, Micksey Hassett was Ned's partner, but in 1934, Joe came in on the left and
from then on, for five years, no pair could 'live' with them. Not that they ever really
trained—they enjoyed handball too much to take it seriously. And any ballcourt was

good enough for them; they would play an All-Ireland final in the same spirit, as they would take on a couple of cattle drovers at the fair of Roscrea.

They began playing ball in the Shamrock ballalley in Nenagh in the early 'thirties'. Now any man who won a Shamrock championship was good because he had to beat good men—Ayres, Bergin, McMahon, O'Gorman—to win through. So when Ned and Joe Hassett stepped into the court for their first All-Ireland final, against the reigning champions, Perry and Mullaney in 1934, they played and won a match which opened the way to five years of glory.

Glorious years they were, when crowded galleries everywhere gave welcome to them—the greatest partnership in the history of handball. 1934, 1935, 1936, 1937 and 1938 went by and still the newspaper headlines kept repeating, 'Hassett brothers win again', 'Hassetts retain title' etc. Tipperary was proud of them, but they belonged to all Ireland, winning friends as they won matches in every part of the country.

God Love You Wedger

By John Lefty Devine
Source: Gaelic Weekly, Mar 14, 1959.

He's gone from this sad world of heartaches and sighs,
From the fields where he hurled with the Tipperary boys;
From the haunts of his childhood 'neath blue Irish skies
The valleys and wildwood of loved Toomevara.

Patrick 'Wedger' Meagher was a legend in his own county and this is remarkable
because he never won an All-Ireland. But he was one of the greatest hurling corner
backs the game has known. He got the name 'Wedger' after he went to work with
John Lewis of Clash who kept some horses and it was while he was with him that he
acquired the nickname 'Wedger'. He was riding one of his employer's horses at
Toomevara races held in Looby's field and having ridden a very strong finish to win
one of the races, he was nicknamed 'Wedger' after a Co. Waterford family of that
name noted for breeding and racing horses.

He was dedicated to the game of hurling. He organised Toomevara with his friend Jim
O'Meara and so began the era of the Legendary Greyhounds. They won their first
county final in 1910 and dominated North Tipperary hurling for the next twenty years.
Wedger won three more county finals in 1912, 1913 and 1914 when he captained the
team. It is said that his organising ability, enthusiasm and leadership was mainly
responsible for the success of the team in the early years.

But all Wedger's talents were not confined to the playing fields. During the years of
the Club's greatest successes there was also a great upsurge of national feeling.
Wedger also recruited, organised and trained the local volunteers, many of whom
were his team-mates and he once again became their captain. He took part in most of
the local ambushes and raids. He was arrested for drilling Volunteers with Jack Harty
and Frank McGrath and spent six months in Belfast Jail. It was during those years that
he was elected Secretary of the North Tipperary county board. In 1920 he was re-
elected. The following year he was elected secretary of the County Board.

Canon Fogarty in Tipperary's G.A.A. Story (p269) pays the following tribute: 'Born
on the outskirts of Toom village, 'Wedger' Meagher belonged to a family that had a
hereditary love for the native pastime. As a child like many a Tipperary youngster, he
paid more attention to hurling than to his books. Daily he went to school with a
"crook" in his hand and a thread ball in his pocket. Some time before 1910 he
marshalled and was the controlling genius of the famous 'greyhounds'. A Gael with
the Fenian outlook, 'Wedger' Meagher was on active service in the fight for freedom,
and therein he lost the blush of youth; so much so that after the Treaty, he was forced
to say 'goodbye' to the arena, but the weight of his powerful personality was carried

into the councils of the Association. On the occasion of a presentation made to him by the County Board on the eve of his departure for the U.S.A. he said: ' My dearest wish was at all times the honour of Tipperary. I gloried with her in her victories; I grieved with her in her defeats. I feel this parting acutely—but though far away my heart will fly back to the venerated scenes amongst which so may of its impressions were moulded.'

In 1926 he travelled with the county team that had won the all-Ireland in 1925. In 1927 he emigrated for good. He worked in various jobs, ran his own drapery store and plumbing business and in 1930 he was appointed sports Editor of the Irish Echo, a position he held almost up to the date of his death. Wedger's impact on the games and on his village was enormous. His friends in New York have ensured that his memory will be remembered in his native parish as the year after his death they donated a baptistry, which now stands in the parish church.

Wedger died on Feb. 20, 1959 at his home 94-09 40th Drive, Elm Hurst, Long Island.

Denis Maher, Killinan

Rev. Bro. J. Perkins, C.B.S. Thurles.
Source: Tipperary Star, Mar. 2, 1991

Another tree has fallen; another voice lies still—
Another grave is covered beside Killinan Hill.
Another name is written upon that cold stone plaque
In the graveyard in Killinan, not far from Mullaunbrack.

A hurler's prayer goes heavenward; there is music in the air—
There is joy and peace around us and happiness everywhere.
It is like the peace of evening when the Munster final's o'er—
We are happy with our victory and the honours that we bore.

In the homes we'll tell the tales of that great and well-fought test,
And enjoy success and glory in the realms of the blessed.
And future generations will gain courage form those tales
Of former hurling heroes and those glorious gallant Gaels.

May the Lord forever guide you
As you tread life's winding track
May the peace and love continue
In the homes of Mullaunbrack.

The Tipperary Star Star, Mar 2, 1991 (Rev. Bro. J. Perkins) wrote as follows: 'Denis Maher, brother of 'John of the Hundred Battles' and James 'Dowse' has died in his 76th year…He may not have the physical strength of John and James, nor their prowess on the hurling field, but he had their presence, their bearing and their character, that love of all things Gaelic, the feeling for the Irish way of life, that longing for that tradition and heritage portrayed in the Mahers of Killinan. Song, story, music, hurling was their life blood, as necessary to them for their survival as the purple blood within their veins or the pure air that came form the fresh skies above Mullaunbrack where Denis and his grand family dwelt for many years.'

Father Bobby Harkin

By Br. J. Perkins, C.B.S. Thurles

In Littleton of hurling fame
They speak of Father Harkin's name.
They've raised to him a monument,
Where Father Bob long hours spent.

In toil, in training Gaelic youth,
To understand the gospel truth.
Full well he loved the hurling clash
The emerald field and the tender ash.

Moycarkey-Borris still speaks with pride
Of this saintly priest and youthful guide.
His soul is at rest in the realms above,
Borris holds his bones with respect and love.

When you pass the Pavilion say a fervent prayer,
For this man of work, great priest and player.
For long we'll remember the work he has done,
Round the hurling homes of Littleton.

On the 24th September 1980, the club had a ceremony in Littleton field when club chairman Liam Hennessy unveiled a memorial plaque on the club dressing rooms to Father Bobby Harkin, who was chairman of the club from 1971 to 1978. Father Bobby was a native of Thurles where he hurled with distinction on several Sarsfields winning teams.

Bro. Perkins was also the author of another verse of commemoration to Fr. Harkin.

> In Two Mile-Borris by the Church
> They laid this man of God;
> And there he sleeps among his friends
> In Moycarkey's verdant sod.
> In Dublin, London, Holycross,
> The Gospel seed he cast;
> The game of life he played with strength,
> Courageous to the last.

In Memoriam - T.J.Keating, Cloneen.

By Margaret J. Costelloe
Source: Received from Liam Ó Donnchú, Ballymoreen, Littleton.

Another June has come the way,
Fragrant with roses, with song birds gay;
Just three Junes now you went away
When God's angel passed along.

The mountain you loved stands brave and bold,
Clad in bright garments of green and gold;
Ah! We'll always remember the tales you told
Of romantic Slievenamon.

And, sure, if you were with us today
'Tis proud you'd be of the grand display
Tipperary still gives in the football fray
Or with clash of the sweet camán.

O! Poet splendid, your loss is keen
You'll be missed in Tipperary for e'er I ween,
And your memory forever will be green
As the grass o'er your hallowed grave.

Requiescat in Pace, true son of the Gael
At the white throne of heaven, now, you will not fail
To ask God's blessing for dear Innisfail
At the trying hour of her dawn.

Tom Keating was born in Brookhill, Fethard on the 13th April 1891—the same townland as Michael Doheny, the Young Irelander. Educated at Patrician Brothers, Fethard, he began writing verse during his school days. He trained as a national schoolteacher, and contributed prose and verse of a high standard to various local and metropolitan journals. A keen follower of Gaelic games he endorsed everything Irish. He was appointed Principal of Cloneen National School in 1927. His health declined shortly afterwards. He died in June 1934 aged 43yrs. (*Slievenamon in Song and Story*: Ed.Sean Nugent (1996)

Michael Bourke

By Rev. Bro. J. Perkins. C.B.S. Thurles
Source:Toomevara G.A.A. 1885-1985:
Received from Seamus J.King, Boherclough, Cashel.

Where are the boys of the rural schools
Who with hurleys roamed playful and free?
Where is the shepherd who guarded his flock
In the green fields around Ballinree?

Those faithful companions of schooldays are gone
Their teacher no more will they see:
How oft in the shade of the schoolhouse they played
Those young hurlers around Ballinree.

But your spirit Michael shall live with them all
No matter where ever, they'll be,
For you love the camán and that love will live on,
With the 'Greyhounds' around Ballinree.

Toom's banners still fly, your name will ne'er die
The green and the gold, long you'll see:
The name and the work of great Michael Bourke
Will forever-live round Ballinree.

We laid him to rest in the place he loved best,
Where many great hurlers find room:
For in this holy ground, the names will be found
Of the great hurling 'Greyhounds of Toom'.

Micheál de Búrca died in January 1982. He was associated with Ballinree N.S. and founded Kilmacud Crokes, GAA Club, Stillorgan, Dublin.

The Bould Rubber Man

By Paddy Power, Drangan
Source: Received from Liam Ó Donnchú, Ballymoreen, Littleton.
Air: The Gay Galtee Mountains

In Tipperary we had some great hurlers they say
From Cashel to Carrick and from there to Roscrea
With Semple's great stalwarts to add to that clan
But the pride of them all was the Bould Rubber Man.

In nineteen thirty-seven, he first made his name
In Killarney that day, sure he had a great game
In nineteen forty-five when Tipp jumped on the van
The star once again was the Bould Rubber Man.

In nineteen forty-nine, Cork were held to a draw
By a fine combination that had not a flaw.
'Twas a joyous occasion to be a Tipp fan
When Ring was held scoreless by the Bould Rubber Man.

And then the replay that went extra time
Those famous Cork hurlers once more they did shine
Ring, he swore vengance, but he failed in his plan
And again was held scoreless by the Bould Rubber Man.

Then in nineteen-fifty, the crown was retained
By a team led by Kenny, both skilled and well trained.
Nineteen fifty-one we were champs once again
It was now number five for the Bould Rubber Man.

For two more long years we waited in vain,
But never again would the times be the same.
In nineteen fifty –three, there came the swan song
When Tipp were led out by the Bould Rubber Man.

In a land up above, they still play that great game
A band of great hurlers, who all won great fame—
There was Rackard and Langton, Mackey, Ring and his clan
What a welcome they'll have for the Bould Rubber Man.

A tribute to Tommy Doyle, Thurles Sarsfields— winner of five All-Ireland medals—
1937, 1945,1949,1950,1951. Tommy's career spanned three decades. He held Christy
Ring scoreless in 1949 Munster Championship for two games plus extra time—
remembered as being one of the greatest clashes in hurling. He was chosen as left-half
back on the Tipperary Hurling Team of the Millennium. He received many honours
including the Bank of Ireland, Hall of Fame award 1987 and the Knocknagow award
1987.

Biography—*A Lifetime in Hurling* as told to Raymond Smith, 1955.

Paul Slevin

By a Team-Mate
Source: Lorrha and Dorrha GAA by Seamus J. King and
Midland Tribune, Sept. 6, 1969

Where the Suir flows down from the Golden Vale
We laid you Paul to rest.
May you sleep in peace in Tipperary soil,
We know you loved it best.
Tho' our hearts were grieved, as the graveside prayers
Echoed a sad 'Amen'
We felt some joy that you had come,
To rest with hurling men.

You graced the field in every game,
When you wore the Lorrha blue
For win or lose you wore a smile,
When the final whistle blew.
Your slight physique belied a heart,
So strong it knew no fear
And the memory of your courage
Helped us stem that brimming tear.

When by the great monastic walls
That told of Lorrha's past,
We bore your coffin shoulder high
The memory will last
Of a silent, mourning, praying crowd,
That spoke in louder tones,
Than funeral march or gun salute,
Of the grief of loving ones.

'God Rest You Paul', is our fervent prayer,
As we bid our last adieu;
'May His grace sustain your family
And give them courage too.

May your memory kindle in our youth,
The will to show like you,
Their sportsmanship and manliness,
When they wear the Lorrha blue.'

'May we all once more play on the team,
Where every game is won,
Where no-one is defeated
And nothing unkind done;
Where the champions who have won the laurels,
Don't boast or taunt the foe,
May we find a place upon that team,
Dear Paul, with you, also'.

People were shocked to hear of the death of Paul Slevin on July 9, 1969. Paul died as a result of injuries received in a car crash at Knockmorris, on the Clonmel/Cahir road when travelling to the Munster semi-final at Cork on June 21. He played with Lorrha and NewYork. At his funeral in Lorrha, his coffin was draped in the club colours and a guard of honour of Lorrha players made it a moving occasion.

The Deeds of Joe Moloney

Anon:
Source: Roscrea Hurling Club Commemorative Programme,
St. Cronan's Park, 1ˢᵗ June 1980

You've heard of Mickey Mackey and the famous Lowry Meagher,
You've heard of famous hurling men, known both near and far.
But in our opinion we the people of Roscrea,
Know we had a stalwart who outshone them in his day.

This gallant lad for many years thrilled the yelling hordes
And many thousands saw his scores mount steadily on the boards.
He was the greatest of them all from Thurles to Ardcroney
I speak of Roscrea's golden boy, right-half Joe Moloney.

To see him bend and lift and strike, to watch his shot soar true
And listen to the thunderous cheer re-echo through Burgoo—
To watch his frees, his lengthy stroke, his dash along the wing
To pull a game out of the fire in one last desperate fling.

And when a game was at its height and you'd hear the hurleys crash,
You'd see Moloney in the midst of those clashing sticks of ash.
And emerge he would triumphantly with ball upon his stick
To send it soaring o'er the bar with that old Moloney flick.

His hare-like dash upon the wing as goalwards he would speed—
Charging backs and crashing ash, to them he paid no heed.
This valiant son of gallant Tipp. made the thousands stare
As he pulled with wild abandon on the ground or in the air.

But alas those days are gone and ne'er no more I'll see
The likes of Joe Moloney as he bent to take a free.
And as I watched the ball in flight, o'er the bar 'twould soar
And the white flag fluttering in the breeze would bring a deafening
roar.

Those were the days that thrilled me in the days of yesteryear
When hurling men were hurling men who knew not pain or fear.
As I watched the scene below , from the brow of Hastings's Hill,
The deeds of Joe Moloney my heart with joy would fill.

Now when they speak of all-time greats of hurling giants gone by,
There is one name when mentioned that quickly lights the eye.
They'll tell you that he was the best from Cork to old Kilcroney,
They'll tell you that there'll never be another Joe Moloney.

The Wade Brothers of Kilcommon

Anon
Source: *Tipperary Star, Jan 13, 1990*

Through the green fields of Cummer no more the Wades will stray
To view the tender flowers that bloom in the month of May.
No more at dance or hurling shall those fond brothers shine,
Or walk on summer evenings to the Anglesea New Line.

Now will you tender Christians for those fond brothers weep
Who in the cold arms of death enjoy a lasting sleep.
And for their hopeless widows, a tender tear bestow,
And may the Lord of Mercy console their grief and woe.

At sweet Kilcommon chapel no more they'll bow in prayer,
Nor meet each kind relation they often met with there.
But when these friends assemble, let them proudly pray
For those two loving brothers that now lie in the clay.

Now to conclude and finish, I hope good people all
That you will take a warning by their untimely fall,
And shun the paths of error where hidden snares are laid,
And may the Lord be merciful to John and Thomas Wade.

The three Wade brothers were tried at Nenagh in the 1840's for killing a man in a row over a turf bank. John and Thomas were executed and Patrick was acquitted.

Tommy Treacy from Killea

By Rev. Bro. J. Perkins, C.B.S. Thurles

In thirty and in thirty-seven
We've seen great hurlers play
But none outshone that noble son
Tommy Treacy from Killea.

He strode across the emerald sod
Ever yearning for the fray;
From head to heel–a man of steel
Tommy Treacy from Killea.

His speed and skill, that fierce strong will
The toughest in his day:
In the gold and blue of 'Young Irelands' too
Was Tommy Treacy from Killea.

Of all the great Tipperary men
Who did their prowess display
None could compare to that daring player
Tommy Treacy from Killea.

That spirit and will is with him still
'Though now he's far away;
You need not fret, Tipp will ne'er forget
Tommy Treacy from Killea.

Mid Tipperary men, gather once again
This great honour to convey;
With the 'Hall of Fame' we honour his name,
Tommy Treacy from Killea.

Killea—near Templemore
Young Irelands—Dublin G.A.A. club which many Tipperary hurlers in the city joined.
Won two senior hurling All Irelands with Tipperary (1930, 1937)

Tony Carew

By E. Murphy, Washington
Source: Received from Liam Ó Donnchú, Ballymoreen, Littleton.

To Jones's road the fairest of Munster's athletes flew
But he who was their bravest no hurley there he drew
Or we'd see the East contriving, before their goalposts striving
To save the frightful driving of the famous Thurles Blue.

Of Tipperary's camán wielders, no forward of their hosts
Could so crush opposing fielders, could so humble all their boasts;
Or send the slitter spinning, his blows upon it ringing
While hats the crowds were flinging as he shot it through the posts.

If only Toomevara had picked the county through,
We'd be playing, 'The harp through Tara' while Kilkenny paler
grew
And there they'd sit bewailing their fortunes they were failing
For they'd get an awful whaling if you were there Carew.

Tony Carew was a famed forward with the Thurles Blues. He won a senior All-Ireland
medal with Tipperary in 1908.
This poem bemoans his omission from the Tipperary team (Toomevara selection) that
lost to Kilkenny in the hurling All-Ireland final in 1913.

Farewell to Connie

By Rev. Bro. J. Perkins, C.B.S. Thurles
Received from Liam Ó Donnchú, Ballymorreen, Littleton.

By Ailbe's walls, 'mong Dúrlas Óg, he walked and talked with truth.
A faithful son of rebel Cork, an inspiration to our youth.
The love of hurling he instilled in many a youthful brow;
His name will live—for evermore in the homes of Knocknagow.
Many a match he refereed and many a hurl he bore.
His name will live—in the hurling homes, with pride, for evermore.

The proud traditions of the past—you received by the banks of Lee.
At home, at school in the far-famed Mon, you gave unselfishly.
You loved the red of rebel Cork, so neat and clean were they—
You were proud we know, when you saw them go to the Railway
field to play.
At song and dance and drama, you were always to the fore.
You did right well—and they did excel in the juvenile Mid-Scór.

As Chairman, Sec. and P.R.O., your great talents too were seen.
In times of crisis you kept calm, you stayed peaceful and serene.
Your great ambition and delight, which always brought you joy
Was to see a hurley in the hand of every Thurles boy.
What care you took of each camán; how you made it look so grand
With linseed oil and varnish, the right size for every hand.

Many a long and tedious hour, I heard the hammer beat—
Many a band you fitted on, so carefully and neat.
Many a hurling ball you gave, in schoolyard, yard or lawn—
Many a boy was tutored well to wield the sweet camán.
You showed them all the basic skills of the world's greatest game.
To catch, to strike, to hook and block that one-day will bring them
fame.

But greater still than all those skills and greater still by far
Is the love of hurling you instilled in many a budding star.

A transformation's to be seen, it is not long in vogue,
'Hurling's the game'—you have restored the name of Dúrlas Óg.
Arise take heart—you played your part, at last we've seen the dawn.
For on each street—each child you meet doth bear the 'ould camán.

Oh! Connie dear—we're glad you're here as we this tribute pay
To a rebel son, who, great work has done in the home of the GAA.
Where're you go—we'd like you to know, be it England or New
York.
We respect, we esteem, that gallant team, the red and white of Cork.
May you fare well, when you shall dwell in your home in
Monasterevan.
We hope one day, together we'll play in the hurling fields of heaven.

A tribute to Rev. Bro.Connie Higgins, Thurles C.B.S. first Chairman of Dúrlas Óg—
1979.

576

Father John

By Jimmy Roche, Ballinard, Cloneen
Source: Received from Seamus J.King, Boherclough, Cashel

We saw him walk the narrow road
To the little village school.
We saw him play the game of ball
And play it strong, yet cool.
We saw him light the Flame that day
The Flame that led him on,
When he joined the Holy Orders
We were proud of Father John.

We saw him step behind the plough,
He walked the narrow sod.
We needed him to lead us
In the harvest field for God.
With warm sun to aid him
'Til the last wee grain was won,
And formed into bread for us
By men, like Father John.

We saw him on that day in June
Of glory, joy and fuss:
Our hands reached out the greet him
And he said he'd pray for us.
His kin, his pals, his people
From Crohane to Slievenamon—
He laughed and shared his joy with us:
We loved our Father John.

Just one short year he laboured here,
Beloved by one and all.
Then on that harvest evening
Came 'The Noble Call'

He is gone on to a better land,
His memory will live on,
While grass grows green on his loved Cloneen,
We miss you, Father John.

These verses were written in August 1983 on the sudden death of Father John Egan,
(40yrs) Garrawkyle, Cloneen. John Egan was a well known GAA player and
administrator and stalwart of his local St. Patricks (Cloneen and Drangan) Club in the
1960's and 1970's. He was honorary secretary of the club for ten years until the late
1970's when he entered St. Patrick's Seminary School, Thurles with a late vocation.
He was ordained in 1982 and served as a curate in Ballinakill-Derrybrien, Co. Galway
until his untimely death in 1983. He was well known in GAA circles in the South
Tipperary Division. He played at corner back for Tipperary Minor Footballers in
1961. Afterwards, he won South U.21 Football with Grangemockler-St. Pats. in 1961
and County J.F. Championship in 1967 with St. Patricks.
He was a nephew of Jim Egan, Mullinahone, who played with Mick Hogan of
Grangemockler on Bloody Sunday at Croke Park.

Scad Lonergan

By Anon
Source: Aherlow GAA commemorative Programme-Official Opening of O'Gorman
Park, 10ᵗʰ June 1979 and Tom O'Shea, Aherlow.
Received from Seamus J. King, Boherclough, Cashel.

There was a one Scad Lonergan, a hero of great note–
He had a brother Darby who was a famous poet.
But Scad he was a jolly soul and a poacher sharp and cute
And as good a man to lash a ball as ever wore a boot.

Of all the greatest exploits in which he won renown
Was the day he marked Phil Doherty in a match against the town.
The greatest deeds were done that day as ever they had seen
When the gallant lad Scad Lonergan contended with Phileen.

Now Phileen was small and handy and as lively as a hare,
And as good a man to pass a ball as any man was there.
His togs were made of flour bags and he wore a jersey green,
Oh, he was the townies' pride that day was Doherty Phileen.

The teams lined up at centrefield opposing man to man–
The backs went back, the ball was in and then the match began.
All eyes were on Phil Doherty to see where he would play
But when they saw him facing Scad there was a wild hurrah.

Now Scad my boy restrain yourself and think you of your name,
For on your toe there rests to day the downfall of Goat's Lane.
For we'll never let the townies back into Goat's Lane to blow,
That they bate the Galtee Rovers in the Glen of Aherlow.

All hotly did the combatants engage them in the strife,
To gain the ball both one and all they risked both limb and life.
So furious was the football that I heard old people say
The serpent up in Loch Bohereen came out to see the fray.

All smoothly for an hour or so did the tide of battle roll
And then Scad slipped in a cow track and Phileen scored a goal.

Oh woeful was the wailing that echoed o'er the place,
And the tears rolled down the old men's cheeks to witness the
disgrace.

But Scad arose like a frenzied bull and dashed into the fray,
And through them all he swept the ball, 'My God how that man
could play'.
All throats yelled on Scad Lonergan as they watched him near the
goal,
'Tis in! Tis in! Dar Fia tis in! poor Scad God rest his soul,
He died in that victorious rush but he scored the winning goal.

Poor Scad is gone, God rest his soul, he lies the earth between,
And as long as grass bedecks his grave, so long his memory is green.
Green in the morning's early dawn, green when the lights are low
Green as old Galtees graceful peaks, smiling down on Aherlow.

And ever since by the firesides bright along the Glen's green slopes,
The fame is sung of the men who won and dashed proud Tipp's last
hopes.
Yes, and many a dad tells his little lad of the victory long ago
When the hero of that Glen-Tipp match was Scad from Aherlow.

This ballad was written in the early 20's by Tomás Ó Laoi, National School teacher,
National School Inspector and later Professor in U.C.C. He was also a Tipperary and
Munster footballer. His father Chris founded the *Erin's Hope* club in St. Patrick's
College of Ed. Drumcondra, Dublin.. This ballad was written in fun, is a piece of
fiction, but a man named Scad did exist but he never played football.

Ode to Michael O'Hehir

By P.O'Connor, Carrick Street, Kells, Co. Meath.
Received from Liam Ó Donnchú, Ballymoreen, Littleton.

The championships are over, there're laurels lost and won;
Some brilliant stars have faded, who oft in glory shone.
Great teams have been defeated, that often blazed the trail,
But better teams replace them, so there is no need to wail.

But there is one outstanding, the champion of them all,
Though he never wears a jersey, nor ever plays a ball.
We have never seen him beaten; he's a champion on the air,
The Prince of Commentators, is the peerless M.O'Hehir.

When Gaelic games require him, he's ever at his post.
His glorious voice rings clearly and loud from coast to coast.
He's never tired of talking; he never needs a rest,
With hawk-like eyes and lungs of steel, that wonder man is blessed.

We need not go to Croke Park; he brings Croke Park to us.
He gives us every puck and kick; we miss the rush and fuss.
The 'seventies' and the 'fifties', the wides and all the frees,
The ebb and flow of battle; he gives them all with ease.

Across the broad Atlantic, to New York and far away,
To every land beneath the sun, goes the idol of our day.
To many a lonely exile, he sends messages of good cheer,
From dear old friends in Ireland and the homes they loved so dear.

You'll find him on the Curragh, where the plains are stretching wide,
Where the Classics are decided, though he never has a ride.
He'll tell us of the fancied ones, the last ones and the slow,
And then he'll give us one-two-three, as past the post they go.

On that far-famed course of Aintree, he stands without a peer
And keeps the old flag flying, with accents sweet and clear.

All other commentators, he'd smother them at once—
He'd tell us of the beaten ones and those that had a chance.

When the war drums beat for battle in nineteen-fifty-eight,
And camáns clash and rattle, when hurlers use their weight.
We hope to see our champion quite as happy on the air.
There may be many champions but there is only one O'Hehir.

Micheál Ó Hehir was born on June 2nd, 1920, He played hurling with Crokes and St.
Vincents. He was head of Sports in R.T.E. His father Jim Hehir, Glasnevin, formerly
of Ballnacally, County Clare, trained the Clare team that won the All-Ireland in 1914.
---'In the 12 years since the first radio broadcast of GAA events, Radio had had
several commentators, ranging from sports journalist Patrick. D.Mehigan ('Carberry')
to Father Michael Hamilton of Clare. Then one day in August 1938, a teenage Dublin
schoolboy, the son of a popular Clare born Dublin GAA official was given charge of
the commentary of the football semi-final in Mullingar. Micheál Ó Hehir became an
almost essential part of the annual Gaelic championship season, bringing the major
games not only into remote rural homes in every corner of this island but also half-
way round the globe to immigrant Irish communities' (Extract from *A Celebration of
Irish Life' –the Story of the GAA to 1990* by Marcus de Búrca)

Green His Memory

By Dáithí Fitzgerald, C.B.S. Thurles
Source: The Mackey Story by Séamus Ó Ceallaigh and Sean Murphy

Ah, bitter death our hero you have claimed
And rent the heart of every hurling man
With savage grief. But still the glorious name
Of Mackey will defy your rapacious hand.
For young men with great dreams have stood
Flushed and proud to have seen him in his day
Scattering his foes with powerful ease like Shannon's flood
Or bounding, deer-like through their ranks away.
In later years, grey-haired, with growing sons
They stood, shirt-sleeved in the sun on Munster Final day
And gasped with awe-struck voice, 'there's Mackey'.
Then laughing as of yore, you went your way.
'Twas sad so great a spirit should be confined
Though in one great body. But now at last set free
To stride Colossus-like the fields of time
Forever young, the fearless hurling Cavalier.
Your memory will be forever green, O noble soul,
Go now, the Master awaits you at the final goal.

Mick Mackey was truly worshipped in life as well as in death. Mackey was a great
hurling hero much admired by Tipperary hurlers and Tipperary hurling followers.
Mackey was serious about his hurling but he didn't give that impression. He was the
laughing cavalier of the hurling fields, a man to whom, every game big or small
brought great personal enjoyment and an intense sense of personal challenge. But he
had a hidden reserve, that was coldly analytical, which extracted every hidden
weakness. Con Houlihan writing in the Evening press said that 'we loved him for
another reason because he played with such obvious enjoyment. He took his craft
seriously but not solemnly. He could laugh and joke on the field...He gave the world
far more than it gave him but he didn't worry too much about that'.

The Mackey Story talks about his shoulders being as big and wide as a barn gate; steel
like hips as armour plating for his powerful frame; a flashing turn of speed; an inner
fire which seldom failed to envelop flagging comrades and a deft skill and control. He
has been described as having 'the strength of a Shetland pony; thorough as a baby
bulldozer, ruthless as a Sherman tank; mobile as a Myra's Fancy; swift as Tulyar and

courageous as a Spanish Toreador. Of him it has been said that you might as well try stopping the Shannon river with a hay-fork; that his playboy approach and bustling assaults were carefully designed to mystify opponents and put them momentarily off their guard; that he had a trick up his sleeve against the best of them; a masterly sportsman with all the attributes and commitment of greatness. On the field he was so formidable that one approached any possible encounter with him in trepidation; that off the field he was so easy going, modest and friendly that one found difficulty identifying the player on the pitch with the Mackey on the field.

He would pick the ball up and tap it on his hurley and allow his spirit to take him on some outrageous solo run that carried through hardship of the kind that would appear incredible to the modern hurler, surging through the field in celebration of the sheer physical strength of the man. He stamped his personality incredibly on the game, caught the imagination of the crowds and was the idol of every youngster in the land long after he had passed his best. Ex GAA President and Cork hurler, Con Murphy, said of him,'Mick Mackey was one of those rare people whose great performances on our hurling fields allied to charisma made him a living legend, who in some peculiar way managed to bridge many generation gaps long after his glittering career was over, Even in the twilight of his days, he always had a great presence in company, who never saw him play or indeed in many cases, were not born when he played. I always got the impression that while he was totally immersed in a game and the overall performance of his team with a keen eye for weakness, he enjoyed every minute of playing. If anything, his relaxed and jovial, if not cynical comment, to an opponent on his performance, could be as devastating as his play, if one did not keep one's head on, and feet on the ground'

Mick Mackey was born on 12th July 1912 and died on the 13th September 1982.

Christy Ring (1920-1979)

By Gerard Ryan, Inch, Bouladuff, Thurles

Majestically he strode across two great hurling decades
Bemedaled, bedecked in a breathtaking career
The leading actor surely in hurling's story
Yet scarcely aware of the magnitude of his role.
What intensity his hurling evoked
The drama lover he never disappointed
One marvelled at the quality of his play
His action had the economy of a lyric.
A sporting life filled with encore after encore
Given for immeasurable pleasure to the hurling fold.
Sleep peacefully now Hurler of Hurlers
Far from the jostling throngs you spoiled
 with your genius.

Extract from the graveside oration given by the Taoiseach Jack Lynch a team-mate.
'Had Christy applied his talents to another code, to another sport that had international
participation, I believe he could have achieved the same degree of perfection as he did
in hurling and would have had world renown…he had inspired literally two
generations of hurlers,…. as a hurler he had no peer. As a friend he was intensely
loyal. As a man he was vibrant, intelligent and purposeful'
Louis Marcus writing of Ring says: 'the crowds that tingled as he walked on to the
field and that exulted in his deeds were enjoying a poetry that they found nowhere
else. For Ring was not simply the supreme match winner. He was a figure of beauty.
Though thickly built and strong as a bull, he moved like a dancer. Ring in action was
taut, spare, compact. Of the thousands of pictures snapped of him in play there is
hardly one where he is not poised in a moment of grace. It was for this gift of Ring's
to gild their lives, that people adored him. But this magic was intensified by his
personal remoteness. There was no television in his time; he shunned Radio and Press
and he didn't speak to strangers.' (*Christy Ring* by Val Dorgan)

Christy Ring's Achievements:

Selected on the Team of the Century 1984
Team of the Millennium and Munster's Best Hurling Team 2000
All Ireland Senior Hurling Medals (8): 1941, '42, '43, '44, '46, '52, '53, '54.
All Ireland Runners Up. (2): 1947, '56.
All Ireland Minor Hurling Medal (1): 1938
National Hurling League Medals (4): 1940, '41, '48, '53.

National Hurling League Runners Up (3): 1949, '60. '61
Munster Championships (9) 1942, '43, '44, '46,'47, '52, '53, '54, 56
Railway cup Medals (18):
1942, '43, '44, '45, '46, '48, '49, '50, '51, '52, '53, '55, '57, '58, '59, '60, '61, '63
Cork Senior Hurling medals (14):
1941, '44, '45, ''48, '49, '50, '53, '54, '58, '59, '60, '62, '64, '67.
Cork County Senior Hurling Medals (Runners Up) (4): 1946, '51, '55, '56
Cork County Senior Football Medal (1): 1954
Cork County Minor Hurling Medal (1): 1938
Cork County Junior Hurling Medal (1) 1939
Munster Club championship 1965
Texaco Awards 1959
Texaco Hall of Fame Award 1971
Rest of Ireland Team: 1952, '53, '55, '56, '57, '58, '60, '62.
Selector and Captain of Cork's 1946 All Ireland winning team
Selector on Cork's All Ireland winning teams 1976, '77,'78.
Played on Cork Senior Hurling Team 1939 to 1963
Played on Munster Railway cup Team 1941 to 1963
Played on Glen Rovers Senior Hurling Team 1941 to 1967
Captained 3 Cork Teams to win All Irelands 1946, '53, '54,

Cuchulainn's Son

By Tom Williams, Taghman/Camross

The challenge of an ancient game
Brought glory, glory to your name.
When March winds blew the crowds still came
To watch you gentle hero.
In life's long march you made us proud
And many's a voice from out the crowd
Called out your name, aloud, aloud
An echo still resounding
And Blackstairs' men who saw you then
Still speak of you in awe
On Corman's Green where you had been
They tell of what they saw.
We watched you on September fields
And lightning was the drive
You were the one Cuchulainn's son
In nineteen-fifty-five.

The hand that held the stick of ash
And the man who led with style and dash
Oh Carrigtwohill once felt the crash
And Bennettsbridge and Thurles
And when in later years you beat
The devil on that lonely street
You showed us how to take defeat
With dignity and courage.
And Blackstairs' men who saw you then
Still speak of you in awe
On Corman's Green where you had been
They tell of what they saw.
We watched you on September fields
And lightning was the drive
You were the one Cuchulainn's son

In nineteen-fifty-five.

The last parade was sad and slow;
The last oration spoken low
And as on green fields long ago
The Diamond stood beside you.
Old friends they flanked you side by side
And the tears they shed were tears of pride;
An ash tree toppled when you died
And scattered seeds at random.
And Blackstairs' men who saw you then
Still speak of you in awe
On Corman's Green where you had been
They tell of what they saw
We watched you on September fields
And lightning was the drive
You were the one Cuchulainn's son
In nineteen-fifty-five.

This is a ballad written about the legendary Wexford hurler Nicky Rackard. The
second verse acknowledges Thurles as a nationally recognised hurling stronghold
and Nicky's victory over his self confessed problem with alcohol. The third verse
writes about his famous Kilkenny opponent P. 'Diamond' Hayden and his other
sporting friends at the funeral obsequies.

Jimmy Doyle

By Gerard Ryan, Inch, Bouladuff, Thurles

I will tell a tale of a hurling star,
With speed, control and style.
He gave us all such value—
His name was Jimmy Doyle.
His hurling was a treat to watch,
He was manly, he was clean—
Old-timers looked in awe at him,
His likes they had never seen.
For four years as a minor,
He held centre-stage.
Again he had no equal,
The best ever under-age.
When hurling men assemble
And they talk of skill and style,
One name will always come to mind,
The greatest—Jimmy Doyle.

Jimmy Doyle was one of the greatest six forwards of all time. His speed to the ball, his deft control, his keen sense of positioning, his adroit use of the open space, the speed in which he could lift and strike in one fluid movement and above all his deadly accuracy in dispatching the leather—all these qualities combined to make him not only one of the hurling wonders of the age but of all time. Selected on the Team of the Century in 1984, the GAA Hurling Team of the Millenniumm 2000 and on Munster's Best Hurling Team 2000. Chosen on Tipperary's Millennium Hurling Team in 1999. He won six All-Ireland medals with Tipperary in 1958, 1961, 1962, 1964, 1965 and 1971(in as a sub). In 1962 and 1965 he was captain of the team. With Tipperary he also won seven National Hurling League medals. He played with the Tipperary minors for four years contesting four minor All-Ireland finals and being victorious in 1955, 1956 and 1957. He won 11 senior hurling county medals with Sarsfields, was awarded the Hurler of the Year trophy in 1965.and holds 8 Railway Cup medals. In all he played in 13 All-Irelands between 1954 and 1971, winning 9 and losing 4. He began his inter county career as a goalkeeper in 1954 and also completed his inter county career as a goalkeeper in 1973.

He won a Tipperary Senior Football Championship in 1960 with Thurles Crokes, 4 minor hurling championships with Thurles Sarsfields in 1954, 1955, 1956 and 1957, a Dr. Harty Cup with Thurles C.B.S. in 1956. And the Dean Ryan Cup in 1955, 1956.

Jimmy Doyle

By Tommie Gleeson, Drombane, Thurles.
Received from Liam Ó Donnchú, Ballymoreen, Littleton.
Air: Davy Crockett-Chorus after each verse

Way down in Thurles upon a summer's morn
The greatest hurler in the land was born.
He learned to hurl and so gifted was he—
He was scoring points when he was only three.

Chorus

Jimmy, Jimmy Doyle, King of the Hurling Field.

In Thurles C.B.S., so there he went to school
' I was there he showed he was nobody's fool.
He learned the tricks of the hurling game—
There he started the legend of his famous name.

With Ray Reidy and Michael Craddock on the minor team
He led those hurlers to fulfil a dream.
The standard of play mounted up and up—
At last Tipperary won The Irish Press Cup.

On Sunday May the sixth at old Croke Park,
The half-time score made things look dark.
But Jimmy and the boys were up there to win
Not even Kilkenny would make them give in.

Two points in the lead, two minutes to go,
Liam Devaney got the goal that staggered the foe.
Tipp were in front and the seal was set,
When Jimmy blew a hole in the back of the net.

Jimmy is the smallest but Jimmy is the best—
He beat the pick of Leinster and the Men of the West.
His name will be listed in the Hall of Fame
And Irishmen will forever remember his name.

See notes on previous poem Jimmy Doyle by Gerard Ryan

Jimmy Doyle

By T.J. Kennedy Callan, Co. Kilkenny. (Formerly Tipp.)

Come all you lads and lassies and listen to me awhile.
I'll sing to you a verse or two concerning Jimmy Doyle.
It's all about this young lad, I'm going to tell ye now,
Sure when it goes to hurling, he's the boy to show them how.

To Thurles town of high renown, this youth he does belong.
His name and fame will yet be known in story and in song.
To wield the ash in style and dash, I think you'll all agree,
His equals Tipp. has never known, now that's a certainty.

In the hurling semi-final, Kilkenny they went down,
Before the onslaughts of this boy from dear old Thurles town.
Tipperary should be proud of him and for that we must allow,
For when it goes to hurling, he's the boy to show them how.

Now we've read in Gaelic records of great hurlers in the past,
But none of them at this boy's age his records has surpassed.
In honours, cups and medals won, in fame he stands alone—
Like a king in all his glory, he sits upon his throne.

So long life to this young hero, may the years upon him smile.
He's a credit to Tipperary and the pride of Erin's Isle.
For I know that in the years to come some stories will be told
Of this brilliant teenage hurler, who wore the blue and gold.

See notes on previous poem.. Jimmy Doyle by Gerard Ryan.

592

The Evergreen John Doyle

Anon:
Received from Liam Ó Donnchú, Ballymorreen, Littleton.
Air: Slattery's Mounted Fut'

We have heard of famous hurlers, who played in days of yore,
Such as Mackey from the Shannon and Langton from the Nore.
The Rackards too from Wexford town, all hurling honours share,
With Ring the wizard from the Lee and big Jim Smith from Clare.

Now those are but a few great names before me in my file,
But best of all I will recall is widely known John Doyle.
He doesn't hail from Cork or Clare, Mooncoin or sweet New Ross,
This man of steel, now I'll reveal belongs to Holycross.

Just twenty years ago, the truth I will unfold,
When John stepped out on green Croke Park, clad in the blue and
gold
To play for his own county Tipp; sure he did nothing wrong.
Some since have died, more have retired; John is still going strong.

Now Ring, he was a genius, likewise John Mackey too,
As the flags did soar, the crowd did roar, when they came thundering
through.
But when it went to showing them how, Jim Langton had the style,
But none I dare will e'er compare with the evergreen John Doyle.

He won all honours on the field—as a sportsman, he was great.
Of All-Irelands he has seven but Christy Ring has eight.
So, please God this year, the crowd will cheer when they meet the
boys of Ross,
And I have no doubt, the loudest shout, will come from Holycross.

Now every year, sure we all hear, no more the ash he'll wield,
But comes the band and sure enough, Big John, he leads the field.
He's feared by all the forward men, when ash on ash doth ring.
Sure you're held at bay with no loose play, when hurling on Doyle's
wing.

So here's to Ireland's brightest star, as a hurler he is great.
We know quite well and time will tell, he'll equal Christy's 'eighth'.
And then go on to beat them all, clad in the blue and gold,
This farmer boss from Holycross, who gets young instead of old.

John Doyles' Hurling Record.

M.H. Munster Medals: 1946, 1947.
M.H. All Ireland Medals: 1947
S.H. Munster Medals: : 1949, 1950, 1951, 1958, 1960, 1961, 1962, 1964, 1965, 1967
S.H. All_Ireland Medals: , 1949, 1950, 1951, 1958, 1961, 1962, 1964, 1965
N.H.L. Medals: 1949, 1950, 1952, 1954, 1955, 1957, 1959, 1960, 1961, 1964, 1965.
Railway Cup: Selected in 1951, 1952, 1953, 1954, 1955, 1956, 1960, 1961, 1963,
1964, 1965, 1966.
Railway Cup Medals: 1951, 1952, 1953, 1955, 1960, 1961, 1963, 1966.
Oireachtas medals: 1949, 1960, 1961, 1963, 1964, 1965.
Representative Games: Ireland v Combined Universities. Selected on the Ireland
Team in 1953, 1954, 1955.
Texaco Hurler of the Year Award: 1964.
Hall of Fame Award 2000.
Tipperary Sports Star Award: 1959
Team of the century in 1984: Team of the Millennium 2000 : Munster's Best Hurling
Team 2000: Tipperary's Millennium Hurling Team.
Club Honours: On Mid Selection county M.H. winners: 1946, 1947, 1948.
Mid. S.H.Medals. 1947, 1948, 1951, 1954.
Co. S.H. Medals: 1948, 1951, 1954.
Mid. S.F. Medal: 1954.
Played for nineteen consecutive years on the Tipperary senior hurling team—1949-
1967 (incl.) Played for Tipperary in all six back positions. He was never substituted
during this period. Doyle was a rollicking, charismatic, forceful, fair and skilled
player, who gave extraordinary and faithful service to his club, county and hurling.
Christy Ring (Cork) is the only other player to have won eighth senior All-Ireland
medals in hurling. He is a legend in hurling circles.

He retired from inter county hurling in 1967, following the All-Ireland defeat by
Kilkenny. He continued to play club hurling until 1969.

He served as a county S.H. selector and as Tipperary's Central Council representative.

Our Hero John Doyle

By Pat Murray, Clonmel
Source: Tommie Barrett, Thurles. Chorus after each verse.

On a fine Sunday morning in the month of July,
A father sat talking to his little boy,
Of legends, of heroes and men of great fame
And of those who brought glory to the great hurling game.
Oh the little boy said,' please Daddy tell me
Who was the best hero you ever did see'.
His father looked down and said with a smile
Son he came from Tipperary and his name was John Doyle.

Oh, promise me faithfully my darling son
That you'll tell your children when I'm dead and gone.
You'll gather them round, bid them rest for a while
And tell them the story of our hero John Doyle.

From Holycross in Tipperary our hero he came—
Eight All-Ireland medals he has to his name.
Eleven League titles you can take from me
And the great Hall of Fame in the year ninety-three.
He hurled on such men as the great Philly Grimes
The Rackards and Ring are the stars of his time.
He defended in style against the great Eddie Keher
And Cork's Paddy Barry a stalwart so rare.

Ah 'tis well I remember those All-Ireland days
When John from Tipperary we'd all sing his praise.
He was strong as Cú Chulainn as tough as they come
The greatest defender we've known in the game.
All the fans in Croke Park would be cheering for John
And the stands would erupt when they'd sing Slievenamon,
As he'd gather the ball and near send it a mile
We'd all shout for Tipperary and our hero John Doyle.

595

John Doyle, Holycross

By Jimmy Smyth, Ruan, Co. Clare

The matchless men of Tipp. were in the forefront
In service to their country and their race
But when we speak of hurling and of passion
John Doyle from Holycross will take his place.
Hardy as the goat on Galtee mountains
Steady as the Rock of Cashel town
Strong as the young steed in Ireland's story
A hurling man who wears a hurling crown.

Eight All-Ireland medals for his county
A record that he holds with Christy Ring
Eleven leagues to treasure for his people
Of Ireland's greatest backman let us sing.
For nineteen glorious years he wore the jersey
Fearlessly he stormed in the fray
At full-back, in the corners and the centre
And on the wings he gloriously held sway.

A hurler to the tips of all his fingers
The crowds went wild when he came into sight
With steely eyes and shoulders set he challenged
A terrible excitement was in flight.
With socks pulled down and hair adrift he hurled
And scattered men who dared stand in his way
He kept the colours flying for his county
And always lived to fight another day.

The matchless men of Tipp. were to the forefront
In service to their country and their race
But when we speak of hurling and of passion
John Doyle from Holycross will take his place.
And when the poets write of hurling greatness
Of the greatest backs that played upon our soil
The verses will abound with hurling stories
And the matchless man from Holycross, John Doyle.

John Doyle of Holycross

By Bro. J. Perkins, C.B.S. Thurles
Air: Dear Old Skibberreen

While green grass grows and water flows
While ash trees their tall heads toss
In the Hall of Fame we'll enshrine the name
John Doyle of Holycross.
In the fearful fray I've seen him play
On many a famous field
'Twas all the same—that noble frame
Was never known to yield.

In forty-nine I saw him shine
When he was but a boy
For sixteen years he nobly played
He has kept our flag on high.
Eight times he (has) won the All-Ireland crown
And gained the Celtic Cross
Eight golden medals adorn the home
Of John Doyle of Holycross.

He is tall and slim and loose of limb
And strong as Cashel's tower
He knows no fear—just see him clear
As men before him cower.
When bodies crash and hurleys clash
Around the enemy square
Where stand the brave their goal to save
John Doyle is always there.

The hand that gripped the stout camán
In work oft gripped the ash
And many a foe full well did know
Those strong hips and that dash.
He's got skill and drive tho' he is thirty five

There's power in those shoulders yet—
May his spirit live on when he is gone
For his deeds we'll ne'er forget.

Then here's to you my brave John Doyle
You still can show them how.
Eight times you've won the major crown
Great star of Knocknagow.
And when at length you will retire
To Tipp. you'll be a loss—
To the young we'll say—'step forth and play'
Like John Doyle of Holycross.

King of the Ash (John Doyle)

By Jimmy Smyth,
Ruan, County Clare.

John Doyle was the man who carried the can
When Tipp.was in doubt or in dread.
He'd face an attack on the flat of his back
With his stick or his head or his leg.
He never was shy and he'd never say die
No matter how tough was the game
This man wouldn't yield but could waltz through a field
And that was the strength of his game.

His courage was pure and his hurling was sure
He sprung from the land as a man
You could never decide as you stood by his side
On a trick or a play or a plan.,
That would give you a chance as you thought to advance
And side-step your way for a score
He was like a stonewall as he faced the ball
And as strong as a barnyard door.

When he played as a back in the midst of the flack
In the years when the going was rougher.
He kept them at bay and stood in the way
And always that little bit tougher.
This isn't to say that this was his way
He was fair but he rarely was bettered
A giant of the ash with the skill and the dash
Of a freedom that couldn't be fettered.

Yes, life can be rough and life can be tough
A little bit more than a canter—
But away from the game John treats it the same
With a smile and a chat and a banter.

But he could inspire and we had to admire
A great heart as he gave it a lash.
The record is there and no one can compare
With John Doyle who was King of the Ash.

Bannon From the Ragg

By Gerard Ryan, Inch, Bouladuff, Thurles
Source: Liam Ó Donnchú, Ballymoreen, Littleton

Across Ireland's hurling fields he strode
Like a legendary Greek god
A striking figure surely
On, and off the sod.

He loved the game he played so well
He was fit and fast and clean
His ground striking left or right
Had a brilliance never seen.

Those heady days on the Ennis Road
Saw him raise many a flag
A supreme hurling stylist
Was Bannon from the Ragg.

Seamus Bannon won three All-Ireland senior hurling medals with Tipperary in 1949,
'50 and '51 as a forward and at centre-field. He was a fast, skilful, effective and
dashing player. He was dubbed 'the most typical Tipperary hurler of all time' and
was a native of the parish of Drom-Inch, with whom he hurled, in his early years. He
later played with Nenagh and Young Irelands of Dublin. He also won national hurling
league medals with Tipperary and Railway cup honours with Munster.

1991 The Year of The Fox

By Jim Leahy
Air: The Fox

The Fox togged out on a summer's day—
He called for the ball to come his way.
And the green and white in tatters lay
When the Fox's teeth were bared-o
Bared-o, bared -o
The green and white in tatters lay
When the Fox's teeth were bared-o.

Next to try, Cork's mighty men
Shot goals and points, eight, nine ten,
But then the Fox came from his den
And evened up the score o
The score-o, the score-o
But then the Fox came from his den
And evened up the score-o

In Thurles town, Tipp looked 'bet'
And Walshe, he thought he'd found a pet
Till Foxy's flick it found the net
And the crowd came through the fence-o
The fence –o, the fence-o
Till Foxy's flick, it found the net
And the crowd came through the fence-o.

Then the Galway hunt came with their flag
And the Galway dogs their tails did wag,
But then the Fox he laid a drag
King Cormac showed his heels-o
His heels-o, his heels-o
But then the Fox he laid a drag
King Cormac showed his heel-o.

Kilkenny Cats they came to fight
And try to win with all their might
But the Fox he beat them out of sight
And Olly blamed the ref-o
The ref-o, the ref-o
But the Fox he beat them out of sight
And Olly blamed the ref-o.

We watched Mike Cleary have his fun—
We thrilled to see John Leahy run
But the summer of nineteen-ninety-one
Was the summer of the Fox-o
The Fox-o, the Fox-o
But the summer of nineteen-ninety-one
Was the summer of the Fox-o.

A tribute to Pat Fox, Tipperary's right corner forward, whom the author considered to
be the hero of Tipperary's winning All-Ireland campaign in 1991.
Verse 3—Denis Walsh , Cork's right-corner back in the 1991 Munster hurling final.
Olly in verse five was Ollie Walsh, manager of the Kilkenny team. Ollie was a
legendary Kilkenny goalkeeper.
Tipperary's 1991 All-Ireland winning team: -K.Hogan, P. Delaney, N. Sheedy, M.
Ryan, Colm Bonnar, B.Ryan, Conal Bonnar, D. Carr (Capt), A.Ryan, M.Cleary,
D.Ryan, J.Leahy, P.Fox, Cormac Bonnar, N.English. Subs: C.Stakelum for Cormac
Bonnar. D.O'Connell for N.English.

Gallant Dinny Ryan

By Jim Armshaw
Received from Liam Ó Donnchú, Ballymoreen, Littleton

The parish of Kilcommon has bred many men of fame,
Whose names will live in history and whose deeds we all acclaim.
But now in nineteen-seventy-one when Tipperary victorious shine,
To that roll of fame we'll add the name of gallant Dinny Ryan.

The green sward of Croke Park has seen great hurlers of renown,
Who, in by gone days set our hearts ablaze and won us many a
crown.
But to night the victory's sweeter still as we all proudly join
And our glasses raise to sing the praise of gallant Dinny Ryan.

The brown hills of his native home re-echoes o'er and o'er
Our cheers for Tipp and victory as never yet before.
Our hearts beat high with pride and joy and in some future time,
Our sons will yet, with baited breath, praise gallant Dinny Ryan.

The mighty throng in Croke Park field is waiting eagerly,
The dash: the clash: the smash of ash and then the ball breaks free.
From nowhere comes a lightning streak that nothing can confine
And like a jet 'tis in the net, that goal from Dinny Ryan.

Kilcommon's proud of you my son, for you will always be,
An inspiration to us all to strive for victory.
To give our best in any test, at any place or time
And bless the kin that gave us men like gallant Dinny Ryan.

Then here's to Tiperary and our hurling men,
Who have kept alive the spirit bright in valley hill and glen.
Who played the game and won us fame and never would decline
The challenge of the hard fought field like gallant Dinny Ryan.

Dinny Ryan of Sean Treacy's club played at left half forward for Tipperary in the
1971 All-Ireland Senior hurling win v Kilkenny.

A Tribute to Nicky English

By John Murphy, Ballinard, Cullen

Tipperary lost the McCarthy Cup the year of seventy-two—
For eighteen years our boys hurled hard but could not win it through.
Then on came Nicky English, a hurler in his prime—
He brought the cup right back again in nineteen-eighty-nine.

As he left home for famed Croke Park, as he'd done the year before
Little did he realise that he'd get a record score.
They say 'God loves a trier' and in Nicky He had one
And when the final whistle blew, He said 'well done my son'.

We've had great men from Cullen, back in the days of old,
But none as good as Nicky ever wore the blue and gold.
Although I often wondered about his hurling fate—
Thank God I lived to see the day his name among the greats.

For eight hard years of sweat and tears of blood and broken bones,
He joined the fray and there did stay for he's as hard as stones.
He's a gentleman, a hurler and always got it rough—
He played the game for sport not fame; he's made of rare ould stuff.

And to his humble parents, I now must say 'well done',
I hope by now you realise, you've reared Tipp's greatest son.
There's only one regret I have as I look at the score,
If you had more like Nicky, we would keep the cup flowing o'er.

Now youth of Tipperary, take a leaf out of his book—
If you are down to morrow or think you're out of luck.
You must always keep on trying as Nicky did before
And then some day, you will achieve another record score.

Nicky English , Lartin-Cullen club and Tipperary and was regarded as one of the most
brilliant hurlers in the country during the 'eighties'. His achievements include one
minor hurling All-Ireland, one under- 21,two senior, two National Leagues, two
Railway Cups, an Oireachtas, five Fitzgibbon medals and six All-Star awards. With
his club he won two West senior football medals, two intermediate hurling medals and
one intermediate football medal. As well, he won county medals in under-21 and
intermediate football, junior and intermediate hurling. He is currently manager of the
Tipperary senior hurling team.

'BABS'

By Micheál Ó Meara, South Tipperary GAA Secretary

From Tipperary's football garden, in Grange outside Clonmel,
Came a mighty dual performer who served the GAA so well.
His name is Michael Keating, as 'Babs' he is best known
And he became a legend, his records stand-alone.

In Clonmel's famed High School, his talent first shone through.
With Ballybacon and Ardfinnan, his skill was matched by few.
The blue and gold soon beckoned; he wore the colours with great
pride,
And as every honour followed, his name spread nationwide.

All-Ireland, League, Oireachtas and Munster medals came his way,
At home in South Tipperary at local level he held sway.
A gifted footballer, he gave his all, and his team-mates he did inspire
But here success eluded him, he failed to grasp the Sam Maguire.

The great success of seventy-one will forever be retold,
But then there came a famine and dark days for the blue and gold.
Until in eighty-six the great 'Babs' once again took command
And thrilled a new generation as we regained the Promised Land.

And now in ninety-four we pay due tribute to his deeds
We thank you 'Babs' for all your work in many fields.
Your skills and your achievements forever will endure
As long as Gaelic games are played down by the gentle Suir.

'Babs' Michael Keating was a legendary Tipperary hurler winning two All-Ireland
hurling titles in 1964 and 1971. He was on the losing Tipperary All-Ireland sides of
1967 and 1968. From 1972 to 1986 (incl) Tipperary failed to win a Munster title —
the famine ended in 1987 with 'Babs' (as Manager) but the team were later beaten by
Galway in the All-Ireland semi-final. Later on, he managed the team to win two All-
Ireland titles in 1989 and 1991. Babs was also an outstanding footballer and
represented his county and province with distinction He won the Texaco hurler of the
Year award in 1971 and won a Railway Cup Football medal with Munster in 1972. .
He was perhaps Tipperary's finest dual performer.

The Ballad of John Leahy

By Paddy Power, Drangan
Source: Received from Liam Ó Donnchú, Ballymoreen, Littleton.
Air: Nóirín Bán

There's a spot in old Tipperary
And they call it Kickham's town
Where there dwells a mighty hurler
Who has brought us great renown.
His name it is John Leahy
Though yet of tender age
He has brought home four All Irelands
And has entered history's page.

When John he started hurling
In his native Mullinahone,
'Twas against a wall in Carrick Street,
He was mostly on his own.
His brother used to join him
For to throw him back the ball
Then his skills were quickly noticed
In the school in Killenaule.

Here's a health to you John Leahy
May more honours come your way
You're the greatest in all Ireland
That's proved now day by day.
You have speed and skill and toughness
And you fear not any man
You're a mighty new addition
To the famous Leahy clan.

Now the year at last is over
And the All-Ireland crown 'tis won
They are singing and rejoicing
Round the slopes of Slievenamon.
To his team-mates all we thank you

Sure you all can take a bow
You've brought honour to your county
And the homes of Knocknagow.

John was the first Mullinahone man to play hurling for Tipperary. He holds three All-Ireland medals; under 21 and senior All-Irelands in 1989: All-Ireland senior in 1991. Two All-Star awards;1991 and 1994.

PART SIX

Miscellaneous Items

Memories of Cashel

By Philip F. Ryan, N.T.
Source: Source: GAA History of Cashel and Rosegreen 1884-1984 by Seamus J. King.

'Twas night, my thoughts in dreams went back some forty years ago
When I, a country lad, to school to Cashel first did go.
I mind the awful anguish when I reached the Ladyswell
I might as well be journeying into the depths of hell.

The old school stood before me, its height gave me a shock
Reaching up to heaven 'neath the shadow of the Rock.
Will we old folk e'er forget it, so stately and so tall
Surrounded like a jailhouse by a great big ten-foot wall.

Do you remember Maurice, I in fancy see him still
O'er the wall a swapping yarns with the lads down in 'the kiln'.
And dear old Francie Phillips, a gentleman so bold
He'll live in Cashel's history, like the famous kings of old.

When the day's work was over and the end of classes came
I thought I'd learn more about this city of great fame.
As I strolled down near the 'Terrace' to the end of Ladyswell
There stood before me gracefully Larry Stewart's hotel.

In Bank Place to view the names a short while I did stop
There was Margaret Dunphys, Katies, and the Sleator's Bookie
Shop.
Dargans, Delaneys, —Jack Cahills' butcher's stall
And Suttons on a great big sign upon the gable wall.

Of Friar Street, I'm quite sure you know the scene quite well
Like a king in regal splendour stood Willie Ryan's hotel.
While the beat of sledge on anvil, the smithy's tuneful sound
As Peter shaped the iron while sparks flew all around.

O'Briens', the barber shop, the harness maker Lee
Mrs Fogarty's restaurant for that grand cup of tea.
George Griffin, Quane the tinsmith, E.D. Ryan of hurling fame
And Quigleys who made boots and shoes, theirs was a household
  name.

Dwyers, the city bar, Dick Conroys, Larry Ryan
And Moloneys where we'd photos took at confirmation time.
Alices for chaney, Downeys come to mind
And there was Burkes the paint shop, who sold paints of every kind.

There was Mulloins for hardware; they sold coffins, iron bars
Buckets, cans and screws and bolts and wood for horses' cars
Those shelves were laden high with wares that now hold shirts
  and socks
While across the street in Costello's we got watches rings and
clocks.

Remember the Market House, sure I remember well
The country folk all gathered there with produce for to sell.
In donkey cart and pony trap each week they came to town
Oh Cashel folk! A shame on you to pull that hallmark down.

I wandered round, back to the 'Pipes' behind the city hall
Where Arthur Ward sold everything from needle to an awl.
I saw the little cobbbler shops; the cobblers beat on last
Those little huts have vanished like shadows of the past.

Shadowing the main street, the Town Hall stood in state
'Twas there the 'Fathers' met to guide and shape the city's fate,
While upstairs in the dancehall the young folk came in hordes
To 'trip the light fantastic' on squeaking creaking boards.

Remember Christy Hickey's and Hannigans for bikes
And Pake English's drapery, we'll ne'er see more the likes.
You'd get a suit there for a 'quid', a tie you'd love to knot
Those names now all have vanished, McInerney's own the lot.

Some names I nearly clean forgot, now that would be a sin
There was Tommy Ryan's bike shop, Bridget H and Cathry Flynn.
John Feehan's drapery, Babe Nash's for a treat
And Denis Hickey's grocery at the end of the main street.

I stood upon the 'Fountain' and my gaze in circle ran
There was Mickey Heneys, Learys, Con Carroll and Moll Dan.
At the end of Boherclough Street, one other shop I found
At the entrance to St. Patrick's was Norah Ryans, 'The Pound'.

I awoke from my slumbers, my eyes were hot with tears
I said 'Oh Cashel what a change in that short space of years'.
You've all just gone and left us like birds on fleeting wings
You're now but part of history of Cashel of the Kings.

The Bansha Hurlers Lament

By Dan Bresnan
Received from Geraldine McGrath, Galtee Rovers St. Pecaun's Club, Bansha. Also
published in the programme of the offical opening of Canon Hayes Memorial Park on
Sunday, 21ˢᵗ May 1978. Received from Seamus J. King, Boherclough, Cashel and John
Moloney, Currana, Bansha,

Where are the lads of the Village to night?
Where are the pals we knew?
Where are the men that sat on the bridge
Or strolled down Lismacue?

Where are the boys who played the first match
Against Carrick below in Clonmel?
Where are the lads that stood to the line?
Oh, it's not easy to tell.

How many are left in the Village to night?
Oh, cruel is the way of the fate
Of some the Grim Reaper has taken his toll,
And others have gone to the States.

Where is George Mahony the first man to go?
So sound and so sure on the backs.
His cousin Paddy was one of the best,
To lead in the forwards attacks.

Where is Tom Compton who minded the goal?
As good and as true as the best,
But alas he is gone to his maker and judge,
May his soul be at peace with the blessed.

Where is young Grogan, light-hearted and gay?
He would lighten our hearts with his song,
But sure at this moment he is far, far, away,
He is one of the emigrant throng.

Where is Mick Ryan who once captained the team
Jack Looby a good man and true?
But they cannot hear us to answer the roll,
For they are in America too.

Where is Ned Roche about whom we should boast?
He showed us some scientific play.
But he is another one Grim Reaper told,
We hope he's in heaven today.

Where is Paddy Dwyer the best man we had?
The best little forward of all–
I can assure you; he was a big loss
The day that we played Killenaule.

Where is Pat Kennedy, Pat Barry, O'Connor
Young Butler and Hourigan too?
But they have exiled to lands far away
We hope they are all well to do.

Where are the lads of the Village to night?
The lads we used to know–
Where are the crowds that went to the Mail
Or stayed around the G.P.O.

Oh, poor Bansha they are leaving you fast,
Your hope, your joy and your pride–
We hope the Lord will hasten the day
They will be all on the homecoming tide.

Where are the lads of the village to night?
Where are the pals we knew?
Where are the men that sat on the bridge
Or strolled down Lismacue?

Sadly, Geraldine McGrath, who supplied this lament, was tragically killed with her
husband John, in a car accident in Bansha, January 2000.

A local lament, with a universal flavour, for the Bansha hurlers, who have either emigrated or passed away. Written in the early 50's. The author was honorary treasurer of the Bansha club for forty years. This lament brings to mind an emigrant's lament by Phil O'Neill (Sliabh Ruadh) included in his *The History of the GAA* 1910-1930 (p275)

No more I'll join the cross-roads dance
Or mow the blooming clover,
Or share the joys with the girls and boys
When the harvest day is over;
No more upon the hurling field
Will Sunday evenings find me,
But far away from all that's gay
And the spot I've left behind me .

The Game of your Life

By Gabriel Fitzmaurice
Source: Poetry Ireland Review, Spring 1988

Whatever way it's kicked out, face the ball!
While wingers await delivery in space,
Centrefield must rise above the maul
And safely field, taking thought to place
The ball of fortune with the chosen one
And will him on to make the greatest use
Of what he's given as he solos on;
Centrefield's involved as play ensues.
For now's the time when great men must redeem
The story of the game from death, defeat:
The game of life's the story of a team
Who cannot rest until their task's complete
To take the cup, the cup that cannot pass
And raise it up in glory for the mass.

The Rural Club

By James Lyons
Source: Our Games Annual 1964

It was an ordinary country place
Where eyes were focussed on the hurling club
As pivot point, the veritable hub
Around which all activities kept pace.
For forty years—but it was no disgrace—
Teams played and lost and tried and lost again
Until one day a stripling among men,
A youth grew up a champion of his race.

He proved his genius on the field of play
In local championship and tournament
And won a medal on All-Ireland day,
His deeds were named at crossroads and in town—
His homeland spoken of where're he went—
A country place but it had won renown.

Give Them a Place to Play

By Denis A. McCarthy, Carrick On Suir.
Source: History of the GAA by Phil O 'Neill (Sliabh Ruadh) 1910-1930

Plenty of room for dives and dens—glitter and glare and sin
Plenty of room for prison pens—gather the prisoners in.
Plenty of room for jails and courts—willing enough to pay,
But never a place for a lad to race—no, never a place to play!

Plenty of rooms for shops and stores—Mammon must have the best,
Plenty of room for the running sores that rot in the city's breast.
Plenty of room for the lures that lead the heart's of our youths astray,
But never a cent on a playground spent—no never a place to play!

Plenty of room for schools and halls, plenty of room for art,
Plenty of room for tour and balls, platform, stage and mart.
Proud is the city—she finds a place for many a lad today,
But she's more than blind if she fails to find a place for the boys to
play.

Give them a chance for innocent sport, give them a chance for fun,
Better a playground plot than a court and a jail when the harm is
done!
Give them a chance—if you stint them now, to morrow you'll have
to pay
A larger bill for a darker ill, so give them a place to play!

On, On with the Games of the Gael

Anon
Source: A History of Rosscarbery GAA, 1887-1990
Air: The Men of the West.

We proudly look back o'er the ages
To that snap of the alien yoke—
To that star, 'mid our country's dark pages,
Made radiant by Cusack and Croke.
That brilliant now shining in splendour,
That flashed forth from Munster's green vale
Whose motto is still "no surrender";
On, on with the games of the Gael.

We spring from the hillside and valley
The games of our fathers to play,
And all loving Ireland shall rally
Beneath our choice standard today.
And here in our forces assembling,
In many a storied green vale,
We shout- not in fear or in trembling—
On, on with the games of the Gael.

The Dream of a Gael

By Eamonn Leahy
Received from Liam Ó Donnchú, Ballymoreen, Littleton.

At the mid-hour of night in the month of July,
I was taken in dream through heavenly sky.
I saw angels take wing from their celestial Ark,
And landing in thousands in dear old Croke Park.

Two teams had there mustered from God's own sweet home,
To play in Croke Park, thirty hurlers had come.
Then the teams took the field, looking eager and keen,
While Archangel Michael played Ámhrán na bhFiann.

The game was then started and speed was the thing.
I heard angels cheering for their 'Christy Ring'
The crowds were all cheering, 'Up Moycarkey', 'Up Glen'
Those angels of God would remind you of men.

They hurled on the ball, one left, then one right—
No harsh words were spoken, no row and no fight.
Good sportsmen, their like, I never have seen.
No catch cries of 'Culchie' or 'Dublin Jackeen'.

When the game was over, such a beautiful sight,
After blessing Croke Park, the angels took flight.
Now Moycarkey had won, spirits gallant and true,
Tipperary's good hurlers in God's gold and blue.

Flag of the GAA

By Michael Madigan
Source: Story of the GAA , by Séamus Ó Ceallaigh, Luimneach.

All flags may change and alter,
Political and national policies may likewise—
But there is one flag and one policy
That knows no vicissitudes
And that is the flag and policy of the GAA.
Hoisted and unfurled in 1884
By Croke, Cusack and Davin,
After ninety long years it still waves on
Unconquered and triumphant.

All flags may fade and fall,
But there is only one that never will
And that's the one we stand beneath.
If ever it bends or falters,
The national and physical resources of the Gaels
Will again uplift it,
And their exiled brothers,
Planted God's world all over,
Will gladly and proudly help
In its resurrection.

May it ever live on to inspire and renew us
With that national and patriotic feeling
That ever it has imparted,
In the trying and tumultuous periods
Of our chequered history.
My earnest wish here is:
May God bless the sons of the Gael—

May he ever inspire them to keep the flag,
The great national insignia
Of our sire's pastime,
Untarnished, unchanged,
Untrammelled and unsullied.

This was also published in the Gaelic Weekly, Sat. Jan.11, 1964 with Joseph C. Smyth as the author.

Native Place

By Criostoir O'Flynn
Source: Centenary, FNT, 1985

No man will love his land and race
Who has no pride in his native place,
Nor will traditions linger long
Where local poets make no song
To praise their parish, street or town.
In exile's homesickness cast down
The sons of Uisneach longed to see
Their native Ulster hills and be
Among their kin and friends once more:
'No matter how great his golden store,'
They moaned to Deirdre in Scottish glen,
'No man can be contented when
His eyes each morning do not rest
On that land in which his birth was blest'.
The men who founded the GAA
Would scorn the modern parasite way
That looks to government grants and schemes
To make reality of dreams.
The Parish Club was the sure foundation
Of their planned nationwide organisation
And thus it spread and prospers still
Because men love their local hill,
Their fields and streams, village and town,
And proudly play to bring renown
To parish and county; no purse of gold
Can buy the hero, brave and bold,
Whose talents, skill and determination
Are used to win the acclamation
Of his own people.

The Premier County

By James Mulcahy Lyons, Clonmel
Source: Slievenamon in Song and Story edited by Seán Nugent.
Received from Liam Ó Donnchú, Ballymoreen, Littleton

Thine in battle's van the bravest slogan ringing,
        Tipperary!
Thine in social hour the voice of gayest singing,
        Tipperary!
Thine the staunchest grasp the hand of friendship wringing
        Tipperary!
Thine deathless love to Irish colleen bringing
        Tipperary!
Thine of Gaelic fields the champion camán swinging
        Tipperary!
Thine the changeless faith to Patrick's gospel clinging
        Tipperary!

Tipperary-An Ode

By Rev. Bernie Moloney, Cashel.
Received from Liam Ó Donnchú, Ballymoreen, Littleton.

Mine are the Premier People:
Royal rulers on Cashel Rock.
Proud princes in castle towers:
Herds heavy with meat and milk
Vales of honey, woodland bowers.

Mine are the Premier People;
Wrenched from home for hard exile.
Blight beggared into famine;
Ore ripped from Silvermines;
Trees torn from Slievenamon.

Mine are the Premier People:
Saints and sages herein dwell.
Heroes' fame on distant shores:
Cill Ruain calls Ailbe's cell.
Keeper Hill greets Galtee Mór

Mine are the Premier People:
Rich with blue of summer hills.
Bright 'neath sheen of sun and moon.
Ripe 'midst gold of autumn fields.
Calm 'side Suir and salmon pool.

Mine are the Premier People:
Deft hands caress seasoned wood.
Shape a wand, gauge spring and grain;
Clash of ash is sweetest sound.
Speed of play: O wondrous game!

Mine are the Premier People:
Swift of horse, run hare and hound.

Win Waterloo and Epsom;
Poets, minstrels much abound.
Sing words both wise and gladsome.

Mine are the Premier People:
Blest by language, land and lore.
Song and prayer rise and ripple:
Thank Providence now and more.
Peal bells from hill and steeple.

Tipperary Far Away

Anon:
Source: Received from Liam Ó Donnchú
Ballymoreen, Littleton.

My home lies in Tipperary,
Round the slopes of Slievenamon
Where the lark and linnet sweetly sing
At the dawning of the day.
'Tis but a small mud cabin
And its floors are made of clay
But my heart lies in that cabin
In Tipperary far away.

By the side of our mud cabin,
The river Anner flows
Where the widow's brown haired daughter
Taught young Kickham's heart to love
Where Rory from the rafters
Took his pike to make the hay
Saying rise up my gallant Tipperary boys
Tipperary far away.

When I think of Charles Kickham
No wonder do I mourn
And dream of where his body lies
In his native Mullinahone.
Where thousands of his countrymen
They fervently do pray
In magnificent Tipperary,
Tipperary far away.

I remember nineteen-thirty
When we won the Triple Crown
We sailed the briny ocean
And played in the Polo Grounds.

We came back world champions
And proud we are to say
Were unconquered Tipperary,
Tipperary far away.

And soon we'll all be sailing home
To the slopes round Slievenamon,
Where the men of old in the days of yore
Could handle pike or gun.
Where the maiden fair with her nut brown hair,
Would sing and dance all day,
In magnificent Tipperary,
Tipperary far away.

Verse Four: The 1930 All-Ireland champions, Tipperary, were invited to New York to play America in the Polo Grounds, New York on September 20th 1931, It was the first of three in a series to decide the hurling championship of the world. A party of twenty-three sailed from Cobh on September 8th. An attendance of 35,000 attended the first of the three games in the Polo Grounds. Tipperary defeated the 'pick of America' by 5-2 to 1-4. The next game was in Boston against a Massachusetts selection. It was then back to New York for the second game in the series and another victory for the visitors. Two games followed in Detroit and Chicago and then the party headed west for San Francisco. The final game was played at Inisfail Park, New York and Tipperary recorded their seventh victory. (*The Clash of the Ash in foreign fields: Hurling Abroad by Seamus J. King*)

Success to Gallant Tipperary

By Tim Crowe, Dundrum- Irish Champion Athlete.
Received from Liam Ó Donnchú, Ballymoreen, Littleton.
Air: Success to dear old Ireland.

Some sing of friendship and Lang Syne, while others praise the
flowing wine
And others sing of love divine but let me sing Tipperary.
I'll sing of Tipperary's hurling men, from Shannon banks to Suir
Mills,
Till echo sounds from hill to hill, success to gallant Tipperary.

Chorus:

Join me in the sweet refrain
Let it ring o'er hill and plain,
We'll sing it o'er and o'er again
Success to gallant Tipperary.

Some sing the songs of far off land, while others praise the patriots
grand
And others sing of Red Hugh's Hand but let me sing Tipperary.
I'll sing of Tipperary's football men, from Slievenamon to Aherlow
Glen
Till echo sounds from hill to hill, success to gallant Tipperary.

In hurling and in football too, Tipperary's dash would thrill you
through
'Twas written on their noble brow, success to gallant Tipperary.
I'll sing of Tipperary's heather hills, its mountains, rivers and its
rills,
Till echo sounds from hill to hill, success to gallant Tipperary

Some sing of those of lyric fame, while others praise the glorious
name
And others sing of wild demesne but let me sing Tipperary.

I'll sing of Tipperary's athletic men, Kiely, Davin and Tipperary Tim
Till echo sounds from hill to hill, success to gallant Tipperary.

Such famous men we ne'er have seen, in blue or gold or emerald
green,
Their deeds are known to you and me, in Ireland 'an' far o'er the sea.
I'll sing of Tipperary's greatest men, in city, town and heather glen,
Till echo sounds from hill to hill, success to gallant Tipperary.

The emigrant will weary sigh, oft' back on Ireland casts his eye;
He's chained by mem'rys golden tie to scenes on many sports field.
As long as time its course shall run, where Irishmen meet beneath
the sun,
They'll think of home and glory won and sing success to Ireland.

Verse 4—Maurice Davin was an athlete of international fame, a founder member of
Cumann Luthchleas Gael and its first president. T.F.Kiely and Tim Crowe (Tipperary
Tim) were champion athletes.
The author, Tim Crowe, Bishopswood, Dundrum was a great athlete. His fame was
mainly due to his extraordinary feats in long distance running. In an athletic career
beginning around 1906, he won over 200 races. He was three, four and five miles
track champion of Ireland, marathon champion and All-Ireland cross-country
champion undefeated in a reign of fifteen years.

A steeplechaser, Tipperary Tim, winner of the Aintree Grand national in 1928, was
named in his honour.

In 1926, Tim Crowe accompanied the Tipperary Senior Hurling team on a tour of the
U.S.A. He was also very talented otherwise being a very successful competitor in
cycling events, a musician and a step dancer of note. Tim died in 1962 and is buried in
Clonoulty Cemetery.

Tipperary

By Edmund Murphy, Washington D.C. August 2, 1909
Received from Liam Ó Donnchú, Ballymorreen, Littleton.

Why does my memory wander so,
Back to those scenes of long ago,
By hill and dale and rivers flow,
    That ne'er will vary.
And think of stories, songs and rhymes,
That cheered us in those olden times,
In spite of England's blackest crimes,
    In old Tipperary?

For if we feared the north winds chill,
To hurl, to jump, or climb the hill,
There was a place where we could still
    Feel light and airy.
'Twas in the forge Tade Call'nan told
Surprising tales and very old,
Of Leprechauns and pots of gold
    Hid in Tipperary.

The Mahers, Kielys, Gleesons, Hayes,
Her fame in every contest blaze
Till people wonder at their ways
    Extra'rdinary.
For who like them can strike the ball,
Before whom all opponents fall—
Where could such men be raised at all
    But in Tipperary?

What men with valour more inspired,
Or what more valiant deed transpired,
When 'Galloping O'Hogan' fired
    Siege train and prairie?
When Raparees on Saxon's dashing,

Their gunners sabring, hacking, slashing;
Exploding guns and powder flashing
   Bespoke Tipperary.

And in our fight for fatherland,
Who made a bolder, firmer stand;
Whence hailed those who a nation planned—
   Kickham and O'Leary?
If e'er again revolt we plan
And Celt meets Saxon man to man,
The county to compose the van
   Will be Tipperary.

Centenary Final Day in Thurles 1984

By Gerard Ryan, Inch, Bouladuff, Thurles
Source: Liam Ó Donnchú, Ballymorreen, Littleton.

The time has come, the stage is set
For this centenary spectacular.
From across this Fair Isle and afar
They'll gather in Thurles,
The Mecca of the Gael.
On this day the mighty Davin
Comes to mind, who contributed
So much at the embryo stage.

A stadium beyond the wildest dreams
Of those Gaelic optimists—
The Founding Fathers.
A century that has seen
Sad and great occasions—
The early passing of Parnell—
Partial freedom.

Now the multitude assembled
Stand in awe.
The anthem is played,
Bringing back memories of the dawn.
The start,
The participants locked in combat
Win or lose, neutral or supporter,
A great year to be here.

Semple Stadium, Thurles was chosen as the venue for the All-Ireland hurling final,
Corcaigh v Uibh bFháilí on Sept 2, 1984 in order to commemorate the founding of
Cumann Luthchleas Gael there.

At 3 o'clock on Saturday afternoon November 1, 1884, Michael Cusack opened the
meeting in Miss Hayes's Commercial Hotel, Thurles, in the hotel billiard room.
See notes attached to the Founders and Patrons.

Centenary Year

By Criostoir O'Flynn
Source: Centenary, F.N.T. 1985

Thus the sad state of our nation's health
When Centenary Year of ' Eighty –Four'
Caused us to pause and count the score
Since that All-Saints Day in Thurles town
When Cusack and Davin and others sat down
In dark days of national frustration
To plan, for the health of the Irish nation,
The Gaelic Athletic Association.
The year of Nineteen-Eighty-Four
Was heralded in literature
When Orwell's novel made this date,
Then distant, symbolic of the fate
In store for freedom of thought and speech.
When dictatorial powers could reach
The citizen's mind; power less direct
Has often proved of more effect:
Subliminal and tendentious slant
Can skilfully in minds implant
Opinions they think their very own
And cherish more dearly than propaganda thrown
Like fire-bombs at a beleaguered town.
To Cusack and Davin and comrades few
Who hoped and strove, but little knew
What fruit would come from their endeavour
For Ireland's glory. Davin could never
Have dreamed that his name would be enshrined
In Áras Daimhín, a building designed
To commemorate this Centenary year
By providing at Ceannáras near
The Hogan Stand at famed Croke Park
New offices and a museum to mark
The part the GAA has played

In Ireland's story. Thus fate has made
Yet one more trinity of fame
By linking at Croke Park the names
Of Cusack and Davin and Archbishop Croke.

The Proud GAA

By Eddie Duggan (Sr) Mullinahone.
Source: Mullinahone Magazine 1984.
Received from Seamus J. King, Boherclough Cashel.
Air: Master McGrath.

Ten decades ago in fair Thurles town
A meeting was called and a plan was laid down
An organisation was founded that day
And is known throughout as the proud GAA.

Could they have known on that day long ago
That the seed they had sown would so fruitfully grow
And spread thru' the land, fulfilling their dreams
And bring to the whole world our great Gaelic games?

The camán, the shotar, the clash of the ash
The leather to leather, the toe to hand dash,
The puck and the kick, the save and the score
Oh, may it all last, for a hundred years more.

This poem was written to commemorate the GAA Centenary.

A GAA Centenary Song

By Jimmy Smyth,, Ruan, County Clare

One hundred years ago or more in eighteen-eighty -four,
When famine and oppression had touched on every door,
When Ireland with its customs, its hurling and its pride,
Had bowed a weary humble head, a nation almost died.

We knew of our distinctiveness but yet we let it ebb:
Our pastimes and our nationhood decoyed to England's web:
Our culture and our heritage, is teanga bhinn na nGael
And hearts were ever heavy since the battle of Kinsale.

Michael Cusack, County Clare, a fair and fearless friend
Decided that the tide must turn, that greatness shouldn't bend.
Inspiringly he led the way and forced a right-of-way
Through every obstacle in sight to found the GAA.

Maurice Davin, loyal and true from Tipperary came,
To lend a hand, to forge a link, to stop this bitter shame
Of Ireland sliding to the brink, athletics in decay.
A father of traditions had come to show the way.

Archbishop Croke from Mallow, the third and vital link:
A voice to guide a sacred ship, that ne'er again would sink:
A voice to challenge men in power, a fighter in the fray:
Another man for Ireland that never would give way.

Our games have prospered with the years and now it can be said
That hurling, Gaelic football, with handball surge ahead.
Let's think of Cusack, Davin, Croke, who faced the ebb and flow
To reach into the depths of man one hundred years ago.

Winning entry for the National Centenary GAA Ballad Competition , 1984

In a letter to the Irish sportsman in 1881, Cusack wrote that the Gaelic Democracy
was pushing the doors of Dublin Castle, that outside of Ulster the ruling class in

Ireland were not the proper people to organise sports and they, 'must make room for a strip of green across their colours and their ground.' (Marcus de Búrca, *The Story of the GAA*, Wolfhound Press, 1990, p.16)

'The definition of an amateur gentleman' was one who never competed in an open competition or for public money or for admission money, or with professionals for prize money, and who has never at any period of his life taught, pursued or assisted in the pursuit of athletic exercises as a means of livelihood, nor as a mechanic, artisan or labourer' (Séamus Ó Riain, 1994, *Maurice Davin* (1842-1927), Dublin Geography Publications, p30)

The general population, including artisans, labourers, and their families, were allowed time off to attend as spectators, but there was no place for them in the track and field events unless by a special dispensation a race confined to labourers or policemen was included in the programme' (Séamus Ó Riain, 1994, *Maurice Davin* (1842-1927), Dublin Geography Publications, p30)

'The rise and development of the GAA in November 1884, was one of the most effective efforts that had been made with unqualified success to check the supplanting of our native sports and pastimes—they were then almost dead. It is only those old enough to remember the uphill fight of the earlier years, who can appreciate to the full the wonderful strides that have been made. (Rev.Canon P. Fogarty *Tipperary's GAA Story*, p14, 1960, published by the Tipperary Star.)

'In its first quarter century the GAA had saved the national game of hurling from extinction; it had revived and standardised the distinctive form of football that had been played in rural Ireland for centuries; it had gained control for nationalists of their athletic pursuits. Above all it had created in the realm of sport a sense of national identity—giving a lead that other bodies like the Gaelic League and Sinn Féin were to follow in later decades with striking success and lasting consequences. (Marcus de Búrca, *The Story of the GAA*, Wolfhound Press, 1990 p.57)

Oh to be in Thurles

By Joseph Senan Considine, Ennis, County Clare.
Source: Liam Ó Donnchú, Ballymoreen, Littleton, Thurles, Co. Tipperary.

Oh, to be in Thurles when the final there is played,
A sight to cheer the hearts of all who wield the ashen blade.
A hosting of the Gaelic clans from districts far and wide
Where age and youth and beauty fair foregather side by side.

Oh to be in Thurles as the rivals take the sward
To weigh their 'form' and pick the team to win the day's award
Then while the Babel voices call each favoured one by name
And lusty clansmen stridently their county's worth proclaim.

Oh, to be in Thurles at the throw-in of the ball
When tense first seconds speechless hold the multitude in thrall
And then to hear reverberate one grand tumultuous roar,
In cadence mixed of joy and gloom to greet the opening score.

Oh, to be in Thurles and to note the pluck and dash,
The scientific striking of those heroes of the ash.
The eager forwards sweeping down, spectacular and fine
'Till the cúlbáire, with doughty drive relieves his harassed line.

Oh, to be in Thurles and to watch some veteran back
Opposing craft to youthful speed beat off each fierce attack.
And when some boy till then unknown reveals his hurling skill
To hear the Gaelic host, as one, applaud with right goodwill.

Oh to be in Thurles as opposing fortunes sway
And in the closing minutes tense, a point divides the play.
Then souls in transport rise above humdrum, mundane affairs,
And hurling takes pre-eminence o'er tariffs, markets, fairs.

639

Oh, to be in Thurles at a Munster final game
Regardless of the teams engaged, the thrills are much the same.
But surely the Olympian gods would ask no finer fare,
Than this sporting epic battle of old rivals Cork and Clare.

The Poetry Reading

By Arthur Broomfield, Irey, Ballyfin, Portlaoise.
Source: Poetry Ireland Review
Issue No.24 Winter 1988

The first poetry reading
I ever attended
Was at Semple Stadium
In the early days
Of my love affair
with Tipperary.

Everyone else thought
It was a hurling match
But I knew it was a reading
When I heard the poet
Rhapsodise the names
of G.A.A. clubs
Through the charged aura
of a hurling stadium
From his bunker
Beneath the New Stand.

Isolated on his podium
By ticket sellers
Counting out their takings
The Ezra Pound of Thurles
Shocked me with the excitement
Of the spoken word.

As he read out the names
Carrick-Davins, Lorrha
Boherlahan-Dualla
Moycarkey, Roscrea
Kilruane-McDonagh
And Borrisoleigh,

The fans cheered their players
and their clubs.

And I cheered the poet
For giving me back
My love of language.

Munster Final Day in Thurles

By Gerard Ryan, Inch, Bouladuff, Thurles.

Munster Final Day in Thurles
Unrivalled atmosphere prevailing
Field improvements undreamt of
By the founding fathers.
The sound of native music, the crowds
Coming over the bridge.
Lads and lassies hand in hand
Stall holders selling their wares
With familiar chatter
The crowded terraces and stands.
The banter between rival partisans
Match time.
Great exponents crowd the mind.
Mackey the colossus thundering goalwards—
Jimmy Smith scoring time after time
Against the odds.
Ring getting the scores
When his team needed them
As no other player could.
Doyle—the Thurles wonder boy,
The greatest ball player.
The beauty of Munster Final Day—
Long may it be.

Munster Final Morning

By John Arnold, Bartlemy, Garryantaggart, Fermoy.
Source: Poems from the Priests Garden by John Arnold

Today is Munster Hurling Final Day
Thoughts of Ring, Doyle, Mackey and Fenton
Dust in the square, the crush of the crowd
Killarney, Cork, Ennis Road and Semple
Hip to hip, pulling hard, ash and leather flying
Blood and bandage, helmets and handshakes
Ham sandwiches, 'ripe apples and pears'.
 Outside this morn the rain is teeming down
The hay is saved but Tipp are not 'bate',
Rain or sun the crowds will travel
Drawn as if to Knock or Mecca or Lourdes.
If the game is lost so is the summer
Victory means O'Connell Street in September.

'Tis only a game, but what a game.

A Munster Final

By Pat Kearney
Source: Slievenamon in Song and Story: Ed. Sean Nugent..
Source: Liam Ó Donnchú, Ballymoreen, Littleton.

A feast of hurling, a sporting venue,
Tipp and Cork were on the menu.
It was Munster final day—
Thurles town was bright and gay.
Crowds poured in by bus and train,
Cars were driving head to tail.
They came from Carrick and Clonmel town,
From Roscrea, Nenagh and Lorrha down.

We went to Hayes's Hotel to be fed—
The place was alive with white and red.
From Doneraile they came and Duhallow,
Bantry Bay, Skibbereen and Mallow.
Then we headed off for the field,
Touts had tickets, twenty pounds each.
Hats or colours the travellers said,
Blue and gold or white and red.

Apples, oranges and chocolates supplied—
The last few minerals the hawker cried.
Official programmes, one pound each—
Schoolboys selling them on the streets.
Ice cream twenty pence a lump—
The more you eat, the more you jump.
We must get in before the match,
The ref was looking at his watch.

The band had finished the Soldier's Song—
Then the whistle blew, the game was on.
Cork were helped by a summer breeze,
But Tipp were playing at their ease.

A low ball came from centre-field,
The Cork men struck, the green flag waved.
A sideline cut went over the bar—
A sixty-five pointed by a Tipperary star.

The second half started at a sizzling pace—
Cork got a penalty but the goalman saved.
The Tipp full forward had it all planned—
He caught the ball in the palm of his hand.
Then he kicked the ball with his big left boot
And as we looked the net it shook.
But like giants of other days,
Cork set about to wipe out arrears.

Goals were exchanged, a point or two—
Cork now had it all to do.
Tipp fought every ball and tussle,
With might and main and every muscle.
Excitement now was a fever pitch,
When the ref started looking at his watch.
The hay is saved and Cork are beaten
But Cork got a point that saved their bacon.

Munster Final Day

By An Br. S. Ó Páircín
Received from Liam Ó Donnchú, Ballymorreen, Littleton.

In days of yore we saw crowds pour, into the 'Cradle' Town.
Men, who toil on Munster soil, toughened, tanned and brown.
By hard work done in the summer's sun, with corn 'spuds' and hay:
They laughed and spoke with the city folk, good-humoured, bright
and gay.

The fiddlers play 'long the crowded way some grand old Gaelic
tunes:
Accordion players mix with the banjo pairs, the bodhran's beat and
the spoons.
An old man sings and his sad voice rings as beggars crave and pray:
The hawkers shout and in and out the programme sellers stray.

I hear the song of 'Slievenamon' of 'Anner's Banks' and 'Suir'
Famed 'Garryowen' and the Treaty Stone, and the 'Valley of
Knockanure':
The 'Rose of Tralee', the 'Banks of the Lee' and the march of
'Clare's Dragoons':
Songs of 'Róisín Dubh' and 'Sliabh Geal Dubh' and the Déisigh's
well-known tunes.

The din and noise, the triumphant cries, as hurling heroes clash:
The sun and sweat, the shaking net, the spine-tingling sound of ash.
The sward so green, the enchanting scene, the banners, flags and
cheers:
'Tis still the same, this hurling game, as it was in bygone years.

The young, the old, the brave and the bold, have memories that will
last;
Of matches played, of skill displayed in encounters of the past:
Though they have seen in sward or screen, the 'stars' of the World
play;
There's none to beat, or can compete with a Munster Final Day.

Hurling Final Glory

By Gerard Ryan, Inch, Bouladuff, Thurles
Source: Liam Ó Donnchú, Ballymorreen, Littleton.

The hurling final—the climax of the Gaelic year.
From the four corners of the land they'll assemble
To see this drama re-enacted again.
What an amazing spectacle to behold?
To hear the sound of Artane music,
See the crowded terraces and stands—
The hive-like murmur of the fans
To complete the pre-match scene.
Enter the combatants
Amid a crescendo of cheering.
They march past in traditional array.
The anthem, the start,
The do or die efforts of the participants,
The throbbing hearts of rival partisans.
The atmosphere prevailing stirs the blood,
Watching the ancient Celt demonstrate his art.
The final whistle.
For the victors —hero worship;
For the vanquished —consolation
In participation.

Semple Stadium

By Gerard Ryan, Inch, Bouladuff, Thurles.
Source: Liam Ó Donnchú, Balymorreen, Littleton.

Gaeldom revels at this revelation—
Edifice to a great figure, on and off the field.
What memories Semple Stadium evokes?
Its sod, its atmosphere, on Munster Final Day.
The actors that have trod its stage seem infinite.
Some great performers come to mind.
Dinny Barry Murphy scoring from his own line.
Stakelum on the ground or in the air.
Finn the halfback supreme.
Phil Cahill scoring in full flight.
Ring without question the most successful player.
Mackey, the colossal, thundering goalwards.
Jimmy Doyle the greatest hurler—
He was the flawless version of the Celtic art.
September sees the climax of Centenary year.
From the Four Corners, they'll come to Semple Stadium.
The kith and kin of all the Gael
To see the ancient Celt exhibit
His treasure of a hundred—a thousand years.

Tom Semple after whom the Stadium was called is a legendary Tipperary and Thurles
hurler and administrator.

'What is your fear boys while Semple is with you,
That gallant old captain who leads in the fray?
Why should you doubt when you think of the past boys
That one word 'Dungourney' ought all trouble allay.
Forward to victory then; on to the Leinster men,
Let Erin see what the 'blue' boys can do—
Practise at dawn and noon, train hard and train soon,
On! On! The battle cry is Thurles Aboo.'

Seamus J. King in his *History of Hurling* (1996) writes about an article in the *Cork
Examiner*, by Carbery (J.D.Mehigan) December 1908: 'Few men playing the game in
Ireland have achieved the fame that the Thurles captain-Tom Semple- has known. As

an organiser and a player he deserves a high place in any story of the progress of hurling during the infancy of the 20th century. Tom is a conspicuous man-there is no chance of mistaking another player for Semple...In build Semple is one of the tall, sinewy type, more of a thoroughbred than a hunter, if I may so express myself. He is well over six feet in his 'vamps'. And like most Tipperarymen, square cut and as hard as nails. Considering his great height he is light all over him particularly at the waist and limbs...

Semple's career stretched from 1897 to 1911, and its height coincided with the success of the Thurles Blues. He led his club to county championship victories in 1904, 1906, 1907, 1908, 1909 and 1911. He was a regular on the county team for many years and led the Blues to all-Ireland victories in 1906 and 1908. In 1906 also he won the All-Ireland long puck championship, sending the nine-ounce ball 96 yards. He was also captain of the Tipperary team that travelled to the Continent in 1910 and played exhibition games at Brussels and Fontenoy.'

A Lad of Young Fourteen

By Joe Healy
Source:The Story of Aughabullogue GAA

It was on an April evening I met him on the road
With his hurley and his hurling kit, it seemed a heavy load.
But his heart was light and his eyes were bright, his hair a golden
sheen
The world was all before him, this lad of young fourteen.

I stopped the car and took him in and said, 'I'll drop you at the cross'
He thanked me then and said, 'that's fine'; I'll be picked up by the
bus'.
And while we drove along, I spoke of hurling times
The Mackeys and the Rackards and Waterford's Philly Grimes.
.

I spoke of goalman Reddan, Tipperary's Tommy Doyle
Of thrilling goalmouth clashes and tempers on the boil
Of the thunder and lightning Sunday when Kilkenny pulled it
through
Of Limerick's Paddy Scanlan, Stokes and Clohessy too.

'Yes, I'd love to see them play, he said, 'those men of yesterday
Especially Cork's great four-in-a-row, they were mighty men they
say'.
'Yes', I said, 'I saw them play in Thurles, Limerick and Croke Park
The Murphys, Lynch and Barrett and Quirkie from Blackrock'

'The Buckleys, Young and Donovan, Campbell and Cottrell too
Kennefick, Mul and Condon and that famed old club the Blues.
We had 'Hitler' from Ballincollig and Micka from the Sars
Bat Thornhill and a gent called Lotty who are now above the stars.

He listened to my ramblings, this lad of young fourteen
With memories full of hurling days, of heroes on the green.

And then he asked the question that rang across the years
Of summer clouds, the thrilling crowds, the flags flying in the breeze

The sound of hurleys clashing, the sliotar flying high
The nerve tingling excitement beneath a clear blue sky.
These are the memories that come to me and the joy it will always bring
When someone asks the question, 'do you remember Christy Ring?

As he went away from me that evening in the spring
I wondered what kind of life would be without that hurling thing.
What would there be to talk about in factory, shop and farm
What other game could we invent to keep the small boys out of harm.

I watched a swallow gliding by, I hear a young lamb bleat
The little primrose raised his head the evening sun to greet.
The foal stood up on its gangly legs it's mother's paps to suck
I heard the ref's shrill whistle and the sound of the hurling puck.

These are the things about Ireland we hold so very dear
All enshrined in God's great plan, all so very clear.
Aye his step was light, his eyes were bright and his hair a golden sheen
And I thanked my God I met him then, this lad of young fourteen.

The Beautiful Game

By Brendan Kane
Source: Micheál Ó Muircheartaigh, R.T.E.

Less than a minute remains on the clock
As I tighten my lace and turn down the sock.
One last chance and it's all down to me,
It must be a goal, for we need all three.

I step up to the ball and look towards the posts.
Is that the crowd I hear, or is it the ghosts
Of men who before me have faced the same test
And never once failed to give of their best.

My father he gave me the love of it all,
When he guided my arms to strike that first ball.
A hurley or football, it's the same (thing) to me,
It's playing the game that matters you see.

From boys in a field to the big crowd roar,
There's never been anything to excite me more.
From the day I could run, till the day I can't walk,
And even then, about the game I'll talk.

The few steps to the ball now seem like a mile,
But a well-placed shot and I'll be carried in style
On the shoulders of team mates expressing their joy,
It's a dream that's consumed me since I was a boy.

My feet pound the ground; my foot sends the ball.
It sails through the air over men who are tall.
Then dipping and curling it finds the goal,
And just for a moment I'm in touch with my soul.

A whistle blows hard and I awake from the dream.
I'm watching my own son play for the team.
And (but) maybe one day they'll announce his name,
As he steps out to play--the beautiful game.

Croppies' Acre

By Roddy the Rover
Source: The Gaelic Echo, Dec. 12, 1941

Under green grass by the riverside growing
Where Dubliners pass beside us unknowing,
We lie in the clay where the foreigner slew us:
Remember and pray, for as Croppies they knew us.

Our pikes they are rust, our banners are rotten,
Our bones they are dust, our names are forgotten
And the tramp of our foe with their vaunting was blended—
And how could we know it would ever be ended?

But at last through the clay that so long did unfold us,
By the hurley in play, new tidings were told us:
Our dust, it could feel that the sons of our sireland
Had lifted the steel and the standard of Ireland.

The crack of the ash, the cry and the cheering,
The break and the dash, O sweet was the hearing!
Comrades leap light, good fortune betide you:
In field or in fight we would fain be beside you.

The field between Arbour Hill and the Liffey, where the soldiers of Ireland played
their Gaelic games, is called Croppies' Acre, since the patriot men slain at Arbour Hill
in 1798 were buried there.

A Team with Spirit

By Gerard Ryan, Inch, Bouladuff, Thurles

Cut them hurls from an Irish glen
And give them a broad green field
A team imbued with spirit
A team that will never yield
Success upon success will come
To such a hurling team
The championship they will win
And realise a dream.

All-Ireland Football Final

By Peadar Kearney
Source: All-Ireland Football Final Programme,
at the Polo Grounds New York, 1947.

There's a nation's proud resurgence where the Gael in friendly fray,
Proves the valour, grit and courage of his race.
The hopes that cheered our fathers' lives are living here today,
A heritage no time can e'er deface.

See the lithe quick moving players; mark the breadth of shoulder
there,
How their keen eyes mark the flight of speeding ball:
Hear the roar of watching thousands, like a war-shout rend the air—
Oh! Ireland's game's the monarch of them all.

Here is Munster, Leinster, Ulster; Connacht sends her hosting too,
They have travelled from the Gaeltacht to the Pale.
They are here to tell the world Irish hearts are ever true,
To the language and traditions of the Gael.

Every street and laneway tells us, every glen and mountainside,
How our fathers held the pass through blood and tears.
From the death fight of Cuhulainn to that later Eastertide,
We are heirs to all the glory of the years.

God be good to all our comrades, gentle, loving, true and brave—
Never more upon the sward we'll watch their play.
Tho' their lion hearts forever rest in many a soldier's grave,
Their spirit lives to cheer us here today.

Peadar Kearney specially wrote this ballad for the All-Ireland football final at the Polo
grounds in 1947 between Kerry and Cavan. Peadar Kearney was born in Dublin in
1883 and his great interest was in theatre and song writing. He wrote the Soldier's
Song in 1907 and lived to see it become the national anthem of a new state. His other
songs include, Down by the Glenside, the Tri-Coloured Ribbon, and Whack Fol The
Diddle. He was also props manager for the Abbey but not before he had finished his
time as a house painter, an occupation he shared with his more famous nephew,
Brendan Behan. He left the Abbey in 1916 and was interned in 1920.

657

Bold Lardy Corbett

By Paddy Clarke
Received from Donal O'Connor, Coláiste Pobal Mhichíl, Cappamore.
Air: The Garden where the Praties grow'

You've heard of many famous men from Cork to Donegal
The Mackeys and the Rackards and Tipperary's Tony Wall
But best of all the bravest men that e'er you've seen before
He was known as Lardy Corbett from the town of Cappamore.

For drinking pints of porter boys, I'll tell you he's a sight
He'll wheel 'come on Tipperary' then whenever there's a fight.
With a plant of ash he carries around he'd lay them on the floor
The one and only Lardy from the town of Cappamore.

He has seen the scars of many wars and famous men put down;
He's walked the roads for miles and miles to fairs in many a town.
At funerals, wakes and weddings, he's always to the fore;
The one and only 'Lardy' from the town of Cappamore.

Through the winter's snows of long ago and the blazing summer
day;
That hardy drover trod the roads to earn an honest pay
We know he'd get a bob or two, betimes a little more;
'Ah! 'Twas money then' said Lardy, from the town of Cappamore.

One hurling day in Thurles town he met with Thady Quill.
He said, 'come out you Corky now, I'll fight you if you will'
Thady looked him up and down an' faith he'd say no more
He dreaded the fearless Lardy from the town of Cappamore.

The match was in the " forties" when the nations were at war;
The only transport on the roads was Lynch's jaunting car.
When Lardy failed to get on board he sat on the axle bar
With the spirit of old Tipperary went the man from Cappamore.

It was on a Munster final way down in Limerick town;
The Cork and Tipperary boys were battling for the crown.
He gave advice to Jimmy Doyle; it was a vital score.
'Over the bar' said Lardy from the town of Cappamore.

In a one-roomed mansion where he dwells, for comforts he has none;
He takes no pills to cure his ills and doctors he will shun.
For porter, Players and Woodbines, he never would ask for more,
'Shure, they'd keep you strong, says Lardy, from the town of
Cappamore.

He's been around for many a year, how long you'll never know
Just like the brook that rolls along, as men may come and go.
And when you speak of famous men, this name you can't ignore;
The one and only Lardy from the town of Cappamore.

Horses and Plough

By Micheál Ó hÓgáin, Caltra, Ballinasloe
Source: P.J. Murrihy, Mullagh
Air: Horses and Plough

Balmy the breezes that blow in the spring
Sweet are the songs that the young thrushes sing
I sigh for a sight that I seldom see now
A man in the field with his horses and plough.

Farewell to the days of my youth long ago
When I harnessed my team near the barn below
Then away to the highland beside Curragow
To tear the hard green sod with horses and plough.

Invoking a blessing I started my day
Bail O Dhia ar an obair that's what I would say.
Asking for guidance to keep my know how
And strike a straight furrow with horses and plough.

Then up at the headland every once in a while
I rested my seisreach all aching with toil
With the sleeve of my shirt wiped the sweat from my brow
As I gazed at the work of my horses and plough.

Then in the evening as the sun it sank low
With the hurley and ball to the sports field I'd go
To win the All-Ireland we'd all make a vow
And seek recreation with horses and plough.

The whistling and lilting and the odd bar of a song
To lighten my labours all the day long
With seagulls around me and crows on a bough
All seeking the bounty from horses and plough.

But the clatter of tractors, pollution and all
Has crippled the OPEC and sad was its fall
While far away -we richly endow
Not counting the value of horses and plough.

Very soon I'll be leaving this valley of woe
To the fair fields of heaven I hope I will go
One request of St. Peter that I hope he'll allow
Eternal employment with horses and plough.

Joe Molloy's Schooldays

Anon:
Received from Willie Hackett, Main Street, Thurles.

I'll tell you a story of long ago about a lad who's name was Joe.
He walked three miles to school each day—that long New Road to
old Roscrea.
With school books covered tidy and neat, I romped along in my bare
feet.
Always on time, I was never late, the first to open the old school
gate.
At the back of the school was the old bare wall, with the rest of the
boys I'd play handball.
Those good old days so long ago, my teacher called me Little Joe.

He could be cross and sometimes nice—if you misbehaved, you'd
pay the price.
When I was naughty or played about, as quick as a flash the cane
came out.
Two of the best, 'come here and stand, look up at the ceiling, hold
out your hand'.
No mercy shown, the pain severe—once I got a box in the ear.
The pain would last for a day or two— I am still deaf —no lies—
that's true.

I'm seventy-two, which is classed as old, about my life a story told.
Those good old days I sadly miss, sure I'd love to sit and reminisce.
The times were hard but full of thrills, when I roamed the fields in
the old Sheehills.
Some pennies scrounged from Mum and Pop, to the Temperance
Hall for the 'four-penny hop'.
A crease in my trousers, neat and grand, I'd dance to Billy Cummins
' Band.
Sure he was the best musician of all to play for the dance in the
Temperance Hall.

662

Well I wonder what it's like today; do they still have the 'Hop' in old Roscrea?
In the old home there, with its battered door, do they still dance 'the Set' on the old stone floor?
When the 'hooley' ended, then off to bed, but not before the Rosary said.
The hardest time for Little Joe was wintertime in frost and snow.
The nights were cold, no turf in the shed, an overcoat for a blanket in bed.

Those times were hard but yet somehow, I was happier then than I am now.
People were honest and lent a hand, to scratch a living from that boggy land.
And many a time at the dead of night, a penny candle I would light.
With brother Jack in our worn duds, to the neighbour's field to steal some spuds.
Those days will never come again— more's the pity, more's the pain.
Then home again across the field, to the winter's cold we would never yield.

But I often wonder when I die, will there be a place for Joe Molloy,
To share with Jack and brother Kevin, just a little corner, somewhere in heaven?
No fancy shroud, just my old duds and the slate wiped clean for stealing spuds.
Lay me to rest by the 'Asses Gap', leave a little space for my epitaph.
Saying, 'No More Hunger, No More Fast, Joe Is Gone, Free At Last'

Another Green Field

By Harry Mullins, the Commons, Thurles.
Source: Commemorative programme—Official Opening of Ballingarry Parish
Sportsfield, 19th May 1985. Received from Seamus J. King, Boherclough, Cashel.

The parish is Ballingarry, it's May of nineteen eighty-five
The venue is the Commons; the hour at last arrived.
The opening of our parish field is hailed with much acclaim;
A credit to the parish fold for all they did attain.
Another green field has been created for sportsmen all to grace.
To give their best in every test against each foe they face.

To all who trod this green, green sod to swing the ash in style
Or kick a ball between two posts or run a record mile.
Take pride in every sport you play, try hard and never yield
Then folk will come to cheer you on upon your green, green field.

The Commons is a small village that nestles in the Slieveardagh Hills with a
population of approximately 200 people. It is noted for its traditions of music, song
and dance. The village is also noted in Irish history as 'The Warhouse' (scene of the
1848 Rising) which is situated a mile from the Commons.. It was in a home in the
centre of the village that William Smith O'Brien, leader of the rising spent the night
on his retreat from the Warhouse and it was here that the national flag was first raised.
In 1948 the centenary celebrations were held in the Commons village and a museum
was housed in the village school. (*Article by Annie Heaphy in the Commemorative
Programme*)

The Jockey

By Liam Ó Donnchú, Ballymoreen, Littleton Thurles

On the Jockey road they travel fast,
With cars and lorries flying past.
Why don't they stop and rest awhile,
And blend with our relaxing style?

They'll meet the men, who hurled the ball,
And those who alley cracked the wall,
The athletes bold who beat the best
And laid a challenge to the rest.

The Inn it stands with welcome door,
As it had stood in days of yore,
When Bianconi- the stage being done,
Food and drink for everyone.

They'll hear of how in eighty-four
We won the 'county' yet once more
With Bergin leading from centre-back
And Tobin throwing away his cap.

The station house in silence stands,
Recalling trains and travel grand,
While gazing down upon the scene,
Old Killough and its woods serene.

If playing at cards appeals to you,
We play the whist and twenty -five two,
We love to chat, the yarn and song,
And often stay up till forty-one.

The farms about are a joy to view,
With corn, beet and barley too,

And cattle grazing in pastures green,
The best in Ireland can be seen.

The Gobaun Saor—he walked this land,
A mason skilled with chisel in hand,
On the Chalice Island of Derrynaflan,
He sleeps amid abbots and saintly men.

We'll dance a set before you go,
And toast your health a time or two,
New life long friendships found will be
In Tipperary's lovely Horse and Jockey.

1899 Tipperary's (Horse and Jockey) winning Team—Tim Condon (capt), Big Bill Gleeson, Jack Gleeson, Dick O'Keeffe, Wattie Dunne, Billie Gleeson, Joe O'Keeffe (goal), Tom Ryan, Johnnie Walsh, John Ryan, Phil Byrne, Jack Flanagan, Mike Wall, Jack Maher, Mikey Maher, Jim O'Keeffe, Denis Walsh.

Verse 3—Where the Horse and Jockey Inn stands to day, in 1740 two thatched cottages surrounded by trees and open fields marked the place. The mail car operated by the British government halted there briefly to water their horses. One of the cabins developed from a shebeen into a licensed inn. Shortly afterwards a new inn was built which had the sign of a horse and jockey hanging outside the premises. It was to give the crossroads village its name.

Verse 4—Moycarkey Borris won the 1984 Tipperary senior hurling championship. Jack Bergin was captain and Jimmy Tobin was one of their staunchest supporters.

—**The Bianconi Stage Coach** was a horse drawn passenger and mail coach that formerly ran on a regular schedule between established stops.

Verse 4—**The Railway Line** from Thurles to Clonmel served the station at Horse and Jockey—goods trains and passenger trains all made a stop there. The people of the village and surrounding area travelled by train to nearby towns of Thurles, Templemore, Fethard or Clonmel and on excursion trains to Dublin or in summer to the seaside. Passenger trains were discontinued on September 9th, 1963 but specials and freight trains ran until all traffic ceased on March 27, 1967.

Verse 8—According to *Fóclóir Gaedhilge agus Béarla* by Patrick S. Dinneen M.A. **An Gobán Saor** was a very clever person. Gobán was a craftsman of genius in Irish folklore, the reputed builder of the round –towers.

666

The **Derrynaflan Hoard** found in 1980 at the monastic site of Doire na bhFlann, Co. Tipperary, contained a decorated silver chalice, a paten received in a fragmentary state but now restored, a hoop of silver, probably at one time attached to the paten as a foot, a bronze strainer and covering all of them a bronze basin. They had been concealed in a pit, probably in the 10th century as the chalice had seen very little use. The 9th century **chalice** is 19'2cm high and 21cm in diameter. The **paten** is of a type unfamiliar to modern eyes . It measures 35cm in diameter and is heavily decorated. It consists of over three hundred components. The **strainer** is of ladle form, almost 38cm. long with a deep bowl 11.5 cm. in diameter and a jewelled handle-terminal equipped with a bronze ring for suspension. Strainers were an important part of the altar service in early times. In the 8th century in Rome two sieves were used, a larger when filling the chalice for Mass and a smaller to take form the chalice the particles of consecrated bread dropped into it at the consecration. The Derrynaflan **strainer** is the attempt of an Irish craftsman using local ideas of design to produce what was once an essential pierce of equipment for the service of the Mass. (*Early Irish Communion Vessels by Michael Ryan,—A National Museum of Ireland Guide 1985*)

Ballingarry

By Dan O'Meara
Source:Commemorative Programme
of Official Opening of Ballingarry Sportsfield, 19 May 1985

There's a spot in old Tipperary
That's so very dear to me
Ballingarry is the place that I was born.
I can picture its hills and valleys
From this land across the sea
As I walk these city streets this summer morn.

I can see the skylark soaring
O'er the slopes of Fennelly's Hill
And hear Grawn river rippling down below.
I can look right down on Kickham's town
At the foot of Slievcnamon
Ballingarry I have loved from long ago.

'Twas there I spent my childhood years
With friends I loved so well
There are some that I may never see no more.
Some are buried in the graveyard
O'er the graves the grass grows green
Some are exiled on a far and distant shore.

Sure I can't forget The Commons
While my memories with me stay
Ballintaggart, Crohane and Garrynoe.
They brought honour to Slieveardagh Hills
On many's a Gaelic field
Ballingarry I have loved from long ago.

I'll still walk out those city streets
Across the Irish sea
In a land I do not love or do not know.
But my heart lies in Tipperary

At the foot of Slievenamon
Ballingarry I have loved from long ago
Ballingarry I have loved from long ago.

Notes: See Another Green Field

Dear Old Newport Town

By Michael Bourke
Source: Newport in Song and Poetry
Published by the Michael Bourke Festival Committee

Here by the Mulcaire banks I stray by the lovely flowers in June—
The birds are singing cheerily and the meadows in full bloom;
When on my boyhood's days I think—then the tears come rolling
down—
For it's in the morning I must leave you, Dear Old Newport Town.

I grow lonely as I think on each lad and comely lass
Who used to greet me warmly on my way to early mass.
With their winning ways and greetings as they passed me up and
down
My heart will break when my leave I take of Dear Old Newport
Town,

Farewell awhile sweet Gortnanoe, where I oft'times chased the hare
Through Caher hills and Carrowkeale and Cully's mountains bare.
And sweet Clare glens, your flowery dells, I oft strolled up and down
Must I leave those scenes and the girl I love in Dear Old Newport
Town.

Farewell Tipperary's hills and dells from you I now must part—
I'll ne'er again roam Cullen's grove—the thoughts near break my
heart.
When I think of the hurling and the dance and the Keeper's summit
brown,
And the days I fished the Turn Hole in Dear Old Newport Town.

How lonely is the pigeons coo and sad the blackbirds lay,
And loud and high the thrush's song on a long bright summer's day.
I'll sit down and cry my fill where the flood comes rushing down
And dashes through the Ivy Bridge in Dear Old Newport Town.

Adieu, adieu, sweet Newport town, once more I say adieu—
Where many's the pleasant day I spent with comrades loyal and true.
And if God spares me I'll return where the Mulcaire waters flow
And when I die my bones wlll lie in lonely Ballymackeogh.

Michael Bourke, the author was born in Newport, County Tipperary in 1879, He is
best remembered for this ballad. He wrote many ballads about hurling the most of,
which are included in this collection. I was he who christened the Toomevara hurlers
'The Greyhounds'. Mick was 75 yrs when he died. He is laid to rest in Castleconnell
cemetery.

Dúrlas Óg

Le Séamus Ó Duibhir
Fonn: The Boys of Fair Hill
Received from Liam Ó Donnchú, Ballymorreen, Littleton.

Is muidne Dúrlas Éile
Is maith linn iomáint is beagáinín peile
An buadh linn go deo Buachaillí Dúrlas Óg.

We are the boys from Thurles Town
Out to win the hurling crown
An buadh linn go deo Buachaillí Dúrlas Óg.

We play with Tipp's hurling flair
On the ground and in the air.
An buadh linn go deo Buachaillí Dúrlas Óg.

We have respect for all our foes
What the ref says always goes
An buadh linn go deo Buachaillí Dúrlas Óg.

All our backs are tough and hard
They can sprint over every yard
An buadh linn go deo Buachaillí Dúrlas Óg.

Our centrefield are fit and quick
They can wield the hurling stick
An buadh linn go deo Buachaillí Dúrlas Óg.

All our forwards love to score
On the puck-out back for more
An buadh linn go deo Buachaillí Dúrlas Óg.

So come all ye boys one and all
Enjoy your game with hurl and ball
An buadh linn go deo Buachaillí Dúrlas Óg.

Dúrlas Óg is the juvenile club in Thurles—founded 1979

Killough Hill

By Patrick Bourke, Moan-na-moe, Holycross
Source: Liam Ó Donnchú, Ballymoreen, Littleton.

At times we read of climbers bold, who topped the towering peaks,
In foreign lands through ice and snow, enough to bring the creeps.
No avalanche assailed me and biting blasts were nil,
But linnets sang in hazel as I climbed up Killough Hill.

But sure those hardy climbers will never once describe
The sights they saw while gazing o'er the valleys far and wide.
The reason is apparent; the view brought them no thrill—
I wished they scanned Tipperary's plains from top of Killough Hill.

For from its highest summit, I thought that view a treat,
Moycarkey's bounteous harvest lay spread beneath my feet.
And as a breeze came playing, the picture for to fill
It waved in all its golden prime for miles round Killough Hill.

I thought of famous hurlers, that parish always knew,
O'Keeffes and Walls and Condon, Purcell and Sweeper too.
And there the same grand tendency to play the old game still
While ash will grow and flourish on the slopes of Killough Hill.

And looking to the westward, all foreign scenes might fail
Before that view so charming along the Golden Vale.
Where fertile fields rich pasture yield with many a sparkling rill,
And raths and forts, old towers and moats in view of Killough Hill.

Ah, what was that 'neath hazy blue I could not see so well,
But sure I knew that always true, down there was rare Clonmel,
Whose very name recalls some fame that's sure to live until
The morning's gleams the shadows fail to chase from Killough Hill.

And memories come crowding of that historic town,
Where Cromwell's mighty Ironsides lost all of their renown.

And where its brave defenders, the tyrant's power did kill—
I felt like shouting 'Up Clonmel' from the top of Killough Hill.

Before I leave my pen away, I'd say to each and all
Don't sigh for great Mt. Everest, don't mind the Alps at all.
That if you stray some glorious day you're safe in life and limb,
The view is great, 'twill compensate to climb up Killough Hill.

Fourth Verse—O'Keeffes refer to Jim, Dick and Joe O'Keeffe, All-Ireland hurlers
with Horse and Jockey in 1899. Mike Wall was another member of this team. Tim
Condon was captain of the 1899 Horse and Jockey All-Ireland winning team. Phil
Purcell was a Tipperary senior hurler and later county GAA secretary. Paddy Ryan,
(Sweeper), Ballybeg, Littleton, Moycarkey and Tipperary hurler of the 1930's and
1940's came from Ballybeg, Littleton.

Skehana's Hurling Field

By Rev, Bro. J. Perkins, C.B.S. Thurles
Received from Liam Ó Donnchú, Ballymoreen, Littleton

Persistent Gaelic voices called:
'Come forth, come forth, alanna;
Come make your way and view today
The green fields of Skehana.'

By Conor's side I went with pride
From Two-Mile-Borris straying;
By meadow's green, where oft were seen
The cream of Borris playing.

We had set our face to that Gaelic place;
Oh! With joy my spirit trembled;
I would see again where hurling men
And great crowds were assembled.

The ten-acre field is still the same
And the slopes where commentators
Could sit for hours 'midst the fragrant flowers
With friendly, fair spectators.

I saw again Ned Hayes' men
As their home-made hurls kept flashing
And o'er the sod, where they often trod
Those brave Borris boys were dashing.

They say, 'now and then, great spirited men
As the midnight smoke is curling,
When the moon is bright all through the night
They're still there, hurling, hurling.'

Verse two—*Conor's side*—Conor Kennedy (Moycarkey-Borris club officer)

Moyle Rovers Abu!

By Rev. Bro. J. Perkins
Source: Liam Ó Donnchú, Ballymoreen, Littleton.

I passed through friendly Fethard where Slievenamon doth smile
And stopped at fair Lisronagh by the riverbanks of Moyle.
Game filled the woods of Lakefield, the pheasant, woodcock, grouse;
I saw foxes, hares and horses round Clonacody House.

I thought of our ancestors and those difficult days of yore,
When the people oft assembled for the Mass at Donoughmore.
But the river Moyle keeps roving by Annsfort lonely ridge
'Till it meets the gentle Anner not far from Thorny Bridge

Giantsgrave all gazed in wonder and Clonmel skies were brown
When they saw the thousands thronging, through Caherclough and
Orchardstown.
The Carrick flags were flying as they passed Kilsheelan side
Where the married Moyle and Anner meets the Suir's bright,
sparkling tide.

In that famed field near the river, Tipp/Kilkenny boys did play
For the opening of your Sportsfield on the twentieth day of May.
May the name of famed Lisronagh and Powerstown ever grow;
May the sky blue flag of Moyle Rovers fly proudly o'er Monroe.

Written for the opening of Moyle Park, Monroe, in May 1990. Tipperary (All Ireland
champions) and Kilkenny (National League champions) played a draw.

676

Kilsheelan's Primary School Team 1947

By Eddie Cummins
Source: Liam Ó Donnchú, Ballymoreen, Littleton.

There's a village in South Tipperary
In its centre a small house stands.
From whence came a primary school team
Known as Kisheelan all over the land.

The goalman P. Hennessy was captain
No better small man could be found
He could save any ball coming his way
Let it be in the air or on ground.

The full back line had everything needed
To stop every ball was their bent
It consisted of three brilliant young hurlers
Tom Hennessy, Tom Larkin and Nugent.

The half-back line also was dashing
Our followers they did enthral.
With Matt Landers and also his flankers
Determined to get to each ball.

If you were watching them playing
And see the ball the midfield pair served up
You'd feel like going to Lynch or Con Cottrell
And say it was time they gave up.

The six that are left for to mention
Are forwards in every sense.
And when their attacks are repulsed
It's done by a stubborn defence.

And now one word of praise for our trainer
James Pender our Hon. Secretary,

For he did everything in his power
To see we were up to the test.

And now we are South champions
Ballylooby and Crough we did beat.
We hope that the spirit will still be the same
In the year nineteen forty-eight.

A tribute to the Kilsheelan Primary School team of 1947, who made a breakthrough
for hurling in the parish by winning the South Primary Schools' title. They beat
Crough, Goatenbridge, in the final.

Slieve Felim's Height

By Rev.Bro. J. Perkins C.B.S. Thurles.
Source: Jack Ryan, Greystones,Limerick (formerly Newport)

From the lovely Suir of the waters pure, with its wild birds, game
and trout,
Past Liberty Square with its hurlers there, I joyfully set out.
I saw horses train by Seskin Lane and Bawntameena bright,
As I set sail from the Golden Vale, to view Slieve Felim's Height.

On Kilinan Hill I took my fill, of the beauty all around
Past Maher's abode and the long straight road towards the Ragg's
new hurling ground.
On a far off brow stood Ballinahow, with its Purcell castle bright
A gem so rare, a land so fair among Slieve Felim's Height.

And by bright Ballycahill where 'Cathaldus'used to go
I saw the school and the chapel, where the lovely flowers now grow.
Castlefogarty lies hidden, as in shame of its sad plight
But the pheasant roams round those happy homes among Slieve
Felim's Height.

I looked into the Clodagh, from the Anglesea New Bridge
Ere I passed by Laffan's Folly and Rosmult' rough riding ridge.
There were cars at Mary Peelers; Templebeg looked clean and bright
From the 'Barracks' and Rossoulty, you could see Slieve Felim's
Height.

The Owen Beg's waters glistened as they rippled o'er each ridge
In the pool the young were swimming at the famous Metal Bridge.
At Poll an Eas the salmon were jumping with delight
At the Mill there's music playing as they sing of Felim's Height.

The little lambs were leaping o'er the lands round Lough na Sceach
There were cows and bullocks grazing on the slopes of
Knockalough.

In the pubs around the village, they're still talking day and night
How their fathers fought for freedom all along Slieve Felim's
Height.

They speak of ghosts and phantoms and oftentimes they see
Atshanbo's Eamon an Chnoic the famous raparee.
Through the roads around Kilcommon all in the dead of night
They hear brave Sarsfield's horses ride through Slieve Felim's
Height.

Through the Milestone men are moving from Nenagh to Tipp. town
Through the village homes of Hollyford where the grand Blackstairs
look down.
Through Curraheen and Piper Hill and lovely Cappawhite
Foilldearg, Doon, Foilaclara, Toom, all around Slieve Felim's
Height.

The Bilboa bright comes from the right by Sean Treacy's field it
goes.
By Mauherslieve, it makes its way to where the Mulcaire flows.
I passed Coonmore where oft of yore when all was calm and quiet,
The poitín smell from some hidden dell spread through Slieve
Felim's Height.

I stopped to pray at the church of Rea and passed history to recall
Where brave men gave their lives to save. when they stormed the
barrack wall.
There's freedom still on every hill and in every home at night
Sean Treacy's name and Dan Breen's fame, ring o'er Slieve Felim's
height.

And Paddy Ryan the Lacken lion still holds an honoured place
Where the deer runs free in the forestry, safe from that murdering
race.
I was not far from Congo Bar when I spied the school on my right
Ryan's Fancy song and his heirs (airs) belong to grand Slieve
Felim's Height.

680

At last I came to the walls of fame and I long kept looking down
On sweet Clare glens that winds and wends its way toward Newport town.
There was Limerick, Clare and clear Mulcaire,Ryan Park and the church so bright
Ahane of old with its hurlers bold are well known through Slieve Felim's height.

When my life is spent and my last ascent is made through the heavenly door
May I have the chance to have a glance around those hills once more.
I will sing my days in song and praise and gaze from morn to night
From the realms above on the land I love—Far famed Slieve Felim's Height.

Moriarity

Anon:
Source: Muiris de Prionnbhiol, Blanchardstown, Dublin (formerly Cork)

Oh! when I was born on a frosty morn
About twenty years ago
I never cried for my young eye spied
A bright thing that made me crow.
'Twas a football shirt and tho' caked with dirt
Still it could not be kept from me
So my father said 'He's a kicker bred'
He's a true Moriarity.

Chorus:

Oh! I've won great fame at the Gaelic game
For my style is a treat to see
And the watchers say when they see me play
'He's a star, Moriarity'

As a growing boy there was no grand toy
I'd prefer to an old football,
And the bouncing sphere could dry every tear
And could silence each sob and squall.
When I went to school I proved no fool
And the teacher looked after me—
If some coddling man asked 'who hurt my lamb'
He'd reply 'Moriarity'.

As I older grew I joined the crew
Who played at the cross each eve
And we'd play non-stop till the stars came up
And the darkness made us leave.
I learn new tricks and practise kicks
And the right way to take a free

682

Till not none there could at all compare
With young Moriarity.

I often dreamed of the county team
And now I'm their shooting star
Though it blow a gale still I never fail
To send her across the bar.
The crowd all roar when they see me score
The young lads go wild with glee
While the ladies stare at my shoulders square
And sigh 'Moriarity'.

When the score is closed and the whistle goes
For the last line-out of all
Then beneath my name write 'He played the game
In all things as in football'
Then the one who waits by the Golden Gate
Will turn with a smile to me
Saying, 'Come across, for you've won the toss
Step inside Moriarity'.

Chorus:

My Grand-Da's Boxty Bread

By Michael A Corry, Castleknock, Dublin (Formerly Killanena, Feakle, Co. Clare.
Source: Clare Association Yearbooks 1985 and 2000

My Grand-Da, Patsy Casey was mad for Boxty Bread.
He ate it at the crack of dawn before he ate his bread;
He ate it in the afternoon; he ate it twice at night
And every year at Christmas-time he went on boxty skite.

He loved the crunchy mixture of potatoes and oatmeal,
Aleavened with egg-white and mead, and flakes of lemon-peel.
He loved the aromatic smell exuding from the cake,
While it lay on the griddle pan to cook, ferment and bake.

He swore that more nutritious food was nowhere to be seen;
He swore that it surpassed flesh meat, white bread and carrigeen.
He swore, in short, that it contained not only vitamin C,
But also vitamin A and B and vitamin D and E.

My Grand-Da's craze for boxty bread was known all over town.
Some feared he'd burst his bowels with it or twist them upside down;
But my Grand-Da frisked just like a youth, without a sock or shoe,
When he played the game of football at the age of sixty-two.

My Grand-Ma swore she'd slaughter him, if he refused to eat,
Some cabbage green or carrigeen or chips of sugar beet,
Because she feared he'd lose his beard or hair from off his head,
If he confined his food intake to 'tay' and boxty bread.

'Why should I change my diet ' says he, 'while it seems right for
me'.
'It keeps me hale and hearty and lively as a bee.
Why should I eat your sugar beet, your peas or cabbage head,
While I can dine, so mighty fine, on wholesome boxty bread'.

My Grand-Da never suffered pain or slept more hours than four:
He never faltered in a game or muffed a chance to score:
'Cause he was healthy as a hound, with limbs as tough as lead,
From bumping bowls of buttermilk and bins of boxty bread.

My Grand-Da lived 'till ninety-six and I would bet a score,
That he'd have reached the hundred mark, had Gran not gone before.
When she passed on he said to Da, 'I might as well be dead,
I can't go on for long without my diet of boxty bread.

Forget your Christmas turkey, your 'pudden' and your ham:
Invest instead in boxty bread in honour of your Gran.
Go get yourself a griddle pan, a grater and a sieve,
And sing with me for Christmas—Let's live again, Let's live—

Bacstaidh (Boxty) according to *Foclóir Gaedhilge agus Béarla* by Patrick S.Dinneen
is 'a bread made of raw pulp of potatoes'

The author gives the following **recipe** and notes for and on boxty bread: —

'Peel about six medium-size raw potatoes of top quality. Crush the solid raw potatoes
with a grater until completely mushed. Then place the lump-free mush in a muslin bag
or cloth and squeeze from it, through the muslin, every iota of its moisture content.
Mix the remaining/starchy/powdery substance with refined/powdered raw oatmeal.
Add a little salt and pepper and knead the mix with the requisite quantity of egg-white
and/or fresh milk, to give you a pasty, malleable dough of sufficient coherence to
enable you to form with it a thin, circular slab of about one and a quarter inch
thickness and about twelve inches diameter. Place the slab/cake on a pre-heated,
greased and lidless griddle (rimless frying pan) on top of a fire or cooker and then
place the lidless griddle on top of a fire or cooker of constant medium temperature for
slowish baking. When the underside of the slab/cake has been fully baked (in about 15
minutes) turn it upside down to bake the other side equally well. Remove the full-
baked slab/cake from the griddle, smear it lightly with butter or margarine and leave it
on a plate to settle and cool. The finished product may be eaten hot, lukewarm or cold,
depending on individual taste, and while most people prefer to eat it while it is hot,
some people do not like to eat it until it is cold.

Individual taste determines the mix ratio. While some people like to use equal
quantities of the mushed raw potato and the refined/powdered raw oatmeal, other
people use twice as much potato as oatmeal and vice versa.

Where refined/powdered oatmeal is not readily purchasable, boxty-makers purchase
granular oatmeal and crush it themselves with a heavy, hard smooth object, such as a

685

strand stone, a mason's hammer or a short thick wooden pole (pounder). A pastry roller might serve that purpose quite well.

Some boxty-makers add to the above-mentioned mix a little honey and/or a little poitín, but that refinement is not really necessary.

Properly made and properly baked boxty is so absolutely delicious that most people tend to overheat it, with considerable consequential discomfort. For that reason I would like to warn all potential boxty-eaters that it tends to generate stomach gas when eaten excessively, and that if an over indulgent boxty eater happened to be constipated at the time he ate it, he would be most likely to develop stomach colic.

As professional medical assistance was not readily available to such patients, in my native parish, in the 'twenties' and 'thirties', the non-professionals tried to cure them by stripping them bare naked and rolling ('rouling') them hither and thither several times, across cold concrete or cold stones to dissolve the colic. I can clearly recall that my first severe fright was caused by one such patient shouting furiously in his agony the words, 'will yez for God's sake rub me and 'roul' me'.

The author passed away in February 1999.

Radio Éireann

By Criostoir O'Flynn
Source: Centenary F.N.T. 1985,

Veterans who had served the G.A.A.
From youth, in council and in play,
The sick, the handicapped, the blind
For whom the radio is God's own eye,
The poor who never could afford
To travel, all travelled on the word
As on a magic carpet to be
Present in Croke Park and see
The black-and-amber from the Nore
Meet rebel red from Lee's bright shore.
And every year from that day on
Ireland in her games was one
When Radio Éireann brought the play
Live to the nation on all-Ireland Day.
No British lines on Ireland's sod
Could cry halt to that wonder-work of God.
That miracle of technology
Cusack did not live to see,
But Maurice Davin, whose fame had drawn
All Ireland to listen to Cusack's call
Was able at eighty-two, to hear
The magic voice that brought to ears
In every corner of the land
A commentary from the Hogan Stand,   **
And when in Nineteen-Twenty -Seven
They met in the green fields of heaven
And Cusack asked 'How's old Ireland
A Mhuiris Ó, and how does she Stand'
He could that tale of marvel tell
And further wonderment compel
With news of how their Association
Was thriving in the partitioned nation

Where thirteen hundred clubs had grown
From the seed those patriots had sown
When that small determined group had planned
In Thurles town a New Ireland.

**The first commentary was from Croke Park on August 19, 1926. It was of the All-Ireland semi-final, Kilkenny 6-2, Galway 5-1. Commentator was P.D. Mehigan (Carbery).

Tay in the Meadow

By Jack Ryan Beechwood Drive, Greystones, Limerick. (formerly Newport)

Oh! times have changed and all the old ways are o'er
I'd love to see horses a mowing once more.
What a memorable sight on a fine summer's day,
To watch the old *Bamford* or *Pierce* cutting hay.
The mower there sitting like a king on his throne
And a man by the hedge—edging blades with a stone.
I remember those scenes, just like yesterday,
Going out to Mount Phillips to the |Meadow withTay.

I think of those days when the 'saving' took place—
When the weather was fine and they worked with great pace.
With the shaking and turning and making small cocks
And the sweat running down from the forehead and locks.
The wheel-rake and 'gatherer' working non stop,
No time for a smoke or a thought for the clock:
The corncrake calling so loudly and gay
When I went long ago to the Meadow with Tay.

All sat in the sun and each man was fed
With mugs of sweet 'Tay' and loads of brown bread.
The pipes were all kindled and fags were alight
And we heard all the news and what happened last night.
Of hurling, of hurlers, all brave men and true,
Who brought honour to Tipp. in the famed gold and blue.
Of Purcell and Treacy, O'Meara and Ryan,
The Powers and the Leahys and the great 'Hawk' O'Brien.
Oh, memories sublime are with me today
When I went long ago to the meadow with Tay.

They traced of Tipp's hurlers and 'who was the best'—
Was it those from the North, the Mid, or the West.
Then Pat he spoke up saying, 'ye are leaving some out,
There were good hurlers too way down in the South.
Willie Wall and Tom and Jimmy Cooney ye knew

All wore with distinction the gold and the blue.
Don't forget Butler Coffey, he is one of our own
And to be a good hurler 'tis bred in the bone.

They spoke of Sean Treacy, Tom Ashe and Dan Breen,
The ambush at Upton, Dromkeen and Rineen.
They would talk of a singer and remember his song,
Kickham, the Anner and sweet Slievenamon.
Debates about Dev. and his Fianna Fáil,
About Labour and Cosgrove, they talked of them all,
Of markets and fairs about each circus and play,
When I went long ago to the Meadow with Tay.

Those days are now finished, no more to be seen,
The súgán, the wheel-rake, the mowing machine,
The Bailer now working so sad and alone
And a man cutting silage and alas so forlorn.
Progress has come to the home and the farm—
Some say 'twill be good and others say harm.
But I'll never forget 'till I'm laid in the clay
As I went long ago to the Meadow with Tay.

The author writes that Mount Phillips in verse 1 was an outside farm, owned by Pat
Humphries of Newport P.O. (a good hurler himself). Jack would bring the Tay out
there in the pony and car in the mid 1940's.

690

The Athlete's Joy

By P. D. Mehigan (Carberry)
Source: Carberry's Annual 1955-56

The athlete's days are joyous days,
Of bounding life and movement free—
I dream green fields and sunlit ways,
Of speed and grace and symmetry.

Long stately limbs, all lightly clad,
The bloom of health on every face—
The maiden's cheer—fresh breath of God!
New thrills assured with every race.

Like deer, fleet runners speed the track,
Scarce bends the grass beneath their tread—
Lo! Neck and neck, adown the back,
Ho! Up the straight, the leader's led.

A breast outswing the race decides,
Nor is young loser cheered in vain!
Some day he'll win the champion's prize
And burst the worsted string in twain.

Lithe bird, yon jumper mounts in air—
Strong muscles heave the missiles far.
That hurdler's hair is wondrous fair—
Slim levered waist athwart the bar!

Clean healthy sport of youth and pride!
The sport our fathers loved to grace—
On foreign fields, at home fireside,
Their fame brought joy to land and race.

For the first few years of its life the GAA was much more concerned with athletics than with games.

The Camera as Referee

By Rev. Bro. J. Perkins, C.B.S. Thurles
Source: Tipperary Star, Sat. June 24, 1995

The power of the referee is gone, the camera's there instead—
You need not fear the man in charge; the lens is the thing to dread.
On Sunday you may think you've won but on Monday 'on the air'
You may see a poke or an accidental stroke on some unharmed
player.

The man behind the camera may zoom on some small foul
And leave disgruntled losers the rest of the week to growl.
For trial by television may be the coming thing
And small things seen 'in camera' may another verdict bring.

We usurp the power of the man in charge and take from his
authority—
He is subject now to 'media trial' and constant scrutiny.
The men behind the cameras though not of the GAA
Can zoom on what they want to see and forget about the play.

We do not want to see foul deeds nor witness unfair play,
But spirit and dash and clashing ash in the thick of the frightening
fray.
The truly Gaelic referee knows well our Celtic soul
And understands the incidents that take place around the goal.

So leave the ruling of our games to umpires and referees
Judge not, by what, the zooming lens of cameraman oft sees.
Use not TV or video, to lower our Gaelic game,
And focus not, on every shot, that may destroy one's name.

Br, Perkins was commenting on the use of TV/Video in the Tipperary /Waterford
Senior Hurling Championship game (first round) on the 21th May 1995 at Cork. As a
result of a row behind the Tipperary goals in the second half, for which referee,
Terence Murray, sent nobody off, two Tipperary players, Michael Ryan and Paul
Delany, were suspended on the video evidence.
Final Score: Tipperary 4-23, Waterford 1-11.

The Chairman

By a Mullinavat Man
Cill Sioláin-100 Years and More of Gaelic Games in the Parish of Kilsheelan and
Kilcash 1884-1988. Received from Seamus King, Boherclough, Cashel.

If you want a thankless job that doesn't pay a bob
And be castigated every night and day
You must plan and plot and scheme to fulfil this empty dream
And be chairman of your local GAA.
Born leaders in this town seeking fame and high renown
Canvassed daily for support in every pub
But no matter how they tried, their despair they could not hide
When elected chairman of the hurling club.

In this sporting town of ours we spend many thoughtful hours
Making plans to land the county's Holy Grail
After every sad defeat they will tell you down the street
Replace the chairman and we cannot fail.
Yes, he has to take the blame after losing every game
All his efforts they will ridicule and mock
That's the price he has to pay when he tried to have his way
As the chairman of the local Gaelic flock.

He must have a skin so thick, poisoned arrows cannot prick
He must take all criticism in his stride
He must listen as dumb fools pass their anti-guide book rules
And against his better judgment then abide.
He must counter foreign games and remember special names
When All-Ireland tickets he must allocate
If he dares to disagree with the folk who pay their fee
He'd be safer blowing the fan in Santa's grate.

In the sunshine, snow and rain he must watch the hurlers train
And ensure a good supply of balls and ash
As they curse and swear and sweat he must worry toil and fret
Preparing for the coming vital clash.

He must search and analyse when the hurlers tell him lies
And call him a dictator to his face.
If he doesn't take their lip that's an unforgiving slip
Pretty soon they'll have another in his place.

Now if by chance they win they'll forgive his every sin
He's the greatest that the club has ever had
But things won't be the same if they lose another game
They lost because the chairman was so bad.
What I'm trying to get across is the chairman as the boss
Will be praised as long as teams gain victory
Though the club be strong and sound they will harass, hunt and hound
If there's not a prize for all the world to see.

Now the moral of this tale is that hurlers never fail
Our supporters and our members can't do wrong.
But the man who's at the top 'tis with him the buck must stop
He must face the anger of the sporting throng.
So if you've got time to spare and you haven't got a care
If you want to see your hair turn silver grey
You don't need much craft or skill this position for to fill
As the chairman of your local GAA.

The Gaels Beyond the Wave

By Phil O'Neill (Slieve Ruadh)
Source: History of the GAA 1910-1930 by Phil O'Neill
Air: The girl I left behind me-Chorus to be sung after each verse.

Whilst love and praise we e'er accord the men of might and brawn,
Who foot the leather o'er the sward and wield the stout camán,
We'll not forget the exiled ones, our brothers stout and brave,
Who plod and toil on foreign soil- the Gaels beyond the wave.

Chorus: -

Then here's to you our brothers true,
Who freedom's slogans crave,
The gallant bands in foreign lands-
The Gaels beyond the wave.

In English fields and mills and mines, you'll find our young men
there,
And where the burning sunlight shines, on Pampas broad and fair,
And 'mid the deep Canadian woods and where the wild beasts rave,
In every sphere, where're you steer-the Gaels beyond the wave.

Amongst the cities famed and fair of Europe they'll be found.
Some hold the highest honours there; some tread the cloistered
ground.
And down by where the Tiber sweeps, where lies our prince's grave,
They are loyal and true, and not a few- the Gaels beyond the wave.

Upon the barren African veldt, you'll find our lads today,
And in Australia, too, the Celt has nobly won his way.
And 'neath the friendly "Stars and Stripes", that oft they died to save,
They are here and there and everywhere-the Gaels beyond the wave.

Throughout the globe on every soil, where human foot has trod,
You'll find the hardy sons of toil from this old verdant sod.
And when our country calls for men, again her cause to save,
They'll come with zeal and hearts of steel- the Gaels beyond the
wave.

The Hurler On the Ditch

By Paddy Power, Drangan
Source: Liam Ó Donnchú, Ballymoreen, Littleton.

'Twas in Fethard's famous barrack field
One evening late in May.
When the farmers were cutting silage
And more were talking hay.
'Twas there I spent one afternoon,
That nearly gave me itch—
I will tell of my acquaintance
With the hurler on the ditch.

First, we queued outside the gate,
No tickets could be found.
He nearly kicked up holy hell
To get into the ground.
And when at last he got inside
And I'm sure he got in free,
He started slagging someone
About the referee.

The teams were Ballingarry
And the famous Carrick Swan.
Two great exponents of the code
Renowned in poem and song.
The game was tough and rugged
And the ball was travelling fast—
I heard a tough reporter say,
'That pace it cannot last'.

When the final whistle sounded
And the crowd, they all were gone
The sun was shining brightly
On majestic Slievenamon.

I stood there in amazement
On a silent empty pitch—
Was I glad that I was parting
With the hurler on the ditch.

The Poor Referee

By Joe Ward, Cratloe

The GAA in its time has had heroes sublime
On playing fields at every level.
In administration too, there's been more than a few,
But there's one poor unfortunate official,
Who's there every day in the thick of the fray
With his stopwatch, his notebook, his whistle.

The most ridiculed man, they call him a ham,
He's biased and blind too, they reckon.
They shout and they howl, "Ref, that was a foul"
At him their finger they beckon.
His pedigree alas, like an old hairy ass
Not fit to be grazing with cattle;
But I bet you to-night, he would be alright
If their team had won the old battle.

Now to err it is human and although you are fuming,
Remember all things he just cannot see.
So give him a break, for everyone's sake
Without him where would we be.
And if your team it is beaten and your hat you have eaten
Please don't blame the poor referee.

The Poor Referee

By Michael D. Ryan, Bawnreagh, Askeaton
An 'Anthology' published by Askeaton Civic Trust
—Ed. Patrick J. Cronin, 1998

A great crowd had gathered and filled up the ground
The game will begin with crescendo of sound.
There are bright colours blazing so lovely to see,
But the man dressed in black is the poor referee.

The man dressed in black will be blamed for all wrong
It is surely his fault if our stars not on song.
If our forwards are hopeless and miss every free,
There is none left to blame but the poor referee.

The sliotar goes flying across the small square;
The ball is waved wide; the full forward goes spare,
There's a hole in the net, which the umpires don't see,
But the book has to stop with the poor referee.

A team takes the field that is poorly prepared;
They were drinking last night but last night no one cared.
They are bet and outclassed to the utmost degree,
And they'll say, 'We'd have won with a better ref'ree'.

The boos and the cat-calls are always unkind;
'Your mother's not married, you're thick and half-blind.
We are playing sixteen men, that's plain for to see,
The other side has paid you, you crooked ref'ree.

The names of the All-Stars are tossed all about;
Some surprises get in, some more famous left out;
But amongst those famed All-Stars you never will see,
The man in the middle, the poor referee.

There's a queue formed up at the grand pearly gate;
Famed sportsmen line up, but St. Peter cries 'Wait!
There's a saint coming towards me, does the same job as me,
Take your place with the angels, you gallant referee'

The Ragged Ball

By Sean McCarthy,
Source: Listowel and the GAA

I remember the lazy days and the lovelight in your eye,
The scent of heather on the breeze that graced the summer sky.
The dusty lanes, with twisted names,soft twilight stealing through,
Leaping tall for the ragged ball, in a meadow kissed by dew.

The smell of pansy on the wind, as night came closing down,
A maple tree, where birds sang free, bedecked with crimson gown,
The ragged ball, by the turf shed wall, it's playing life near done,
With cloth and string, it will rise again, to soar in the morning sun.

Yes, I remember the drowsy eyes, when youth was on the wing,
A thrush at play in the new mown hay, a church bell's lonely ring,
The haughty pose of a wild red rose, that burst into awesome flame,
And the hillside green, where we picked the team, to play the
football game.

The Runaway Bookie

By Michael Mackey, Nenagh
Source:Kiilruane MacDonaghs and Lahorna De Wets 1878-1916
Chorus after each verse:

There was a hurling tournament
In Nenagh town of late
The gathering there was famous
And the match was up to date.
The people came from far and near,
The weather it was fair
And hundreds came by special train
From Limerick and from Clare.

Then a bookie stepped into the ring
A man by the name of Tom Flynn
And boldly laid odds 'five against one'
That Clare the great victory would win.

Out came the purses cheerfully
And money went around.
Some men there backed fivers down,
Whilst others bet a pound.
He handed each his ticket
Whilst he gathered in the swag
And then tied up the precious stuff
In a great big calico bag.

The game was played and De Wets won
So in hundreds they gathered around
In search of the amiable Tom,
He couldn't be found
So the cry went around
'Be Jabers-the bookie is gone'

There followed great confusion, swearing etc.
So boys when you're betting again
Beware of that infamous Flynn,

Move quickly along,
When he cries 'five to one'
For 'tis then that he's rubbing it in.

The team was called Lahorna De Wets in memory of the famous South African general De Wet, who had given the British forces such a rough time in the Boer War (1899-1902)

In February 1906.the Nenagh GAA club held a tournament for seventeen medals. (Church Tournament) The teams were to be De Wets v Tulla (Co. Clare), Castleconnell (Limerick) and Coolderry (Offaly). Great interest was shown in the Tulla-De Wets encounter. Fabulous odds were offered for and against both teams, which were eagerly snapped up: Lahorna De Wets won 2-10 to 2-6 but alas, when the winners went to collect their money, they found that the bookie had fled.

Lahorna De Wets—J. Dwan, (capt), M. Conway, C. Brewer, D. Whelan, M & J Darcy, Tom Ryan, P. Kennedy, M. Maher, Dan Ryan, D. Hogan, J. Meara, P. Williams, M. McLoughney, T. Ryan, M. Walsh, Mick Reddan.

The Set Dancers From Kilcommon

By Michael Ryan T. Knockahopple
Source: Received from Liam Ó Donnchú, Ballymorreen, Littleton, Thurles.

Of our dancers from Kilcommon
We can sing in praises loud
Of those young champion boys and girls
Tipperary can be proud.
All o'er the Isle for grace and style
They proved all Ireland's best
In the Gaiety in Baile Átha Cliath
They won their final test.

Now Ireland's best upon their breast
Long may their medals shine
The scroll of fame will hold their name
O'Brien, Dwyer and Ryan.
Those girls and boys will now revise
Our ancient pastime gone
The fame of Kickhams, Knocknagow
And homely Slievenamon.

Round Keeper and Slieve Felim's hills,
In the happy days of yore
When old and young all danced and sung
Around the kitchen floor.
They brought us back the old time craic
Our Céilí sets and reels
And Róisín Dubh feels proud of you
All round her four green fields.

Scór Sinsear 1989 All-Ireland final. Names of set dancers. **Ladies**: Carmel O'Dwyer, Claire O'Dwyer, Margaret O'Dwyer, Sadie O'Brien. **Men**: Corrie Ryan, Fran Ryan, Paul Ryan, Carl Ryan. Sean Treacy's GAA club (winning team) represents Kilcommon, Rearcross, and Hollyford.

Scór and Scór na nÓg are talent competitions with an Irish flavour devised by the GAA to create winter social activity. The competition was initially a senior competition but later on it was decided to have a special competition for the youth. The word Scór has no special significance apart from the fact that it is an attractive short sounding name but the word has now attained a special meaning of worth in the dictionary of GAA activity.

'The initial idea came from a Clare club. The actual setting up was passed in 1969—Cork motion. Derry Gowan (Cork) and Tony Williamson (Down), together with Séamus Ó Riain (Tipperary) appear to have been credited with pushing it in the early years. The first actual year of competition was 1969/1970' (*Letter dated 23 Iúil, 1997, from Liam Ó Maolmhichil, Ard-Stiurthóir, Cumann Luthchleas Gael)*

The Sweet River Suir

By Rev. J. B. Dollard (Slievenamon)
Source: Gaelic Days (Illustrated Handbook) published by Gaelic Athletic
Publications,
San Mairead, Ballinacurra, Limerick.

From Devil's Bit to Thurles, from Cashel unto Cahir,
By Castle–crowned Ardfinnan running pure.
Past Carrick and Kilsheelan, ever sparkling ever wheeling,
Flow the waters of the sweet river Suir.

The Galtees and Slieve Ardagh send their torrents to its flood—
Bright Anner comes from storied Slievenamon.
The sunshine and the shadows follow fast across the meadows
'Til the dew o' the morning all are gone.

By rich flowery fields of the pleasant Golden Vale,
By the broken Norman tower and hamlet white.
The laughing of the Suir, man or maiden would allure
When its glad waters dance in the light.

The winds sough and sob thro' ruined Abbey walls—
Weird music echoes from the fairy mound.
And sad mystic rhymes of long forgotten times
In the crooning of the Suir resound.

In cool sheltered glens where glossy hazels nod
The wild linnet pipes a happy lay.
Blithe thrush and blackbird singing, joyous melodies are flinging
Through briar-scented groves all day.

'Tis there that I dwell for my heart is ever there,
Where Ormond and wide Ossory stretch out—
Where the rival Gaels are dashing and eager hurlers clashing
Make din above the throng's great shout.

I know a sunny meadow, gently sloping to the tide,
Where clover blossoms welcome the wild bee—
By a castle old and hoary, there I'll dream of Erin's glory
While the hushed waters run to the sea.

Ah, dear to me Killarney, where God's smile is ever seen,
And fair thy leafy woodlands, Glenmalure.
But when this life is ended and when earth with earth is blended,
Let me rest by the Sweet River Suir.

The Thurles Emigrant

Anon:
Source: Willie Hackett, Main Street, Thurles.
Air: I'm sitting on the stile Mary

They sing a song of County Down
And Cork upon the Lee;
Of Killarney too and Donegal
And one of Doonaree.
Bundoran, yes and Kerry
And the hills of Donegal,
But they sing no song of Thurles town,
The finest of them all.

How oft I've walked out by the Mall,
When I was but a lad,
To play and fish in Lady's Well,
What fun we always had.
And the games played in the hurling field,
Where Thurlesmen won fame,
Ah, what I'd give to puck a ball,
On that fine pitch again.

In the Quarry now, called Mitchel Street,
And in Kickham Street, the Pike,
I left the dearest friends I had
Ah, you'd never meet the like;
In sickness or in trouble,
They would never let you down;
Yes, the finest people that I know
Are those of Thurles Town.

I'm lonely and I'm homesick here,
My heart is ill at ease,
But soon I know that I'll be free,
To settle where I please.

Then home I'll go to my Helen,
Mo cailín deas mo stór,
And far off hills and foreign shores,
Will beckon me no more.

A Song for the Gaelic Clubs

By Ellen O'Leary
Story of the GAA By Séamus Ó Ceallaigh, Limerick

Come forth! Come forth! My gallant Gaels
Be upright, fearless, steady—
Before calm strength rude discord pales,
Make ready boys, make ready.
Uphold your laws; defend your cause,
And let your watchwords be,
Honour and truth and stainless youth,
They'll make old Ireland free.

Come forth! Come forth! The hour is nigh,
Your giant strength to mould—
With steadfast hearts and courage high,
March onward, firm and bold.
For no true Gael can ever fail,
If these his watchwords be,
Honour and truth and stainless youth,
They'll make old Ireland free.

Come forth! Come forth, let each man's hand
Grasp comrade as a brother—
By no harsh word let strife be fanned,
Forbear with one another.
'Tis for the right you all unite,
Then let your watchwords be,
Courage and youth and stainless youth,
They'll make old Ireland free.

Ireland United

By Criostoir O'Flynn
Source: Centenary, F.N.T. 1985

But ever and always the GAA
Kept Ireland united and one in play,
No border or banner can divide the nation
That proudly cherishes its soul's salvation
In games and culture. The Ireland Act
Blew empty wind when Casement Park
Was opened in Belfast in 'Fifty-Three',
Named for a patriot whom foul decree
Had doomed to hang for so-called treason,
Adding to that imperialistic reason
Vile defamation by forger's art
To antagonise those who might impart
Dignity of office to any appeal
From hangman's noose. Parnell had seen
The letters printed in his name
And thus was able to disclaim
The work of Pigott's poison pen.
Solitary in his condemned cell
Casement demanded that he be shown
Diaries that had been deviously thrown
Open for predictably scandalised eyes
Of King and Archbishop: the wise
Home Secretary refused his plea
And Casement died on the gallows tree
Reviled by hypocrites; his body thrown
In quicklime grave, his soul had flown
To Antrim glens where now his name
Is honoured by our nation's games.
The nation made symbolic mark
When earth from Thurles and Croke Park
Was brought by athletes to be sealed
As one with the soil of Casement's field.

Hurling Final

By Donagh MacDonagh
Received from Liam Ó Donnchú, Ballymoreen
Littleton, Thurles.

It's not only crowds thick as sand
Nor billiard table field of Irish green
Nor the familiar, well-drilled, strutting band
Spellbound forever at the age of fourteen,
No, nor the coloured hats, rosettes and flags
Mingled and hostile, nor the cries and cheers
Futile advice and joy like paper bags
Puffed out and banged and bursting in our ears;
The hour is all these things, yet more than these:
It is delight in movement as exact
As music, or Euclidean syntheses
Where theory once accepted becomes fact;
It is the beauty of the perfect act
When moving bodies can become abstract.

The author, Donagh MacDonagh, (1912-1968) was a poet, dramatist and lawyer. Born in Dublin, son of Thomas Mac Donagh signatory of the Proclamation of Easter Week 1916. Called to the bar 1935. Practised until 1941 when he was appointed a district justice. Had a varied career as poet, dramatist, ballad writer, folklorist, broadcaster and editor. His poetry appeared in two volumes, *The Hungry Grass* (1947) and *A Warning to Conquerors* (1968). With Lennox Robinson he edited *The Oxford Book of Irish Verse* (1958). He died on the 1st January 1968.

His father Thomas MacDonagh (1878-1916) was a poet and revolutionary. Born in Cloughjordan. Co. Tipperary. Educated at Rockwell College, Cashel and University College, Dublin.He had a life-long involvement with the Irish language movement. Helped Pádraig Pearse found St. Enda's School at Cullenswood House, Ranelagh in 1908. Co-founded the Irish Review, 1911 and the Irish Theatre, 1914; founder member of the Irish Volunteers 1913 and was its Director of Training 1914; organised the O'Donovan Rossa funeral, 1915; joined the IRB, 1915 and was co-opted on to its Military Council. In April 1916. signed the Proclamation of the Republic: commanded insurgent forces at Jacob's factory and was executed by firing squad on May 3 1916. A British officer said,' They all died well but MacDonagh died like a Prince'. *Poetical Works and Literature in Ireland* appeared posthumously, 1916. He published five volumes of poetry, two in prose between 1903 and 1916. Since 1934, all North Tipperary championship medals have as their centrepiece the bust of Thomas MacDonagh.

A Second Century

By Criostoir O'Flynn
Source: Centenary, F.N.T. 1985

So we can start this century new
Renewing our faith in our heritage true,
With hope and courage and national pride
Remembering those who have lived and died
To make this land a nation free
That we might grow in liberty.
We trust in God and his Mother blest
In Pádraig our apostle, who could not rest
Until he returned to bring our race
The gospel news of redemption and grace,
In Colm Cille, Bríd and all whose praise
Brought glory to Ireland in ancient days,
That revival in spirit once more may bring
New life and renewal in everything.
With hope in the new generations to come,
With thanks to the courage of all that are gone,
Let us wish for old Ireland, in our own native speech:
'Go mbeirimid beo ar an am seo arís!'

The concluding line of the poem is the traditional Irish prayer for any special day or
occasion which it is hoped to see next time round. It says 'May we live to see this time
again'. As the penultimate line says, the wish is not for the poet or his readers, that
we might linger on like Rip Van Winkles to totter into Croke Park for the bicentenary
All-Ireland in 2084 but for the future well-being and prosperity of the Irish nation, its
people, language and culture.

TIPPERARY G.A.A. BIBLIOGRAPHY

Club Histories

Club	Title	Author	Year
Anacarty-Donohill	*Anacarty-Donohill: G.A.A. History 1886-1986*	Eileen O'Carroll	1988
Arravale Rovers	*The Arravale Rovers Story The G.A.A. in the Parish of Tipperary*	Tom O'Donoghue	1995
Ballingarry	*Commemorative Programme & Brief History of Parish*	Ballingarry G.A.A.	1985
	Ballingarry 1887-1987 100 Years of Gaelic Games	Dick Molloy	1988
Ballybacon-Grange	*Ballybacon-Grange Hurling Club 1928-84*	Fr. Pat Moran, OSA	1985
Boherlahan-Dualla	*The Tubberadora-Boherlahan Hurling Story*	Philip Ryan	1973
	Boherlahan and Dualla: A Century of Gaelic Games	John G. Maher & Philip F. Ryan	1987
	Tubberadora: The Golden Square Mile	John G. Maher	1995
Borrisoleigh	*A Century of G.A.A. in Borrisoleigh*	Lar Long & Timmy Delaney	1987
Cappawhite	*The Cappawhite G.A.A. Story 1886-1989*	John Kelly	1989
Cashel	*G.A.A. History of Cashel & Rosegreen 1884-1984*	Seamus J. King	1985
Clonmel	*St. Mary's Hurling Club, Clonmel 1929-1989*	Sean O'Donnell	1989
Drangan	*History of the G.A.A. in Drangan & Cloneen, 1885-2000*	Eamon Hall	2000
Emly	*The Parish of Emly History of Gaelic Games and Athletics*	Michael O'Dwyer	2000
Fethard	*Fethard, Coolmoyne & Killusty Centenary G.A.A. Story 1887-1987*	Michael Ahearne	1989

Club Histories

Club	Title	Author	Year
Glengar	*The History of Glengar G.A.A. Club and Area*	D.J. Treacy	1986
Golden-Kilfeacle	*Golden-Kilfeacle: the Parish and its people*	Willie Ryan	1997
Gortnahoe-Glengoole	*The History of Gortnahoe-Glengoole G.A.A. 100 Years*	John Guiton	1985
Holycross-Ballycahill	*Gaelic Games in Holycross-Ballycahill 1884-1990*	Bob Stakelum	1990
Horse & Jockey	*All-Ireland Hurling Champions 1899 Centenary Commemoration*	Liam Ó Donnchú	1999
Kilcommon	*Kilcommon My Home. Mountainy Men at Play*	Bill O'Brien	1978
Kilruane	*Kilruane-MacDonaghs and Lahorna de Wets 1884-1984*	Rev. E.J. Whyte	1985
Kilsheelan	*Cill Sioláin: 100 Years and More of Gaelic Games in the Parish of Kilsheelan and Kilcash*	Sean Nugent	1988
Lorrha	*Lothra agus Doire 1884-1984 Iomaint agus Peil*	Seamus J. King	1984
Marlfield	*Marlfield Hurling Club 1946-1996*	Catherine O'Keeffe	1996
Moneygall	*Moneygall Hurling Story 1885-1975*	Seamus O'Riain	1975
Moycarkey-Borris	*Moycarkey-Borris G.A.A. Story*	T.K. Dwyer & Jimmy Fogarty	1984
Newport	*1886-1986 By the Mulcaire Banks The Story of the G.A.A. in the Parish of Newport*	Michael Collins & Denis Floyd	1986
Roscrea	*Roscrea Hurling Club*	George Cunningham & Tom McCarthy	1980
	The Red Years: A Roscrea G.A.A. Publication	Seamus O'Doherty	1984
Suir View	*Suir View Rangers 1895-1898*	Peter Meskell	1997

Club Histories

Club	Title	Author	Year
Templemore	G.A.A. History of Clonmore, Killea & Templemore 1884-1988	Martin Bourke	1988
Thurles Sarsfields	Official Opening of Social Centre	Liam Ó Donnchú	1977
Toomevara	The Green and Golden Years of Toomevara G.A.A.	Donal Shanahan	1985
Two-Mile-Borris	Two-Mile-Borris All-Ireland Hurling Winners: Souvenir History	Jim Fogarty	2000

Other G.A.A. Publications relating to Tipperary

Title	Author	Year
Tour of the Tipperary Hurling Team in America 1926	Thomas J. Kenny	1928
Conventions or A Dozen Years with the Gaels of Tipperary	Rev. J. J. Meagher	1938
A Lifetime in Hurling	Tommy Doyle	1955
Tipperary's G.A.A. Story 1884-1934	Canon Philip Fogarty	1960
Hurling	Tony Wall	1965
Report on the Commission on the G.A.A. in Tipperary	Michael Ryan (sec.)	1978
A Century of Gaelic Games in Mid-Tipperary	Michael Dundon	1984
Official Opening of Semple Stadium Souvenir Programme	Liam Ó Donnchú	1984
Tipperary's G.A.A. Story 1935-1984	Seamus J. King	1988
Tipperary's Bord na nÓg Story	Seamus J. King	1991
Bloody Sunday 1920-1995	Mícheál Ó Meara	1995
West Tipperary Board G.A.A.: A History	J. J. Kennedy	2000
Tipperary G.A.A. Yearbooks 1970-2000		
County and Divisional Annual Convention Reports		
Centenary History of the North Tipperary Board G.A.A. 1901-2001	Seamus J. King	2001

Ciobraid Árann Abú